In Whose Image?

In Whose Image?

*Political Islam
and Urban Practices
in Sudan*

T. Abdou Maliqalim Simone

The University of Chicago Press
Chicago and London

T. Abdou Maliqalim Simone is associate professor of clinical and
social psychology and African studies at the Medgar Evers College
of City University of New York. He is the author of three books,
including *About Face: Race in Postmodern America.*

The University of Chicago Press, Chicago 60637
The University of Chicago Press, Ltd., London
© 1994 by The University of Chicago
All rights reserved. Published 1994
Printed in the United States of America
03 02 01 00 99 98 97 96 95 94   5 4 3 2 1

ISBN (cloth): 0–226–75869–9
ISBN (paper): 0–226–75870–2

Library of Congress Cataloging-in-Publication Data

Simone, T. Abdou Maliqalim (Timothy Abdou Maliqalim)
    In whose image? : political Islam and urban practices in
Sudan / T. Abdou Maliqalim Simone.
        p.   cm.
    Includes bibliographical references and index.
    ISBN 0-226-75869-9. — ISBN 0-226-75870-2 (pbk.)
    1. Islam and politics—Sudan—History—20th century.
2. Sudan—Politics and government—1956– 3. Islam—South
Africa—History—20th century. 4. Islamic fundamentalism—
Sudan—History—20th century. I. Title.
BP64.S73S57   1994
320.5′5′09624—dc20   93-32289
                                                  CIP

♾ The paper used in this publication meets the minimum requirements of the American National Standard for Information Sciences—Permanence of Paper for Printed Library Materials,
ANSI Z39.48–1984.

Contents

Contents

Preface

The lingering power and attraction of Africa for Europeans and Americans is that much of its collective life defies explanation. This is not an inherent condition, certainly not the essence that defines an inherent condition, certainly not the essence that defines Africa for Africans. At times what is alarming is not the fact that so-called objective conditions of African existence appear immune to coherency, but that Africans come to internalize Western bewilderment and exasperation. Western responses have, in most ways, been invented to reproduce themselves. The West interacts with Africa in ways that serve to intensify the old characteristic beguilement. Thus when it observes Africans, the West observes its own limitations and complicity.

Instead of allowing Africa to draw us in, provoking a greater resilience in our analytical and interactional capacities, our general tendency as Euro-Americans is to retreat reassured with the illusion that there exists a place undominated by our habits. The price Africa pays for this "freedom" is to be permanently fixed in Western consciousness as the exemplar of the irrational, the object of a necessary therapeutic process that may never end. What we miss, consequently, are the potentialities and intelligence displayed by many Africans, occasioned by the very "pathologies" themselves. Instead of interacting with this resourcefulness, and conceptualizing developmental agendas and external resource inputs on the basis of them, most Europeans and Americans focus solely on the sicknesses they have diagnosed.

There is of course a well-documented legacy of Africa ignoring and destroying much of itself. There probably is little it can do to alter its current situation as long as it does not deal directly with this legacy. Western imperial practices and attitudes of indifference have contributed substantially to Africa's tendency to defer and, at worst, excuse itself from this self-confrontation. National consensus and integration is exceedingly difficult for peoples able to coexist and collaborate and equally able to ignore, exploit, and kill one another as well. The immensity of the land, the fluidity of social movement, the constantly shifting configurations of polity and household, and the relative abundance of resources have historically positioned Africans in a psychological situation where it is difficult to stay put, to build upon what already exists or is invented. Not used to being cornered, Africans now find themselves cornered by an international economy leaving them few options.

But Africans at all levels persist and continue to diligently carve out a place for themselves in an internationalized world. If nothing else, this book is an attempt to take these indigenous productions seriously, not only in terms of what they indicate about the home context from which they ensue but in relationship to the political imagination in general.

The book explores the ways in which one African society, Sudan, comes to grips with the multifaceted problems of shaping a viable social order. Particularly significant in Sudanese politics is the linkage increasingly made between religious integrity and economic development. The dominant ideology of recent years has emphasized that the economic welfare of the Sudanese masses cannot be enhanced unless the labor, governance, and everyday conduct of people are firmly inscribed within religious practice.

If Sudan were a culturally and religiously homogenous society, perhaps this linkage would indeed engender unequivocally significant transformations in the political and economic parameters of everyday life. But Sudan is one of the most culturally diverse nations in the world, and the insistence of one sector of its population on the sustenance of this linkage brings about a host of delinkages based on competing religions, regions, and races.

What on one level may perhaps guarantee progressive development undermines it at another. It is within this and homologous structures of complexity that African societies are situated. Although as a Muslim and social psychologist I may be critical of the many aspects of the Islamic movements that insist upon the linkage of religious and political practice, I do not consider these to be highly significant aspects of the kinds of popular social movements that are the key to effective significant social change in Africa.

What has been clear historically is Africa's unwillingness to consolidate itself in institutional self-images and cultural frameworks it finds lacking spiritual expansiveness or humor. Contrary to appearances, Africans have tended to invest in the realization of possible futures more heavily than is comprehensible to us. There may exist a fine line between "take what you can now" and "protect all you can for later" attitudes in the African psyche. In light of all that has been stolen, absconded with, and wasted, it should be surprising to note all that is shared, made accessible, exchanged, opened up in the day-to-day inter-actions of Africans.

During the nearly two years I spent as both academic and consultant to the Islamic movement in Khartoum, it was the hundreds of small indi-vidual efforts to survive and put together a meaningful life without mas-ter schemes or abstractions from which I took the most significant learn-ing. Although this is a book about social movements and large-scale politics, the analysis is constantly informed by and indebted to these efforts, which any strategy or program of social transformation must respect and take seriously.

Part One

Struggles for the Familiar

Chapter One

Religion, Islam, and the State in Africa

Religion has been an integral part of Africans' attempts to sustain a process of indigenous cultural and political development—to evolve a worldview that stays close to traditional concerns and yet is able to enhance behavioral and cognitive resilience. Such resilience has been particularly necessary in light of the successive interruptions of this process by colonialism and postcolonial dependency.

Religion is a major focus of African concerns and passions. The attempt to continuously reaffirm and reshape the nature of the human relationship with the divine and the spiritual penetrates African everyday life. Part of the nature of this penetration is that before God Africans are not passive subjects. They strive to make God "adapt the arrangement which follows his desire to live."[1] Connections to the past are a noncontingent reality that needs only to be reaffirmed, not represented; communication between the secular and the spiritual is to be direct and incessant, one of "perpetual osmosis."[2]

Given the vulnerability of African life to dislocation, drought, and disease, the nature of a person's relationship with God has become increasingly important, if only as a space where a symbolic control of everyday life can be exerted. Religious frameworks imposed by colonialism became a context amenable to the survival and reworking of African cognitions and inclinations. Religious ideology became the means by which Africans could actively take apart the logic legitimating Western domination and undermine its spiritual authority. The West's aim of religious conversion concealed its attempt to reengineer cultural practices and modes of thought. But by defining their own particular connections to Christian universality, Africans disrupted its political aims and used it to camouflage resistance to colonial rule.[3]

Religious movements were used to undo the ideological and procedural bases of colonial apparatuses and at the same time to embody the cultural capacities of an oppressed people. Many works discuss how colonial and neocolonial political realities required that political resistance

3

be played out in seemingly apolitical domains. As such, a political order and worldview is sustained, reproduced, and changed through a variety of everyday religious practices that do not necessarily entail explicit political discourse.[4]

Religious interactions cannot be subsumed as simply correlates of larger political forces even though the religious and the political each reciprocally affect the other. The assumption of Christianity by much of sub-Saharan Africa was not simply a by-product of colonial political and economic domination but also addressed the needs that were particular to African religious concerns.[5]

African cultural development has been frequently viewed as static, hopelessly interrupted by colonialism. Often neglected are the substantial complexities of internal dynamics and struggles prior to colonialism and the ways in which affiliations with colonial institutions were viewed by sectors within African societies as a way of resolving local contradictions.

James Fernandez, in particular, seems to give voice to this use of religion as the rubric under which African thought has attempted to alter and to preserve itself simultaneously:

> In religious movements we discover displacements in which the outer has become a greater reality than the inner. We miss the heart of such religious thought if we neglect the fact that this de-centering and the acute sense of peripherality it produces is imaginatively negotiated in primary images . . . and only secondarily in theological or "logic of science" idioms. What we have pointed to here are approaches which are ontologic . . . such approaches keep us focused on the African struggle to maintain the integrity of their worlds in transitional circumstances and they enable us . . . to be most profoundly in communication with what <u>development</u> really means to Africans.[6]

African societies, far from being merely haphazard conflations of static conventions transmogrified by colonialism, still adhere to worldviews which largely see bailing out of the past as necessary to the fulfillment of an essential human character.[7] Despite the very real liquidation of cultural orientations perpetrated by the colonial legacy and the stratification by class of contemporary African societies, any assessment of these societies must in large part be based on the recognition and saliency of this worldview.

The anarchic and repressive ways in which African states often push to exceed themselves, the hastily negotiated deals with transnationals that deplete national assets, the manipulative improvisations compensating for bureaucratic ineptness, the rampant disregard for borders or legal transactions, and the apparently wasteful expenditures on pomp and frivolity all contain within them a desire to upend and enlarge every conceivable social and political relationship. What becomes sacred is fluidity and ambiguity.[8] The ambiguity of religion is often the very factor that solidifies devotion.[9]

In the postcolonial era, analyses of the political implications of religious attachments have basically been divided between those that affirm the persistence of primordial attachments[10] and those that see religious tradition as a resource for self-conscious political engineering or the empowerment of civil society in general.[11] In the former, political units are projected as the embodiments of deeply embedded religious communities. In the latter, the nature of religious identity is readjusted according to varying patterns of socialization, degrees of coercion, and perceptions of efficacy. Generally, religious practice must be assessed in terms of a society's efforts to come up with a framework for defining normative group activity and constituting ideals through which people will interpret social and political events. In this way, religious identities are considered applicable to and explanatory of particular social phenomena but are considered inappropriate in other domains.[12]

Additionally, religion in Africa is frequently seen as a vehicle for symbolic reconstruction, a means of healing experiential dislocations that derive from the failure of prevailing social discourses to provide adequate models for achieving a sense of self-sufficiency.[13] It also serves as a vehicle to exit state control; e.g., witness the Kitawalist movement in Zaire, a community that has moved deep within the bush to avoid taxation and any affiliation with state structures.[14]

Any valuable examination of the instrumentality of religion in African life must confront the understandings and distortions Eurocentric social theory has encouraged in the general attitudes held about it. In most ways the exoticism of the animist is more palatable to us than the austerity of the Muslim. Our own ingrained compartmentalization of the secular and the religious in the West provokes us to view the so-called "encroachment" of the religious upon politics with alarm. Intensifications of religious concerns and practices tend to be interpreted as preoccupations with the past and impediments to modernization. Islam is especially viewed as an inflexible despotism that fosters terroristic single-mindedness or fatalistic passivity in its devotees.

THE FOREGROUNDING OF ISLAM

Much attention has been paid to the use of Islam as an instrument of political and social change. Within specific Muslim nations these efforts have been popularly known as "the Islamic movement." In some contexts the movement takes the form of a political party; in others, it is simply a designation referring to loosely linked extraparliamentary groups. Overall, the Islamic movement connotes a cultural and symbolic orientation adopted by an increasing number of Muslims who remain unaffiliated to any specific group.

Although explicitly Islamic movements are, in large part, a response to the particular problems of state politics in the Arab world, the sensibilities and orientations of these movements have increasingly penetrated the Muslim world in general, including Africa.

Variously known as Islamic "fundamentalism," "resurgence," or "renewal," these movements are seen by the West as a retreat to traditional values or an archaic escape dictated by religious fanatics unable to cope with the modern world. The underlying assumption of these designations is that "something which has been dead has returned to life."[15]

The cultivation of a ruling elite and civil service during the colonial periods introduced a strong secular thrust into certain sectors of the Muslim World. Yet, Islam has been a persistent, unyielding focus for the bulk of Muslims. There are many instances of popular, Islamically inspired social movements.[16] Western impressions of Islam were based primarily on the fact that, for decades, most of the *ulema*—the religious class of theologians, clerics, and teachers—accommodated themselves to a host of various regimes more interested in perpetuating their rule than in addressing the social, economic, and spiritual needs of the people. The rulers, caliphs, and sultans did not abide by Islamic principles for the most part but upheld the religion as religion.[17] Centuries later, in the anticolonial struggles, predominant emphasis was placed on nationalist aspirations and radical political ideologies, e.g., Pan-Arabism, Pan-Africanism, and Marxism-Leninism.

Although initially as much a methodology for practicing politics and configuring a social order as a theology, Islam had found itself increasingly compartmentalized in consonance with Western conceptions of religion. Colonial rule had progressively accorded religious practice a substantial degree of autonomy as long as it did not interfere with the process of accumulation and political consolidation.

The revival of Islam can be seen as an attempt to restore a developmental process interrupted by colonialism—an effort to reconstruct religion as an aspect of larger efforts to ensure greater political accountability and more productive economic activities. As such, Islamic movements do not envision so much a return to a glorious mythical past as a determination to relink to their histories and substantiate a sense of identity that is self-sufficient and less influenced by the West. The designation "Islamicist" will be used here to connote this use of traditional sources for the simultaneous pursuit of a modernist agenda and preservation of cultural integrity.

As Hudson points out, there has been much reconciliation of modernism with Islam already.[18] From Sayyid Jamal al-Din al-Afghani and Muhammed 'Abduh in the nineteenth century to Muhammad al-Muwayhi and Muhammed 'Amara today, there has been a strong intellectual tradition of trying to bridge the gap between Western science and Islamic ethos. Many so-called fundamentalists have advanced degrees in science and mathematics.

The source of the depression and dissatisfaction currently expressed by the bulk of the Muslim world is that things are not modernizing at a quicker pace—not that a pristine past has been denied. The resurgence of Islam does not signify a deferred end of traditional political community, but rather the activation of ideological conflict and opposition in frequently stagnating political contexts.

It is true that aspects of this process of relinkage portray themselves in an often anachronistic light. As such, popular Western conceptions tend to impose a notion of fundamentalism—an idea the West is familiar with in terms of Christian evangelical movements and reactions to the sweeping theological changes taking place during the past twenty-five years. These conceptions confuse the Islamic method of relinking with traditional sources of authority (as the moral basis of progress) with the strict Protestant emphasis on the literal inerrancy of scripture.

But as Hugh Roberts states, applying the designation "fundamentalism" further projects Western understandings of religion onto Islam.

> The Bible is above all a collection of histories. Christian fundamentalism characteristically asserts the literal truth of the Book of Genesis as the history of the creation of the world and of Man. But the Koran is not a collection of histories, but of prescriptions for the social order. To apply the term "fundamentalist" to radical Islam is to stigmatize it by means of the connotations of anti-scientific eccentricity appropriate to fundamentalist Christianity.

But there is nothing necessarily anti-scientific or eccentric about the insistence that the prescriptions of the Koran be taken seriously.[19]

In some parts of Africa, Islamic ideology has facilitated the process of class consciousness and labor activism, as well as providing a means of adaptation to the restructuring of everyday life precipitated by accelerated urbanization.[20] Functional adaptation to and maneuverability within a progressively internationalized economic and political space may necessitate confidence in the continued vibrancy of tradition. Although there has been much analysis that sees Islamicism as a retreat from the modern world, it may actually be an attempt to reconceptualize local identity in terms of transnational concepts—a means of establishing the psychological parameters through which the larger world can be engaged more actively and effectively.

In Sudan, the Islamic movement provides a mechanism for the increasingly marginalized sector of civil servants and educated youth to address their particular urban positioning in an international framework. The idea is to provoke these skilled yet ghettoized people to look at themselves as international actors and to think about the nature of their life in Khartoum in larger terms without getting stuck in simply viewing themselves as Third World victims and the oppressed.

The question becomes, once this *jinsiyya* (political identity) is adopted, what is to be done with it? What forms of expression are to be utilized? Once people have conceptualized their lives in terms of a global picture, what implications does this have for how they behave, how they act with the unfamiliar, or empower themselves in the face of economic forces largely outside of their control? These are questions without easy resolution. Even if there are not yet substantial answers, the fact that they are being posed by Islamic movements certainly takes us a long way from viewing Islam as merely a desire for the archaic.

The West tends to underestimate Africa's fear of a virtual recolonization. In Sudan, especially, there have been for years widespread concerns that International Monetary Fund–facilitated structural readjustment and privatization policies were occasions for the direct reassertion of Western economic domination. The fear is that national territory and resources will be taken away once again. Indeed, throughout Africa, national assets are being sold off to foreign interests and sovereignty attenuated in the subsumption of policy-making to the conditions set by international financial institutions. As the Sudanese are fond of saying, the West "went through the front door but came back (like a thief) through the window." As a result, the Sudanese are frequently preoccupied with the idea that they must psychologically prepare themselves for this eventuality. Such preparation means coming to grips with the complicity of their ancestors in the colonial enterprise.

There is a tendency in the Muslim world to conceptualize difficult situations as internal problems demanding rectification. Muslims often internalize the Quranic injunction that they are responsible for their own fate.[21] Accordingly, many Sudanese believe that they did not help themselves sufficiently in order for Allah to help them avoid colonialism. A people should do whatever is possible to strengthen their capacity to exist as they want. Thus, the intensification of Islamic identity is seen as the most comprehensive means of preparing for the Western powers sneaking back to dominate Sudan.

The Islamic movement in Sudan attempts to effect social and cultural transformation through adherence to "indigenous" conceptions of religious practice. The movement takes the form of a political party, the National Islamic Front, and a wider extraparliamentary tendency to actively find ways of rooting all aspects of public and private life within Islamic principle and discourse—a tendency that cuts across political parties and social classes. Formal leadership has come primarily from urban academics and educated merchants; much of the movement's power base has been derived from the support of youth, both the highly educated and the illiterate.

The Sudanese Islamic movement believes that religious integrity and a reconnection to the purported Islamic foundations of Sudanese society will enhance social development and, conversely, that social development has been limited because of inattention to Islam in the recent past. In this belief, the Sudanese movement may seem like the overeager revisionist-minded students of Weber, who consistently considered religion in the context of cultural change and new definitions of identity and selfhood.

The question is whether the assumption made by Islamicists in Sudan is a valid one. Much depends on the kind of social development envisioned. The Sudanese Islamicists have stated that they aspire to the ideal of an Islamic, democratic, free-market society without the so-called contamination and callousness of the West. But what must be considered is whether this purported moral decline is the by-product of (1) structural arrangements of capitalist production, (2) a particular failure of Western societies to complement economic progress with substantiated forms of cultural meaning, or (3) the necessary characteristic of transforming a society with unequal levels of capitalist penetration and a marginal relationship to the world economy. For example, the "cure" may accelerate the very processes that produce the moral demise feared.

Whether religion can maintain a distinct religiosity while being used as an explicitly political instrument must be evaluated in the convergence of the particular of the Sudanese context and the hermeneutics of Islam itself. It is virtually impossible to identify the crux of any religious manifestation in order to demonstrate its salience to broad socioeconomic issues. Most past attempts to assess the role of Islam in different societies have tended to assert some kind of core kernel of truth to the religion that coheres Muslim behavior everywhere. But given the wide diversity of Islamic sensibilities in the Muslim world, what coordination exists depends on what Muslims themselves do with the religion as a social construct.

Before approaching such a context-specific examination of these issues, I will outline some general questions raised by the broad definition of the Islamic project in Sudan—questions that will be pursued in depth later. It is clear that Islamicists in Sudan attempt to compensate for the relative paucity of political procedures and guidelines in Islam by interpreting the domain of religious practice in overcoded and seemingly precise definitions.[22] Although religion is not conceptualized as a discourse or state of being separate from other aspects of life, how it should be experienced and lived tends to be strictly defined.

Several questions are raised by this assumption. Observers of religion have frequently shied away from attributing a definition to religion, sensing the possibility of losing the real scope of its operations by chaining it to specific constructs. Weber is the classic example of this position. The academic trend has been to identify specific manifestations of faithfulness and religiosity in all secular fields of human activity.

Partly this trend reflects the situation in the West, where religious belief appears to no longer define particular associations or practices— where belief built out of specific socioreligious bonds has vanished and is, instead, dispersed throughout a highly mobile and overdetermined social body.[23] Belief finds itself operative in a network of microcultural tactics and maneuvers that infiltrate the secular and, while doing so, reframe those institutions still bearing the "religious" designation either as "museums" or the "railhead" of traces of religiosity whose effects are deployed elsewhere. Although these notions are most relevant to the status of religion in the West, their implications for the Third World must be assessed in such a way as to consider whether the resurgence of religion connotes the demise of religiosity.

In attributing the developmental lag of Sudanese society to the absence of Islamic vitality, the Islamicist may be reiterating the Orientalist tradition of associating the dynamics of socioeconomic development in the Muslim world with the structure of religious practice—albeit in a controverted manner. The ways Islam was thought to be relevant to the development of capitalism, as conceptualized by the Orientalists, have been thoroughly challenged.[24] Underdevelopment, far from being explained by the persistence of "static" religious practices and traditions, is as much attributable to the onset of capitalist agrarian development and the cultivation of Muslim states as monocrop-exporting agricultural societies.

Yet, internal cultural dynamics do play a role in economics. They engender worldviews that inform the appropriateness and efficacy of individual actions and their place in the world. But the resultant conceptions are highly complex—the terms themselves used to posit cause-effect and/or dialectical relations embody great ambiguity. By insisting on the primacy of religion as the guarantor of social progress, many Islamicists may actually miss the locus where belief, cultural identity, and economic practice intersect, especially in a world where religious belief has been progressively delocalized.[25]

Although Weber's details about non-Western religions were often not adequate,[26] his theoretical work does constitute a base from which to continue explorations of the relationship between Africa's place in the world system and the internal dynamics of African cultures. Particularly important is his attention to the role of religion in developing adequate structures of consciousness and legitimation for particular modes of production and social organization, and how particular forms of domination are able to "seize" the consciousness of individuals. At the same time, the value rationale and ethically motivational claims to legitimacy associated with religion can undermine and circumvent an existing social order by providing the basis through which individuals can engage in more loosely knit opportunities for social solidarity.

In this latter role, Weber emphasized the nonsocialized and nonsocializable aspects of individuality. These aspects have enabled religion in Africa to serve as a vehicle of resistance and a harborer of reworked indigenous values. Accordingly, the question is, what becomes of the vitality and efficacy of religious sensibility when it is harnessed as a self-conscious socializing agent—a way of training citizens to be more productive—and when its motivation is perceived as externally imposed rather than as a manifestation of individual commitment or desire?

In attempting to refute the Western charge that Islamicism is simply a reverting back to tradition disguised as a force of progressive change, the Islamic movement may be neglecting the least problematic role of religion in contemporary society, i.e., as a vehicle for the sustenance of tradition.[27] The West too often represents tradition as static, without embodying the dynamism, conflict, and transformative qualities that were once a crucial facet of what was seen as "traditional." At the same time, the dynamism that does exist within societies is often deprived of a discourse or manifestation that has the apparent concreteness and steadfastness associated with what is today considered to be "tradition." It is precisely this juncture that the Islamic movement seeks to bridge.

What is often forgotten is that modernity is already a diversion and redeployment of social structures inherited form tradition. Religion, far from being a recalcitrant hallucination of continuity, signals an inevitable resilience and openness of the present—a series of possible futures all potentially applicable and livable to a particular people.

The Sudanese Islamicists have elevated traditional religious practice and law to the center stage of Sudanese political life. But by adamantly qualifying this move as simply the most pragmatic way of engaging the Sudanese population, the Islamic movement may engineer tradition into the very calcified notions it attempts to dispel. For if its image of the future does not spring fluidly from its very particular reappropriation of traditional forms, then tradition will hasten the loss of that faith in a collective will which these contemporary reconnections of society to tradition are expected to restore. The focus on tradition doesn't necessarily mean that people are unprepared for the demands of contemporary life.

THE ROOTS OF TRADITION

Sudan experienced one of the three explicitly Islamic regimes that existed in sub-Saharan Africa during the nineteenth century—the others being the Sokoto (Nigeria) and Futa Jallon (Guinea/Senegal) states. The caliphate instituted by Muhammad Ahmed al-Mahdi shortly before his death in 1885, which lasted until the reassertion of Anglo-Egyptian rule in 1899, remains the most significant aspect of contemporary Sudanese history.

Yet the legacy of the Mahdi cultivated a pronounced dependency of much of the Sudanese peasantry on the Mahdi family and their political and economic aspirations—a dependency that has frequently bordered on blind obedience. The Islamic movement, indirectly influenced by the Muslim Brotherhood (Ikhwan) of Egypt founded in the 1940s by Hassan al-Banna, has attempted to translate the religious commitment and fervor embodied by the Mahdist tradition into the development of a modern state, intersecting a largely rural population's significant educational and material needs with religious and social discipline.

The core assumption of the Sudanese Islamic movement is that only through strict adherence to Islamic principles can a worldview be engendered that will permit social practices that can simultaneously achieve economic advancement and political autonomy. This book explores the potentials and problems inherent in this use of Islam as an ideology of political and economic development.

Sudan is not unique in facing these challenges of political and economic vitality. Its problems must be considered in the larger context of the structural positions assumed by most African states in the international economy. Additionally, it is important to conduct a thorough review of contemporary Sudanese politics, with particular attention to the 1985–88 period of democratic rule following the overthrow of Jafaar Numayri and the intensification of the civil war between the so-called "Arabized" North and the "Africanized" South.

STATE AND CIVIL SOCIETY

Religious discourse and social movements have played an increasingly important role in national political life and governance throughout the Islamic world. Much of the contemporary understanding of this process is based on the West's historical tendency to assume a fundamental disjunction between state and civil society. But in many settings, the process of consolidating rule and configuring power in a context of diminishing material resources and cultural upheaval has made unequivocally clear distinctions between state and society increasingly problematic. Despite the historical particularities that largely account for Sudan's present political dilemmas, it is important to expand the scope of reference and situate the current political role of contemporary Islamicism within the dynamics of forging functional governance and social development throughout Africa.

In most of Africa, the formations of state and civil society are thoroughly entangled, preying on each other even when acting at cross purposes. "Self-help" often becomes "help yourself" to the state kitty and other resources, while traditional institutions become parties to "joint partnerships" in order to avoid state repression or to substantiate their own authority. In much of Africa the strength of both civil society and the state is limited to demonstrating the weakness of the other and affirming the failure of the postcolonial Nkrumahist injunction: "Seek ye the political kingdom . . ."

Regimes consolidated their authority by elevating access to state organs as the key to material accumulation, status, and wealth—where dispensing favors, largesse, and opportunities substitutes for the cultivation of social solidarities. In the meantime, communities retreated into reconfigured associations and "neotraditional" practices of accumulation outside the state realm.

On the other hand, the coherence of state-society relations in many African societies has seemed, for centuries, to depend on ambiguating territorial jurisdictions, formal designations of power relations, and the very boundaries distinguishing social formations from one another. Governance did not depend so much on functional social contracts among unequivocally distinct parties as it did on the opportunities vigorously pursued by elites to build alliances outside of their communities and thus rearrange the existing social fabric.

As Bayart indicates, the move by elites to consolidate regional hegemonies or enter into a multiplicity of shifting alliances reflects an ongoing tendency to "compensate for their difficulties in consolidating and intensifying the exploitation of their dependents by deliberate recourse to the strategy of extroversion, mobilizing resources derived from their unequal relationship with the external environment."[28] Hegemony is secured by (1) pursuing linkages to outside religious, military, and commercial groupings; (2) elaborating trade routes; and (3) reconfiguring ethnicity as a mechanism for asserting a politically expedient sense of "commonality" among diverse peoples. Bayart indicates that this practice of "extroversion" characterizes both colonial and postcolonial relations—as the management of dependence emanates just as much from African practices as it does from Western impositions.

Associational life in civil society has been largely shaped by the precolonial practices through which state power was disseminated. When government failed to protect African societies from the terror of the slave trade, a new era of understanding of state power was ushered in that has carried over to this day.[29] Postcolonial states frequently adopted repressive means in order to "capture" societies having no need for a centralizing mechanism, and were, as well, increasingly unable to guarantee the security of everyday life or provide for basic needs. To defuse arbitrary power and repression, Africans tended to treat the entire concept of governance as an elegant joke, a ready-made mechanism of acquiring importance without really having to do anything.

Government became inflated ritual, presided over by prefects, generals, ministers, mayors, attachés, official hostesses, and so on. Government invented positions and titles. Here, the possibility of assuming multiple identities—provided by the reproduction of empty, yet authoritarian, epistemologies of everyday official life (in speech, dress, social networks, cults)—accounts for the willingness of people to dramatize a certain subordination to the state. By acting as if the power of the bankrupt state is incontestable, one might be able to better play with it and modify it where possible.

Governments became objects of ridicule and obscene gesture. In light of people's fundamental distrust of government and state, regimes increasingly reverted to what Mbembe[30] calls the domestication of political power—power itself was made obscene and carnivalistic so as to make it fit the forms of resistance used against it. The restoration of national cohesion and effective governance requires, therefore, the location of adequate sources of moral authority to persuade people that there is a common good that can be achieved. The most important task of contemporary African politics is to reconvince a long-cynical populace that they do have the capacity to govern themselves.

The extent to which this capacity to govern relies upon a consensual clarification of national identity remains unclear. It is true that many African societies seek to posit a vital or clear sense of their own places in history. Yet the African experience has forced diverse societies to live between the constructs of rationality imposed by the West and the collective memories of a tradition that required incessant reinvention and masking in order to survive. African societies have managed to reproduce a semblance of social coherence while operating without certainty of reference. Knowledge has been produced under conditions of incessant displacement and within a global order that has continuously diminished productive capacity.

Such conditions have engendered a process throughout postcolonialism in which people invest in a multiplicity of identities—frequently operating at cross-purposes to any effort to systematize populations as citizens, public servants, workers, and so on. These identities usually allow more latitude and flexibility for managing survival, advancement, and cohesion than do other national or administrative roles.[31]

The legacy of a marginalization engendered by a form of colonial rule generally separated from the values and morality of both its European authors and its African subjects has made postcolonial governance appear rootless, without grounding. Civil societies, instead of putting "the best of both worlds" together, have been forced to act against the grain of the expectations generated by both Eurocentric and local cultural understandings.

A fundamental discontinuity exists in most of Africa between identity change and value change.[32] The making of "in" and "out" ascriptions is a shifting process that signals little about the existence of shared values or cultural processes, but rather takes on an increasingly pragmatic function in social negotiations. Common and divergent orientations to community, authority, conflict resolution, system change, and distributive justice are not outlined in terms of fixed individual or communal identifications. Ethnic identity may have great importance in an individual neighborhood but mean little in the workplace. Ethnic identity may itself be emphasized by individuals with marginal historical relationships to it, who are most unaware of the value systems "traditionally" ascribed to it. Yet, ethnic identity cannot be reduced to other types of categorization or stratification.[33]

The salient features that constitute ethnic identity are often disputed and are frequently mobile and elusive. Multiple identities that seem on the surface to be contradictory and mutually exclusive are often sustained without difficulty by individuals participating in a network of vacillating loyalties.[34] Yet despite the great fluctuations in ascriptive identities, they remain important in contemporary African life. Despite great movements of populations and changes in economic activities, authority patterns on both micropolitical and national levels have remained largely stable during periods of modernizing change, as have community cultural practices.

But the apparent continuities should not be mistaken for a seamless persistence of tradition. Rather, many African societies conflate reinvented memories of cosmological orientations and practices with the projected contents of Eurocentric ethnography to piece together discourse strategies that address this fundamental position of "inbetweenness."

Instead of focusing on a unifying concept of society, the African emphasis has been on articulating discourses and approaches that, on the surface, seem to be miles apart and don't fit together at all. Yet, by focusing on circumventing a seeming incommensurability of practices and orientations, a workable sense of cohesion can be located within an expanded set of possibilities—where one would least expect to find it.[35] After all, the socioeconomic conditions of the continent have not allowed waiting for ideal solutions.

There are many examples of such practices. Several African states have long tried without success to discourage and repress the use of sorcery discourses. In fact, these discourses have become a major facet of African social and political life—in part because of their extreme flexibility in simultaneously legitimating and discouraging new forms of material accumulation and labor control. Within such discourses conventional loyalties can be suspended and rearranged, and persons linked to one another regardless of position, social standing, or identity. As such they are as capable of aggravating past envies and conflicts as they are of rectifying disparities in material accumulation and mitigating overambitiousness. The same vehicle that permits material excess and greed, the fragmentation of moral authority, and circumvention of family responsibility also offers one of the few persuasive guarantees of equity and moderation. This flexibility largely reflects the need to maintain the integrity of familial and kinship structures and, at the same time, link them to "the modern trajectories of accumulation and disaccumulation."[36]

While people often violate every sacred principle to make sorcery work for them, it also enables societies, pushed and pulled, scattered and dissipated, to conceptualize their situations and actions within an often enormously comprehensive reading of their social ties to others across vast distances in space, social stratification, wealth, and experience.

Unlike the West, where postmodernity has made the development of a self in dissolution the only sustainable social project, the progressive unraveling of the economic foundations of African social solidarity has simply produced a wholesale borrowing—of religious forms, fashion cults, and other pastimes—from the West. These borrowings act as vehicles to reinforce individual engagement with kin, clan, religious group, and ancestry.

African identity has usually been constituted at the interstices of some local-global articulation, so there is no essential project to be realized, no cultural authenticity to be preserved, even if a totalizing language, such as sorcery or Islamic fundamentalism, is used.[37] Access to health and material well-being always must go through channels, must be channeled through a nexus of social relations with whatever means at one's disposal.

As indicated earlier, there may be more important sites than the state where power relations are negotiated. Perhaps the strongest institutions in Africa are the church and the mosque. Their strength may be due to the way African societies have worked out a functional ambivalence toward them—a way of seeing their existence as "foreign objects" that can be used to advance intrinsic concerns and viewpoints. Unlike the state, their cultural distance has proved functional, i.e., as a "safe" context in which to try out new provisionalities in practice and outlook.[38]

The church and mosque command the greatest loyalty and capacity to mobilize resources quickly. They are the locus of resistance to taxation, repression, and arbitrary rule. Despite the fact that they often compromise their political role, the church and mosque become the context where tradition is reconfigured and redeployed. They are the places where African societies attempt to engender a workable sense of plurality and infuse society with an operational diversity often precluded by the needs of the contemporary state in the world system.

Although religious institutions may be more trusted than the state in terms of their ability to function, caution should be exercised in attributing too much incompetence to the state. Its apparent incompetence is also the product of a situation where the management of political relationships takes place primarily outside of the state—where the state becomes simply the occasion and the arena for activating an often vast, overdetermined network of patron-client relations. These less formalized social transactions are often competently played out as a means of maintaining some notion of internal political coherency but are usually unable to coordinate the relationship of the internal economy to the world system.[39]

Social rivalries, sexual jealousies, and family disputes frequently become political ones, sometimes interacting with the state and at other times not. When such conflicts link themselves to competing external interests, they are frequently converted into irreconcilable polarizations. At times, attempts to accommodate conflicting groups by localizing authority and restructuring administrative boundaries spur intensified competition for patronage among new group alignments in light of the multiplication of administrative units.[40]

At times, the state compensates for the absence of real control by an emphasis on ceremony and/or repression. Large sums are spent to mark anniversaries of survival—witness the Basilica of Yammousoukro, testament to the everlastingness of Houphouët Boigny. The state also becomes the broker for outside development moneys. Tanzania, Burkina Faso, and Niger are largely dependent on foreign aid in order to survive. Internal policies are largely designed so as not to jeopardize the availability of such funds.[41] During the regime of Thomas Sankara, who assumed the role of spokesman for marginalized peoples throughout the world, it was difficult for the Burkinabe government to raise money even to reconstruct the central market. But following his assassination and replacement by Blaise Compaore, a more palatable figure to Western interests, not only has a new market been constructed, but building projects throughout Ougadougou suddenly found financing.

In most African societies, the capacity to treat people well—your neighbors, kin, friends—is the organizing ethos of social networks and requires the ability to give in moments of marked scarcity. In this way, a sense of possibility is continuously maintained no matter what. State corruption then often becomes a stretching mechanism of exchange in response to the expanding interconnections of people, all doing their best to maintain "good neighborliness."

Good neighborliness and social cohesion have become increasingly difficult to maintain. There is a growing dissociation between the paid productive activities carried out "elsewhere" by, most usually, men and the maintenance of social ties, which continues "at home" as the burden of women. Material survival often takes the constituents of households and kin groups far from identifiable "home base" and across several national boundaries.[42]

Associational groups, such as secret societies, ethnic clubs, syndicates, and religious brotherhoods, are instrumental in helping urban Africans to maneuver from their ghettoized positions. Despite being zones of incarceration for the poor, urban shantytowns in much of Africa keep people alive by acting as nodes in a network of highly variegated, if tenuous, transactions with other sectors and communities. New modes of social interconnection supplement existing affiliations of kin and ethnicity, providing people with additional channels for sharing resources.

Although a variety of tactics and conduits of exchange are employed to maintain some sense of cohesion in this dispersed structure, it does become harder to sustain relations of a consistent character among "neighbors" and "co-residents." Home base becomes subject to a myriad of diverse inputs and influences brought back by returning kin.

As a result, communities become webs of relationships seeking to intersect and mediate parochial concerns (sustaining family interest and habitat) with those of managing globalized identity, in which the maintenance of individual and social units transpires across what were formerly distinct cultural, political, and ethnic zones. Because "home" and "community" may no longer be a physically identifiable place or entity, its continued existence is increasingly an act of social imagination.[43]

In Africa, the cultural construction of community takes place within a specific space of political and economic relations that enforce their own determinations and prescribe circuits of actual movement and influence: the dedevelopment of agriculture, international price structures, domestic price controls, labor market regulations, termination of food subsidies, trade liberalization. Additionally, Africa possesses half of the world's refugees.

The combination of dislocation and ghettoization is more intense than at any other time in African history. Urban residents, in particular, are forced to deal with a high-density diversification of social relations and a distribution of primary social ties over a large distance. The calls for delinking from the international economy frequently made by "progressive" elites are especially problematic in light of the economic spaces configured by citizens on the ground. In an ironic way, this situation of dispersement may roughly parallel aspects of precolonial social relations, although it is unclear what the long-term effects of this process on the consolidation and development of discrete African nations will be—though it perhaps posits the incipient forms of new regional configurations.

Despite the large degrees of marginalization inherent in these African circuits of dispersion extending across the globe, it is in the status of Africans as "international actors"—as opposed to ethnographic particularities of specific communities—that the most radical sense of Africentricity is being reworked. Ethnic and national origin acquire new significance, albeit in contradictory directions. Civil and regional conflict is frequently ethnically based, sending refugees across borders (where home is uprooted and reimagined). At the same time, these conflicts occasion new forms of interethnic and international collaboration.

Take Sudan. The civil war has precipitated contexts where "undercoded," often clandestine, collaborations between Northerners and Southerners have become a crucial feature of urban survival. A major multireligious, multiethnic theft ring operates out of Khartoum—bringing together Mahass, Dinkas, and Nubas, groups known for their past hatred of one another. Equatorians and Rizaygat—archenemies in the present civil war—run a lucrative smuggling operation between the Central African Republic and Khartoum, exchanging red mercury for electronic equipment stashed in tattered sheepskins. The war, along with religious, racial, regional, and ethnic animosity, provides a cover for activities the state is hard-pressed to control, let alone understand. Religious convictions, ethnic identification, distinct worldviews are all very real—allegiances are not merely cynical convenience.

The African map today juggles the ever-fuzzier delineation of discrete states with the fluid boundaries of transregional civil societies and intensely localized particularisms. Some territories have ceased even to function as states, while others are on the way to substantial rearrangements. In some countries, such as Liberia and Togo, the state has been effectively split into hostile factions engaged in a constant "slow burn." The economic debilitation of almost all states has meant that national boundaries mean little, and to a large extent religious networks, ethnic ties, and syndicates have become the real government.

With African populations increasingly unmoored from the specificities of a home base, developmentalists and policymakers are forced to try to understand what contemporary African social formations and practices might be on their own terms, instead of seeing them as simply deficient from conventional Eurocentric ideas of what they ought to be. As Roitman points out, "The conceptualization of the state and market as reified entities which function in a predefined, ideal way precludes examination of African states and markets as anything but deviations from a model."[44]

Increasingly, there is a demand for democracy in Africa—but it is not always clear what kind of democracy is being demanded. Part of the issue is that the nature of democracy in the West has been changing over the past two decades. African communities and local units now enjoy a semblance of the Western autonomy of decision making and operation, but this autonomy is based on the relative dysfunctionality of government, rather than on a reaction to its hegemony over decision making as holds in the West—as people demand a right to a meaningful existence.

Often it appears as if the West seeks to impose a model of democraticization increasingly moribund in the West itself—one that would strengthen the state's ability to engineer accumulation and distribute opportunities for productive activities. Privatization measures and structural readjustment programs implicitly advocate for the clear redemarcation of state and civil society. Yet, as Melucci points out, distinctions between state and civil society have also become increasingly ambiguous in the West:

> The state as a unitary agent of intervention and action has dissolved. . . . It has been replaced, from above, by a tightly interdependent system of transnational relationships . . . from below, into a multiplicity of partial governments, which are defined both by their systems of representation and decision-making and by an ensemble of interwoven organizations which combine inextricably the public and the private.[45]

Both the absence of democracy and its attempted imposition into seemingly anachronistic and situationally dystonic forms fuels many of the anti-system movements taking place in Africa. Some movements advocate a stronger insertion of religion in the running of states, others advocate a return to traditional forms of governance, and still others appeal to a nebulous syncretism of a variety of ideologies. All seek to "invent" a way out of increasingly desperate circumstances and find new frameworks of social agency.

Though Islamicism in the Sudanese political arena may be the completion of a long-term "social contract" with the Sudanese people, a return to traditional values, a framework of religious repression over altered gender relations, and the mythologizing of religion in times of political chaos, it is not simply these things. The above outline of the key dynamics of state–civil society relations throughout Africa clearly points to Islamic resurgence as being one of many efforts under way throughout the continent to "put influences, languages, ideas, memories, movements together that don't belong" into some kind of workable bridge between the inadequacy of state authority and the excessive resilience of civil compensations. All throughout Africa, societies are trying to retain the flexibility and creativity of their adaptations to colonial and postcolonial space, and, at the same time, are being pushed and pulled, fragmented and stretched nearly beyond their ability to maintain coherent social ties and public life. The Sudan experience, thus, should not be seen as reversion to a past or as the culmination of the essential, but as a work in progress aimed at the superficially contradictory aspirations of reconnection and upheaval, of healing and radical reform, of engaging and disengaging from the globalized culture.

RELIGION AND POLITICAL PRACTICE

It is within the context of organizing new forms of social agency that the use of religion as a political instrument will be considered. The complexities of African governance and the consolidation of coherent relations of production must be kept in mind in any effort to assess the directions of contemporary political Islam in Sudan.

Islamicism in Sudan embodies several contradictory tendencies that reflect the general ambiguity concerning what to make of Africa's predicament—its confounding intersection of stability and disorder, rigidity and resilience. By advocating the salience of past religious practices, Islamicists in Sudan affirm the need to reconstruct active linkages to underdeveloped sources of political knowledge and circumvent the anxiety-ridden self-evaluations nurtured by enforced attention to Western "competence."

At the same time, they reproduce a certain Western blindness by not acknowledging potential areas of sense and resilience in the ways Sudanese attempt to survive. All the while, the possibilities for real economic vitality and maneuverability in the international arena are quite limited. People are increasingly aware of what they don't have. There are a seemingly overwhelming number of issues to be addressed and no really apparent clear-cut responses. In recent years, the stated priority has become developing Africa's most valuable resource—its people.

How this development of people is to be done remains vague and challenging. Whatever its limitations, the Islamic movement is primarily concerned with taking steps to enhance the resourcefulness of this resource. In the end, the movement is interested in shaping Sudanese minds and commanding their loyalty. Will this nurturing of loyalty enhance Sudan's long-term prospects, or will it accelerate a process of decline? This is the question to be taken up here.

Chapter Two

Sudan: The Search for Political Coherency

Sudan has often been referred to in order to illustrate a variety of sociopolitical issues. Touted by itself and others as an intersection of religious, ethnic, and cultural worlds, it seems endlessly available to be used and abused by Western academics and development workers. They have been intrigued by the near impossibility of Sudan's establishing itself as a coherent and functional political entity. It is said that if national integration could work here, it could work anywhere.

I take up the issue of cultural and political coherency here not to draw general lessons from it, but to examine what such coherency really means and to argue that it can be found in Sudan (and elsewhere in Africa) in locations and experiences which on the surface appear inimical to it. In Sudan, any prolonged period of stability will require a transitory intensification of the instability characteristic of recent years.

I was sent to Sudan as a Muslim academic, and it is from this position that I write. My agenda there was ambiguous: to work with Islamic activists that were beginning to turn away from the movement. I am not at all clear or confident about what this position, Muslim academic, entails. There are no strict guidelines. At times all it means here is that I will take positions, be both critical and empathic, in ways not usually associated with academic riting. At the same time, I am always directed by a certain academic sensibility. Since Sudanese cultural life has recently been dominated by conflicts over the application of Islamic law to all questions of national development, it may be useful to examine these issues of political coherency through the experiences of a Muslim who himself is trying to come to grips with the extent to which his own life should be informed by that law.

To write as a Muslim precludes opting for a separation of identities. In Islam one cannot speak sometimes as a Muslim and other times as a social psychologist. For Muslims are embedded in the totality of their profession of faith, and it is on this basis that I choose to interact with Sudan—perhaps better able to address it as a dialogic partner than as a distant observer.

There has been a great deal of dialogue taking place in Africa for a long time. Despite the imperial incursions, the dominations, and the incorporations of African political, cultural, and economic life into a Western orbit, Africans have never stopped trying to constitute and reconstitute themselves. There have been and will continue to be intense debates and conflicting forces at work to determine what societies will look like, regardless of the positions taken and the powers exerted by the West.

For centuries there have existed conflicts between tendencies to consolidate disparate polities and identities and tendencies to amplify particularisms—emphases on local, parochial identities and politics. My work is an attempt to explore the political dynamics of Sudan within this framework of conflicting indigenous orientations and their articulation with current international trends in the postmodern political era.

SUDANESE IDENTITY

Any discussion of Sudan today must inevitably begin with the nature of its cultural and political position within the international arena. Being both inside and outside the Arab world, inside and outside the African world, Sudan sometimes appears located in a state of fixed indecision, condemned to suffer through the absurdity of its colonial demarcations. It is a multireligious, multilingual country of twenty-two million people. It covers a vast geographic territory. Although the nation encompasses widely disparate ethnicities and cultures, Arabized ethnic groups, primarily from the Northern regions, have dominated the visible representation of the whole. Roughly 65 percent of the population is Muslim.

Links of trade, language, and religion have oriented Sudan to the Arab world. Despite the fact that Sudan borders Zaire, Uganda, Kenya, Chad, and the Central African Republic, its national relationships with sub-Saharan Africa remain cursory. Part of the problem is one of infrastructure. The lack of roads and telecommunications limits the possibilities for opening up these relationships. In fact, the regions at the convergence of these borders remain some of the most underdeveloped in Africa. At the same time as the majority of Sudanese intensify their identification with Islamicism or orthodox Islam, there is a nascent recognition by many that Sudan must substantiate its relationship with Africa.

Embedded in this question of identification is a lingering confusion in Sudan over what to call various types of Sudanese. The designations Northerner and Southerner (the most frequently employed references) refer to much more than regional distinctions; they also encompass race, religion, language, power, and worldviews. The relationship between religious identifications is so thoroughly ambiguated as to be of little explanatory value. Despite the efforts that Francis Mading Deng, the renown Sudanese intellectual and diplomat, has made to posit the cultural basis for a valid national identity, when Sudanese state, "we are all Sudanese," what is invoked is more a hollow abstraction than a confident conviction, though at times it is an idea deeply felt.

Since independence in 1956, Sudan has deferred resolution of the racial, regional, and religious divisions that now render it nearly ungovernable. Civil war has resumed and intensified; the differences that constitute Sudan have been brought into a greater and more explosive proximity as a result. Within a few years, Khartoum has rapidly become one of the largest cities on the continent with an estimated six million people; as many as half that number have migrated to the massive shantytowns that have encircled the city during the past ten years. Basic staples are either in short supply or, when available, carry a price beyond the reach of most. Eighty percent of the population is unable to read, and mortality rates for all ages are some of the highest in the world.

In 1983, Jaafar Numayri, in his fourteenth year in power, instituted a form of Islamic law, popularly known as the September laws, in response to the increasing power of the Islamic movement and his own preoccupation with death. Although roughly based on the *Shari'a*—a systematization of the practice of the Prophet Muhammed and revealed knowledge in the Quran undertaken by four schools of legal scholars in the eighth and ninth centuries—the September laws emphasized the *hudud*, the aspect of the *Shari'a* dealing with criminal punishments for personal aberrations. The more predominant aspects of Islamic law—those dealing with the codification of family and political responsibilities as well as individual moral behavior—were largely ignored or constituted rearticulations of customary practice. Instead, the excision of limbs for crimes of thievery, flogging for alcohol consumption, and stoning for adultery were imbued with great symbolic value, forced to operate as indications of an Islamicized society—in large part because of expediency and the neglect of other issues. The laws proved unpopular even though public desire for the full implementation of *Shari'a* has intensified, since it is perceived as the obligation of Muslims to do everything possible to adhere to and institutionalize its practice.

While working in Sudan I heard many voices. Almost all expressed frustration. Soon after arriving I met with a group of journalists writing about cultural issues for some of Khartoum's ten daily newspapers. I would meet many people from different walks of life, but I initially sought out this group because they were closest to being my peers, and because I wanted to understand Sudan as part of a collective effort, a process of coming up with a shared point of view. Most were unsympathetic to the actual mechanics of Islamicization, yet believed deeply in the ideal of a Muslim society. For several hours they presented a sweeping and, at times, idiosyncratic critique of Sudanese culture. Although each expressed particular points of view, there were many common threads in their thinking.

Although often critical, their thoughts come from an unequivocal commitment to the pursuit of knowledge that underlies their faith in Islam. Like El-Affendi, who completed a study of the Sudanese Islamic movement for his doctorate, they see Islam's applicability as universal— not just a defense of "turf." Therefore, they believe that self-criticism is an essential aspect of enabling a heightened contribution of Islam to universal human endeavor. Moreover, they come to this position as an aspect of being within the *Din*, not outside it. In this pursuit, El-Affendi concludes, "you often have to make a fool out of yourself, so to speak, in order to make sense."[1]

As a starting point for my own critical discussion, I have attempted to summarize the thinking of these journalists. Participants included: Mohammed Mahjoub, Fatah Gabboushi, Salih Hassan Salih, Najat Tag al-Din, Shams al-Din Yunis Najm al-Din, and Abu Gassim Goor Hamid. At the end of our discussions we decided to continue talking about these issues with people in various sectors of Sudanese society, to form a mobile seminar engaging people in a multitude of settings—a method affectionately referred to by the group as "cruising Khartoum."

I wish to begin my discussion with their critique because my aim is to examine what factors contribute to the making of such a critique. Because of the complexity of Sudan today, it seemed useful to organize my work around positions taken by others and then relate them to points of view that differed but yet were generated by actual dialogue and interaction with the original positions taken. Here, the aim is not to create a definitive explanation of the objective conditions of Sudanese culture but to look at how political culture is shaped by the intersection of different positions and worldviews—where harsh and devastating critiques open up opportunities to discover resourcefulness and resilience perhaps otherwise not recognized.

In the long run, political coherency in Sudan, and perhaps in much of Africa, will manifest itself not in efforts to coordinate and find commonalities among particularisms and divergences, but rather, in the process where the intensifications of local orientations and plural worldviews exhaust and undo the capacity of each diversity to maintain an antagonistic position in relation to the others. In other words, if each group in civil society feels that it has the relative psychological autonomy to act as if it can develop its own agenda and way of life without having to refer to what other groups are doing, it is possible that each micropolitical entity will move toward intersections with the others on their own accord.

CULTURAL CRITICS

According to the group of journalists, Sudan has learned little over the years. Sudanese culture, they claim, is like an empty pocket resewn time and time again. While embodying so much ambiguity within it, the culture demonstrates little tolerance for ambiguity, yet is always willing to hold up the ambiguity of its Afro-Arab heritage as a calling card to the rest of the world. There is no system of political accountability. Oppositions are defined, aligned, and then incorporated to share state power as a means of displaying the ineffectiveness of all political players. Everyone jumps at the opportunity to govern, to be inside, yet then finds himself without authority—that which will guarantee orderliness and the rule of law, regardless of whether this proves beneficial.

The chaotic flow of improvised resourcefulness, long a trademark of Sudanese survival, now seems only a prudent means of circumventing the prohibitions and strictures of the state, not a propelling method for institutionalized democracy. The state, always referring to the popular will as the basis for its actions, is hard pressed to distinguish the popular will it invents from the will of a populace now increasingly uncertain about what its fellow citizenry actually thinks about things. The capital has grown so fast that no one is quite certain if a well-defined majority continues to exist within it—which is partially why the regime has driven so many periurban residents farther into the desert. The political game played by a cast of overly familiar faces has tended to accelerate the populating of Khartoum as the provincial regions are increasingly neglected. During the period of democratic rule, 1985–89, bodies became numbers at ballot boxes in the fight for control of the capital—formerly a game between brothers-in-law (Sadiq al-Mahdi, former Prime Minister and head of the Umma Party, and Hassan al-Turabi, the present de facto head of state and head of the National Islamic Front). The urban nightmares in part prompted by this power struggle led most to prefer rigged elections—it would have saved the city a lot of head-aches.

The racial struggle between Northerner and Southerner has tended to eat away at the interior of each individual ethnic group. People are more vicious toward other tribal groupings because they find it harder to get along among themselves. Some of the journalists view the cessa-tion of intermarriage over the years as having arrested the Sudanese character. The previous existence of racial interpenetration produced a self-conscious recognition by Sudanese individuals of themselves as disparate, unfixed people. This recognition, in turn, prompted a kind of spiritual nomadism, a search for connections and an interweaving with others. Alliances based on the amplification of commonalities were of-ten invented. The aim was not a consolidation that would have to be defended, but the maintenance of an ability to enter and exit fluid social configurations.

The group of journalists maintains that identity making is now overly declarative, too much "I am this and not that." The thrust of contempo-rary Sudan is to protect, amplify, and distort differences. But in Sudan, the group argues, these differences make no sense removed from a tradi-tion in which cultural identities of subgroups were established on the basis of how various ethnicities related to and interacted with people they considered themselves not to be. For example, Dinka and Baqqara were not differentiated historically on the basis of a mutual recognition of fundamental racial and religious distinctions, but rather maintained differences because they made possible a collaborative division of labor that was highly adaptive to the environment in which they both had to operate.

The difficulty, the group points out, is that cultural vitality looks too much like a cartoon—a matter of putting on *jellabiyya* (traditional Arab robes) over Western clothes or discarding *jellabiyya* for *dashikis* (long Af-rican shirts). Too little attention is paid by both Arabs and Africans to how each behaves at the intersection where the unfamiliar is con-fronted. The strength of Sudanese culture was once that people and ideas circulated; people were highly generous with what they ex-tended outward.

Now people have become increasingly closed off, sedentarized in their societies and faced with a collective depression as a result. Ac-cording to the group, the Islamic movement acts to protect this depres-sion. It does not restore something essential that has been lost, but insti-tutionalizes its absence as a permanent fixture so that one's devotion is to the vacuum. That is why Islamicists repeatedly say, "We need Islam because we are lost." But such a citation comes precariously close to implying that the condition of "lostness" may be essential to the power of Islam's attraction in the present situation.

Shariʿa becomes a fetish of rules; people know it has changed and will change things but few are able to detail just exactly how their lives will be different as a result. Among the educated, the justification used is that *Shariʿa* will reconvince Sudanese of who they are so that they can proceed to energize themselves for the key tasks of socioeconomic development. The group argues, however, that identity is not a matter of reimposition, but rather a process of negotiation and structured conflict. The belief by both Northerners and Southerners that their cultural identity has an essential core has frozen them into a majority and minority as if neither shared any common experience.

Tribal groupings in Sudan are the key to both the survival of the central government and the fight against it. In a policy adopted by a former deputy defense minister, Gen. Burma Fadala, tribal militias were armed to fight one another and regional governments were split into smaller regimes.[2] This process of divide and conquer, fragment and dissipate takes its toll on the psychological integrity of the Sudanese, dissociating them from any clear sense of purpose or even history. The fragmentation is internalized. A common question asked by university students is, "Is there any connection between where we have come from and where we are now?" For many, *Shariʿa* is the symbolic link, but a link that so far remains more of a name tag than an actuality.

ISLAMIC TREND/AFRICANIST TRENDS

Given this critique, where does one begin looking at what these points of view mean in Sudan today? Worldviews not only reflect a set of assumptions and experiences, both personal and social, but are articulated instrumentally as well: they are proffered in order to accomplish something. Many young Sudanese seek to get around the ways in which racial, religious, and cultural designations have become polarized into static oppositions. They try to find small ways of disrupting the polarizations of race, religion, and politics by assimilating and then colliding them within the scope of their individual lives. At times they will simultaneously out-Islamicize the Islamicists and out-Africanize the Africanists, exaggerating (and thus exasperating) such terms beyond recognition and thus creating occasions for identity making that are then able to operate outside the entrenched matrix of ethnic, racial, and religious conflicts.

The thrust of this effort is directed at creating a language of politics outside of nationalist, ethnic, and religious discourses by incorporating all of them. As of now, these efforts are highly provisional and frequently awkward. But they are important to acknowledge lest we mistake these grapplings as simply signs of an immature and potentially fanatical idealism.

Before discussing the process through which these provisional modes of self-conception and political method are forged, it is necessary to review the various political and cultural forces shaping Sudanese cultural life today. This discussion includes the nature of the Islamic movement, the political attitudes of the young, the history of the present racial conflict, the mushrooming of urban shantytowns in the capital, and the subsequent assault upon the urban poor.

The story of Sudan today is in most ways the story of the increasing "African" character of Khartoum. Civil war and the starvation and displacement it has provoked have resulted in an enormous influx of Southern Sudanese into the capital. It is disconcerting to most Northern Arabs to witness an increasing number of Southerners in their midst who, for all intents and purposes, are either the "enemy" or sympathize with it. There is a reluctant accommodation of them, partly because they are fellow citizens, hard workers, and can be treated as physically present objects of derision—surrogates for the enemy that seems distant and removed. Sporadic outbreaks of violence are intense because the resentments are enormous. Hostilities that had been dormant during the period when the South was granted a large measure of political autonomy (1972–1983) have been fully reawakened.

Neither the Sudanese army nor any of the now various factions of the Sudan People's Liberation Army (SPLA), the Southern guerilla army formed from Battalions 104 and 105 of the Sudanese army in 1983, appears to have the military capacity to win the civil war outright. It is not clear what the terms of a settlement might be. Until the SPLA split in 1992, the war was not one of secession. The political arm of the SPLA, the SPLM, states that the abrogation of *Shari'a* is the main prerequisite for a cease-fire, with other substantive issues for a permanent settlement to be worked out at a constitutional conference. Past governments, under pressure from the Islamicists, have repeatedly backed down from accepting this proposal. In fact, the government of Sadiq al-Mahdi fell the day it was to officially accept such conditions. Meanwhile the war is draining the treasury of nearly a million dollars a day—provoking closer ties to a domineering Iran.

During the Mahdi government, newspapers called every day for a stronger government. Some felt the Islamic movement was strong only because it was easier to deal with religious concerns and issues of personal demeanor and behavior than with economic structures. When it is difficult to envision what to do to ameliorate the material conditions of everyday life, at least the causes of the hardship and demoralization can be deliberated. As solutions to the problems of national identity and coherence become more elusive, the emotional investment in Islamicization as a way of displacing the question of identity altogether grows.

Islamic theology subsumes issues of race and culture; it states that such differences are insignificant, not worth paying attention to. However, something else is going on as well. Although more Sudanese are explicit in describing themselves as Arabs, many so-called "Arabs" reject such identifications, preferring to cite ethnic particularisms such as Baqqara or Mahass. Particularisms among Northerners, however, are viewed as dangerous since they potentially contribute to an undermining of Northern hegemony.

Even though Southerners are tribally split and religiously divided (historically, Catholics dominated the east bank of the Nile and Protestants, the west), they are conjoined through their status as the oppressed and through a growing yet vague Pan-Africanist identification. Religious focus in the North implicitly becomes a way of managing identity, a way of reaffirming certain elements of a collective selfhood among disparate ethnicities without doing so explicitly. It becomes a means of effecting and enforcing cultural homogeneity at a time when the alternating pulls of Westernization and Africanization are exerting a heightened force. Religious focus thus becomes a means of consolidating arabization—a process which probably could not otherwise occur.

Religious preoccupations also acquire a kind of magical quality as a means of cushioning Sudan's decline into solid Third Worldism; they reflect a dearth of political alternatives at the same time as they constitute the most accessible means of significant political transformation. Politics in Sudan has always been closely associated with religion. The two political parties have been largely rooted in the two predominant *turuq* (Sufi religious sects), the Khatmiyya (The Democratic Unionist Party) and the four million strong Ansar al-Mahdi (the Umma Party). It is expected then that much political opposition would take place on the basis of existing anti-Sufist religious dogma—as embodied by the

Jabhatu Islamiyyah al Qawmiyyah (the National Islamic Front), or "Jabha" as it is popularly known.

The failure of Arab secularist movements to effect the revitalization of Arab culture, provide clear and united leadership in opposition to Western and Zionist interests, and rechannel the Arab preoccupation with cultural authenticity into a clearly distinguishable political agenda looms large in the attention of Sudanese intellectuals. The Islamic movement has found fertile ground here. Intellectuals are particularly attracted to the Islamic notions of economic justice. *Shari'a* theoretically forbids currency speculation, black marketeering, and hoarding. But Jabha's coffers have grown through these very practices; merchants who finance the NIF are highly dependent on the second market.

Drug smuggling and alcohol brewing took on increased economic importance as the city grew. Jabha's economic program remains vague outside of support for a mixed economy. Despite its longtime opposition to IMF-administered structural adjustment programs, the current regime has implemented a homegrown policy of fiscal restraint nearly identical to them. This policy has driven many urban dwellers deeper into illegalities in order to survive. At present no African city can survive economically while adhering to the full strictures of *Shari'a*. In part, this is why the institution of the *hadd* punishments takes on great symbolic importance.

The September laws of Numayri permitted amputation of the hands of one who steals public property, although according to *Shari'a*, not the *hadd* but *ta'zier* (discretionary punishment) must be upheld because of the *shubha* raised by the ownership of such property. The enforcement of *hudud* and *qisas* (retribution) requires an absolute prerequisite of social justice and a rational economy:[3] everyone must have access to viable economic practices. These conditions obviously do not exist in Sudan. Yet every Muslim must bring about *Shari'a*. The economic options are very limited. An interpretive framework ensues whereby Sudanese think that the economic conditions necessary to realize *Shari'a* may, given the nature of Sudan's relationship to the international economy, come only through a "premature" adherence to it.

THE SUDANESE ECONOMY

Until lately, Sudan was frequently referred to as an example of how not to run an economy. Faced with an ever-increasing national debt, now estimated at sixteen billion U.S. dollars, its long-term prospects appear dim. Only recently has Sudan been restored into the good graces of the international financial community for its "self-initiated" efforts at fiscal austerity. Yet much of the recent "miracle" of attaining an officially almost nonexistent inflation rate appears more the connivance of expert local accountants than a real indication of economic health. Whereas late in the last decade Sudanese still had the purchasing power to buy basic staples, which were in constantly short supply, the substantial increases in the availability of foodstuffs have been of little use to the bulk of urban residents, who have seen the real value of their incomes plummet.

The country is still paying for the exorbitance of the Numayri regime, which spent large sums to buy the loyalty of the military. During the latter part of this regime an estimated twenty-five thousand security personnel came under Numayri's direct command. They were heavily involved in such schemes as the Military Housing Corporation, Military Industrial Corporation, and Military Agricultural Corporation, which were set up to guarantee profits and provide cheap services for military personnel. Much of this expenditure was hidden in state budgets under items labeled "Other"—which constituted the largest line item in budgets between 1979 and 1982.[4]

In a related fashion the current Ministry of Finance has been able to utilize the injunction against *riba* (interest) in the predominant Islamic banks to obscure real levels of internal indebtedness, reframe outstanding portfolios as capital investments (subject to rapid levels of depreciation), and engage in hidden transfers to mask defense spending. The long-term health of the economy is being held hostage in significant ways to the sheer appearance of declining shortfalls.

Between 1970 and 1982 prices for major export commodities fell, at annual rates of 4.1 percent for groundnuts and 1.9 percent for cotton, eventually leading to a decline in net barter terms of trade of 30 percent between 1980 and 1982.[5] In 1983, the Paris Club consolidated all overdue amounts up to the end of 1982 and all amounts falling due in 1983 on loans contracted previously into a sixteen-year-old loan with a six-year grace period, which brought the debt service ratio to 30 percent of exports.[6] Since this time, debt service obligations have climbed to 85 percent of export and service earnings.[7]

Economic restructuring policies have been a sensitive political issue, especially given the large role the state plays in subsidizing basic commodities. When Sudan broke with the IMF in December 1985 over repayment schedules and austerity measures, it lost access to $3.5 billion in potential aid and $900 million in balance of payments support.[8] A shortage of imported inputs prompted a large increase in domestic prices, making production for the internal market increasingly profitable, thus further exerting a decelerating pressure on export production. Sudan was unable to take advantage of price increases on export crops during the 1970–78 period due to declining volume triggered by insufficient inputs, aging infrastructure, and structural financial discriminations that favored foodstuff cultivation (thought to reduce import bills); thus very few inputs such as machinery and equipment went into the productive sector. Manufacturing remains less than 10 percent of the GDP.[9] In 1980–81, exports earned $479 million while imports cost $1.63 billion.[10]

Political neglect, corruption, and the organization of agricultural production combine to undermine the development of Sudan's agricultural potential. Twenty percent of the total seven million hectares of arable land is under cultivation; 50 percent of the water potential is used.[11] A common joke is that if you plant a man in the rich soil of Equatorial Province, he will grow. Yet, almost all agricultural schemes have been developed in the North. The few that have been attempted in the South were poorly planned and nearly all failed. In the Jebel Ladu scheme, for example, 30,000 feddans (1 feddan = 1.088 acres) were to be cultivated for sorghum. Millions were spent on equipment, but nothing was done to make the ten-mile road from Juba to Jebel Ladu passable during the rainy season.[12]

Much of the problem lies with the development of large-scale agricultural schemes, in which farmers become owners of a tenancy rented from them in turn by the scheme. Under these arrangements, such as the one at Wad al-Abbas in the Blue Nile Region, farmers are required to grow certain crops on specified acreage. Irrigation is provided against the cash crop account. Farmers exercise almost no control over the means of production; decision making rests with the scheme's managers, who tend to favor monocropping. Profit sharing is more apparent than real since the farmer pays for production costs. In 1980, only 6 out of 1,597 farmers received a profit from the year's cotton harvest.[13]

With the emphasis on cotton growing as a year-round activity and the need to also grow sorghum for internal consumption, a heavy emphasis is placed on the introduction of hired labor, often at prohibitive wages. Household labor is overextended, contributing to poor yields and the threat of eviction from the land as a result. Since land can be neither bought nor sold, farmers are converted from independent producers to unpaid proletarians.[14] Since profits to the state derive from the total outputs of labor and not from yield efficiency, the state ends up profiting from the least profitable system, irrigated production, since it controls irrigation and water delivery.

The erosion of livelihoods in the Western regions, Darfur in particular, has sent a large proportion of the population to Greater Khartoum. Here many are recruited for jobs on agricultural schemes. Although they manage to eke out a better living doing agricultural work than living in the city (earning as much as $2.50 a day as compared with $1.20 in Khartoum) they easily become "captives" on the schemes—forced to buy expensive provisions, pay high rents, and accrue high levels of indebtedness.

Corruption and disorganization have also contributed to economic weakness. When an IMF team visited Sudan in 1983, there was no full account of its loans available in the Ministry of Finance. Different ministries were negotiating different contracts without informing the Bank of Sudan or the Ministry of Finance about the details. There were also marked discrepancies and inconsistencies in the regulatory policies applied to the national, private, and Islamic banks. Faisal Islamic Bank, for example, was exempt from profit taxes and foreign exchange controls, and operated outside of IMF-negotiated credit controls.[15] Export licenses are often no more than hurriedly scribbled pieces of paper bearing the semblance of an official stamp. Elaborate networks of extortion and racketeering exist for those who wish to avoid custom duties, especially at the time of hajj when many Sudanese visit Saudi Arabia. Under-invoicing and hoarding are common practices that distort the prices of basic staples. While the informal economic practices of the poor are frequently blamed for distorting national economies, it is important to keep in mind the thorough entrenchment of Sudanese economies of scale in structures of "informality."

Throughout the substantial political and regime changes during the past decade, the civil service has largely remained intact—partly because civil servants have vigorously protected their own interests rather than pursuing rational economic policies. Additionally, alliances have existed between civil servants and some of the major merchants. The latter are frequently awarded government contracts which finance entrepreneurial projects rather than the development schemes for which they are intended; for example, tractors sold at one-third discounts through international development aid contracts reappear on the market bearing face-value prices.[16] Often projects are conceived that make little sense (or should make little sense): an onion dehydration factory was built in Kassala and then closed because fresh onions were available year round; a sugar scheme was developed in El Gunied, a place where sugarcane cannot grow; factories were built in Babanousa without provisions for an adequate power supply.[17]

The public sector consists of some thirty industries, primarily those producing sugar, yarn, textiles, cement, food products, and paper. Most suffer from poor planning, problems with the provision of water and electricity, and failed capitalization agreements.[18] Although the private sector once contributed up to 80 percent of the industrial budget, by 1985 it had declined to 5 percent as individual investment laws removed incentives.

Since 1978 the Islamic banks have stepped in to become the major organizers of the economy. Due to the relaxation of currency controls and the minimal state supervision accorded these banks, they operate with relative autonomy. They have proved popular with many as an alternative to the feudal *shail* system, in which the large merchants, financed by the traditional banking sector, lent farmers money at exorbitant rates of interest. This system became a major source of rural impoverishment. Under the principles of Islamic banking, account holders receive shares in the bank, and the bank engages in joint projects with borrowers. In agriculture, the bank enters into a partnership (*murbahah*) with the farmer who owns the land. The bank charges no interest (*riba*) for its investment (loan), but retains 30 percent of the profit and owns the equipment utilized. The bank then acts as the marketing agent for the crop—a function which allows the bank to take a "hidden" profit since it alone determines the cost for this service.[19] In addition, if the bank's profit margin falls below a certain level, the farmer is usually obligated to make this up in the successive harvest. Although successful in altering patterns of capital distribution in a few areas, the Islamic banks too often have simply constituted a new merchant class no more committed to long-term development of viable agricultural infrastructure than the older ones.

The selective application of strict currency controls has also been used by the present military regime to reconstitute the prevailing merchant class. Since almost all the major merchants are dependent on the "illegal" acquisition of foreign currency, major transfers of capital assets have been effected simply by executing several prominent businessmen with over-close connections to the Democratic Unionist Party. The international Islamic social welfare and propagation agencies play a major role in the circumvention of currency and import controls. The new mansions of Manshiyah in Khartoum North testify to a new generation of merchants—many who have acquired vast wealth almost overnight. But even within the Islamic movement itself, there have been repeated instances in which the "Islamic" state coffers have been plundered by prominent Sudanese and other Arab supporters.

There are different degrees of capitalist penetration in the country. Some regions, such as Gezira, are sources of raw materials for capitalist industry; others, such as the Northern Province, have experienced transitions from subsistence to commercial agriculture in ways mediated by exclusively local initiatives—where mercantile capital is invested in productive capital.[20]

In his book on agricultural practices in the Donagla region of Northern Sudan, Omer talks about the persistence of the *sagiy* system of production. The concept is an overdetermined one, referring simultaneously to a manually operated lever for raising water, the land to which the water is fed, and the social unit working the land, as well as a structural system for the disposal of surplus. Subsistence agriculture became commodity agriculture with the introduction of merchants who trade goods and market crops, and who invest in the introduction of new crops and larger yields, necessitating wage labor. Family-based production units were converted into sharecropping systems when the household had saved enough to invest in more animals or cultivate unused freehold (*milk*) land. This would, in turn, spur migration by one or several household members to accumulate income to annex more land. A variety of limitations, such as lack of rainfall, mechanical irrigation, and labor, led farmers to initiate cooperative companies; as a result, kinship relations are no longer determinant of land rights and ownership of capital equipment and assets. Yet the mode of distribution continues to be that of the *sagiya;* with resources for animals, sharecroppers, owner, overseers, animal drivers, and level handlers all taking a predetermined share of the surplus based on a logic that has persisted for decades.[21]

The Sudanese economy has long been dependent on foreign earnings—estimated to be between $500 million and $1.3 billion per annum. Every extended family has one or more members who have worked in Saudi Arabia, Libya, Iraq, and other Gulf states—from academics to engineers to laborers. These foreign earnings are responsible for nearly 75 percent of all construction starts in Sudan. In the aftermath of Sudan's support for Iraq in the Gulf War, many Sudanese lost their positions due to the collapse of the Iraqi economy and retribution by the Saudis, who had employed the bulk of Sudan's foreign workers.

Under the Bashir/Turabi regime economic policy floundered until Abdel Rahim Hamdi was appointed Finance Minister in 1990. A former senior executive in Al Baraka Islamic Bank, Hamdi instituted a series of radical liberalization policies. Much of the state-owned industrial sector was privatized, with major firms such as Sudan Textiles and the White Nile Tannery sold off at cheap prices, usually to NIF interests. Sizable retrenchments in the civil service, wide-open trade and investment policies, and massive reductions of government expenditure were the cornerstone of this indigenous structural adjustment program. Subsidies on staples such as sugar, bread, and gasoline were withdrawn, prompting immediate price rises of 75 percent.

A program of national economic salvation was initiated which devoted sizable financial resources and arable land to domestic wheat production. Although the availability of wheat for domestic consumption grew, this policy cut severely into the production of cotton, Sudan's chief earner of foreign exchange. Though increased wheat yields were supposed to compensate for massive food shortages, 97,000 tons of sorghum still found their way to European Community markets in 1990.

In September 1990 the International Monetary Fund accorded Sudan noncooperation status, since the country was not paying on arrears totaling $1,586 million in special drawing rights. As a result the regime was anxious to curb inflation, control capital goods and imports, and address the liquidity crisis in domestic financial institutions. During 12–18 May 1991 the bank exchanged new 50 and 100 Sudanese pound notes for old ones, but at a markedly distorted rate—£1,000 in new notes was exchanged for £5,000 in old notes, and those with under £5,000 were given £500. The balance was then deposited in frozen accounts.[22] Even this swap wasn't able to bring down inflation to the satisfaction of the IMF, which continued to defer decisions to expel Sudan. In February 1992 a new currency, the dinar, was issued, constituting an effective 600 percent devaluation.

A classic post–structural adjustment picture takes hold. The shops are full but no one can afford to buy anything. For a poor urban household, the simple provision of a month's supply of wheat exhausts most of the household income. Health and education costs have skyrocketed. In the city, workers grab whatever opportunities are available in the informal service sector. Often one young boy who shines shoes supports more people with his earnings than does a state bureaucrat. At 1989 figures, civil servants on average were paid £500–1,000 per month. A shoe shiner, if he shines an average of forty pairs of shoes a day at £1 each, stands to make £1,040 a month. A cigarette vendor who sells 30 packs a day at £10 (for which he pays £8 a pack) will make £1,560 in 25 days. A person who washes 10 cars a day, with roughly one-half being a full wash (inside and out) at £10 and the others at £5 will make £1,820 in 26 days.[23]

Southerners and Westerners tend to do this kind of work, as well as guarding homes and offices, making tea, brewing alcohol, hawking consumer goods, and washing clothes. In some of the settlement areas bulldozed by the government during 1991–92, up to 80 percent of the households had a member with continuous formal or informal employment. But before anyone thinks that these workers do quite well and are able to live a good life, one must take into consideration the fact that some of them are supporting up to twenty-five people, spread throughout the country, on their earnings. Estimating that it now costs about £25 a day to feed a person, these earnings still fall short of what is minimally necessary. Health surveys conducted by CARE indicate that 40 percent of children in Khartoum fall below the 80 percent height for weight ratio. But the fact that the urban poor are at least able to diligently identify and exploit opportunities for some income generation in the midst of a devastated official economy is one of the reasons that the Islamicist regime has targeted them for removal to the outskirts of Khartoum.

Chapter Three

The Civil War

Conditions of civil war have persisted in Sudan since independence in 1956. During the last thirty-seven years there have been numerous agreements, political arrangements, and workable solutions. Each has been sabotaged. During 1986–89 the war reached its fiercest intensity, with the SPLA making significant gains in the number of garrison towns seized from the Sudanese army, and building a fighting force of nearly twenty thousand. The SPLA, led by Dr. Col. John Maribor de Garang, has for the past nine years carried on the latest in a long line of armed struggles against Northern hegemony by the South. The discontent of the South historically emanates from external domination of the local economy and the vastly unequal allocation of development resources that has primarily benefited the North. The Sudanese state has in many ways perpetuated the "divide and rule" politics of the British colonial apparatus, which terminated intertribal collaborations between North and South, particularly in the areas of grazing land and water rights.

Ethnic tensions have been exacerbated during the past nine years by the government's policy of organizing and arming tribal militias among peoples either residing in or contiguous to Dinka areas, where the bulk of rebel activity has been located. This practice has resuscitated ancient enmities and culminated in occurrences of slave-taking by Rizaygat and Baqqara nomads.

The military strategy of the SPLA, a primarily Dinka-based organization, has appeared to be to make the three Southern regions, Equatoria, Bahr al-Ghazal, and Upper Nile, as unlivable as possible. It carries on a kind of "slash and burn" warfare that has devastated former agricultural schemes and commodity estates, forcibly extracted cattle and grain from villages, and most importantly, cut off these regions from contact with the bulk of the outside world. The SPLA has blown up most key rail bridges and has shot down both civilian and military aircraft, making the transport of essential supplies highly precarious and frequently impossible. Although Juba, because of its proximity to the Ugandan border, is still sporadically supplied by convoys coming through Uganda or Zaire, the provincial capital of Upper Nile, Malakal, had been virtually cut off from external supplies for two years. Even in Juba, an estimated forty thousand people died of starvation in 1988.[1] In February 1993, a tentative agreement was made at the urging of international relief agencies to provide safe passage for barges transporting food from Khartoum to Juba—even though it is thought to be a ploy to allow the Sudanese army to transport military hardware for a new dry season offensive.

Over the past several years, the SPLA claimed much of the countryside in the three Southern provinces, including eight major garrison towns. It did not, however, effectively institutionalize its grip on these ares. It has not formed an adequate administrative system nor has it established revolutionary or alternative institutions. This is primarily due to the range of territory within which it had to operate and the distance of many of its military units from their former administrative bases in Ethiopia. Since its forces were diffused over great distances, the SPLA, numbering roughly forty-five thousand at its peak, did not have sufficient manpower to institutionalize a stationary presence. Equipped with new supplies of military hardware from Iran and China, the Sudanese army was able to make major gains during 1992 and retake most of the garrison towns.

Limited to widespread guerilla operations, the SPLA destroys and disrupts what it can, since Garang's stated intention is to extend incursions into Kordofan and Darfur as a way of making the war more intensely felt by the Northern regions. Garang has also claimed to believe that the war's definitive shift in his favor will come about when the black Muslim ethnic groups of the Western provinces connect their own deep-seated hostilities toward arabized Northern ethnicities with Southern efforts.[2] So far this has not happened, as many of these groups are more interested in what takes place in Chad, with which they have greater affinities of ethnicity and kinship.

Garang has stated that the objective of the liberation struggle is not simply separation or autonomy for the South, but a change in the governance of all of Sudan.[3] But now desertions from his "Torit" faction have altered Garang's position. After the Ethiopian People's Revolutionary Democratic Front ordered refugee camps in Gambella, Ethiopia, closed following the overthrow of Mengistu in May 1991, thousands of displaced Southerners began trekking across the South in search of safety. These population flows have exerted pressure on the SPLA to move toward some kind of resolution of the conflict. Since they have suffered a string of military defeats, a faction known as the "Nasir" group, headed by Riek Machar, Gordon Koang Chol, and Lam Akol, has emerged in favor of separation. During a 31 August SPLA commanders' meeting in Kapoeta, it was announced that Garang had been deposed, an event Garang denied several days later as the factions moved to regroup in their respective strongholds.

In May 1992 secret talks between the Nasir faction and the government were held in Frankfurt, prior to the formal talks between the two factions and the government sponsored by Organization of African Unity chairman Babangida in Abuja, Nigeria, during October 1992. If anything, the Abuja talks forced the two factions into an on-again, off-again reconciliation. Despite the fact that Garang backed away from his former demand for a unified, secular Sudanese state—in favor of "self-determination" for the South—there continued to be great enmity and suspicion on both sides. Many Dinka came to believe that their rival Nuer clansmen were collaborating with the government in the latter's battlefield success. Although there may have been areas of cooperation, the intense hatred of the North among civilians in the Upper Nile region, as well as the intention of Riek to represent a more civilian-oriented voice in the SPLA, would seem to limit any substantial collaboration.

A prevalent belief throughout the Southern neighborhoods of Khartoum is that the Nasir faction intentionally cultivated this impression of collaboration in order to lull the government's defenses and stage a daring seige on Malakal. Whether they were actually able to take Malakal for any length of time or not—in what would have constituted the greatest Southern military operation of all time—the success of the Nasir group was widely believed. It was evident by the end of 1992 that Garang's leadership of the Southern movement was over.[4]

Any resolution of the war must take into consideration a plethora of internecine conflicts between ethnicities that have gotten out of hand in wake of the arming of tribal militias. In Bahr al-Ghazal especially, a large number of arms have found their way into the hands of roving bands of children. There are random ambushes of villages and nomad encampments by displaced and homeless teenagers armed with AK-47 assault rifles, and who have no real tribal or political affiliation. Armed skirmishes frequently break out between these roving bands of youths. They usually have no idea who anyone is or who they're shooting at.[5] The combined efforts of the SPLA and the state to disrupt any semblance of normal life have engendered a situation of intense implosion, where different tribal groups, their herds decimated, villages burned, children enslaved, and kin scattered or starved, escalate and settle conflicts with sophisticated weaponry.

SPLA recruits, once taken from refugee camps at Itang, west of Gambella on the Ethiopian side of the border (which they had often trekked for twenty-one days through the bush to reach), were often sent back immediately into the bush as fighters.[6] Although the SPLA is equipped with surface-to-air missiles, hand-held grenade launchers, and an array of automatic weapons, it lacks many non-hardware supplies such as medicine and uniforms. There are many stories about naked Dinka *kic* (renegades) wandering through the bush dazed and psychotic, unable to be resupplied. There are shortages of field commanders, and Garang for most of the past three years has spent most of his time in the field attending to rifts within the ranks—a process which his dictatorial style and frequent recourse to torture seems to have exacerbated.

The recent factional split was a long time in coming. During 1988 there were an increased number of intragroup conflicts. Even within the Dinka, a large tribe constituted by various agnatic lines and spread over a wide area, divisions have become more vocal, as witnessed by the animosities between the Jarad and Murmur groups. In August 1988, Joseph Oduho, the best-known Southern separatist and leader of the struggles of the 1960s, a member of the Latuka tribe, was arrested on Garang's orders, as was Scopas Lugoro, a Kuku, who had ordered the execution of a Dinka officer for raping a ten-year-old girl in Torit. In May 1988 two prominent SPLA figures, Carabino Kwang and Major Arok Tan, were arrested in Addis Ababa for supporting peace negotiations with the government.[7]

Although Garang has done much to cultivate support among neighboring black African states, opening offices in Nairobi, Kampala, and Lusaka, much of the leadership of these states remains wary of Garang personally and skeptical about the ultimate settlement obtainable. They continue to distrust Garang's motives in refusing to negotiate with the transitional government following the May 1985 overthrow of Numayri. It is generally believed that had Garang returned to Khartoum at that time he would have been given the vice presidency. Additionally, the singularly Dinka orientation of the SPLA does not bode well for the elicitation of foreign support.

Despite many attempts and political vehicles, no effective alliance has been forged among Southern ethnicities and political groups to fight *Shari'a* and Islamicization. The state has been successful in the past in playing upon ethnic and Christian divisions, enticing elites with symbolic political positions and property in Khartoum. Until recently, most of the Southern administrative posts were occupied and run from the capital, contributing to a major vacuum of authority in the major Southern cities, such as Wau and Malakal.

Much of the South has become virtually depopulated through migration and famine. An estimated seventy thousand people left Juba alone in October 1988.[8] An entire generation of Southerners has been deschooled and fragmented. Southerner migrants in the North, as well as households that have been established in the capital for years, feel increasingly between a rock and a hard place, hating both the government and a liberation movement that has failed to win much of anything and, in the process, has left them more economically and politically vulnerable than ever before.

As Northerners grow tired of the war and alarmed at the increased number of Southerners in their midst, there is growing sentiment for some kind of "final solution"—a professed willingness to concede to a permanent division of the country. There appears to be a continuing split in the present regime on this issue: On the one hand, most know that the last decade has made the South fundamentally ungovernable for years to come and that even the most rudimentary Northern control of the South would cost lots of money. On the other hand, the South is potentially rich in oil and agriculture—so rich that a "Southern nation" could become a Black Arabia. Although the extent of the oil deposits is itself a matter of debate, there is an emerging view that a Northern state could make a Southern state dependent on Northern capacity and infrastructure in order to capitalize on any reserves. Those who hold this view believe that the Sudanese army should make one last, all-out effort to win the war and, failing that, cut their losses and quickly assemble a client state, whose leadership would be adequately armed and availed of ample opportunities for self-enrichment.

Meanwhile, there is a general commitment on both sides to keep fighting the issue out simply because fighting it out has become so much part of the dynamics of Sudanese political life, a kind of legacy that cannot be parted with. In its determination to end the war, the military regime has come to increasingly rely on "volunteer" popular defense forces and has appropriated the "martyrdom" ideology prevalent in Iran to sustain their numbers. A common sight in Khartoum is pictures of recent "martyrs" ascending into a special place in heaven from the Battle of Torit or the Battle of Kapoeta. The divisions between Northerner and Southerner have remained so great that the impossibility of resolution has become the only shared national belief.

THE CONFLICT IN HISTORICAL PERSPECTIVE

In 1955, the Southern Command, formerly the Equatoria Corps, was constituted with Northern officers replacing British officers. During this time, a strike at the large Zande agricultural scheme in Bahr al-Ghazal prompted the intervention of the army. The Southern Command killed six people. This incident of Southerner fighting Southerner left a deep scar in the region's psyche. Rumors were quick to incite violence. A battalion of Northern troops was dispatched to Juba in response to rumors that noncommissioned officers in the Southern Command were operating in concert with Egyptian agents. When a company of the Southern Command was ordered to Khartoum to march in the independence celebrations, rumors spread about the imminent arabization of the military forces in the South. Tensions culminated in a mutiny by the company stationed in Torit. A bloodbath ensued in which Northern merchants and military personnel were slaughtered throughout the area.[9]

Widespread repression of Southern civil life followed this mutiny. Education was completely disrupted.[10] Southerners, who had been persuaded to agree to Sudan's independence by British assurances that the North would fully include them in the running of the country, initiated the first of many exoduses out of the country. They saw the signs of their exclusion in the Sudanization Committee, established on 20 February 1954 by the transitional government of Isma'il Azhari to run of the state until formal independence, on which Southerners received eight positions out of eight hundred.[11]

Most Northern politicians have continuously denied the existence of a "Southern problem," seeing the conflict as inspired by foreign Christian elements. Initially, the focus was on Europe; more recently it has been on East Africa. Immediately following independence in 1956 there existed a mood for national integration. Despite the widespread tensions in the South, this mood contributed to Southern representatives in the parliament agreeing to independence. Implicit in both Northern and Southern thinking was the prospect of a federal government. However, the persistence of the Catholic Church in maintaining control over Southern educational policy, the underrepresentation of Southerners on constitutional committees, and the preoccupation of the North with exerting political control led to the ascendancy of more separatist groups in the South.[12]

In 1962, William Deng, Joseph Oduho, and Aggy Jaden formed the Sudan African Closed District Union, with an office in Kinshasa. This organization was later reformed as the Sudan African National Union (SANU) with offices in Kampala and Addis Ababa. It contained two rival factions, one of which called for the advent of armed struggle in the South. In 1962, the officers and soldiers who staged the Torit mutiny of 1955 regrouped under an umbrella organization known as Anya-Nya—a conflation of a Madi language word meaning "snake poison" and a Moro language word meaning "soldier ant." In September 1963 the first military operation was conducted inside Sudan. Although tenuous connections existed between Anya-Nya and the various political groups, it remained outside of the political maneuvering taking place until 1971.[13]

Following the overthrow of the regime of General 'Abbud in October 1964, serious negotiations were conducted for the first time since independence. The Northern political parties found themselves united in their stance against either federalism or separation, and the main Southern groups, SANU, the Sudan United Party, and the Southern Front (a group of teachers, professionals, and students who had remained in Sudan) were seriously divided in their approach to the situation. Between 1964 and 1970, five different governments in exile were to be formed by different Southern factions. The Azanian National Front, formed by Oduho in April 1965, tried unsuccessfully to integrate the various factions under a common banner.[14]

This divisiveness reflected the great heterogeneity of the South and its lack of regional political and social institutions that transcended tribal affiliation. In 1928–1930, the British, at the instigation of civil secretary Harold McMichael and financial secretary Sir George Schuster, began to administer the South as a bastion against the spread of Islam and prepared for its eventual linkage to the East African territories. English was introduced as the official language, and drastic measures were taken to uproot Arab and Muslim influence from the region. Particularly brutal were the efforts of R. C. G. Brock, District Governor of Bahr al-Ghazal.[15]

Bahr al-Ghazal is a flat plain full of marshes and swamps, sporadically populated by refugees from a wide area—people sick and desperate, forced into a wide variety of provisional alliances and collaborations that are always shifting and reforming. The so-called Southern policy of the British had the effect of breaking up these shifting collaborations among distinct ethnic groups and polarizing the area along ethnic and religious lines, which previously were being displaced as salient factors in the region's social organization.

Even though this policy was reassessed by the new Governor General, Sir Steward Symes, in 1934 and eventually terminated, its ramifications are still felt in the nature of the conflict today.[16] The policy was shifted in favor of integration with the North, leading to the resumption of Arabic as the lingua franca and the return of Northern merchants and civil servants to the region.

For a time following the 1964 revolution, Clement Mboro, a prominent Southern politician, was appointed Minister of the Interior. Splits in the Southern political movements continued to plague attempts to find a political formula for resolving the conflict. A formal split in SANU was effected over proposed talks with the government and a proposed cease-fire, with William Deng supporting a framework for Southern autonomy. At the March 1965 peace conference, the Sudanese Communist Party took a strong role in advocating for a strong central government to power economic development. Southerners offered a variety of proposals, but in the end no resolution was attained. Several months later mass killings and retributions in Wau and Juba acted to further harden the respective positions of Northerner and Southerner.

A Southern Sudan Provisional Government (SSPG) was formed in August 1967 but proved to be an exercise in formalism, and was unable to integrate the various political groups into a coherent constitutional structure. Frustrated by the vicissitudes of interethnic collaboration, Dinka politicians formed the Nile Provisional Government in March 1969 as a vehicle to coordinate their activities. Following on its heels, Anya-Nya was renamed the Southern Sudan Liberation Movement, headed by Col. Joseph Lagu, signaling the political ascendancy of soldiers conducting the armed struggle within the country.[17]

THE LONG REIGN OF NUMAYRI

Following the may 1969 coup by the Free Officers Movement led by Jaafar Numayri, a series of steps were taken to address the Southern problem. But it was several years before these efforts were to culminate in any structured dialogue among the parties to the conflict. The exiled Southern leadership was still highly distrustful of Northern intentions. Radical elements within the Numayri regime, led by Communist member Joseph Garang, prioritized the acceleration of socialist development over regional considerations.

Although more Southerners were now involved in national political life and regional administration, the bulk of Numayri's efforts were directed toward consolidating political power, in light of attempts by Imam al-Hadi al-Mahdi to mobilize forces on the Right and the active efforts of Abd al-Khaliq Mahjub, General Secretary of the Sudanese Communist Party, to institutionalize a solid leftist framework within the regime. Finally, when both Left and Right were effectively suppressed, Numayri made significant moves to involve the various Southern forces in substantial negotiations. Discussions were held in Ethiopia which culminated in the signing of the Addis Ababa Agreement of 27 February 1972. The agreement provided for the establishment of a regional government in the South with its own executive and legislative agencies.[18] The central government retained control over foreign policy and revenue collection. Anya-Nya forces were to be reintegrated into the national army. Subsequently, Abel Alier became the first president of the High Executive Council.

Although the formal structure of a resolution to the conflict was in place, the agreement never really addressed the fundamental problems, even though it remained in place and provided a measure of stability for eight years. Interethnic rivalries still existed and were readily exploited by the central government. The agreement came at a time when Numayri was at the height of his political popularity, and subsequent economic disasters and Northern political discontent undermined the central government, which required substantial support to keep the agreement in place. Southerners were overly content to manipulate the structures of regional government and did little to establish themselves as a political factor in the national arena.

According to Mohammed Beshir Mohammed, the aftermath of the Addis agreement actually exacerbated the political schism between North and South as Numayri's personalized rule detracted from the development of ideological alternatives.[19] Additionally, the South possessed a greater number of political institutions than the North and more relative freedom to participate in them, making national reconciliation all the more difficult.

Increasingly, the South became a power base for the Numayri regime and his own only base of popular support. Regional autonomy for the South in large part rested on the continuation of the regime. Since the regime lacked ideological clarity and substance, the internal politics of the South remained ideologically impoverished themselves, vulnerable to the exacerbation of ethnic and tribal tensions.

The Nuer, particularly sensitive to fears of Dinka domination, reactivated Anya-Nya (II) in 1975, initially as a check on perceived Dinka attempts to dominate the autonomy process. Joseph Lagu, a longtime rival of Abel Alier, began pushing for consideration of subregionalization. Lagu was elected to the High Executive Council after Numayri persuaded Alier not to contest the second election. In an attempt to buttress a rapidly deteriorating political situation in the North, Numayri provisionally dissolved the HEC in February 1980. Abel Alier was returned to power, while Lagu continued to promote redivision in order to seize control of Equatoria. In October 1981, the Regional Assembly was dissolved again, this time in the context of the Regional Covenant Act, which divided Northern Sudan into five regions.[20] Gismella Rassa, a Muslim Southerner, was appointed by Numayri to head a provisional administration. The April 1982 election was won by a Lagu supporter, J. Tomburu, who took a pro-divisionist stance. Southern politics at this time was plagued with incessant feuding and manipulation. A vote of the regional Sudan Socialist Union Congress (Numayri's political organization) was altered to report a majority favorable to redivision. Finally, in May 1983, the South was divided into the Bahr al-Ghazal, Equatoria, and Upper Nile provinces and functionally lost much of its former autonomy.

At this time Numayri also announced his intention to integrate the Sudanese armed forces. No longer would Northerners and Southerners be stationed in their home regions exclusively. A large contingent of Southern soldiers were to be transferred to Khartoum, and the military command in the South was to be equally shared between Northern and Southern forces.

The proposed plan threatened to disrupt the economic practices through which Southern soldiers and their families were able to stay afloat.[21] In the Southern regions, patrols were accompanied by extended families and some animals, and the $15 per month salary was supplemented by family activities and reliance upon family ties spread throughout the region. Although this planned transfer precipitated the mutiny of soldiers in Malakal—and was repeatedly cited by Sadiq al-Mahdi as the reason for the resumption of the civil war—other factors were at play.[22] The rescinding of the Addis agreement, in addition to the rapid Islamicization of political and social life and the perceived arabization of the armed forces, also prompted many Southern soldiers to take to the bush. The mutiny was also fueled by rumors that Southern soldiers were to be sent to Iraq to fight in the Iran-Iraq War.[23] Interestingly enough, the three garrisons that mutinied at Bor, Pibor, and Pachella were the only nonintegrated battalions in the South.

THE NATIONAL ISLAMIC FRONT

The NIF has its historical roots in the Ikhwan reformist movements of Egypt that came to the fore in the 1940s and 1950s. Yet, during this time, a group of Sudanese academics in Cairo started meeting to consider the direction of Sudanese society and to provide an Islamicist perspective to anticolonial movements in the country—in contrast to the unionist background of most Ikhwan activities. Based on liberal, almost quasi-socialist theoretical underpinnings largely influenced by Babikr Karar, the Islamic Liberation Movement attempted to give voice to the rudimentary framework of a new Islamic order.

Many of the members of this grouping moved into the Islamic Front for the Constitution, a single-issue, nonpartisan pressure group devoted to ensuring an Islamically inspired postindependence constitution, headed by Al-Rashid al-Tahir. The members of these early movements were primarily students and the offspring of well-established sectarian families. The IFC was split by conflicting political leanings and relationships with military rule, as well as growing tension between those who saw Islamic movements as the most effective ways of advancing radical political objectives and those who were basically interested in uplifting the moral standards of the country.[24]

The return of Hassan al-Turabi, Sudan's first Ph.D., had a substantial effect on the development of the Islamic movement and signaled the end of politically leftist tendencies in the leadership. The formation of the Islamic Charter Front began a long-term strategy of putting pressure on the traditional political parties, which derived much of their legitimacy from association with Sufi religious orders. The IFC also consolidated itself in provoking a ban on the Sudan Communist Party in 1966, a move that opened up a major conflict between the legislature and the judiciary. This would prove to be a significant wedge in allowing greater Islamic influence in both.

Ikhwan throughout the Arab world emphasized cadres of a tight-knit, disciplined elite proficient at indoctrination and infiltration of educational, religious, and welfare organizations. Turabi led much of the Islamic movement into being a broad-based political apparatus, capable of drawing membership from a wide range of sectors and backgrounds. Turabi believed in democratic deliberations and popular participation in decision making—policies that contrasted sharply with Ikhwan's organizational style. There was great confusion as to who was in the end accountable to whom. At an IFC conference called in 1969 to debate the future of the Islamic movement, Turabi's emphasis on mass politics won the day after days of fierce contestation.

After the Numayri coup of May 1969, the Islamic movement was dormant for several years, as much of its leadership was detained. By 1972, the movement was reorganized and participated in a broad front of opposition to the regime, culminating in the failed Shaban uprising of 1973. Discontent over the tenuous nature of alliances within the broad opposition convinced Ikhwan that it increasingly had to fortify its own position. When Numayri offered a general reconciliation with oppositional forces in the late 1970s, Ikhwan seized the opportunity in order to win space to rebuild the organization and acquire necessary governmental experience.

The emphasis of Ikhwan was increasingly to keep Numayri strong enough until they were prepared to take over the reins of power—an expedient course of action that became transparent to the general public and cut into their popularity. Ikhwan-based trade unions split from the central leadership and began to oppose Numayri in 1982. Although Ikhwan had nothing to do with the implementation of *Shari'a* laws in September 1983, and disagreed with much of their content, the movement decided to support the legislation, and Turabi was appointed Attorney General. Ikhwan believed it could use the *Shari'a* issue as the locus around which to build a new coalition of political forces that would diminish the role of the traditional Sufi parties—an agenda which failed to materialize.

Again the overarching political method employed was oriented to buying time. Ikhwan knew that they lacked the popular support to win any election outright, and instead opted to build a solid base of administrative experience and a close relationship with the growing Islamic financial institutions in the country. Ikhwan concluded that there was not much to gain by vociferously opposing Numayri, even though by 1984 Numayri began to crack down on the movement. The Ikhwan-allied Supreme Court justice al-Mikashfi Taha al-Kabbashi became a law unto himself, completely ignoring Numayri's authority. Numayri restored the power of the former leftist core of the Sudanese Socialist Union, in particular, Omar Muhammed al-Tayyib, who led a massive crackdown on Islamicists.

There is much conflicting opinion over the actual role Ikhwan played in the 6 April coup that toppled Numayri, since the organization did not play a visibly active role in the broad front of opposition that was engaged in daily antigovernment demonstrations. Whatever their role, the Transitional Military Council, led by Suwar ad-Dahab, permitted a rapid reconsolidation of the Islamic forces, which culminated in the formation of the National Islamic Front.

The NIF, intended as a front joining Ikhwan with various civil societies and Sufist organs, again showed patience in the political arena. The National Gathering for the Salvation of the Homeland (NGSH), a coalition of basically left-wing forces opposed to the NIF, immediately played for high stakes and lost, in the end solidifying a closer relationship between the NIF and the army.

Even though the NIF proved to be only the third strongest party in the elections of 1986, they were the dominant force in Khartoum and entered the new political arena with the most proficient organization, the most international connections, and the most administrative experience.

THE ADVENT OF THE SPLA

It is unclear just what Garang's role actually was in the 1983 mutiny. Officially he was sent by the armed forces to Bor to mediate the dispute, but he either joined the rebels after having been captured or joined them voluntarily, as he claims. According to Garang, the mutineers essentially preempted a rebellion that he himself had been planning.[25] Whatever the details, the SPLA and the SPLM were formed at this time:

Form its inception, Garang exercised almost total control over the armed movement, but only gradually was able to exercise his dominance over the political wing. Initially, this control was shared with members of at least two other groups that had been in opposition to the Addis accord. First, there was the alliance of the Sudan People's Liberation Party with Anya-Nya II, a Nuer-dominated fighting group that had been conducting low-level guerrilla activities since the mid-seventies, headed by Aquot Atem and Lt. Col. Samuel Gai Tut. A year following the formation of the SPLA, Anya-Nya split, estranged over the perception of Dinka domination, and later was converted into a progovernment militia.[26] The second group, the Southern Sudan Liberation Front, headed by Ladu Lokurange, was responsible for the Boma incident earlier in 1983 in which seven members of a Christian aid group were kidnapped.

As part of the government's plan to export crude oil, a billion dollars had been invested by 1983 in a project to construct a pipeline from the oil fields at Bentieu to the Red Sea. This decision reflected the government's attempt to avoid a politically sensitive question of where to refine crude oil. An initial decision had been made to build a refinery at Kosti in the North, a decision based primarily on the cost-effectiveness of the location over Southern alternatives, but one interpreted by many Southerners as yet another example of resources being drained from the South. The government had secured extremely favorable terms for the financing of the pipeline: the government's share of the investment was to come from future proceeds.[27]

The oil fields became a focus of guerrilla activity. In November 1983, three American Chevron workers were killed by young armed bandits—robbery being the most probable motive. In February 1984, however, a group of twenty guerrillas, perhaps led by Aquot Atem's faction, attacked a Chevron accommodation barge, killing three. By 2 April 1984, Chevron suspended all of its operations due to a lack of security.

The disruption of this highly significant economic investment was not the only disaster Numayri faced. During the droughts in Kordofan between 1983 and 1985, the region lost a quarter of its residents to death and migration; most livestock was sold or lost. One of Sudan's chief exports, gum arabic, declined by nearly 80 percent in the course of one year, 1983 to 1984. Al-Ubayyid, the region's main city, experienced rapid depopulation due to the severely curtailed supply of drinking water.

On 16 March 1984 a lone Libyan-made jet dropped bombs near the Omdurman broadcasting station. Much speculation resulted as to the intent and source of the mission. That the speculation could take so many directions became a sign of the potential fragility of the Numayri regime. There was even some talk that Numayri had staged the bombing himself. A master at deflecting attention away from economic issues, Numayri was not above suspicion of arranging false attacks upon himself. Reviewing all the speculation, Gurdon thinks it is most likely that the bombing was planned in cooperation with Libya by Joseph Oduho, a power in the SPLM at the time, as a means of testing out the extent of the existent military pact with Egypt.[28]

A period of marked vacillation in Sudanese politics followed the bombing incident. A period of an intense application of the *hadd* punishments progressively came to a halt. The ban on *riba* (interest-accumulating capital) was relaxed and selectively applied. Following the execution of Mahmoud Muhammad Taha, perhaps the most significant religious and political figure in Khartoum (and the political fragmentation of his party, the Republican Brothers), Numayri inexplicably rehabilitated the long-dormant Menshevik faction of his original May 1969 regime. The Muslim Brothers, Numayri's former allies, were increasingly ostracized and the September laws subjected to officially sanctioned criticism. Singled out in particular was al-Mikashfi Taha al-Kabbashi, who headed both the criminal court and court of appeals. In March 1985 many Islamicists were placed under arrest.

THE RETURN TO DEMOCRACY

The National Gathering for the Salvation of the Homeland (NGSH), a coalition of forces from the trade and professional unions and the Broad Left, a loose affiliation of Baathists, Nasserists, and Leftists, began staging daily demonstrations in early 1985. By April the country seemed to be veering out of control. The economy was in tatters and the SPLA was extending its base of influence. In the midst of the Uprising in April, the army deposed Numayri while he was returning from a medical visit to the United States and replaced him with the Transitional Military Council headed by Suwar ad-Dahab. Numayri took up residence in Cairo, where he remains to this day. The TMC committed itself to a return to democratic rule within the year and a negotiated settlement to the civil war.

Although a deeply religious and moral man, Dahab did not move quickly enough to make a definitive break from the Numayri regime, and effectively lost the opportunity to exert dynamic leadership shortly after the coup.[29] Within seven days of the coup, 29 political parties and 77 trade unions had been formed. By late May there was only one policy initiative regarding the South. The TMC seemed content to continue playing the game of sowing Dinka-Equatorian antagonism. The Equatorians were indeed anti-SPLA for the most part, but they were even more anti-North.

The NASC was subject to too many internal splits to exert substantial political direction. In March 1986 they met with the SPLA in the Ethiopian resort town Koka as a preliminary step toward a national constitutional conference to be held in October of that year. However, with the exception of the Umma Party, none of the other major political parties signed the resultant Koka Dam accord.[30] The Islamicists emerged into the vacuum as the best-organized political force. With generous funding from their primary patrons, Mohammed Yusuf Mohammed (an influential lawyer and businessman) and Osman Khaled (a merchant who controlled much of the sesame and millet markets) and connections with international Islamic banks, the Islamicists had the money to continue building an effective political machine.

The return to democracy in 1986 coincided with an escalation of the fighting. The successful incursions of Maj. Gen. Deng Ajuong beyond the Bahr al-Arab (the dividing line between North and South in the

Western part of the country) led the new prime minister, Sadiq al-Mahdi, to arm Messeriyya militias under the direction of 'Ali Nimr el Muglud, the paramount chief.[31] Once, upon meeting the chief's brothers, I was struck by the vehemence of their words. Stealing cows was equated with stealing sexual power, which had to be compensated with a certain thickness of blood covering the ground in the sight of women. What had been aroused seemed like a passion for death.

Where the borders of Dinka and Messeriyya territory had once constituted innumerable opportunities for cultural diffusion, negotiation, and compromise, the present conflict now seemed to deconstruct the historical moderation as the submergence of a volcanic hatred in which sex, death, food, gender, and god are brewed into a wild intoxicant. Certainly the burning to death of ninety Dinka in July 1986 by Rizaygat in Ed Da'ein was an indication of this passion.

Throughout his first year in office, Mahdi coupled promises to replace (not cancel) the September laws with the need to "wage a real war."[32] Juba, the largest city of the South, was under seige, and Malakal, as of November 1986, had been under siege for almost two years. Anya-Nya II patrols encircled the town, kidnapping labor to work their fields and then selling *dura* (sorghum) in the market at exorbitant prices. In July 1986 Mahdi met with Garang in Addis and pressed for a quick resolution of the conflict. Garang insisted on the abrogation of defense pacts with Egypt and Libya, the abolition of all *Shari'a* laws, and the lifting of the state of emergency as preconditions to a constitutional conference. Following the meeting, the SPLA announced that all military aircraft flying into Southern airspace would be shot down. On 17 August, the SPLA downed a civilian Sudan Air plane over Malakal, believing that it was transporting military personnel. The government then ordered that no direct talks were to be held with the SPLA, an edict which was soon violated by the National Islamic Front.

When asked to assess the failure to negotiate an accord during this time, the head of the NASC, Taysir Muhammad Ahmad 'Ali, attributed the hardening of the SPLA's attitudes to the following factors: During the civilian government of Jazuli Daf'allah prior to the elections of 1986, Garang was deliberating whether to join a transitional government and participate in the elections. After first ruling it out, it was reported that he was reconsidering his position. The prime minister indicated his willingness to talk seriously with Garang and was impressed with certain indications offered by the SPLA of their seriousness about reconciliation. This was dampened, however, when Daf'allah, on a trip to Egypt and the West, criticized the SPLA for lack of sincerity.[33] Taysir also felt that Mahdi was overeager in pressing Garang for quick results during their initial meeting. While the NIF met with the SPLM during a government ban on such meetings, more moderate groups were prevented from exerting a mediating influence.

During 1987, the crystallization of a coherent Southern policy was hindered by preoccupations in Khartoum with attempts to form a national government. Mahdi's strategy for staying in power was to initiate a process in which he could direct the mutual manipulations of various factions and parties. Deeply divided over negotiating stances toward the IMF, Shari'a, the conditions for negotiating with Garang, and what to do about a deteriorating security situation in general, the government simply deferred decisions to other bodies and councils.

The Constituent Assembly, Sudan's parliament, failed to function for the most part due to absenteeism, the lack of accountability of ministers to legislative committees, and ambiguity over delegated authority.[34] Each party was divided over the issue of power sharing with the other parties—a problem that seemed to weaken the governance process in general. The capture of the Northern border town Kurmuk in December 1987 served to whip up a substantial measure of war hysteria, and various Arab countries were enlisted in a needed infusion of arms. Yet, the SPLA continued to capture more garrison towns. They held Kurmuk only briefly, but seized Kapoeta and later Torit, which they eventually lost during the Sudanese armed forces offensive in 1992.

THE FAILURE OF DEMOCRACY

As Migdal points out, the emergence of a strong state can only occur with the exercise of a tremendous amount of social control. Heterogeneous state institutions are necessary to consolidate the state's ability to mobilize the population so as to enforce its agenda. Too much power in too few institutions itself leads to the risk of the lack of state cohesion.[35] There exists a well-elaborated network of rewards, sanctions, and incentives that engender levels of affiliation to the state and coordinate productive capacities. However, diffusion of power, often a strategy for the survival of a particular regime, produces a situation in which the state lacks the political capital to enforce its own agenda and relies on the preemptive shuffling of cabinet posts and ministries.

Political life in Khartoum consisted of the conflation of both these tendencies in a mixture that seemed to guarantee permanent volatility. The organization of political parties centered around the dominance of particular patrons that had been on the scene for decades. The function-

ing of the parties relied heavily on the constant attention of those patrons and leaders. Whatever dissention existed was, for the most part,
not granted a space of negotiating influence. In the three main parties,
the fundamental decisions continued to rest with Mahdi, Mirghani
(DUP) and Turabi (NIF).

Within the state arena, each party was constantly trying to out-
maneuver and accommodate the others, resulting in an almost constant
reorganization of the government during the three years of democratic
rule. The composition of the ministries was always being changed and
their functions redefined. Because the government during those three
years always consisted of at least two of the three major parties,
different interests controlled different ministries—their focus being to
undermine the power and latitude of the others instead of developing
their own roots in civil society. Power was structurally and operationally diffused, making decision making a drawn-out and painstaking
process.

Given this situation, the government found it nearly impossible to
generate a viable negotiating position that could bring the civil war
to a close. Even in ancillary aspects of the conflict, the state did little to
intervene. The war served as a pretext for merchants to intensify black
marketeering. Whatever policy was directed against it, the state confronted the fact that such activity was being conducted by those most
necessary to the state's efforts to enforce political order and provide supplies of essential commodities. The "Little Amira" incident of 1987, in
which a 14-year-old girl was abducted and killed by police, served to
"prove" that the government was unable to guarantee even the safety
of children.

In March 1987, after eight months of deliberation, Mahdi formed
an Interim Council for the South to administer Southern affairs. The
formation of the council was widely challenged by most Southern political forces. Accountable to the Office of the Prime Minister, the council
was viewed as lacking any functional autonomy or authority. The ap-
pointment of Matthew Ubur, a Shilluk and political independent, was
viewed by most Southerners as an attempt by Mahdi to skirt having
to make any substantial affiliations with Southern political parties. The
actions were viewed as a continuation of divide-and-rule politics, and
the Southern forces moved decisively against those who cooperated
with the government in this regard. William Deng, who assumed the
governorship of Bahr al-Ghazal, was expelled from the Southern Sudan
Political Association, as was Aldo Ajo Deng, who became Minister of

Irrigation. The Sudan African Congress expelled Walter Kunijok, who became Minister of Labor and Civil Service.[36]

During 1987 and 1988, the Council had no real function and little influence in terms of formulating policy. It became a vehicle for the dispensation of patronage and government allotments of basic commodities such as sugar, which Southern politicians sold at exorbitant rates on the black market. Most Southern politicians had not operated in the South for many years and often had little sense of the degree of suffering and devastation taking place there. Not accountable to any constituency, since the war had precluded representatives being selected during the 1986 election, their behavior was often oriented toward advancing their own self-interest, which usually meant finding vehicles of complicity with the state's agenda of deferring resolution of the conflict.

Following the DUP's agreement with the SPLA on 15 November 1988 on a basic framework for ending the conflict, there was a renewed sense of optimism in Khartoum about the prospects for peace. Both sides seemed to be in the mood for some resolution since the situation was rapidly deteriorating. Although the SPLA seemed to score one military success after another, latent internecine battles were coming to the surface. In the liberated garrison town of Torit, interethnic battles were fought as the SPLA attempted to seize control.[37]

The NIF vehemently opposed the negotiation accord, which called for the indefinite suspension of Islamic laws until a constitutional conference could deliberate the question of Sudanese national identity. There were countervailing demonstrations that erupted into sporadic violence. A strike by engineers and technicians shut down water and electricity. University lecturers, journalists, and judges walked off their jobs.[38] Mahdi wavered over supporting the accord and finally decided against it. On 21 December he directed the Constituent Assembly to reject the agreement.

In December, the SPLA began secret discussions with Egypt, tacitly approved by the NIF.[39] These talks were later confirmed by Egypt's president, Hosni Mubarak, on 27 February, at the time when crucial political negotiations were taking place over the formation of a new government.[40] In late December, the DUP announced its withdrawal from the government. After repeated attempts to get the party to rejoin the government, a new cabinet was formed on 2 February 1989, which included Hassan al-Turabi as foreign minister, Aldo Ajo Deng as deputy prime minister, and Abdallah Muhammed Ahmed as economic minister— three men despised by Southerners. Two weeks later, Rt. Lt. Gen. Abd al-Majid Hamid Khalil, the defense minister, resigned, stating that the army needed half a billion dollars in order to remain functional. At the same time, the government issued a report in *Al-Wakh* (Manama) that a secret meeting had taken place between Garang and Moshe Arens, the former Israeli defense minister, on Sudanese soil in January. This was an apparent attempt to marshal support from the Arab countries. On 12 February, Juba came under heavy bombardment from the SPLA.

THE ARMY ULTIMATUM

As garrison towns in the South started falling at a quicker pace, the military became alarmed at the way arms supplies from the Arab states were drying up. Before he resigned, Khalil made a secret tour of Arab countries for the purpose of securing arms. Returning to Khartoum empty-handed, he told the army that the message from the Arab states was clear: get the NIF out of the government and distance yourselves from Iran and Libya.[41] On 20 February 1989, 150 top officers from all the armed forces, in a letter to the Council of State (the supreme governmental body), gave the government a stern ultimatum: either take certain steps within one week or resign. They demanded that the army be supported and supplied in such a way as to enable it to win if the war was to continue. Additionally, they demanded a broad-based government including trade unions and a more balanced foreign policy.

Within two days of the ultimatum, Col. Abu Bakr Yunis Jabar, commander in chief of the Libyan armed forces, visited Khartoum, further inflaming the situation.[42] Mahdi, in the meantime, initiated a highly theatrical process of trying to save his job, conducting a series of well-publicized meetings with different sectors of the government and civil society. He asked the military to make a commitment not to stage a coup and threatened to resign if the army did not offer such a commitment. On the same day, Torit was finally seized by the SPLA; Nimule was soon to follow on 4 March and Jummayzah on 7 March.

Ahmad al-Mirghani, chair on the Council of State and brother of the DUP patron, supported the army ultimatum in his formal capacity as Supreme Commander of the Armed Forces. Mahdi then announced his intention to enlarge the cabinet to include the modern forces, i.e., trade union representatives and other extraparliamentary groups. On 27 February gunmen opened fire on Mirghani's house and the army reiterated its ultimatum.

In early March, Mahdi opened up negotiations with thirty-eight political parties, trade unions, and federations in an attempt to form an expanded government based on the military demands of developing a "national course in government." Muhammed 'Uthman Jama, head of the Sudan Workers Trade Union Federation, the largest labor organization, refused to join the government because Mahdi would not extend minimum wage increases offered to public employees to the private sector and insisted that the unions commit themselves to not striking as a prerequisite for joining the government. Suwar ad-Dahab and Jazuli Daf'allah were enlisted as mediators in the attempt to form a new government.

On 14 March, Turabi announced that the NIF would not participate in the new government because the commitment to *Shari'a* was not part of its platform and because the government included two Communists. Additionally, the party disagreed with Mahdi's acceptance of a United Nations proposal for a one-month cease-fire.

With the implicit support of the military for the circumvention of the *Shari'a* issue, the new government took measures to reverse the legislation already approved by the Constituent Assembly and the Council of State. A 60 percent rate of inflation and severe commodity shortages, coupled with constant rumors of coups, meant that some progress had to occur. On 1 April, the Constituent Assembly voted to suspend implementation of the Islamic penal code until a constitutional conference was convened. This action prompted the resignation of the Speaker, Mohammed Yusuf Mohammed, and all fifty other NIF representatives.

The security situation in Darfur rapidly deteriorated. On 1 April, a coup attempt was staged against Hissein Habre, the then President of Chad, by former army chief Hassan Djamous and former army commander Idris Debry. The Chadian army pursued rebel forces some two hundred miles into Sudanese territory.[43] The interethnic war between the sedentary Fur and the nomadic Arab tribes escalated, resulting in the ambush of a Fur village at Kas where perhaps as many as three hundred people were killed. Khartoum newspapers reported large-scale defections from the army, and the military demanded that the press curtail reports on its activities.

On 2 June, Sadiq al-Mahdi reported his intention to abrogate the mutual defense pact with Egypt—one of the SPLA's conditions for negotiations. This followed a one-month period during which the SPLA basically adhered to a unilateral cease-fire it declared on 2 May. On 6–11 June, talks were held in Addis Ababa between the government and the SPLA. September 18 was set as the date for the convention of a constitutional conference, although there existed some divergence of opinion over whether the defense pact with Libya would be abrogated.[44] In

Washington, Garang announced that the cease-fire would be extended to the end of June.

Basically, Mahdi was still a reluctant player in this acceleration of the peace process—which probably was his undoing. Egypt appeared to take an increasingly significant role, ensuring that concrete steps were taken to move the process along. On 19 June, the government announced its discovery of a coup attempt being plotted by Numayri loyalists. Brig. Gen. Salah al-Dawiyy, fourteen army officers, and fifty civilians were arrested. There was general disbelief in Khartoum as to the reality of this attempt.[45]

Following a massive demonstration in which tens of thousands marched for peace in Khartoum on 8 June, it was reported that Mahdi's concern about being brought down in a popular uprising intensified.[46] He felt that Egypt had long ago taken an irrevocably hostile position to his continued rule. Reports of the coup attempt further strained Sudanese-Egyptian relations, especially after Mahdi offered asylum to Khalid 'Abd al-Nasir, son of the former Egyptian president, who was wanted in Cairo on charges of terrorism.[47] The DUP announced that six brigadier generals arrested were among the group of senior officers who had issued the ultimatum in February. Reports circulated in *Al-Sharq al-Awsat* (Cairo) that Numayri was on his way to Chad to conduct antigovernment activities.[48] Numayri did appear in Chad, but it seemed that Egypt was simply taking advantage of the situation to exert pressure on the Khartoum regime.

In the meantime, Khartoum National Unity Radio, the broadcast station of the armed forces, initiated a series of commentaries pointedly hostile to the peace process. The NIF organized rallies to support the army, but these were not well attended. On 28 June, the army denied a report published in *al-Usbur* (Khartoum) that it had issued an ultimatum to the government to either try the detained officers within seventy-two hours or set them free.

THE END OF DEMOCRACY

On 30 June 1989, a group of junior officers led by Lt. Gen. Omar Hassan Ahmed al-Bashir staged a successful coup, which dissolved all political constitutions and bodies and established Al-Harakah al-Qawmiyyah li Tashih al-Awda (National Movement for the Rectification of the Situation), led by the National Salvation Revolutionary Command Council (RCC)—a fifteen-man junta that included three Southerners.[49] The coup came on the same day the Council of State Ministers was to have met in an emergency session to consider a document that would have effectively abrogated *Shariʿa*.[50]

Bashir, who had just returned to Khartoum from an extended trip to assess the conditions of soldiers in the South, was apparently quite alarmed at what he had seen. Additionally, it was thought that the coup may have been a preemptive strike, since it is clear that others in the military were preparing to make moves.[51] Much speculation took place over the extent to which the coup was NIF-inspired. The presence of a close associate of John Garang in the ruling junta was used to downplay this factor, although both the timing of the coup and Bashir's announcement that he would subject the *Shariʿa* to a referendum served to indicate the possibility of substantial NIF influence.

It is likely that a convergence of interests and factors was at work. Divisions between a new generation of Islamicist soldiers and the entrenched leadership had been growing in the military for some time. Given the highly fluid and conspiratorial political climate, whose murkiness seemed to grow exponentially with each passing day, the NIF was clearly the single most cohesive political force in Greater Khartoum, and was also seen by many in the military as the guarantor of the army's integrity. Thus there was a turn toward the Islamicists by many middle-ranking officers simply due to their proficiency as organizers, rather than out of ideological loyalty.

From another perspective, the way the Mahdi regime seemed to toy with the army alarmed many, enabling the NIF to seize the issue of ensuring the integrity of the military. Whether sections of the military and NIF used each other to support their own singular interests or engaged in more direct collaborations remains a subject of continuing speculation, despite the fact that the NIF was clearly calling the shots.

In support of speculation that the coup was NIF-inspired was the removal of Gen. Fathi Ahmad ʿAli, Commander in Chief, and twenty-nine other senior officers thought to be primarily aligned with the DUP. All those officers detained because of the prior alleged coup attempt were released.

Whatever the NIF role, it was clear that a major move was necessary. Although most in the leadership of the movement were sincere in their belief that the transition to power should be effected legally and peacefully, this commitment did not obviate their taking advantage of any means that circumstance presented. Associated with too many failed coups, in 1973 and 1976, and election defeats, in 1964, 1968, and 1986, the movement had accumulated a myriad of compromises that continually threatened to undermine the very moral authority that is largely its reason for being. Yet, as El-Affendi[52] points out, that very moral leadership also has prevented the movement from mobilizing a wide political base, since it is perceived as self-righteous and arrogant. Conversely, the compromises incumbent on a political party tended to make the movement even more unpopular. However, a social movement whose goal is engineering the social order into a fuller alignment with the religious framework that defines the moral order cannot expect to survive without taking on the functions of governance.

Indeed, it was the latter assessment that led the movement in 1976–77 to make the gradual control of state power its central strategy. Faced with a political situation in 1989 in which the NIF was increasingly identified as a scapegoat and in which the movement's longtime enemies, the modern forces, were brought into the government to prop up a faltering Mahdi regime, the NIF may have concluded that they were in a "now or never" situation. Because the NIF was widely perceived as weakened, perhaps debilitated, by many in the outside world who were hoping for a coup, the NIF may also have concluded that the time was right to collaborate with sectors of the military, since they could use their purported "weakened" state to "mask" any subsequent influence.

An important aspect of the NIF's alliance with the military is that it has provided them the space to greatly expand their own security organs, known as the Amm ath Thwara. These security forces have their own arms networks and command operations, and are generally responsible for the practice of detainment-release-redetainment in unofficial prisons ("ghost houses") that has characterized NIF's response to its opponents. These security forces are able to curtail movement inside and outside the country, and have especially concentrated on monitoring actions within the military.

Although Arab states thought they could engineer a gradual separation of the Revolutionary Command Council from the NIF, the NIF's security branch engaged in repeated preemptive strikes, engineering the impression of coup attempts in order to purge possible sectors of dissent from the military. In 1991, 137 police officers and 91 army officers were expelled and replaced with the NIF hard-liners. There is growing resentment even among Islamicists in the military that these organs are compromising military interests. The reported execution of several prominent Southern military officials, including Peter Cirillo, former governor of Equatoria, and Machur Arok (brother of a major SPLA figure) by the NIF security branch in November 1992 was said to have prompted great dismay in the Southern ranks. When Mahdi gave indications that he was ready to reconcile with the RCC, and then changed his mind following discussions with the NIF, a supposed coup attempt on 27 August was foiled, giving the regime a pretext to purge many of the remaining Western Ansar officers. In the recent concern over Turabi's health, members of the security branch, Nafei 'Ali Nafei in particular, have risen to prominent de facto leadership positions.

The security branch has kept a tight lid on the dissemination of information. The security organs attempted to mask the massive casualties among the popular defense forces of civilian volunteers sent to the South—until all the hospitals in the Khartoum area became full. More importantly, they have attempted to conceal the true nature of food shortages and the vulnerability of much of the country to widespread famine.

After the takeover, all previous legislation and agreements were suspended. The issues of Islamic legislation and a constitutional conference were to be gradually resolved, and newspapers, local democratic structures, and trade unions were to be gradually permitted to function again. The only area in which the RCC moved decisively was against black marketeering, arresting many prominent merchants and announcing price controls and strict currency regulations.

Sadiq al-Mahdi, in hiding during the week following the coup, was arrested on 6 July and placed in Kober Prison with all the other prominent political leaders who had been detained. It was announced that trials were to be held for all of these individuals. Hassan al-Banna, Umma Party member and vice chairman of the Council of State, was the first to be tried, and was sentenced to forty years imprisonment for economic crimes. During the flood of August 1988, it was reported that Banna had diverted truckloads of foreign aid to his personal possession. Also arrested were National Alliance leader Taysir Muhammad Ahmad 'Ali (the major protagonist of the Koka Dam accord) and Ushari Mahmoud (co-author of the 1987 book on the Ed Da'ein Dinka massacre).[53]

On 5 July, the RCC proposed a one-month cease-fire and general amnesty. Initial meetings, however, on 19 August between the RCC and the SPLA were unproductive, and Garang announced in a speech to the nation of 17 August that he saw neither competence nor goodwill in the new regime.[54] In the twenty-one-member civilian cabinet announced at the end of July, there were eight NIF sympathizers included, most prominent among them Hassan Ismail el Bieli, the architect of the economic policies for the Faisal Islamic Bank, as minister of justice. Two prominent merchants who controlled much of the import-export business and were the NIF's top financial backers, Shaykh Abdel Basri and El Tayeb al Nus, were appointed to the Economic Commission. The only union allowed to function openly was the Khartoum University Students Union, dominated by the NIF and actively supportive of the new government. Even if the coup attempt had not been planned by the NIF, the lack of political acuity and of managerial and administrative competence clearly evident in the new regime allowed the NIF—the most proficient political structure in Khartoum—to take advantage of the situation and exert predominant influence behind the scenes.

During the year prior to the coup, there appeared to be significant splits in the NIF over future political strategies, with some "progressives" arguing for an ongoing commitment to democratic process and serious negotiations with the South, while others saw opportunities to both intensify and take advantage of the political chaos as a means to gain state power. Several prominent "progressives" left the country in late 1988, and several of the top NIF leadership were initially detained in the aftermath of the coup, including Hassan al-Turabi. During the early stage of the RCC, Ali Osman Mohammed Taha, NIF deputy general secretary and head of the party's militantly "radical" youth wing, was the most powerful man in the country.

It was thought by many observers in Khartoum that the NIF was split over how to deal with the new situation. At the end of July, women were removed from many public positions, including the renowned judge Aminah Awad. Certainly the movement contained many contradictory opinions about the role of women in public life. It is probable that different party factions were also using the new regime to undermine each other. The party exhibited conflicting signs of reconciliation and militance. For example, the BBC reported on 1 August that when fights broke out in Kober Prison between Northern and Southern members of the Mahdi cabinet, prominent NIF members took the Southern side.[55]

The Bashir regime was in no rush to move toward a settlement, holding out to assess the substantial gains being made by the Eritrean People's Liberation Front and Tigrean People's Liberation Front against the Ethiopian government, the primary benefactor of the SPLA. Reports began to circulate in mid-September 1989 that Ethiopia had made the decision to halt assistance to the SPLA and that its operations were being gradually moved to Uganda.[56]

Meanwhile the regime moved to buttress its military capacity so as to take advantage of the increasing disorganization in the command structure of the SPLA. Significantly, it began to clamp down on migrants, Southerners, and periurban residents in Khartoum. A 7:00 P.M.–6:00 A.M. curfew was imposed; this was reduced gradually to 12:30 A.M.–4:30 A.M. by 1993. Checkpoints proliferate throughout Greater

Khartoum, and policing of the periurban informal sector—particularly alcohol brewing, tea making, and hawking—has intensified, depriving many of the urban poor of their basic livelihoods.

Although actual hostilities in the civil war never reached Khartoum, the massive growth of both Southern and Western presence in the capital was implicitly utilized by a range of antigovernment forces as a possible point of destabilization. Many in the SPLA believed that a rapidly expanding Southern presence in the capital was symbolically a means of laying claim to a predominant role in national life. As long as the South was a distant reality, Northerners would never be compelled into significant power sharing.

The conglomeration of diverse ethnicities and walks of life in the sprawling shantytowns also constituted a nexus of shifting alliances and economic collaborations that disrupted the stability of fixed identifications—Muslim versus non-Muslim, Southerner versus Westerner. Traditional ethnic antagonisms and separateness continued to manifest themselves in the organization of neighborhoods and social affiliations, but they came to increasingly coexist with practices that undid ethnic allegiances and generated a willingness among people long kept apart to work together.

The growing informal sector in the periurban areas, which both relied upon and occasioned these new collaborations, became fertile ground for rearranging the traditional assumptions former peasants and marginalized urban workers had about traditional frameworks of social power. Although the Islamic movement had also challenged many of those same assumptions, having for decades sought to be a mass-based movement, these challenges often appeared more of an expedient to accelerate their chances at state power. In assessing this apparent change of focus, it is important to keep in mind that although Turabi is perceived to be today's "ruler," he is not free to rule as he wants. The "progressive" ideas regarding women, the poor, and social transformation may have been sustained, but Islamicism in the current military is not the same set of assumptions and experimentation it was in the hands of university students or the Ikhwan elite. Just as leftism in the Sudanese military produced overly concrete and stolid manifestations in terms of social policy and governance, much of the same rigidity can be found in the military's own appropriation of Islam as a ruling ideology.

For example, the foreign minister, 'Ali Ahmed Sahloul, announced on 20 April 1991 that 800,000 refugees in Greater Khartoum would be resettled back to their original regions or in camps farther outside the city. The government moved on 23 December 1991 to bulldoze urban settlement areas where houses did not possess legal title to the land, appropriating and distorting a long-term urban development plan authored by the World Bank and the United Nations Development Programme. Although Numayri had resorted to this process of *kasha*, never before had it been used on such a massive scale. Established areas in Hag Yousif, Hillat Kushur, and Hillat Shuk were decimated and hundreds of thousands of residents were relocated to unserviced desert sites 8–45 kilometers removed from Khartoum. Employment and income were thoroughly disrupted as people attempting to work in the city were subject to dusk-to-dawn curfews that effectively made it impossible for them to keep their jobs.

Displacements were also selectively applied in order to foster divisions among Southern ethnicities—Nuer versus Shilluk versus Azande versus Dinka—disrupting what was emerging as a moderating force on interethnic tensions in the South. Increasingly convinced that the SPLA was losing the war and thus was progressively incapable of attenuating their vulnerability in the capital, Southerners reverted to ethnic particularisms to negotiate small concessions from the regime. The regime moved to use the propagation of Islam as a carrot, providing special food relief and employment to those converting to Islam and/or offering themselves for circumcision.

This assault on the urban poor constitutes perhaps the most significant "domestic policy" of the new regime and indicates its intent to enforce a strict ethnic and cultural, as opposed to religious, territorialization of the country—since Western Muslim groups are as much an object of displacement as are Southerners, evidenced by the removal of eighteen thousand households from Dar es Salaam, 40 percent of whose population comes from Darfur.

After nearly two years of floundering in power, the Bashir regime moved to simultaneously normalize its international status and entrench Islamic rule. On 5 February 1991 a federal system of states was established, basically corresponding to the former regions. The intent was to devolve a large measure of authority to the states in the hope that this would attenuate Western and Southern discontent. On 31 January Bashir announced his intention to implement a version of *Shari'a* legislation and criminal codes, which took effect on 22 March. At the same time an Islamic Fund of $440 million was set up to accomplish the social upliftment that would enhance the efficacy of *Shari'a* legislation. A hand-picked national conference to deliberate the future of Sudan was conducted on 29 April–2 May; the conference, in turn, became a sitting "parliament."

The *Shari'a* law itself seeks to be a succinct and unequivocal rendering of optimal moral behavior. Legislation implemented by the Bashir regime was to apply only in the North, although within the criminal code there are several areas where regional distinctions are specifically referred to in terms of differing penalties. Much of the law would be familiar to most of the West, with significant differences resting in a few key areas.

Hudud offenses are stated as drinking alcohol, apostasy (*ridda*), adultery (*zina*), defamation of unchasity (*qazf*), armed robbery (*hiraba*) and capital theft. Offenses relating to alcohol and false defamation are punishable by whipping; adultery and apostasy, execution by stoning; and robbery crimes, by amputation of the arm, except where robbery leads to murder, in which case, execution by cruxifiction is provided for. In actuality *hadd* punishments continue to be held in abeyance—largely because when *hadd* punishments are determined there are few provisions for their retraction. The law does provide for a complex series of qualifications in almost in all instances but *hiraba*. For example, the evidentiary requirements to establish adultery require the witness of four persons in demonstratively sound mind without trace of ulterior motive. There are even provisions that require the instance of adultery to be ascertained as an initial act—as if repeat "offenders" are technically immune from strict application of punishments. Cases of capital theft are exempt from *hadd* punishments "where the offender is in a case of necessity and does not take from the property more than what is sufficient to satisfy his need or the need of his dependents for the sake of food or treatment, and not exceeding the *nisab* [a standard usually determined as 4.25 grams of gold]."[57]

In instances of assault and homicide, the law provides for direct retribution (*qisas*) to be undertaken by either the victim or his family, and in cases where the *qisas* is remitted or in instances of negligence, *dia* (financial restitution) is deemed applicable.

It is the area of personal morality that is generally seen as the most problematic. Although drinking is forbidden to Muslims only, the state of being intoxicated is punishable if it is deemed offensive to anyone. A person who "conducts" himself in an indecent manner contrary to public morality or wears an indecent or immoral uniform which causes annoyance to public feelings shall be punished with whipping not exceeding forty lashes or with a fine or both."[58] Repeated homosexuality is punishable by life imprisonment or death.

The laws contains provisions for basic human rights, religious freedom, and the protection of privacy. Qualification of culpability is widely extended to include ambiguous provisions for "necessity"—if the act was essential to maintaining the integrity of the person or his honor. In most instances there is seemingly wide latitude to question the grounds of any offense and, concomitantly, perhaps excessive judicial latitude to mete out justice in ways potentially prejudicial to the uninformed.

The significance of the existence of these laws of course goes far beyond the content of the criminal code itself. The laws constitute points of absolute loyalty and antagonism, and serve as the locus for crystallizing concerted opposition to the regime as well as limiting its effectiveness.

A government in opposition, the National Democratic Alliance, was formed at the beginning of 1991, comprising a broad coalition of opposition forces, including the SPLA. Under this umbrella, Mubarak al Fadl al-Mahdi, Sadiq's nephew, was able to reconsolidate much of the support of Kordofan and Darfur for the banned Umma Party. Former commander in chief General Fathi Ahmed 'Ali formed a military wing of the NDA, the Legitimate Command, that was responsible for various small guerrilla operations in Gezira. Once again, however, the effectiveness of the NDA is being limited by its inability to agree what to do about *Shari'a*, and it is maintaining its cohesiveness primarily because of the general alarm expressed by increasing Southern sentiments for complete separation.[59]

Despite the repression it carried out, the NIF faced opposition in various guises. In April 1991, the Khartoum University Student Union, a secular grouping that had defeated Jabha in the recent student elections, sponsored a daring anniversary of the execution of officers in a purported coup attempt a year earlier. The children of the executed were mobilized to parade at the university in T-shirts displaying the picture of their dead fathers—an action which prompted the temporary closing of the university.[60]

In 1992, the regime attempted to institute a form of popular representation in local government—a system of ward committees that would determine the development needs of each community and, in consultation with the national state, established administrative mechanisms best suited to the plan of action determined and the resources and capacities of each community. It was hoped that this system would be a concretization of the principles of *shura* (consultation) and *ijma* (consensus) long held as the basic foundation of Islamic governance.

Jabha believed that, within Khartoum, people would seize the opportunity to entrench local Islamic activists within these committees, since they offered the political clout necessary to advance improved service delivery. In the select communities in which formation of the committees was subject to democratic election, people used the occasion to express their discontent with the national regime. In the Khartoum wards where elections were held in October 1992, the NIF was roundly defeated, leading it to institute an across-the-board one-half plus one rule for hand-picked Jabha cadres.

Jabha's headaches were further compounded when the linchpin of the NIF's Southern strategy—in the person of George Kinga, a Taposa Labor minister who managed to switch the support of much of the Taposa region from the SPLA to the government—applied for political asylum in Egypt, stating that the process of Islamicization in the South was a guise for Arab control. The demands of the regime in late 1992 that a pastoral letter written by Catholic Archbishop Paolino Lukudu Loro— condemning the RCC for its total callousness about protecting the fundamental rights of non-Muslims—be withdrawn mobilized the Vatican into action, culminating in a visit to Khartoum by the Pope in February 1993. This visit enabled the world to see a portion of the sizable and desperate community of non-Muslims living in the capital.

Despite repeated assurances by Col. Muhammed al Amin Khalifa, the RCC negotiator, that the government was prepared to go a long way in making the talks work, the Abuja conference went nowhere. On 13 December 1991, Iranian chief of state 'Ali Akbar Hashemi Rafsanjani paid a four-day state visit to Khartoum, bringing with him 157 officials, including a large entourage of security and military advisors. During this time, the two countries concluded a deal in which Iranian advisors would be attached to the army, which would also receive training in Iran. Iran would also provide large infusions of military equipment and facilitate negotiations with China for the provision of more. Not only did this reflect a renewed effort to win the war, but just as significantly, countered any moves factions within the RCC might have been contemplating to distance themselves from the NIF.

In May 1992 Hassan al-Turabi was attacked by an exiled Ansar karate expert in Ottawa while on a speaking tour. Although he has made a miraculous recovery, having sustained severe neurological injuries, the attack demonstrated the extent to which Turabi was important in keeping the various factions of the movement together. During the time of his recuperation, it seemed that the NIF increased its dependency on Iran—for petroleum and more arms, and more significantly, for its messianic emphasis on martyrdom and salvation. President Ministry chief

Col. Ibrahim Shams al Din, returning from the recapture of Torit, spoke about how he saw angels carrying the dead up to heaven. Increasingly, the regime has been under the gaze of the international community. During January 1993, the United Nations General Assembly passed a resolution condemning Sudan for the forcible relocation of its citizens, and prospects for substantial increases in international pressure to resolve the civil war were mounting.

THE CONTEXT FOR RESOLUTION

A basis for the solution of the civil war has yet to extend beyond the concept of federalism, which the RCC unilaterally imposed during 1990. Although federalism is an administrative arrangement which for all practical purposes Sudan is unable to afford economically, actual secession by the South continues to seem unlikely despite its increased support in the SPLA. First, there exist substantial confirmed oil deposits in the upper Bahr al-Ghazal region that could potentially make Sudan self-sufficient in fuel and thus lessen its dependence on the vicissitudes of Saudi and Libyan generosity. Second, the state still has the intention of completing the Jonglei Canal, a 36-kilometer bypass linking the Nile at Bor with the White Nile at Malakal—a project that would speed up the passage of water from the swampy Sudd to the North and earn increased hard currency from water-starved Egypt. The completion of the canal has been opposed by many Southerners because it would seriously impede pastoralism in the area. In October 1974 there were major riots in the area over rumors that 2.5. million Egyptians were to be resettled near the canal.[61] Third, Southerners have historically provided the North with a cheap source of labor. In most ways Southerners are the Sudanese "best prepared" for wage labor. Due to the influence of missionary education, a propensity for hard work, and their status as an "alien" population, Southerners have been depended upon to play an important role in construction work, light manufacturing, manual labor, vehicle repair, housekeeping, and security—work in which Northerners rarely engage.

Historically, much of the Sudanese economy has depended upon the importing of migrant labor for the development of the major agricultural estates and cotton schemes. The structural asymmetries of wealth and power that characterize North-South relations have ensured the availability of a non-proletarianized laboring class to perform the menial tasks avoided by Arabs. Even today, Southern office workers are expected to stand in line for the boss's bread and fuel supplies, repair basic equipment, and draft letters. Yet, they own almost no businesses or property, and are allowed limited opportunities for social gatherings. Even prior to the coup of 1989, it was only through the intervention of a Sudanese entrant in the Olympic boxing trials that Dinkas from Wau were allowed an afternoon every week of music and dancing. Assemblages of youth are difficult to pull off, not only because of the watchful eyes of the security organs, but also because people live great distances from one another in areas that transport usually stops servicing by 8:00 P.M. Southerners have few opportunities for higher secondary or university education. Southerners constitute about 4 percent of the university population and approximately 88 percent of the prison population. Over 60 percent of Southerners were underrepresented in the last democratically elected parliament by virtue of the impossibility of conducting elections.[62]

Despite the religious and racial overtones of the war, the NIF is basically correct when it states that the problem is one of economic underdevelopment. The South has always faced shortages of building materials, foodstuffs, and petroleum supplies. Almost all development initiatives, such as the Melut Sugar Scheme and the Tonj Kenaf Factory, have floundered in incompletion. The Southern share of the nation's development budget in 1977–78 was 14 percent, and dropped to 11 percent the following year.[63] What development has taken place has most often been perceived by Southerners as a tool for their eventual acculturation into the North.[64]

In some ethnic communities in Khartoum, for example, among Nuba in Mayo, there is virtually no formal employment; entire neighborhoods live off the proceeds of theft. Even for the relatively well educated young sons of the Dinka elite in Khartoum, cigarette hawking and the import of African printed cloth from Nairobi have proved the most successful economic ventures.

The past nine years have torn substantially at the social fabric of Bori, Dinka, Azande, Torit, and Nuer life. Even if there had been no war, non-subsistence economic opportunities in the South still would have been practically nonexistent as the South bore the brunt of Numayri's disastrous economic policies. Lack of opportunity at home forces the youth to extricate themselves from tightly bonded family structures and insert themselves into alien territory (Khartoum), generating frequent rifts between fathers and sons. A few, such as the brother of Francis Mading Deng, convert to Islam and find their careers subsidized by the NIF, while others scheme to find a way to get to Cameroon, where economic opportunities are believed to be plentiful.

Language differences raise artificial barriers. The rational outlets for migration, Uganda and Kenya, are functionally foreclosed because of political volatility in the former and tight immigration controls in the latter. Southerners see themselves as locked in. Most would return to their home regions if they could, but even if the war ended, the political and economic structures that would functionally permit such a return are many years away. In Khartoum, only the relative indolence of the "arabized" and the tentativeness of the African-identified forestall major clashes. Despite the fact that the NIF implicitly hoped that the imposition of *Shari'a* would produce an effective division of the country into two federated regions, it is the "definition" of the capital that remains a key focus of seemingly perpetual antagonism, especially given the fact that the infrastructural needs of the country are enormous and the available resources meager.

Part of the difficulty is that the Sudanese have internalized the view that their dilemma is intractable. Talking about the problem as impossible becomes a readily available reference for conducting disputes, expressing frustration, and interpreting events that potentially could be accounted for in other ways. Sudan has been courting disaster for so long that to imagine things being better itself becomes a source of anxiety.

Because Sudanese so often expect the unworkability of hoped-for outcomes, daily interactions tend to be viewed through the lens of this futility. As the possibilities of resolution appear close, one or several parties to the conflict usually can be counted upon to insert unreasonable demands or invoke procedural requirements that have little substance. For example, the SPLA's demands in 1988 that the government's agreement with the peace accord negotiated by the DUP be submitted to a vote by parliament before a cease-fire only served to complicate the issue and compel antagonism from those only looking for face-saving mechanisms.

A culture is created that compels people to adopt to the conflict as an almost permanent feature of life. In 1989 Khartoum was full of examples of people who had come to use the civil war, and religious and ethnic antagonism, as a mask to make money. Syndicates began to crop up that brought together Mahass and Equatorians and Nubas—all officially bitter enemies—relying upon the impression that they could never work together in order to forge a variety of "joint ventures"— smuggling, theft rings, transport.

RECIPROCITIES AND DIFFUSIONS

A generative process unfolds despite the predominance of cynical self-fulfilling prophecies. Streets, buses, stores, neighborhoods, and cinemas are being occupied by both Northerners and Southerners together in ways that are more functional than not. The arabized Northerners, though quick with their insults and derogations, deliver the invectives with more ritualized obligation than passion. The Southerner's passivity stems more from indifference than from fear or compliance. Arguments on buses turned into racial disputes are as often occasions for welcome humor as they are struggles for superiority. Police in Erkoweit Qharb have been known to issue traffic summonses to a Dinka woman who serves illegal brew to customers sitting in four wrecked cars "parked" in her compound, instead of arresting and lashing her.

More attention must be paid to those ethnic intersections that operate functionally. Although quickly activated and potentially vitriolic, the racism of the Sudanese is a hollow legacy, something easily fronted without great commitment. Such mutual recrimination, after all, does not reflect completely the capacity of each group to deal with the other. Accommodation and assimilation do not proceed in planned ways on a linear curve. There are always starts and stops, leaps and hesitancies, and an often silent diffusion of cognitive and behavioral styles able to alter basic relations among distinct groups.[65]

The respective behaviors of Northerners and Southerners set up situations that must be addressed by each group if effective individual functioning is to be possible. In their adeptness at displaying a tolerance for intense commercial activity and their enjoyment of public gatherings, the Africanized Sudanese compel styles of social interchange from the Sudanese Arab heretofore unfamiliar and unpreferred, yet now available in the carnivalesque attitude of the central city—even under military control. In their enclosures of private space behind mud walls—where personal relations retreat to personal quarters themselves highly segmented and territorialized away from the highly regulated public domain—the Northerners compel the Southerners to become more familiar with the structures of reflection and private withdrawal.

Of course each group has numerous ways of circumventing and improvising upon the social, commercial, architectural, and behavioral practices of the other. But complete detachment, autonomy, and separation from each other are implausible. Therefore, the differences signified by each group, now living in relatively close proximity to the other, provoke and elicit a range of behavioral alternatives from each group not previously seen as possible.

Any group living under changed conditions, where it faces the necessity of having to reinvent itself, tends to fall back on often exaggerated and abstract features of a past identity. It often insists upon the continuity of what are now only fragmented elements imbued with and conveying the larger fabric of a past coherency or cohesiveness. That past identity itself has also been most probably fraught with conflicts and contradictions.[66] What emerges from this situation are social tensions that are more professed and felt than acted upon.

In the past it has been difficult for young educated Sudanese to have a clear idea about what being African meant—they simply possessed a vague intellectual understanding and inclination to manipulate gross symbols. The increased cultural "Africanization" of Khartoum forces them to interact with people who "offer" themselves up as the embodiment of that Africanity. Despite the fact that this offering intensifies the perceived threat to Islam, the history of the tradition of Islamic practice seems to make such threats somehow necessary to its very survival. Past threats, including colonialism, secularism, and militarism, have not significantly altered the terms of Sudanese religious practice.

Sudan, long having sought political and economic mileage in international arenas with its special blend of Afro-Arabism, is beginning to realize the bitter actualities of this heterogeneity long after other African and Arab countries have concluded this legacy is mere artifice. The Southerners, for all the acquired trappings of township urbanized "ghetto" youth, know the Arab better than they know other Africans, and use their informal position as the disseminators and arbiters of urban culture in Khartoum to convey an arrogance and pride probably unavailable to them in any other African situation. Arab youth, for their part, have started to "move in crews," adopting much of the slang of their Southern counterparts—a style of behavior that itself was derived from the nature of the Southern migration to Khartoum, i.e., where young men came in the beginning without their families and thus coalesced with other peers for support and protection.

These diffusions and mutual shapings are not posited here as counterevidence to the serious racial dilemma that Sudan faces, nor to attenuate the blistering reality that Southerners are denied access to a feasible and meaningful socioeconomic existence. These concepts are offered simply to elaborate the complexity of the situation and posit several alternative futures. How people conceptualize and represent their experiences affects the way they shape or respond to political reality. Yet, people often resist their own conceptions, taking opportunistic actions seemingly at odds with how they understand what they must do to act appropriately or successfully, and seeking out even minimal forms of contact with the various sources of danger that characterize the parameters of everyday life.[67] Especially in an urban setting, what is witnessed and confronted is frequently not assimilable to preconceived ideological notions; motives must be concealed and rationalized, or disguised by workable self-explanations.[68]

Tribal allegiances are being constantly invoked, but only because there is a plethora of intertribal interaction and intratribal differentiation taking place. In interactions among historically related people who share basic symbolic frameworks of intelligibility, connections must be seen at those junctures where individuals are conducting their lives in ways that could be perceived as disruptive of intergroup connections.[69] Each group justifiably wonders about its autonomy within a national political culture and seeks to interact with the state in a way that facilitates or keeps the state as distant from its sectarian concerns as possible.[70] It is the maintenance of collective indifference, then, that becomes the primary signifier of group coherence.

The cultural homogeneity of the North has been penetrated and disrupted. People react defensively, feel threatened. On the other hand, the maintenance of this homogeneity had never resulted in the development of a coherent political culture and a viable economy. The diversification of Khartoum acts as a wedge, an opening of differentiation for a social body where dissenting voices and political conflicts have been suppressed for over a decade. The homogeneous is not so homogeneous. There has been a recognition of "safe" divergences in a people strongly united by religion and language but equally peculiar in the particularisms of their styles and outlooks. In the North there is increasingly broad agreement that the state has been preoccupied for far too long with the question of the national and ideological character of the country and has used the indeterminacy of these issues to either prolong the rule of a particular region or to wage power struggles against it.

ISLAM AND IDENTITY

Islam is a relatively simple religion, and the fervor that it generates is born out of this simplicity. The terms of identification are minimal and clear; there are no great anxieties about the extent to which one has understood or abided by religious principles. "Who are you? We are Muslims," embodies a restrained elegance and clarity that is cherished by most of the *umma*. What is valued is not the systematics of law or codes of behavior but rather the experience of trustworthiness and mutual respect that these laws and codes connote.

The extent to which Sudan should be tied to the vagaries of Middle East politics is of little concern to the majority of Sudanese. The problem is that the ambiguity inherent in the complexion of the national political character is continually seized upon as the means through which specific political factions attempt to advance their interests. Instead of the undecidability of Sudanese identity inserting itself as a productive force in national life, it is engineered as a problem that must be resolved, a problem on which the existence of the bulk of political life is dependent. Essential differences are framed as oppositions and obstructions that must be simultaneously "cultivated" and suppressed in order for the political game to continue. What also ensues is a gradual willingness to torture and wound—all major sectors in Sudan today have demonstrated a callous and cynical attitude toward basic human rights.

Although most Muslims accept the ordinance that they, as Muslims, must at least envision the implementation of *Shari'a* at some point in their collective life, they possess little doubt about their capacity to be Muslims even if such laws are not forthcoming as national laws. Much of the obsession with *Shari'a* comes from the intellectuals who worry about their own conflicts and the politicians who depend on these questions of Islamicization as a mechanism for seeking access to the state and as a means of reconfiguring alliances when ethnic and regional ties among the urban educated are loosened.

Whereas part of the populace will support *Shari'a* as a religious duty or the culmination of an existential aspiration, the way the current conflict over its implementation has become a juggling act is increasingly being perceived by many Sudanese as diminishing the legitimacy of those assuming the religious authority to introduce such laws. While Islam makes little distinction between religious and political life, the way the politics of *Shari'a* has been conducted may have precipitated the very disjunction between religion and politics that *Shari'a* was intended to bridge. More than any other factor, it was the commitment to ensuring the unity of the religious and the political that accounted for the relative tolerance of many Sudanese who held their demands for *Shari'a* in abeyance during late 1988 when an agreement to end the war seemed close.

In other words, most Sudanese assume no *political* duty to support *Shari'a*. As far as Arab identification is concerned, Sudanese readily identify with the label "Arab" because they are Muslim and speak the language. This does not imply, however, that they perceive themselves to be fully integrated or subsumed into the Arab world.

HOW ARE WE ARAB?

Identity is not a permanent commitment; it is a cultural acquisition that serves a pragmatic function in terms of staking claims for access to resources and opportunities.[71] The growth and wealth of Saudi Arabia maximizes the usefulness of claiming Arab identity for the Sudanese. But the extent to which this is actually done is another question. On the national level, the Sudanese belief in Pan-Arabism cost them heavily when they attempted to become the breadbasket of the Arab world— the region's supplier of foodstuffs.

During most of the century, agricultural development was oriented toward seasonal wage labor on large estates rather than peasant cash crop producers. Production was geared then for a large internal market, which necessitated an implicit commitment to the well-being of prospective consumers—something that fundamentally changes in export-dominated production.

The large-scale development of capitalist agriculture during the 1960s and 1970s disrupted what had been a fairly balanced system of crop rotation and food distribution in Sudan. It undercut the seasonal practices of nomadic herding, which led to rapid nutrient depletion of much of the arable land. This, coupled with the alteration of crop selection practice demanded by the expansion of the cash needs of agricultural workers and peasants, eventually contributed greatly to food shortages even before the resumption of the civil war.

In the South, the destruction of subsistence plots and household savings (in the form of cattle) forced farmers into an impossible dependency on the market with its limited stocks and artificially inflated prices.[72]

During the period of capitalist agricultural expansion, the Arab states were willing to make initial investments in Sudan but did not provide sufficient support to cover ensuing balance-of-payment adjustments, resulting in the accumulation of massive indebtedness and inflation.

When grumbling was heard shortly after the RCC took power that the country was more concerned with supplying food to other Arab states then at home, the regime announced plans to increase both the domestic availability of food and its export to Muslim struggles throughout the world. It was the pursuit of these plans that was often cited as the justification for displacing entire periurban communities to the desert—since more agricultural land was needed. Again the basic needs of localities were subsumed to the rulers' pursuit of some "broader" identity.

Even though Arab identification is sustained because of its historical connotations of elevated social status (to the extent that genealogies are frequently reinvented to affirm Arab lineage), Arabs are not fondly regarded. They are frequently resented as exploiters of Sudan's dependence on petroleum and perceived as using much of the merchant class and agrarian capitalist class as their personal agents to extend their land holdings and opportunities to get rich. The massive swindle of state coffers pulled off by a Jordanian syndicate in 1992, which forced a substantial revision of exchange controls, is simply the latest in a long line of manipulations by other Arabs. Sudanese resent the time-consuming and laborious process entailed in obtaining Saudi work permits and the extent to which Sudan is regarded as a permanent "backyard," endlessly manipulable and ingratiating. At one point Gen. Bashir even accused Saudi Arabia on a television address of supporting the SPLA.

The persistence of Sufi traditions in Sudan is explained by many factors. But certainly one contemporary motivation for their persistence is that they constitute a form of resistance to the domination of the orthodox Wahabi movement in Islam embodied by the Saudis. The Bruhani sect in particular, with its lavish and muscular forms of ecstatic worship, is a continual affront to Saudi sensibilities.

Sudanese identity, and implicitly the framework for the end of the civil war, rests in a series of convergences and disjunctions, in which each points out the possibilities of the other. The African must come to see that the Arabs are not as Arab as they might appear to be. The Arab must come to see the Southerners as not as "African" as they might appear. The labels are full of holes. And though this situation at times appears hopelessly bleak, provisional forms for new intersections and collaborations have consistently emanated from the protracted conflict, despite being the "real" target of the Islamicization campaign.

Part Two

Out of Bounds
Islam and Transformation

Chapter Four

Indigenous Solutions
Islamicization and Postcolonial Identity

Throughout Africa, people are calling for political practices that emanate from within. A common assumption is that political life doesn't work in Africa because the framework around which it is organized is essentially foreign and inapplicable to local realities. The question becomes: What will this indigenous solution consist of? Essentially, it is a work in progress, something that must be made up as state politics goes along. If the indigenous is not to be construed as the arbitrary artifact of the ruling regime, however, it must be rooted in a consensually recognizable form or image of tradition, something which appears to transcend the authorship of the dominant political figures.

Many intellectuals in Sudan see an Islamic movement as the basis for an indigenous national solution to the intractable problems of national development. They also view the existing movement as a work in progress. The work adheres to a series of guiding principles but they are acknowledged as insufficient to the development of a comprehensive political strategy. This in no way, however, detracts from the belief that Islam must be at the core of whatever strategy is devised.

The movement has combed a wide range of ideologies to gather those that are seen as compatible with these principles. *Shari'a* provides the anchor and the content of the political vision, even though many in the movement do not actually believe that *Shari'a* can become a political reality. Yet it must be maintained as the inevitable reference, the tradition that grounds the practice in a framework of shared objectives.

Additionally, placing *Shari'a* as the centerpiece of the new political agenda justifies the movement's appropriation of "Leninist" tactical models. They are used as a method of operation in a context otherwise disillusioned with both Marxism and trade unionism. Because most Sudanese now despise Marxism as one of the causes of the disruption of public life, the Islamic movement had to use *Shari'a* as its raison d'être in order to have used mass mobilization, strikes, and sometimes subversion as tactical models. Mohammed Mahjoub Haroon, a leading figure in the NIF, told me, "if it wasn't for *Shari‘a* we could never ask people to do most of the things they are now willing to do."[1]

Since trade syndicates and occupational groups have traditionally wielded substantial power in Sudan—playing a national political role that exceeds their organizational interests—the growing power of the Islamic movement has been achieved partly through forcing consideration of specific issues, such as *Shari‘a*, that can provoke debilitating ideological splits within the syndicates and thus limit their efficacy as national players.

Islamic movements are often associated with hordes of young people carrying placards calling for the government of God. The leadership of the Islamic movement in Sudan is acutely aware of the need to do more than revolve the movement around a series of platitudes and slogans. Lacking a fully realized socioeconomic platform to implement, the movement must point to something that their assumption of power would immediately make different. The so-called guiding principle, although elaborating an ideal Islamic state with well-articulated social and political relationships, remains for the most part only a set of ideals.

What becomes feasible in a developing country such as Sudan is an emphasis on criminal code and procedure, which is used as the primary signifier of a larger commitment to bring about a fully Islamic state. The emphasis on the *hadd* laws becomes the most accessible means of demarcating a clear "before and after," a harbinger of what is to come.

By emphasizing its role as both the purveyor of radical difference and the restorer of an essential identity, the Islamic movement can legitimate its claims to state power without ever having to substantiate an economic program in the short term. State power is viewed as necessary in order for the movement to consolidate the vision and formation of an Islamic *umma* (community). The movement assumes that Sudanese are seeking to live with their religion fully. What the state must offer in order to justify its existence is to become the concrete manifestation of this aspiration. State power is not claimed on the basis of a specific socioeconomic agenda. Rather, the attainment of state power will actualize social and economic relationships that are already immanent and intact in all communities professing themselves as Muslim.[2]

The state is to become the very instrument of Islamic propagation, not simply the engineer of policies amenable to it. It is to provide the context for people to change themselves and, in doing so, change society. State, society, and people are levels of conceptual distinction that do not exist Quranically. The Quran only designates the people—those who either receive or reject faith. No reference is made to the use of the faith as an instrument to engineer a particular social body.[3]

In some ways, this emphasis on religion is part of a process of making the state familiar in contexts where historically the state has acted more as an arbitrary imposition. Past colonial realities have done little to foster interdependence between state and civil society, and so the Islamicization of the state must be based in the general context of finding ways to make the state relevant.

The Islamicization of politics signals a rupture or break from having to make reference to Western political culture in a geopolitical framework where any clear manifestation of autonomy or economic independence for Third World states seems otherwise impossible. Yet, at the same time, it accepts Western categories of political identity—i.e., the differentiated notions of the nation-state, civil society, state-society relations. Previously, the issue was primarily the moral quality of the rulers and the ruled and their answerability to God as persons. There was no sense that it was the duty of the rulers to reform the hearts and minds of the people.[4]

The National Islamic Front says that even though the criminal codes of *hudud* appear archaic, they emanate directly from God and are, therefore, unchangeable. Dr. Hassan al-Turabi, leader of the NIF, has said many times that he wishes that the law would not appear as it does but that it is impossible to intervene in it if one has truly submitted oneself to Allah. The insistence upon this aspect of *Shari'a* is the amplification of unchangeability, an unchangeability that becomes the guarantor of the essential cultural and psychological autonomy of Sudanese society. That which has been intact throughout history, unmodified by even the most dominant of political forces, becomes the best means of ensuring distinctiveness in a world where foreign ways and interests dominate. Adherence to the very archaic qualities of the *hudud* comes to signify an overarching commitment to cultural identity. Despite the fact that the immutability of *Shari'a* is as much fiction as fact, its apparent impermeability to reshaping connotes that the survival of Islam ensures the survival of Muslims through all situations.

The Islamic movement anticipates areas of criticism against it and incorporates these criticisms as a basis for elaborating its own position as a differentiating force in Sudanese society. Anticipating its critics' condemnation of it as repressive of human freedom, the movement asks: Would people rather engage in the freedom of individual expression and innovation, or participate in the collective freedom of a culture restored to its wholeness and integrity—the freedom of a social body living by its own cherished values? The very terms in which this issue of freedom is raised increase the fervor of commitment to either modality of freedom and conceptually polarize the issue in ways that make reconciliation or synthesis extremely difficult.

This situation incites the movement's critics even more and turns them into an opposition against which the movement must be vigilant. Whereas notions of freedom need not be polarized in such terms, this is not really the point. Rather, the movement converts the defense of individual freedom, something conceptually compatible with Islam, into a veiled attack on Islam. This construing of a call for the preservation of individual freedom as an attack on Islam then justifies the curtailment of that freedom—something otherwise difficult to reconcile with Islamic principles.[5]

Although professing a complete political vision and methodology for governing, informed by both the actual practice of the Islamic state in Medina during the time of the Prophet and the codification of governance generated by the legal schools of the ninth and tenth centuries, the political vision of the Islamic movement is still sketchy. It must deal with a wide variety of contradictory forces and influences. Much of its organizational apparatus and style has been appropriated from the experience of leftist movements. As a political party the NIF is an umbrella for a wide diversity of sentiments. Consensus on specific political and economic issues is usually difficult to attain. The NIF is always careful not to alienate its nouveau riche merchant supporters (who would be adverse to any radical restructuring of the economy and thus their privilege). At the same time it must commit itself to providing people with food and other essentials, which may require radical economic restructuring.

A STRUGGLE FOR POWER

The struggle for state power is a messy and nasty business. Entrenched regimes must be immobilized, their legitimacy weakened in the eyes of the masses. The former coalition government of Sadiq al-Mahdi had not been able to solve the basic problems of war, security, and the provision of basic resources. The Islamic movement, although a coalition partner in this government in 1988–89, did much to discredit it. This practice did much to advance the NIF's own interests as a political group, but did little to motivate faith in the political process.

The cyclical history of failed democratic governments followed by harsh military rule, coupled with the problems of tying together the large physical terrain of Sudan, has led most Sudanese to view state politics as largely irrelevant to their lives. Given this attitude about politics in an increasing number of Sudanese, the NIF risks institutionalizing itself as the purveyor of an indigenous solution turned to not for its own vitality but in the face of an impoverished political discourse everywhere else. Silently, Islamicists wonder whether Islam is strong only because other forms of political consciousness and practice are so weak. By implication, if other well-conceived political alternatives existed, the current ascendancy of Islam in Sudan might not have occurred. Such overly self-conscious concern about the nature of its growing influence and power may make any social movement more defensive.[6]

Islamicists make sure to ward off this deep-seated anxiety. Yet this understanding creeps in, and at those times the NIF becomes highly distrustful of debate and diverse opinions, especially among university students—those to whom it has often turned as spearheads of the movement. Students often complain that the NIF is reluctant to include them in key policy-making decisions.

This anxiety stems in part from the fact that the historical interweaving of political struggle and religious development in Islam engenders a common perception by Muslims that their political defeats are insults to their religion intentionally organized by non-Muslims. The purveyors of Islam must then demonstrate religious superiority as an intrinsic aspect of a renewed political consciousness. The wolves are always howling at the door. The spectacle of a former Minister of Information and Culture speculating that the Khartoum floods of 1988 were part of a Christian conspiracy does not bode well for Islamicist claims that they can tolerate a diversity of religious practice.

KHARTOUM AND THE CULTURE
OF THE CITIES

Can the NIF and its organizational proficiency as a movement make Khartoum a workable city now that it is the government? After all, Khartoum is the stronghold of the movement. The movement faces major difficulties in this regard. It relies upon a religious framework that emphasizes the engineering of a certain homogeneity of social life and public behavior, but it operates within an urban environment increasingly full of a wide range of both Arab and African particularisms. The thrust of Numayri's actions was to control as much of this heterogeneity as possible, to drive people into their private domains and exert homogenizing strictures over the diverse populations pouring into Khartoum.

This tendency has not been altered substantially in the years since Numayri's overthrow in 1985. As Abu Gassim Goor Hamid, a cultural critic for the former daily *Al-Wan*, puts it, Khartoum is essentially an urbanized village, yet the urban has abstracted out the surface social mores of the village and generated a series of mannerisms drained of both classically urban and village rhythms, where the edges, passions, and margins intrinsic to both urban and rural life have been cancelled out, suspending inhabitants in a kind of cultural dormancy.[7] When people then have to contend with bread shortages, power cuts, and gasoline lines, the quest for new ideas and solutions is abated.

There are some persons in the Islamic movement who worry about its inability to interact with the urban mix. Instead of taking the time and attempting to understand the multiplicity of lifestyles, expressions, worldviews, and personalities that intersect in the urban arena, the movement tends to quickly insert and impose traditional standards of judgement upon them, i.e., this is forbidden, this is objectionable. Islamic ethos in such a climate, they say, becomes too much a surface fashion, a series of etiquettes, injunctions, and demeanors. There is then a danger that Sudan will become that parody of Islam proffered by the West, a kind of cartoon character. As a result, unwarranted substance will then be inversely contributed to a Western ethos.

Countering this point of view, Zeidan Nur, a journalist for *al-Rayah*, states that it is precisely the apparent foolishness of the movement—that which the West cannot understand—that is the proof of its unyielding endurance. The reformers may think that such Islamic actions embarrass them in their dealings with the outside world, but instead they signal that the Muslim community cannot be touched by the outside world.[8]

Because the Islamic movement finds it difficult to extend its organizational proficiency to actualizing a multifaceted socioeconomic vision, it is knowledge of Islam that is prioritized above and beyond all other knowledge. Rule and stricture take precedence over the individual's intention to abide by them or to be faithful. How things look becomes more important than what people are actually doing or feeling. There is no sense of consensually agreed upon developmental stages for how Islam will grow in this context where it has supposedly been operative all along. In such circumstances, social movements frequently become more repressive in their demands, and must increasingly compel by decree because they lack context-specific ways of nurturing the people that are their primary resource.

The contrast of Sudanese Islamicism with a West African Islamic ethos is particularly revealing about the implications of the emphasis on possessing a knowledge of Islam. Although most West African Muslims know little about the theological content of Islam as a system of thought, such ignorance has often become a way of thinking that continuously reinvokes the applicability of pre-Islamic worldviews. Submission to Islam also meant having Islam submit to their own way of life, permitting both cognitive cohesiveness and flexibility, uniformity and diversity.[9]

On the other hand, it needs to be said that in West Africa the ever-present dangers of fragmentation and internecine conflict are never far away. The absence of a thorough knowledge retards the use of Islam as a substantial catalyst for socioeconomic development. West African Muslims remain creative, but they also, for the most part, remain poor.

Many Islamicists in Sudan dismiss the potential dangers of cultural reification and anomie. They essentially say: look, the idea is simply to feel close to God, to stay close to the power that created us. But the conceptual inextricability of politics and religion has not always been intrinsic to Sudanese culture. As Shams al-Din Yunis Najm al-Din of the Ministry of Culture points out, in ancient Meroe civilization (located in what is now the far northern region of Sudan) centers of religious and political power were kept physically separate so that the links between them had to be renewed upon the change of each political dynasty. No succeeding king could rule without this linkage, but at the same time, the basis of rule remained a linkage and not a merger, not a conflation.[10]

THE RELATIONSHIPS OF THE RELIGIOUS AND THE SECULAR

The search for the rule of law presently taking place in Sudan is intended to rectify a situation where the religious and the secular "have been out of sight of each other for too long"—a common expression of Osman Abd-al-Majid, a Sudanese Islamic activist. Although Islamicists conceive the implementation of *Shari'a* as a cure for the acute suffering of the masses experiencing the tugs and pulls of different worlds, the majority of Sudanese seem to experience the religious and secular as unbridged domains rather than as active antagonists.

As Omar Haroon, a psychology lecturer at the University of Khartoum, points out, the intensification of the Islamic focus can be partially attributed to a tendency in Sudanese culture to deflect contradiction, to engineer a separation between the religious and the secular rather than integrating them.[11] In Khartoum, worlds are hidden from each other. There are men who drink alcohol, smoke marijuana, and consort with prostitutes, but will go to the mosque or religious rally and demand the implementation of Islamic law. When asked about this apparent inconsistency, they will claim to feel no conflict or contradiction.

The watchful eye, the surveillance conducted by kin and family and the strong public ethos defining acceptable behavior, contributes to this surface deception. Personal and social conflicts likely to emanate from the incursion of the secular into the religious domain, and vice versa, must be curtailed. Sudanese are exceedingly resourceful in devising secret ways to fulfill individual and idiosyncratic desires. But because secretiveness is a fleeting and provisional activity (the secret acts being strictly and repeatedly forbidden) only a limited sense of personal and social change is likely to ensue from it. No institutionalized and reliable cognitive foundation is established on which to incorporate the vast plenitude of momentary "rebellions" into a transformed public position or way of being.

Unlike the social demeanors of many other societies in which there exists an implicit agreement that the illicit will transpire without interruptions as long as everyone pretends that nothing is going on, disclosure of the illicit in Sudan poses great social and psychological dangers. Family and friends must at all costs literally not find out about certain events. There can be no hints, no pretense. A young woman cannot afford to take the remembrance of her lover's kisses into her home or hum the songs of Black America while cleaning the dinner dishes. Everyone must act as if there are no lovers and interpret this appearance as if it is the absolute truth.

But this does not mean that lovers are not kissed. Ever so briefly, fingers and lips will become very active in an abandoned market stall or ditch, and for five minutes men and women will bite and claw their way to a temporary freedom that brothers and fathers cannot touch. Yet it is unlikely that such actions will be repeated between the same partners twice. Collaborations are brief and volatile complicities; the repetition of such illicit acts gives them an expanding significance, for it means that one is more tempted to give oneself way, be known, and become differentiated from a safe anonymity.

For many Sudanese, the emphasis on law represents the continuing failure of the culture to build links between the secular and religious domains. This is a particularly difficult conceptual and emotional issue for a people raised in a way of life that scripturally does not acknowledge such a separation. Although religious discourse now permeates every aspect of cultural and political life, its spread often seems able to only further polarize the dichotomy it seeks to subsume.

But Sudanese have become accustomed to bridges being broken. Even the implication of a constitution, which would have symbolically connected the diverse populations after independence, was repeatedly interrupted and deferred. The drafting of a permanent constitution during the government of Abdallah Khalik was interrupted in 1958 by the coup of Major General 'Abbud. The process resumed in 1964 following 'Abbud's ouster, only to be interrupted by the 1969 coup of Numayri, forty-eight hours after all political parties in the Constituent Assembly had finally agreed on a constitution.[12] The finalization of the proposed constitution was again delayed in response to the coup attempt led by former Free Officers Babiker al-Nour, Farouk Hamidallah, and Hashin al-Atta in 1971. The first permanent constitution was implemented in 1973, only to be amended following a coup by the Ansars in 1975 and the so-called national reconciliation of political forces in 1977.[13]

THE NEED FOR A VERSATILE RELIGION

The challenge the Islamic movement faces is how to generate forms of religious expression that are compatible with the personal understandings and processes by which individuals submit to God. The tendency of the current Islamic thrust is to converge the religious and the secular by relying heavily on the potential remoralization of the society as a means to work out and address secular issues. Islam must be able at the same time to address the distinctiveness of the two domains and not simply act to get one to "cover" or rectify the other.

As 'Ali Shari'ati, the renowned Iranian sociologist whose writings had great significance to the Iranian revolution, has indicated, man is two-dimensional, godlike and human at the same time. He demands a religion that is two-dimensional, both profane and inspirational.[14] The implementation of Islam must have a two-dimensional character so that the specificity of discrete political and socioeconomic conditions will generate a set of responses guided by the prescriptions of the religion. What ensues is a sense of oneness. This oneness is not inherent in the conditions of life or religious principles, but is actively constituted by Muslims themselves.

What is necessary, according to Egyptian religious scholar Sayyid

Qutb, is the aesthetic vitality to reproduce the immediate experience of Islamic being by engaging in actual movements with others (*baraka*) and not by the free rein and application of doctrine. Islamic method (*minhaj*) is represented in a dynamic organizational concrescence.[15]

In their affirmation of Islamic identity, both Qutb and Shariʿati talk about how circumstances are to be addressed through an interpretive framework engendered by religious structure. But according to them, this structure is itself re-created by the nature of its actual use in Muslim hands. Religion thus "finds meaning in or creates meaning from a commonly shared, Islamically derived repertoire of imperatives to personal and social action."[16] The ability of the *umma*, the Muslim community, to be responsive and active and to energize itself to conceive of solutions to a situation that has generated widespread dissatisfaction is the key to fulfilling its religious obligation.

Although most activists in the NIF admit to the primacy of the pragmatic aspects of the attempt to get *Shariʿa* implemented, at times it appears to be a questionable pragmatism that is cited. The success of the attempt will empower the party, but the extent to which it will empower the larger community is not clear. Shariʿati states that the political impact of the fight for *Shariʿa* is to be this larger empowerment.[17] Whether or not *Shariʿa* is implemented is not crucial to determining whether the fight for *Shariʿa* is successful. Rather, the key point for Shariʿati is that the fight for *Shariʿa* will bring forth an enhanced consciousness in the masses. Consciousness is inscribed within an Islamic cognition such that a reassertion of Muslim coherency is produced through this continuous invocation—a sense of definitiveness and a commitment to acting creatively and morally that will ramify across all areas of life. The unity of Islam and the inextricability of the religious and secular, then, is not manifested as a conceptual construct but as a dispersion of passion and commitment.

In Sudan, however, this emergent consciousness finds itself baffled and overwhelmed by a multiplicity of situational contingencies. The peripheralization of inner spiritual reality that concerns so many Africans continues. People are forced to make do on rapidly declining purchasing power; shelves may now be fuller than in years past, but the prices are beyond the reach of many. Television brings images of a prosperous life that is unattainable. Recent political history consists of divergent governments fallen to a common impotence. The issue is not so much now that Islam is unable to help rectify this situation of the spirit. Islam is turned to now as an overarching umbrella under which this sheer multiplicity of agendas must be addressed in some coordinated fashion—a tendency not unlike that occurring throughout Africa.

At one and the same time, Islam is being expected to deal with the fears of recolonization, to undo the psychological and cultural splits that have occurred due to the incorporation of the Third World into an international cultural and economic order, and to provide some clarity to the murky process of economic development. Additionally, devotion to Islam is expected to structure the historical fascination Africans have had for worlds outside of themselves, guiding that process in which individuals attempt to exceed what they know themselves to be. In the hypervisible space of an international economy based increasingly on the production and circulation of information and media, Islam is expected to offer practices for how individuals put together an image of themselves for themselves, their social networks, and the larger world.

Given this situation in which the Sudanese must simultaneously address a multiplicity of issues, the question is not whether Islam can be reasonably expected to play this role as a coordinator or coherer of discrete discourses. Rather, the issue is whether there can be any coordinated political practice able to effectively and simultaneously deal with the feelings of personal inefficacy, the cynicism about political power, the dispersion of accountability, the dissipation of moral congruity, and the increased difficulty of economic survival.

The ascendancy of Islam points to the ascendancy of the following questions: How can local understandings and responses be articulated to broad sociocultural transformations? How can psychological linkages to familiar levels of political community be maintained while allowing individuals to explore other provisional and more globalized forms of self-representation and instrumentality? These seem to be the significant political questions to which Islam is being applied. Regardless of whether Islamic thought and practice (as it is understood in the myriad of settings in which it is engaged) can effectively deal with these questions, it is appropriate for Muslims to now envision Islam as an instrument of social change. Islam has offered itself as a way of life and therefore must find ways to address life in its totality. Whereas the bulk of Islamic history necessitated an emphasis on the unification and integrity of the *umma*, the challenge today is that such unity may be irrelevant or easily accommodated in an international arena interested in maintaining coherent ghettos.

The question is not whether Islam has any business actively dealing with the complex economic and political problems that characterize postcolonial Sudan, but rather, what discursive and theological forms Islam can use to strategically engage with that complexity. For this there can be as many Islams as there are Muslims, and the danger is that the ideological framework of the religious as political instrument is rendered so diffuse as to be superfluous to its mission. If it is about anything then it ends up being about nothing. Here, Islam's comprehensiveness may impede rather than facilitate the Quranic vision of its versatility. Care must be taken to make sure that the myriad expressions of Islam are not simply pragmatic substitutions for processes that are more relevantly considered in terms of social class or particular apparatuses of power. It may be more useful to interpret the Quranic vision of oneness not as a totalizing rubric that coheres divergent aspects of life by subsuming them to a fundamental interdependence or symbiosis, but rather as an exterior complete unto itself yet always assembled to fit every occasion of sociality. Here Islam is the boundary or limit to all strata or institutions that introduces new inputs from the outside and provides sociality the occasion to exceed any particular manifestation of itself. To view Islam as a nonreducible supplement or as exterior to political formation and practice may enhance rather than obviate its contemporary role.

Shaykh Amadou Dina, a Guinean religious scholar, said to a group of visitors in 1977 that "Islam is about nothing; it neither adds to what exists or takes away from what exists. . . . Islam is rather how we see that existence, how we know for sure that this existence is nothing but itself." What is being indicated in the shaykh's words is that Islam, as a political discourse, is neither the skeletal structure nor the compelling or overarching framework in which political activity is to be conceptualized. Islam does not represent an intrinsic order but instead sets discrete things in relationship to one another; it is the condition of their visibility and the medium of their appearance. Islam's power is an occasion in which disparate things are brought together and reborn (*nahda*) as inextricable links to one another.

THE RELEVANCE OF TAWHID TO AN ISLAMIC POLITICS

Islam has been highly mobile, penetrating the urban and the rural, the political and the theological. Many conceptions have been brought to it, and it has been used to accomplish a wide variety of agendas. Folk conceptions of Islam dealt with direct reflection on the order of the world rather than the actual statements in the Quran or by the Prophet. Conversely, the literate conveyed the concreteness of textuality.[18]

All conceptions nonetheless convey a sense of *tawhid*—a sense of oneness within diversity; the apprehension of a systematicity to the world, of a fundamental wholeness in creation. The implication of this concept is that no individual or society is to approach the Quran or the world claiming a definitive authority of meaning over them. There is to be no privileged reference or discourse because both individuals and society are to be directed by the Quran itself.[19] Even though it is practically impossible for a reader to approach the Quran with this absence of authority, a specific message is clear: the Quran, in order to be the direct word of God, retains the authority to "throw" the reader out into the world in highly varied ways which cannot be pinned down or predicted. The repetition of reading is the repetition of variation. Diversity, far from obviating the doctrine of divine revelation and immutable knowledge, can be the only confirmation of it. The Quran is to be accessible from any point of view—a common sense, a common position.

A potential trap for contemporary Islamic movements, with their emphasis on the integrity and rebirth of a "true Islam," is the possibility that they will vitiate the universal aspects of Islam in their attempt to buttress its universality. In other words, the Islamicist effort to preserve the *Din* as the method for reinvigorating Islam as a salient politics for the Muslim world may detract from the very universalism that is Islam's most powerful and relevant connotation. According to the Arab anthropologist Abdul Hamid al-Zein, Islam is what is always left over after the political, economic, and cultural analyses have been explored, not as an independent, predefined entity but as a facet of political, cultural, and economic systems—a facet of the world over which we are responsible for implementing God's will.[20]

The universalism of Islam, then, rests in this situation in which it can be added onto everything that has been created. This is a process that compels the particular and multiple differences among the domains of everyday life to harmonize with Islam in order to be in harmony with one another and yet retain the distinctiveness of their differences. The immutability of Islam is this adding on, the supplemental. Although reformist movements in Islam that have pointed in the direction of this understanding have faced seemingly insurmountable difficulties in conveying this sense of universality to the masses, this does not mean that a populist reassertion of the symbols of tradition is the only way to convey universality.[21] Instead of getting lost in abstractions, the bearers and conveyors of this radical sense of Islamic universality will have to build such an understanding through engagements in the peculiarities of specific Islamic communities—exactly what Ikhwan has done so proficiently in the slums of Cairo. This universality is generated by Muslims beginning to address a wide range of superficially nonreligious issues and by their dealing with people, issues, and experiences not within the traditional purview of Islamic practice.

Although often dominating the attention and energies of the Islamic movement in Sudan, the political fight for *Shari'a* is not the only place where radical Islamic work is being done. The organization of a network of social services, the mobilization of women for economic development, and the limited attempts to forge collaborative relationships with non-Muslims in community development projects are areas in which a provisional knowledge base for popular social movements will be built, where people will begin to garner a sense of new Islamic tradition. One of the key factors in the Sudanese situation is that the Islamic movement has not retreated from the West. Although it resents the West for its imperial character and its continued undermining of indigenous aspirations, the movement has not closed itself off from dealing with a wide range of Western institutions in civil society. This position has been maintained despite the increasing siege mentality and heavy reliance on Iran demonstrated by the Bashir regime. The maintenance of this engagement is important since the West has been successfully interpreted for its own multiplicity, for being many things at the same time. This failure has in the past deterred the Muslim community from acting out its own tradition of plurality.

For now, the politically anachronistic dichotomy between modernization and populism is likely to continue reasserting itself and causing popular social movements in Islam to focus on a symbolic return to a tradition untainted by Western morals. Even though this focus is not the main characteristic of what is occurring in such movements, this surface impression of what is taking place will persist for the time being. Rather than preoccupation with religious purity, it is the increased participation of Islamic movements in areas of everyday life where Islam has not had a presence in several generations that holds the key for radicalizing the Muslim community's understanding about the nature of its own universality. This is why the protracted struggle in Sudan to forge a sense of national identity is such an important manifestation of this process.

There are some in the Bashir regime who understand this dynamic and who have been instrumental in focusing attention away from legislation and penal codes and toward these development activities. Yet it is perhaps cruelly ironic that in order to accomplish this shift in focus, they have made deals that provide institutions and sectors more concerned with Islamic mores, dress, and traditions greater access to non-

Muslim communities in Khartoum—tacitly permitting forced conversions and the selective distribution of social welfare benefits—so that they might "get on" with the process of effecting the kinds of understandings outlined above.

DEMANDS FOR AN ISLAMIC STATE: BEGINNING OR END?

For now, aspirations of universality will find expression in demands for an Islamic state or for the imposition of Islamic law. Sudan presently has institutionalized a home-grown version of both. But as the *umma* accelerates its involvement with the larger world, it will increasingly find opportunities for renewal in the particularistic innovations it brings to civil society which are not subsumable to customary stratifications or explanations. As Ashis Nandy, the Indian psychologist, points out, the forces of domination always try to make their object self-conscious about who it is, to deliberate on its own integrity, and to worry about its proximity to the dominator.[22]

Certainly, many aspects of the Islamic movement have fallen into this trap and have been too concerned about living out a true Islam. The most vital aspects of the Islamic movement in Sudan have been those that have plunged into the fray trying to make things happen without always being sure of what either the political or theological implications might be.

A vibrant universality will be built on these myriad situational particulars—by finding ways of distributing bread, delivering health services, reducing the cost of marriage, understanding the dynamics of periurban life, or mobilizing the energies of youth working in the informal economy. All of these are currently activities of the major elements in the Islamic movement—but always placed in the "shadows," always compromised in the negotiations to retain unity in the ranks.

Many doctrinal struggles that have not taken place in the recent past are beginning to emerge.[23] Muslims may find, as Berque indicates, that the politicization of Islam has constituted a displacement of those struggles. But as Hassan Hanafi, the Egyptian sociologist, states, those struggles will inevitably strengthen the capacity of Islam to deal with the postcolonial world and to fully emerge from the prison psyche that has often led radical Muslims to maintain separatist cultural and political positions. Since "the masses had been made a field of experimentation for all ideologies except their own, namely Islam," it is unreasonable in Hanafi's eyes to expect the masses to apprehend the complexities of mobilizing effective social movements without first going through some symbolic form whereby their cultural foundations are reasserted.[24] But once this has been done, it is reasonable to expect that Islam can be converged with a large range of strategies and movements for national development, thus demonstrating the potential viability of Islam in all political situations.

For over two decades, the agenda of the Islamic movement in Sudan has been to resist state domination by taking over the state apparatus. The idea was that only by occupying state structures could it remove the state as an impediment to development of an Islamic society and an Islamic social subject. However, as Jean-Francois Bayart explains in his ground-breaking work on the politicization of civil society in Africa, "Civil society can only transform its relation to the state through the organization of new and autonomous structures, the creation of a new cultural fabric and the elaboration of a conceptual challenge to power monopolies. . . . This can only be achieved by means of ideological and institutional 'mediations,' and 'mediations' of new categories are nothing less than schemes for the reconstruction of identity."[25]

Although on the surface, the Islamic movement has followed this advice precisely, it has oriented much of the development of such autonomous structures to the overarching objective of seizing state power as if that power were ultimately necessary as a guarantee or enabler of the movement's social agenda. Such an orientation complicates the movement's eventual goal of dismantling much of the state's central position in public life, since to dismantle its power as presently configured risks attenuating the efficacy of the movement which seems to link much of its development to it.

As recent events have demonstrated, the Islamic movement finds it difficult to reconcile two parallel political agendas that have frequently been set against each other by competing political actors: (1) the fundamental and existential demand for a politics of redemption and moral integrity—a politics that will restore a sense of purpose and efficacy to the individual; and (2) the balancing of competing power centers, channels of accumulation, and political agendas. On one day in 1988 the young would pour into the street demanding the rule of *Shariʻa* and on the next day march in support of a peace initiative that would require the indefinite deferral of *Shariʻa*.

Giving up *Shariʻa* as the centerpiece of its political ideology would reduce the Islamic movement to one more political party and obviate its role as a transformational force. But, at the same time, not having at least postponed adoption of *Shariʻa* until substantive discussions of a new constitution could be held would have tended to render this transformational effort as simply another symptom of imminent political disintegration.

Like socialism in other states, indigenous political formations in the Third World will find it nearly impossible to exist within current geopolitical arrangements. No matter how democratically constituted, an explicitly Islamic state in the post-Iran era will confront enormous obstacles to staying in power. The current regime, although it has implemented a form of Islamic law, has continued to hold back many of the *hadd* regulations in their entirety, partly as a concession to Western pressure. There are still many in the movement who are not enamored by the need for the movement to be so thoroughly wrapped up in the process of national governance, preferring to deal with small collectives and programs rather than parties or parliaments. There is clear resentment on the part of many of Jabha's former young supporters that the Islamic movement has not really revitalized Islam but rather the state—giving it a new lease on life as an instrument of alienation.

Chapter Five

The Sociality of the Capital
The Transformation of Khartoum

Khartoum lies at the confluence of the White and the Blue Nile. A 1983 census put the population at 1,343,651, but now most Sudanese believe that the population is somewhere between five and six million. It is a city that still retains some of the characteristics of a village. The urban area is actually made up of three towns: Khartoum, Omdurman, and Khartoum North—each manifesting a different function and character. Khartoum itself is the administrative center of the country, traditionally the site of the offices and residences of civil servants and merchants. Omdurman is the spiritual and cultural seat of the country, the place of the Ansar—the followers of the Mahdi—and the former seat of the Mahdist caliphate. It is the major commercial area and the largest of the three in population. Khartoum North is the site of most industries in the capital and contains the largest numbers of non-Muslims.

Historically, Khartoum has been a city of traders, merchants, and their retainers. Each merchant family would also typically have plots of land just outside the city. They raised crops for their own consumption and for the market as well. Many of them live in stately, almost palatial homes in Khartoum II and the new quarter of Amarat, and now Al Riyad. The earnings of expatriate workers in Saudi Arabia and other parts of the Gulf are frequently turned into large four- and five-story homes built in the new subdivisions of the city, many standing empty for years. Workers in the trades and petty civil servants have historically lived in working-class areas such as Deim, Sahafa, and Saganna. Simple brick or mud wall–enclosed compounds are the typical structure of residence. Men's and women's quarters are usually separate, and each compound usually has a receiving area for guests, separate from the private quarters. Most cooking and food preparation is done outside.

In the poorer quarters, the compound may consist of a simple one-room mud structure where belongings are stored. Most living takes place outside, and in the summer months especially, everyone sleeps outdoors. Compounds may also typically contain a few animals, goats or chickens, plus quarters for servants—usually retained by most Sudanese families with any kind of steady income.

Although in most Sudanese families men are protective of women kin, men and women have limited contact and often do not have a psychological closeness. Khartoum households are obligated to host visitors from the rural areas and so most households usually have a variety of extended family members in residence throughout the years. Some civil servants even take up cramped government quarters so as to diminish these obligations. As the maintenance of both kinship ties and personal networks is highly important, a great deal of visiting takes place among households, and a substantial amount of a household's income must be used to cover the costs of hospitality.

The Mahass have historically been the predominant group in Khartoum, having originally settled in the area now known as Kelakla. They were joined by other Northern Arab-related groups, the Donagla, Shaygiyya and Ja'aliyin. There has also always been a Southern presence in Khartoum, as merchants imported slaves to assume the role of domestics, soldiers, and bureaucrats. During the drought of 1983–85, large numbers of Western Sudanese, all nominally Muslim, poured into Omdurman, particularly the quarters of Umm Baddah, El Fetihab, Radmia, Masalma, and Marzuk. These consisted of Fur, Berti, Zaghawa, Borgu, Midab, and Massalit. Westerners have also filled the urban second economy. As loyal adherents to Mahdist traditions and the Umma Party, Westerners were implicitly encouraged to settle in the capital to win parliamentary seats for the party. On several occasions Numayri had them expelled from the capital, but they came back.

The maintenance of social ties in the preeminent activity in Khartoum. Such ties ensure access to opportunities and resources. It is often thought that the Sudanese do not work hard, yet the maintenance of such ties is implicitly an economic activity and a labor-intensive one. Additionally, the extreme heat of the city makes long hours impractical, especially given the six-day work week. Work usually begins at eight o'clock in the morning with a break for breakfast at ten. Lunch takes place somewhere between noon and one, and by two or three, most workers begin the usually long trek home. Khartoum does not have sufficient buses for its working population. At the end of the work day, piling onto a bus (or on the roof and through the windows) and fighting and clawing for any available space becomes a daily routine. During peak hours, if one does not board at the original place of embarkation, it is highly unlikely that one will go anywhere for hours. Additionally there are a limited number of service roads, and traffic in and out of central Khartoum is jammed for much of the day.

With an increased population, there has been a great strain on available human services. Many schools run in two or three shifts. Medical offices frequently remain open past midnight. Increasingly many neighborhoods have become dangerous places after dark, limiting people's mobility and socializing. At the same time, more and more activities have been relegated to the night and to the early morning hours following *fajr,* the Muslim prayer that precedes sunrise. This is due to the scheduling and transportation problems of the day and the increasing complexity of work. Those with cars are often on the road at 5:00 A.M. looking for basic provisions and supplies before work. In recent years, everyday life has been further complicated by incessant power cuts, water shortages, long gas lines, empty shelves, and long bread lines. Rumors circulate about particular merchants who may have eggs or bread in stock.

Price rises have cut into disposable incomes, which in turn affects the markets. In Souk Shaby, Saad Gishera, and Souk Shaggila, stall after stall may not make a sale all day—the new dress for a cousin's wedding, or a new *jellabiyya* for *Eid* (festival) will have to wait. Greater emphasis is placed on smuggled items. In Souk Libya (named after the source of many smuggled items) on the outskirts of Omdurman, almost anything, including hand-held missile launchers, is for sale behind the facades of goatskin blankets and baby clothes. Second-hand markets have also sprung up all over the city.

Women have increasingly entered the work force as clerks and secretaries in order to boost household income. After the 1989 coup, many were "retrenched" for "religious" reasons, but they have mainly been allowed back as long as they dress in the proper Islamic attire. Young men also fill the central city, few with steady jobs. Some find work pushing carts, carrying tea, running errands, shining shoes, loading trucks, carrying parcels, and picking pockets on overcrowded buses. The Sudanese civil service running the government bureaucracies is overstaffed and highly protective of its positions. Part of this is due to the fact that Numayri, ruling for seventeen years, had no constituency and so built a large, unwieldy state apparatus full of duplication. Recently the state has encouraged early retirement and used domestic structural adjustment programs to substantially reduce the size of the ministries.

Class distinctions, always marked, have grown more pronounced. Unlike class disparities in other African countries, which, though existent, tend to be limited, class disparities in Khartoum are omnipresent. In such an exceedingly poor country, it is bewildering to see so many people driving Mercedeses and BMWs and having access to large sums of money. Currency speculation, especially with the repatriation of externally earned incomes, has contributed much to this accumulation, as has the maintenance of quasi-feudal structures of agricultural production. The contrast between rich and poor in Khartoum is as stark as anywhere else in the world. This disparity has become one of the prevalent issues of Sudanese everyday life, a topic of constant conversation and a source of seething frustration.

At the same time, religious brotherhoods, 'ishra or subha (men's associations), bring rich and poor together in an intersection of class levels that simply does not take place in many other countries. These associations occasion the display of generosity greatly valued by Sudanese culture, but do not obviate the basic inequities in the process of accumulation and distribution.

In recent years, land values have risen faster than the values of buildings, leading to an accelerated deterioration of much of central Khartoum. Low-density residential areas have been redeveloped for commercial use. More and more households are subsequently pushed out toward the periphery of Khartoum. At times, an owner of housing stock will build a simple structure in one of the many shantytowns and live there while renting the house in town for income. New areas for housing are allocated and subdivided using the same basic grid layout and classification system used during the colonial period. This has greatly complicated the rational provision of basic services and planning for the urban area as a whole.

The governance of Khartoum is based on 367 neighborhood councils organized into 31 town councils and 10 specialized councils (for the industrial areas and markets), which are, in turn, organized into 3 autonomous city councils.[1] Income is accumulated from tax revenues collected by the central government, local taxes, licensing fees, a percentage of rental value on all shops, sheds, and specialized markets, fees for special services, bank loans, local development schemes, and grants-in-aid from the central government (by far the largest source of income).[2]

Much of the actual provision of services for each neighborhood, however (i.e., the building of local roads, schools, water pumps), relies on the efforts of the residents themselves. The problem is that much of what is started is often not maintained. There is an excess of decision-making bodies, and budgetary allocation procedures tend to be overly complex and politicized. Khartoum also has extreme infrastructural deficiencies. There are two sewage systems in the city (in El Gaz and Hag Yousif), which serve only 5 percent of the population.[3]

Urban life has begun to take its toll on family coherence. Mental health clinics at the three major hospitals are full of people suffering from what is usually a variety of depressions and anxieties related to family conflicts. The incidence of divorce has increased, and young sons and daughters arrange to leave the country, not only for economic opportunities, but to get away from their families.

EXTERNAL REALITIES: THE DENSITY OF CIRCULATION

The tragedy of the African situation is that the resourcefulness of its people finds few expressions at home other than the effort to survive. Although any observer should be careful to impose terms of assessment that make cultural sense for African situations, Africans nonetheless are compelled to interact with definitions of personal and social development engendered by the West. The interaction demonstrates not a lack of capability but of opportunity. Africans search for viable staging areas, precipitating a widespread desire on the part of both the educated and uneducated to leave home.

For Sudan, leaving home has been institutionalized as an aspect of state policy. The earnings of workers abroad continue to constitute a significant portion of the state's hard currency earnings, despite economic and politically motivated retrenchments in the Middle East and Gulf. Sudanese communities in the United States and Canada have mushroomed in recent years.

What has been interrupted in the postcolonial era is population flow over broad distances and regions. The diminished economic capacities of African states make cross-migration untenable for most. More migrants head to the West, which has tightened its immigration policies as a result. The inability of African capitals to absorb increased populations, which drain what limited services they can provide, transforms the life of most of the urban population into a constant search for food, transport, shelter, and bureaucratic forms. Hours are spent waiting for transportation from home to office, office to office, lining up for basic staples, permits, clearances, authorization letters, stamps, and forms—a process that undermines any sense of productivity at the same time as the definition of what it means to be productive is being assimilated as changed.

This process of urban living reinforces the apparent solidity of social ties—loyalties to kin, tribe, and fraternity. But these ties have become truncated versions of themselves. Their continued power rests not so much in the vigor and resourcefulness of the bonds but in their operation as compensatory mechanisms. Among the young, there is little faith in the capacity of the social system to constitute an adequate or satisfactory context for the realization of their aspirations and needs, yet they perceive that there is little opportunity to alter the terms of their participation in society if they are to maintain any sense of personal efficacy. Economic and intellectual success must be framed as a familial and/or ethnic matter if it is to be attained at all. Psychologically, even though many young Sudanese prefer to "go it alone" or negotiate through personally constituted social networks, the maintenance of quasi-traditional structures of social ties remains the only defense against increasing chaos. This is the case even though the lack of resilience in these structures contributes heavily to that chaos which must be defended against.

At times the "genetic" foundation of much of the Sudanese social system necessitates minimal outputs and efforts to keep it going. The dynamics associated with the physical assemblies of related people is the key factor here. Since such assemblies often entail large numbers of people, efforts to maintain smooth contact and harmonious interaction are paramount. Although bickers frequently break out and ensue from the demands (both explicit and implicit) that kin place on one another, they are almost always subjugated to the requirement of presenting a harmonious appearance.

Arguments take on a ritualistic quality in that they seldom transform or rectify difficult situations, alter mind-sets or courses or actions, nor are they usually disruptive of cooperation or alliance. Political and ideological splits, although common among kin, rarely manifest themselves in domains where actual decisions and alliances are made, especially in the key area of the distribution of resources and opportunities. In a context of limited individual maneuverability, few Sudanese are willing to be "talked about" in disparaging or scornful ways. It is this power to talk and disseminate impressions that ensures some level of accountability within kinship ties.

During the flood disaster of August 1988, Sudanese relief workers were frequently put in a difficult conflict between ensuring a fair distribution of relief supplies to the neighborhoods of their responsibility and resisting kin pressures exerted upon them to direct resources to family members. Relief workers frequently said that their extended families had little idea about why they did the work they did, or why they felt it important to perform that work with a sense of ethical responsibility.

Coupled with the massive need and the general politicization of the relief effort, the kinship demands made on these workers made it difficult for them to maintain a perspective concerning their work. Interestingly enough, it was this inability to maintain a perspective that most angered the relief workers about their dilemma.

Although family members are physically and socially close, this closeness does not produce a sense of personal intimacy as it is understood in a Western context. When I asked groups of urban youth whether their families "know" them, that is, possess accurate understandings of what they think and feel, know their worldviews and motivations, most said no. They indicated that in Sudanese society it was not important to know such things until now. They were also apprehensive about the implications for the social system if indeed their families did know some things about their individuality.

Osman Hamid Ibrahim, a man of forty-five who had spent most of his life as a community organizer of youth in Omdurman, expressed his desire to spend the next ten years of his life, if Allah granted them, having the opportunity to observe what was going on around him, to see beyond the political imbroglios and economic hardships, to acknowledge some other dynamic of the means through which people were dealing with their lives. What was clear to him was how specific individuals and families were managing to put food and shelter together, however limited. But what was not clear was how the massive shantytowns, as some ad hoc collective, managed to hang together as wholes. He was convinced that there was something about the way this amalgamation of the desperate survived that was important in deriving concrete mechanisms of social policy and planning.

Certainly on the surface, it is difficult to conceive how such shantytowns as Umm Baddah, Masalma, Mayo, and Radmia are able to function. The land on which they are built is either state-owned or *habous* land (inalienable land given in perpetuity to religious foundations, families, or charities). In the most peripheral shantytowns the land is simply squatted on. In parts closer to the central city, plots, often pirated from state holdings, are subdivided and resold under a contractual agreement that allows the tenant to repay over time and provides him with building materials. At times, owners of a plot who are without capital for construction will subdivide the land to raise money for a dwelling. Oftentimes tenancy is traded for labor. Illegal tenancies are frequently legalized through political connections. One plot might be legally held with the owner then subdividing and selling adjacent plots. Certain owners have acquired large holdings in this manner, accumulating capital and status that enable them to become power brokers in their communities and arbiters with the state for the provision of social services, in effect legalizing their tenancy on officially illegal lands.

Whatever vitality exists in the shantytowns stems from building an economy on the limited provision of services that the state does not provide and on the circumvention of the economic controls it mandates. Water must be often carried as far as five kilometers from wells by donkey cart. The water is sold to buy feed, which is often collected and transported by foot. *Marissa*, an alcoholic beverage made of sorghum, is brewed by about 30 percent of shanty residents and is sold and consumed as both beverage and foodstuff. The legal banning of brewing enables the police, who for the most part are residents of the same shantytowns, to collect bribes to supplement their meager incomes.

The peripheral locations of the shantytowns provide smuggling, usually financed by outside sectors, with a haven from official detection. Even though it is general knowledge that much arms and drug trafficking is conducted in these areas, their relative invisibility and impenetrability constitute at least a psychological barrier to the policing of the state. The state is basically forced to destroy the entire neighborhood as its only effective counterresponse. Additionally, the informal economic operations become the only source of credit for those without access to banks and other landing institutions—which makes entire neighborhoods complicit in these operations, regardless of whether they actually smuggle or not. The lack of health services is compensated by traditional healers, *faqir* and *tkedjir*, who, in turn, buy up quantities of sugar and charcoal to sell locally. The threat of theft emanating from these communities itself provides them with economic opportunities, as most of the *gaffir* (watchmen) are drawn from the shanties.

In a mutually profitable complicity, many of the cultural injunctions concerning sex, intoxication, and *riba* generate viable avenues for income generation. Those with some money frequently look for opportunities to buy sex and alcohol. The large security apparatus necessary for a state that has not really consolidated centralized power finds an additional means to support its personnel in "crackdowns" on these activities. Although the quantity of income generated by these activities is limited, it is the networks and density of circulation of resources that are the keys to survival. The close proximity of different ethnic groups and their simultaneous distinctiveness and sectorization allow for both the dissemination of survival strategies and the enclosed protection of limited resources. Berti and Marsalat can reside contiguously to Shilluk and Nuba, and interact in the souks, yet maintain an impermeability of intracultural contact and relative social autonomy.

The conflation of drinking, smoking, and prayer, seemingly incongruous activities, actually emerges as a key ingredient in defining the cultural differences that must be paid attention to if only to preclude the dismantling of one's way of life. Joined in the drinking house and separated in the prayer house, the co-residents of the shantytowns sustain demarcations that generate both a relative sense of safety and social transformation. Whether this situation leads to a common recognition of class interests is questionable, but it clearly provides for an arena of interchange that maximizes individual knowledge. Even the ensuing frictions provide this.

Once while drinking *marissa* in a brew house, a Christian from the Azande called a Muslim from the Zaghawa a "son of my father's whore." A brawl ensued. Both sides went to get reinforcements. The Azande prepared for war. They rubbed their faces in flour given to them by a Christian relief organization. The Zaghawa sharpened their knives on the belt of a generator that had been stolen from across the Chadian border. After a little bloodshed, a settlement was worked out. The flour and generator were brought together to start a small bakery on the border between the two ethnically divided neighborhoods. In the coming weeks both groups enjoyed a steady supply of bread. Late one night an Azande man and a Zaghawa woman went into the bakery to have illicit sex, but were caught. The woman's father, an orthodox Muslim, was urged to apply a strict (and distorted) rendering of Islamic law, and a line of men was formed to throw stones at the girl (even though this was illegal). However, the Azande man's sister and cousins intervened and encircled the woman to protect her body. The Muslim men were puzzled by this. Why protect someone outside one's own tribe? Had spirits commanded them? They put down the stones and started debating the issue. Equally puzzled were the Azande elders watching the scene; why risk injury for a Muslim who is getting what she deserves? Finally, both Azande and Zaghawa retired to the brewhouse where they talked together about how strange the younger generation had become. A Zaghawa elder remarked that they had to do more to keep the younger generation busy, and together, the men agreed to pool their resources and buy wholesale cigarettes and batteries for their children to sell on the street.

After the flood of August 1988, when almost all shelter in Khartoum's shantytowns was destroyed, Western ethnic groups, at times overly fatalistic and resigned to destitution, found the motivation to mobilize and rebuild their shelters from neighboring Shilluk, who were quick to reassemble their living quarters.

For all the resourcefulness, these areas are rampant with early death, sickness, and the behaviors of victimization (the three coexisting in an almost parasitical relationship). As the productive capacity of Sudan in general diminishes, the shantytowns are the most seriously affected. At the same time, a system of political elites that has depended upon the fractiousness of ethnic groups may be faced with an increasingly "Africanized" urban population turning away from "Arabized" cultural references and agendas.

THE POLITICS OF AN INTERNAL FOCUS

As with Osman Hamid Ibrahim, for whom the shanties represent the inaccessibility of some functional perspective, the fight of the young is not only an economic one, but a fight to achieve some perspective about where the society is moving. Their own difficulties finding employment, accumulating funds to marry, and maneuvering through the system give the situation an intractable character. Political "dinosaurism" is the term they often use to describe the current state of affairs.[4] What will ensue is rarely even surmised. Although it was once comforting to externalize the anxiety and attribute difficulties to a hostile international economic system unresponsive to Third World realities, this explanation appears hollow to many young Sudanese regardless of its truth value. They have considered their history and wonder to what extent their history will consider them. They live in a city that has been the site of great struggles, of a constant shifting of religious and political power. The young feel that once again they are positioned at the cusp of realignment of these forces, and feel forced to assemble an internal focus, a different level of connection to themselves.

Indeed, it is this need for an internal focus that has led to a resurgence of Islamic concerns and the need for moral rectification. But even when professed and supported, the imposition of Shari'a is deemed only an initial step, more of a catalyst for a kind of collective self-knowledge that remains out of reach.

Cognizant of the political volatility of the young, a large sector of the political elite has seized upon the impetus for an Islamic "direction" in order to define the terms of Islamicization so as not to lose (and in many cases so as to maximize) its privileged position. The relative inability of the Islamic movement to effect changes in the economic con-

duct of the state reflects its inability to generate coherent economic policies and its indebtedness to a sector of merchants and speculators who
view Islamicization as a means of consolidating their economic relationship to *Ikhwan* business networks internationally. Even though it is frequently irritated by its status as beneficent patron to an inept government, Saudi Arabia is still willing to dispense large sums of money to an
assortment of journalists, financial consultants, entrepreneurs, religious
professionals, and politicians.

Because the state has proved unable to control economic processes,
the revitalization of Islamic tendencies, long an integral aspect of Sudanese political culture, constitutes an autonomous space for the generation and accumulation of capital for emerging elites.[5] There is nothing
new in this development, as Islam in various forms has continually been
used for many different agendas and appropriated by both the dispossessed and elites as a means of protest and of aggrandizement,
respectively.[6]

In Sudan, the Islamic experience has traditionally entailed individual
identification with Islamic institutions, which have survived remarkably
through a turbulent political history but have become increasingly
anachronistic in the postcolonial period.[7] Accompanying the rise of the
Islamic movement has been the strengthening of various Islamic welfare,
education, and propagation institutions—the largest operating almost
as self-contained governments. They are richly funded by the Gulf
states and have proved to be proficient organizers of services and distrib-
utors of various fiscal resources.

The proficiency of such institutions has fortified the attraction of the
Islamic movement in general. Muslims in Southern Sudan, perhaps once
the most marginalized group in the country, found their position radically changed (and complicated) by their rapid access to schooling,
community development, and economic opportunities. They became
some of the most fervent supporters of the Islamicization process—
which in turn convinced many in the NIF that the problems of national
cohesion could best be addressed by intensifying Islamic propagation in
the South.[8]

In Sudan, those who control the terms of religious affiliation and expression manifest real political power. This is the case even though deep
in Sudanese pre-Islamic history there existed a fundamental and ingrained psychological tendency to maintain politics and religion as distinct zones of power and substance. However proximate religious expression is to basic political concerns in Sudan, there have existed

countervailing practices within the culture that preclude the total subsumption of one by the other.

Even though the efforts of Muhammad Ahmed al-Mahdi to consolidate diverse religious tendencies in the Western and Gezira regions produced one of the greatest anticolonial resistance movements in Africa, its also spurred a host of other messianic populist revolts basically hostile to it.[9] Following the defeat of the Mahdist caliphate in Omdurman in 1898, there arose a variety of sporadic, populist anticolonial movements organized around different preachers and Sufi brotherhoods. Once the Mahdist movement secured state power, its dogmatism tended to weaken its capacity to resist hostile forces. Khalifa Abdullah, who assumed the reins of power following the death of the Mahdi, insisted upon the ideology of *jihad* (war of purification) and demanded that the Ethiopian emperor accept Islam as a prerequisite for a joint alliance against European encroachment. This position defused both countries' ability to ward off imperialism.[10]

In the figure of the Mahdi's sole surviving son, Sayyid 'Abd-al Rahman al-Mahdi, the British constituted the Mahdist movement to play an anti-Egyptian role in the Condominium. After Egyptian personnel were expelled, Abd-al Rahman was expected to return to an exclusively religious role, even though religion had been the basis through which the Mahdist political organization had been formed. In return for his cooperation with colonial structures, Abd-al Rahman was allowed to acquire over fifteen thousand acres of land between 1938 and 1935 and develop large agricultural estates in the riverine areas of Gezira. The followers of lingering anticolonialist movements in Western Sudan were gradually consolidated into a labor force working the expanded estates of the Mahdi family.[11] The oneness of religious and political mission and the belief that Sayyid embodied the spiritual authority of his father enabled the Mahdist movement to appeal to both the illiterate masses and urban intelligentsia.[12]

As indicated above, it would be inaccurate to view the political process as directly subordinate to religious dynamics. Religious particularism has frequently been used as a cover in base political power struggles. Colonial authorities never really understood popular Islam and were always trying to elevate tribal leaders to counter religious ones, not seeing that often there was no distinction between them. For example, the Khatmiyya sect of the Ali al-Mirghani family from the Kassala region of Eastern Sudan emphasized its religious distinctiveness primarily as a ploy to keep the dominance of the Ansar in check and not because it embodied some essential Sufi orientation. Following World War II and the anticipated renegotiation of the Anglo-Egyptian accord, the Khatmiyya radically downplayed its religious specificity in order to constitute the core of a nonsectarian party.[13] Even in the late 1980s, the Khatmiyya and the Mirghanis continued to overplay and underplay their religiosity in order to carve out new political roles for themselves.

The former ruling coalition dominated by the Umma Party, founded by ʿAbd-al Rahman at the end of the World War II and until 1989 led by Sadiq al-Mahdi, has depended almost completely on the loyalty of the *Mahajirun*, the Western tribes, and the "genetic" right to rule fostered by the Mahdist movement. Yet there was an inherent volatility in this arrangement that constantly necessitated the direct intervention of Sadiq himself in order to make the political process work. Although in large part sympathetic to the principles of *Ikhwan*, Sadiq often presented himself as the man able to operate inside the machinery of power and thus commanded the loyalty of the Islamicists. After all, when attempts were made to ban the Communist Party in 1967, Sadiq ignored a Supreme Court directive to lift the ban. But later his initial willingness to cooperate with Numayri and subsequent accommodation of the leftist-oriented modern forces fostered great suspicion on the part of the Islamic movement.

Despite the popular perception that Sadiq was a politician determined to rule at any cost, his attention to matters of state was continuously being diverted by the daily needs of holding his party together—balancing the interests of the Gezira Ansar, the *Mahajirun*, and urban-based civil servants and professionals. This balancing act reflected a key turning point in traditional political organization—traditional groupings were becoming launching pads for radically changed interests that competed politically, but which were not yet consolidated sufficiently to engineer new parties or movements on their own.

Overlaid on this process are the existing antagonisms among professionals, civil servants, educated elites, and the merchant class. The state political machinery has long been dominated by merchants. Although aware of common interests, they do not form a corporate group as they come from diverse socioeconomic backgrounds and different educational levels.[14] But they have funded political competition for state power and occupied key positions in the leadership of political parties. This activity stems from the entrepreneurial practice of cultivating "followings" among employees and retainers, and the liberal use of patronage.

During 1988, Sadiq's attempts to appoint younger educated members of the party to key national and regional positions provoked deep splits in his constituency, long dominated by the offspring of native administrators, i.e., *shaykhs* who continue to command the allegiance of illiterate peasants and nomads. Consternation had also been provoked over his collaborations with the NIF, whose increased popularity among the Khartoum *Jellaba* (as urban Arabs are referred to the *Mahajirun*) precipitated renewed attention to tribal consolidations in the West. For example, the Baqqara, one of the key ethnicities loyal to the Mahdist movement, repeatedly took any steps necessary to protect ethnic interests. In response, Sadiq was forced to elevate a Baqqara to Army Chief of Staff over several other senior officers.

If the Umma Party was to maintain its position of national predominance, it had to make efforts to attract and cultivate support in the capital—a process which tended to alienate its Western base. At the same time, its former coalition with the Khartoum-based NIF was based on Sadiq's need not to be outflanked by the NIF as the proponent and guarantor of Islamic values.

Until proposing itself as the party of peace during the initiatives of early 1989, the Democratic Unionist Party, the original partner in the 1986 governing coalition, had lost power and sought to become the vehicle for secularists threatened by the domination of the so-called religious right. But as a secularist party it did not possess even the semblance of a political ideology that could be invoked to coordinate its internal affairs. For example, in the latter part of 1988, the party was preoccupied with the personal conflicts between Mohammed Yousif Abu Harira (a former commerce minister popular for his attacks on the black market) and Mohammed el Hassan Abdullah Yassin (one of five members of the Supreme Council of State—Sudan's collective presidency). Mohammed Yousif exposed Mohammed el Hassan's importing of drinking glasses from Israel, and the latter was forced to resign from the Council. The DUP then proposed one of the most hated men in Sudan, Ahmed al-Sayed Hamed, a former advisor to Numayri and go-between with Egypt, for the vacant seat. This move further split the party, allowing the election of Mirghani el-Nasir, from the tiny Islamic Socialist Party, to the Council of State and thus hastening DUP's exit from the government at the end of 1988.[15]

That no political party had a national base sufficient for it to rule alone necessitated a seemingly endless series of governing coalitions that found consensus difficult and were unable to draft substantive policies to address the issues of economic chaos and civil war. Each party tended to maintain its support among various sectors of the merchant class, which politically ruled out any effective economic restructuring.

NOT WAITING FOR THE ANSWERS

By the beginning of 1989 disillusionment with the political process was rampant. Many Sudanese longed for a return to military rule, partly since the military provided the only semblance of a national institution. The intensified competition among parties had generated massive corruption and a significant drain on state expenditures to the extent that the state had ceded the bulk of economic activity to the second market. Soaring prices fueled sporadic unrest, in response to which the political parties, especially Umma, did not hesitate to use violence. Thirteen children were murdered in front of an Umma Party office in Omdurman in October 1987 during a demonstration against price increases and repeated school closings. Tires were frequently burned on major roads, and on any given night, there would be diverse forms of social protest ranging from demonstrations in Kelakla over the preponderance of alcohol drinking to demonstrations in neighboring Jabra over the police harassment of *marissa* brewers.

In all likelihood, the fight over the banning of alcohol—between those who favor tighter controls and those who favor relaxation of them—has become a displaced fight over national identity. Alcohol consumption has become a not-so-hidden form of political protest in an environment where there is relative freedom of political expression but no effective means for altering existent political practices. The widespread diversity in Sudanese culture generates a sullen homogeneity of social demeanor which renders often lively and intense political debate an exercise in incessant circulation of gossip and opinion without instrumental efficacy. This is not to say that such gossip doesn't bring down governments.

Part of the political dilemma rests in the language used to construct political identity. Still the considerations remain: "Are we African or Arab, or if we are Muslim, then our responsibility is to build an Islamic society, but by whom, and for whom, should this be imposed?" Political power in Sudan was diffused by being widely dispersed. No sector had either the interest or capacity to establish a truly national agenda. Each sector could only maintain its limited interest in preventing other sectors from dominating the process. The political process became a game of incessant subterfuge and undermining of the capacity of other parties and sectors to advance substantially beyond their current positions.

Territorialized in terms of constituencies, foreign alliances, and control over different ministries, the political parties coexisted in a symbiosis built on relative impotence. An example of this was reflected in the state's inability to stop the electrical workers' union, one of the few remaining syndicates controlled by the Democratic Front (Communists and leftists) from subjecting the capital to repeated power cuts. At the same time, the union was unable to secure wage increases from the state. Finally, in March 1989, the conflict was defused by simply bringing the union into the government—a ploy that Sadiq had self-destructively relied upon some two decades before.

People on the street constantly speculated as to what the politicians were actually saying to one another. Within a democratic framework of political expression, they asked, why is there no movement, why do the leaders find it so easy to lie to one another, why do alliances dissipate almost as soon as they begin? The absence of an ability to attain a viable perspective on what is going on engenders a system of political practices that makes gaining such a perspective all the more difficult. Although the predominant motivation for getting out of the country continues to be economic, leaving Sudan is increasingly the actualization of a desire on the part of individuals to achieve some sense of what is happening in their country. Many Sudanese expatriates say that it is impossible to gain such an understanding at home. The only way to understand Sudan is to be away from it.

It can be argued that the achievement of a viable political understanding entails a collectively organized series of experiences, discussions, and socialization processes contributed to by family, peers, and educational institutions. Yet it is the socialization process in Sudan itself that is being held up for questioning. Young people are asking why they should have to vote for their fathers' candidates; young Northern Arabs fantasize about marrying Southern Dinkas; young women demand their own mosques; university students celebrate each power cut at night with sudden urges to "go to the library" (i.e., have a romantic rendezvous).

For the Sudanese young, two divergent forces must be continuously reconciled—the need for personal autonomy and the need to experience religious integrity. The compensatory mechanisms characteristically adopted by the culture, i.e., the splitting off of one force from the other, are no longer sufficient and are seen by some educated youth as the source of much of the contemporary dilemma. It is ironic that many youth support the Islamic movement not as a process leading to the culmination of an Islamic society, but as a methodology that, by being a totalizing framework for everyday life, can lead Sudanese society into a more comprehensive, integrated secularism.

So often lost in the focus on Africa, in the staggering pessimism of underdevelopment, in debt figures, gross reductions in per capita income, and infant mortality rates, is the nature of the questions and personal needs emanating from individuals confronting the particularity of their own process of surviving. Of course, the focus on primary human needs—food, shelter, and health—takes precedence. Yet in all situations of deprivation, desperation, and confusion, there are psychological realities of substance and practices of "interrogating" the world which contribute something to our own sense of what the world is, and which can partially help us to understand the divergent motivations and behaviors of the internationalized arena within which we all operate.

THE URBAN FRONTIER: KHARTOUM AS THE WILD WEST

What Khartoum is today is in many respects a result of processes it set in motion a thousand miles away. When one reads the early colonial accounts of the Bahr al-Ghazal region and looks at the interaction of Arab and African in that region today, one gets the impression of a region that has become a devolved frontier—an endless murkiness that has simply intensified during the last century. At the time when colonial adventurers joined the private commercial armies of Khartoum merchants, Bahr al-Ghazal seemed like America's Wild West.

Life in Bahr al-Ghazal was dedicated to the pursuit of quick profit. Human life was itself the primary source of this profit. Both Arabs and Africans engaged in the slave trade with the aim of fortifying their respective states. For roaming Messeriyya nomads, slave raiding was insurance against the uncertainty of climatic effects. For the *wakil*, the soldiers and agents of the Khartoum trading houses, entire lives had often been inscribed in slavery—they had been raised since childhood in the cultural and educational systems of the North.

For the Africans, who entered into often involuntary alliances with the fortified *zariba*, outposts where raiding parties were launched and trade organized, the arrangement was a guarantee against their own enslavement and a source of income, since they took a minor share of all booty.[16]

For the *jellaba*, the petty trader, the commercial system relieved him of having to negotiate the terms of his trade alone and of having to pay tolls to enter specific territories and arrange his own armed retainers. He could be comfortably ensconced in the role of middleman, marketing the basic commodities necessary for life on the frontier and taking a share of the larger enterprises. He usually functioned as the man of religion—the imam, qatib, moulana. He had his autonomy and did not have to share it.

The *zariba* was an outpost of Islam, but an Islam that for the most part manifested only the wilderness of the marketplace, the intensity of business. Religious practice was a necessary punctuation to the endless circulation of goods and bodies. On Fridays, Arabs would break for prayer only a few yards away from their tributes and slave armies breaking to eat the bodies of fresh captives.[17] There was not much of an effort to bridge the worlds—the contradictions existed side by side. Brothels were next to mosques, drinking houses next to *medressas*. Islam seemed to be only a container through which the barely faithful recognized their lingering sanity. The Arabs would say that the pagans were not ready for Islam. Perhaps the Northerner simply did not know what to do with it. In the humid flatness of the land south of the swamplands known as the Sudd, there was little effort expended to build anything that would last. Rather, the site was a factory for raw materials and passions that propped up the institution of culture elsewhere.

In Bahr al-Gazal, neither the Northern Arab nor the Southern Azande (the most powerful African army in the region) ever conquered the other. The Dinka, focused on their cattle and their religion, played the side of whoever could ensure the integrity of both. At the same time, they were the most likely to be snatched by their Arab counterparts, the Baqqara cattlemen.

Now, over a century later, Bahr al-Ghazal is a wasteland. In some parts the SPLA has brought some order, but in recent years factionalism has lessened its impact. Otherwise, it has been a free-for-all—a place of starvation and disease. Young kids roam the bush with automatic weapons. Rail lines have been destroyed, bridges burned. Violence can explode anywhere at any moment between anybody.

The leveling of Bahr al-Ghazal has displaced some of the aspects of this former frontier to Khartoum itself. Khartoum, once an orderly city of river gardens and clean streets and a civility unmatched in the Arab world, now embodies the murkiness of that frontier. Arab and African orientations push against each other, becoming fiercer in their solidity as the push goes on. There is a seepage of cultures but little mutual incorporation. Orthodoxy and decadence cling to their respective positions side by side—all shades of blackness take all sides, assume all positions, and as such, perhaps amplify rather than diminish the salience of race in the configuration of Sudanese society. Economically, most people in Khartoum pursue not great profits but simply a way to stay alive. Wind blows dust and dirt, as the city seems to sink into some invisible river running beneath it.

The positions of Islamicist and Southern revolutionary are taken up in order to clear up the murkiness that has characterized ethnic and religious relationships ever since the outsider, i.e., the colonialist with his technology, enabled the Sudd to be penetrated and a corridor to be established between the North and South. Some Islamicists proclaim that Muslims lost their opportunity to propagate Islam in the South a long time ago. For others this lack of diligence in the past must now be compensated by an unwavering persistence. Southerners say that unless the reins of power are thoroughly nationalized, Northerners will be nothing but money men using Southern bodies for profit and for illicit sexual happiness. The Northerners, running out of potential African retainers, are reluctant to take the Southerners' concerns into consideration. They are not pioneers hoping to settle and raise families at the frontier.

Yet in Khartoum, the past comes back to haunt the offspring of the great merchant houses, i.e., the commercial class. The orderliness and tranquility of Khartoum is gone; it has become a wild, uncontrollable city full of crime, thieves, drunkards, whores, hustlers, homeless, shills, and terrorists, which all the various security organs and religious police are hard-pressed to "tame."

Let the Azande take over their kingdom once again, some Northerners remark. Yet others are not so sure. They fly to Wau to keep business contacts and build hospitals. Some make the slow trek to Rubek in search of a buck. They go where they do not belong, and a few are killed. The *jellaba* still feels that the South is his to do business in. War never makes any difference—there has always been war. In war the money is better anyway.

These undercurrents characterize Northern attitudes today. On the one hand, the Northern Arab requires big spaces to operate in—lawless and contested domain. On the other hand, the relocation of the murky frontier to Khartoum scares people; it makes them feel that a way of life is coming to an end. It is better to cut one's losses and live a more circumscribed existence, and to concentrate on speeding up a fuller incorporation into the Arab world.

THE TALK OF CITIES

There are many people in Sudan suspended in a timelessness that renders almost every aspiration strangely obsolete. For many Sudanese, there is nowhere to go, little to do. Some are ready to seize every opportunity to take whatever is weakly guarded. It is an existence that thrives on rumor and on long journeys undertaken to raise sufficient funds to journey somewhere else. It depends on the absence of documentation, gaps in surveillance, fueled by indifference it neither sought nor warranted. Births and deaths are unaccounted for; strangers mix with other strangers; people are willing to do almost anything. There is little money but plenty of ideas for getting it.

African towns once incorporated the phoneme "ka" in their names in order to represent the encapsulation of the essential life force. Kaduna, Kameroon, Kairo, Lusaka, Kampala, and Kano are some of the examples of this symbolic unification of the continent. Today this naming practice has given way to the predominance of Texas, South Bronx, Chicago, South Central, and 125th Street/Harlem as the designators of the spirit of the continent. These names, taken from American media, embody popular notions of the urban wilderness. There is a burgeoning awareness on the part of African urban dwellers that they are merely parts of an American ghetto that extends across the globe; a kind of international underside and excluded sector that is essential to the maintenance of tree-lined streets with elegant mirrored buildings elsewhere.

As the lives of villages and towns have been transformed, the best available framework with which to understand what is occurring is the image the West generates of "danger zones" from which rational social orders must be protected. That danger ensures that those who are "normal" continue to engage in the rigors of modern competition and do not ask too many questions about the moral significance of their actions. For those Africans once ensconced in the clarity of traditional law and universal dignity of everyday conduct, the demise of that order finds its only compensation in images of lawlessness and a bravado that must be at least feigned if one is to emerge from the fray with anything more than the shirt on his back.

Homeboys must be simultaneously trusted and killed. Almost every morning I would emerge upon the streets of my Umm Baddah neighborhood and find the body of a trusted son, companion of somebody held in general esteem by the neighborhood. A process of equalization is initiated whereby those who manage to succeed in either happiness or material gain do so only to the extent that new scams are introduced but never stabilized to the exclusive advantage of a few. A pervasive sense of tragedy must be institutionalized so as to produce an economy of compensations that will dominate lives on the verge of dissipating into Western parodies of poverty.

There is a shantytown outside of Khartoum known as Gatati South Mayo whose main thoroughfare is called 125th Street. Initially conceived as a place where the police could build large, inexpensive housing compounds, Mayo quickly became a place where police seldom ventured. During the last years of the Numayri regime, there was a half-hearted attempt to raze the shanties and displace the residents, but the community resisted fiercely, using weapons stolen from the local police station and spears. In 1992, the military went into one section, Dar es Salaam, in full force, destroying tens of thousands of households. In one sense, Mayo is an invisible community. One must drive on a dirt track twenty minutes past the last southern road of Khartoum across desert scrub. The place is populated by a little bit of everybody, too poor and too tough to make it elsewhere.

While evening prayer is being said throughout Khartoum, there are sections of Mayo where the daily ritual is the beat of Dinka drums. Prevented from establishing independent churches outside the formal religious organizations, some residents take up the search at sunset for secret impovished worship services conducted quietly in some opening in the narrow maze of hastily constructed mud compounds. Young girls filter out onto the main drag to canvass for the daily earnings of the small merchants ready to part with a little cash for "favors." Students from the African Islamic Center five kilometers away make their way en masse for a rollicking night at the "White House," where the refugee daughters of Idi Amin's victims help them spend the scholarship money the Saudis have liberally spread from Algiers to Johannesburg to bring young Muslims to the center.

Whatever is available becomes part of a network of exchange. A man will place a few notes in the hands of a woman for a bottle of local gin fortified with battery acid. The woman will give the money to her husband, who will pay the customer's daughter for sex. The daughter will give the money to her father, who will return to the woman for more drinks. This circuit is interrupted only by the proceeds of a son who has siphoned off a liter of gasoline from police trucks and bought tea and sugar for his mother to sell to traveling preachers, who do their best to convert the son to religion. He may also join a party of young men setting out for a three-hour walk across the desert in an attempt to ambush a passing truck that must slow down for a checkpoint.

By mid-evening, the drunk and the desperate in Mayo commence a nightly ritual of physical blows, and the tailors remain busy into the night sewing the linen wrappings for the casualties. Donkeys carry bundles of hashish to the outskirts, where they will be picked up by Egyptian gangs shortly before *fajr*. A Zairois boy from Kisangani has waited months for a compatriot bringing three grams of red mercury to be eventually smuggled to Jidda. A mother permits herself a rare moment of speculation with her daughter about her six-year-old boy whom she threw out four months ago because he wanted to go to school. A man whose wife has just died of tuberculosis picks up a stray goat and breaks its neck with his bare hands, while his aunt runs with a new Bible through the alleyways to a local *tkedjir* (shaman), imploring him to make sure that everyone who witnessed the act will now suffer from temporary amnesia.

Young girls avoid infections; the few with radios go to sleep early. A Nuba man recounts the names of his ancestors in a moment of intimacy with a newborn child. A Baqqara shepherd finds that he is unable to bring his prayers to a close. A merchant of Nigerian descent reconvenes the search for two fifty-pound notes he is positive he placed in a crack in the northeastern corner of his crumbling mud dwelling. Some of my informants boast of their ability to remember the names of every woman they ever slept with, despite the fact that the great numbers involved must have left them with many different impressions and perhaps confusion. Even though life was much too difficult, they took comfort in their ability to remember these names, seeing in it an affirmation that the clarity of their thinking remained intact. Places like Mayo had a purpose, they said. "God will be forced to intervene at an earlier date than was originally intended not because he is angry, but because he is curious," remarks Ateh Niyo. After translating these thoughts to his fellow Nuba companions, another Nuba boy indicated instead that when Americans ran out of space in their own country, they'd be able to feel right at home in a place like this. Yes, he knew that Americans would be horrified at the absence of their accustomed comforts, but he was sure that Americans like slum life, otherwise why would they make so many movies about it?

There are households where the chores of survival are conducted in total silence. Conversely, there exist households where the chatter of voices rarely ceases, engaged not so much in conversation but in the incantation of lists and indelible narratives that surmount the experience of social fragmentation. What indigenous institutions exist in Mayo are provisional arrangements designed to survey all who enter or leave. A precariousness of community boundaries is maintained. Whatever is taken is returned in a different form through other networks. The only rule is to do everything possible to maximize your advantage and be open to whatever fleeting external alliances are available.

What often passes for a state of permanent unconsciousness is rather the assumption of a calculated indifference. Many of the residents of Mayo believe that their worsening conditions are being engineered by a government hoping that they will start an insurrection so it can wipe them out in one fell swoop. Instead, the *tkedjir* counsel deception and supply the powders that are able to put middle-class households in the city to sleep while their possessions are being removed. A Nuba *tkedjir* points out a Dar Hamid merchant sitting in front of his stall reading the Quran with one hand and turning five round stones (an animist practice) with the other. This, he points out, is a sign that Islam has failed to capture the soul of the *jellaba*. Theft may be wrong, but it is necessary in order for the tribe to have opportunities to hold onto their magic and practice a religion which lives only on stolen time.

Thomas Sankara, the former leader of Burkina Faso, stated on a visit to Harlem in 1983 that 125th Street is the spiritual Mecca for African peoples. Now 125th Street has been deterritorialized, finding itself in different climates and continents, and is barely recognizable, yet present, in the desert slum, Mayo. But on Mayo's 125th Street, there is the sense that even for a people stripped of their custom, livelihood, and coherency in a universe stripped of definition, the reality of some intricate force of spirit remains.

If, despite the terrifying emptiness of this existence, some instrumental social mind is being honed—a creation vicariously enabling bodies and sensibilities to survive despite the odds—the outsider will have to begin to listen to a language he will be forced to relearn constantly. For even as the world's people come to have more immediate contact with and access to one another, distinct "species" are being created, not in a university laboratory, but in the shantytowns that surround almost every major city of Africa. As a movement that also seeks to create a new kind of human being, it is no wonder that the Islamic movement sees these shanty "laboratories" as a threat—something to be removed at all costs.

ISLAM IN THE CITY

Islam can be a powerful force for organizing the disaffected and the disparate. Because it links the local with the transnational, and the transnational with the divine, it enables people to view themselves in terms beyond their immediate experience. In its adamant specification of duty, Islam attenuates many of the uncertainties and ambiguities engendered by social orders that simultaneously change too rapidly and whose change is all too limited in both speed and scope. The basic elements of the religion constitute a universal continuity and a reassuring ideological emphasis on consensus as the mechanism for structural adjustments and transitions. At the same time, Islam justifies militant and uncompromising positions in relationship to injustice.

Islam does not institutionalize a systematics of theology, a chain of command, a religious power structure, or even a rigidly defined notion of heresy.[18] Behavioral uniformity is allowed to exist precisely because there are no fixed judicial injunctions determining how Islam is to be applied in a particular situation. At the same time, any Muslim is theoretically able to elaborate his or her own zone of operations and mission. Although the syntagmatic constraints (those that define specific actions as Islamic) are tightly structured, there is a legacy of freedom for personal initiative and endeavor. The historical difficulty confronted by Muslim societies is how Islam, as a complete way of life, is to be introduced within specific political frameworks.

Frustrated Muslim aspirations for the unification of distinct Muslim states—sentiments which informed the jihads of the nineteenth century from Futa Jallon to Aba Island—are a mirror of the frustrations inherent in coalescing different sociocultural groups within a single national boundary. Islam proves particularly adept at mobilizing people's energies against the state, yet it has had limited opportunities and conceptions available for managing the state. In fact, many instances of Islamic reform throughout African history indicate that the religious macrocosm has been at odds with the political microcosm—a situation destabilizing states that seemed to function efficiently within strict political terms.[19]

Once initiated, the move for Islamicization is almost impossible to attenuate or compromise without engendering a sense that the religion itself has been compromised. It is one thing for a program of Islamicization to be defeated or restructured by outside forces, as for example by colonial conquest or military takeover, and quite another issue if such a trend is volitionally modified because it is perceived to be insufficient or inapplicable to current socioeconomic realities.

For even though the Prophet Muhammed implied that the complete Islamicization of society is predicated on the existence of certain prerequisites, Khartoum Islamicists find it almost impossible to compromise on the question of *Shari'a*. Having compromised on many things, the irony is that Islamicists have chosen to concentrate on that aspect of Islam whose universal applicability seems to generate the most dispute.

Even the obvious terms of compromise, i.e., the exemption of the Southern regions and the capital from *Shari'a* (terms that were themselves two years in the making) raise a seemingly irresolvable quandary—even though the new Islamicist regime has basically ruled Southerners by those exemptions. The Islamic movement can reluctantly agree to the exemption of the South because they perceive it as virtually a separate country, but to exempt Khartoum would be to admit that the "center" of the nation can never avail itself of "God's law." There is another strictly political concern for the Islamicists. Because ideas concerning Sudanese nationalism are weak and ambiguous, democratic institutions limited in experience and loyalty, tribal identifications strong and persistent, and the economic prospects exceedingly bleak, Islam appears to be the only vehicle for mobilizing the energies of the population for long-term development.

The economic and religious needs of a culture are more parallel than they are often made out to be. The degree of religious fervor is frequently a barometer of economic dispossession. This linkage certainly exists in Sudan even though the Islamic movement is led by intellectuals and urban elites. In the long run, the self-sufficiency of the *umma*, its ability to develop the resources available to it, is a more important Islamic value than the legislation against alcohol consumption. Even if the masses reverse such priorities on a symbolic level, it is the responsibility of the elite not simply to play upon symbolic affinities.

In mosque after mosque following the August 1988 floods, worshippers at Friday prayer reiterated that they must take their lives into their own hands; that the blessings and guidance of Allah ensue from His people struggling together to build the social frameworks through which the capacity to serve God can flourish. Conditions of everyday life have always been precarious in the harsh Sudanese climate and have fostered attitudes of resignation and fatalism. One waits for spiritual redemption. Yet there have been clear political agendas in many of Sudan's past messianic religious movements. Therefore it would not be culturally dystonic for religious agendas to prioritize the attainment of self-sufficiency in food—something which the availability of arable land coupled with sound economic policies and political accountability could achieve. Perhaps the only way to attain such self-sufficiency would be to make it part of a religious agenda—as the Islamicists have now done.

The challenge of Islam is now to frame economic justice as a necessary element of religious devotion and to actively address the situation of those Muslims driven from their lands, herds, and livelihoods. Some of the most viable productive units currently in operation are religious communities organized around a Quranic learning center, where up to several hundred men and women are housed and work large plots of communal land. Although most of these centers amass substantial profits for the resident *shaykh* and are clearly exploitative of the devotion of the adherents, a few engage in a form of shared profit distribution that allows participation real opportunities to accumulate savings.

There are emphases in the current Islamic movement that have significant social potential, such as a focus on group marriages, which defray the exorbitant and often prohibitive costs of dowry, and the provision of short-term free housing, which provides couples time to get to know each other without having to reside with one of their parents. Women are being encouraged to open businesses and produce for the market by the provision of credit schemes for initial capitalization. Until the new regime cut back on female enrollment, women were well on their way to outnumbering men at the universities—in large part due to the work of the Islamic movement itself.

It is true that much of the groundwork for these social transformations was laid by the strength of the leftist movements operating in Sudan during the 1960s and by a vocal and determined women's movement. But that these issues have been adopted by at least a segment of the Islamic movement indicates that farther-reaching economic agendas might be possible, portending as they do some form of inevitable conflict with the vested interests of the merchant class. Much depends also on the degree of tolerance displayed to the plurality that such movements are bound to engender.

MORE THAN BREAD ALONE:
ASPIRATIONS IN CITIES

As recent developments across Africa show, the young want food and work. Where food and work are unavailable, they will either take direct militant measures to challenge the authority of the state, or pose indirect challenges to it through widespread criminal activities. It is important to ask not only how adequate employment and basic commodities will be provided, but also what has happened to these youth during the time such opportunities have not been available.

How have youth regarded their lives? How have they explained their circumstances, felt about their capacities, attempted to produce some satisfaction for themselves? In Sudan, as in many places in Africa, some youth have a tendency to "throw" themselves against their situation like a revved-up engine, hurling themselves into all available interactions with an aggression and single-mindedness that seeks some kind of reward in each confrontation, now or in the future. There is no hesitation. Cars will be immediately repaired, wasted, or stolen; rubbish will be collected with other rubbish, then converted, packaged, and sold. There is little time to ask questions, get permission, curry favor, explore the field. One throws one's body into the first available situation where it could make a difference and produce a little money.

In interactions with peers, demands and opinions are quickly put forward. This is a process that toughens and energizes one for the actions needed to get through the feeling that one is constantly walking on a cliff and observing others falling, unsure about just what is enabling them to make it and hindering the others who don't.

Then there are those young who delink themselves from everything familiar, adjusting to the consequences as the very means of attempting to conceive of an existence that is worth something. Ansaf, a 14-year-old girl, sees a movie on television about a street in Bombay. She thinks about it every day. She looks for someone who goes to the university in order to find some books about the city. Having found a book in English she cajoles one of her uncles to translate it for her. She asks the merchants if they know what goods are sold in Bombay, which businesses women are able to run. She begs an American Muslim to teach her some English because she hears that it is spoken there. She asks a travel agent the price of a ticket. She finds the Indian embassy in Khartoum and sells her circumcision gift, a gold bracelet, to buy information from the embassy guard. He introduces her to the consul's son, who has some influence and some money; she has sex regularly with him after school. She is saving her money.

There is a group of small children in a suburb whose name means "we have been cheated" who are told stories every evening after evening prayer by a young man called Ali. He tells them about their region, Darfur, and its connection to the rest of Africa. Their market mothers are too weary from long days of selling to shape their memories.

Then there are other children whom Ali instructs to forget their memories. Approximately a hundred thousand children are homeless in Khartoum. The *shamasa*, as they are called, wash cars, beg, steal, and are the objects of study by local and international organizations. What is known about how they live indicates that they have formed gangs with tightly knit hierarchies and rules. For several years, Ali has been the "godfather" of one of the largest and most productive gangs. He has accumulated a large percentage of their earnings from both legal and illegal activities. Although he continues to live in a run-down compound with his family, he has built basic living quarters for these kids who have worked for him a long time—under the condition that they do not try to contact their families.

With his capital, Ali has invested in marijuana and now controls about 30 percent of all distribution in the city. In order to follow the circuit of the latest karate movies, the *shamasa*, carrying packets of marijuana, ride atop trains on long journeys between Khartoum and Port Sudan, or Khartoum and Atbara. A network of independent taxis serve as mobile "fences" for stolen goods. Ali has imported the tools necessary to make these cars nearly invincible. He has cultivated his good looks and charm to develop close relationships with expatriates working in the country, taking advantage of their diplomatic privileges to get things in and out. He plans to retire next year to devote himself to religious study.

Hamza is a shepherd. He herds sheep into Hillat Kuku Suq each evening. He is still bewildered by the speeding cars on the service road. Illiterate, with wild uncombed reddish hair and a *jellabiyya* that is rarely washed, he makes a point of traveling to a different neighborhood every day to say *Asr* prayer before returning to his flock after sunset. His aspiration is to recite a prayer in every one of the hundreds of mosques scattered throughout Greater Khartoum. He does this to make his presence felt and to pray for the salvation of all of Sudan.

In no way are these youths whose stories I have summarized indicative of some general trend or discernible collective direction. They are not offered as exemplars of an emerging courage or political consciousness. Idiosyncrasies have been embedded in all historical conditions, all macrocosms. Yet these youths and untold others are to be considered as an aspect of an emergent African urban reality.

Probably the response to African underdevelopment cannot feasibly consist of optimal plans for social engineering and economic restructuring. The provision of basic needs is indeed Africa's primary problem, and its people its most valuable resource. The maximization of this resource and the facilitation of its capacity to function and create means more than just the all-too-needed establishment of adequate health care, access to drinking water, livable wages, basic skills, and appropriate technologies. It means more than simply consulting the peasants on how to increase productivity and engender culturally syntonic forms of distribution.

For while these agendas are crucial, the economic debilitation of African states has provoked a range of intrapersonal and interpersonal dilemmas: there are questions concerning (1) the practice of morality; (2) the content of motivations; (3) the procedures of friendship; (4) the values of self-concept. These issues precipitate tentative, often singular and idiosyncratic, responses and strategies that require some framework of intersection and mutual elaboration. Yet, such responses constitute the raw materials for reworking the cultural underpinnings of everyday life.

As African societies inevitably change, these tentative responses will be the means of revitalizing and reinventing the social fabric. Even though it is difficult for a man, woman, or child to imagine, reflect, conceive, or create on an empty stomach, empty stomachs do not terminate the existence of the imagination. The question will continue to be how these endeavors of the imagination can be incorporated into national and institutional life as aspects of a coherent cultural project.

Chapter Six

The Discursive Practices of the Islamic Movement

M y interest in the Islamic movement is not in simply reviewing its ideological underpinnings but in assessing how it understands its relationship with the larger world. How does the movement cohere its agenda; organize talk among its members; configure political space? What does the political strategy of prioritizing *Shari'a* signify about what the movement understands about its location in Sudanese and international politics? What is the relationship of political understanding to the practice of politics in Khartoum? These are some of the questions considered in this chapter.

Individual and collective experiences are represented in the ways people talk and in other nonverbal semiotic forms. In each culture, there exists an overarching framework that attributes particular and shifting value and significance to the actions of its members. Not only must variable understandings be marked and conveyed in differentiated representational forms, but differences in understandings must be accounted for and explained—and these "explanations" themselves represented. Therefore, differences among persons within a community—divergences in the nature of their intentions, obligations, rights, duties, and their relative access to basic resources, social institutions, and information—are manifested in distinct practices through which they attempt to make sense of their lives.

The variations in how people represent their lives correspond roughly with variations in how individuals engage with their social environments. As such, individuals possess and use more than one representational system. Since individuals cannot simultaneously pay attention to all the salient factors affecting their lives, various social arrangements are generated to divide responsibility and focus—in which the efforts of individuals complement one another and act to establish a range of behavioral and conceptual alternatives. All understandings concerning individual and group identity are multifaceted, reflecting the fact that the arenas and communities in which persons conduct their lives are themselves parts of larger communities and spheres of influence.

The work of Michel Foucault has gone a long way toward developing notions of how communities construct the terms through which they understand themselves and the world around them. In Foucault's work, however, this understanding is not a representation of a single objective order or an essential rationality. Rather, the tacit regularities in what a community considers and practices as "possible" are concrete statements of contingent and arbitrary configurations. Whatever regularities are sustained stem from a community's discursive practices, that is, the characteristic ways of speaking that constitute the particular objects and situations that a person considers and conveys to others.[1]

In Foucault's conception, the terms of understanding and the possibilities of meaningful behavior change without strict adherence to either ideological necessity, awareness of internal contradiction, or conscious collective decision. All facets of any local order are instead wrapped up in shifting and diffuse networks of talk—the citings, questionings, commentings, and mentionings through which people are engaged with one another.[2] These discursive practices are incessantly provisional, yet powerful, ways in which a community attempts to organize many people talking at once in conflicting exchanges.[3]

The terms of political understanding are thus made up of a plurality of aspects, techniques, rhetorical moves, struggles, and entities that co-exist, intersect, and mutually elaborate and compel one another without being tied to or explained by some overarching unity or metadiscourse.[4] The motivation of political movements is not, then, the realization of fundamental aspirations and identities, but a constant skepticism about and resistance to the categories in which people are defined/confined.[5] An integral aspect of political activity is the steps individuals take to exceed what they know about themselves and to generate forms of "counter-talk" through which these attempts at resistance are deployed. Therefore, political talk, the locus through which political understandings will be considered, is not simply talk about politics. It is also the talk about how talk in general should be conducted, who it should reach, and the effect it should have.

In evaluating the political behavior of the Islamic movement, I must take into consideration its discursive practices—how participants in the movement talk to one another; how talk is managed and delimited; what constitutes acceptable and efficacious modalities of talk. In this chapter, a few observations will be made about how talk in the movement is interpreted and deployed. From these observations I will deduce the larger patterns of interpretation embedded in the construction of the Islamic agenda.

TALK AMONG THE BROTHERS

Islamicist political discourse in Khartoum has been shaped on several levels. In a political movement without a fully elaborated political ideology, there is tendency for group political discussion to fall back on what is familiar. Since Islam is to be the centerpiece of political ideology and the source of its legitimation, frequent reference is made to the invocation of Islamic principles as opposed to the discussion of the principles themselves. At times, the Islamic agenda is referred to as if it were self-encapsulated body fully coherent and understood by its proponents. Although Islamicists experientially act as if this is the case, their deliberations reveal wide disparities in particular applications of the understandings of this agenda.

Importance is given to the fact that key scholars, associates of the Prophet and teachers, established certain widely used hermeneutical systems. Here, the "who" takes precedence over the "what," since shared knowledge about the authority of the exegete provides a more substantial basis of commonality than does the particular content area discussed. In part, this tendency reflects the legacy of Islamic education, where theological knowledge tends to be organized in terms of specific interpreters as opposed to content areas.

Within the confines of Islamic schools and universities, interpretations previously validated are usually unavailable to prolonged criticism. Rather, discussion about them constitutes another occasion in which deference must be shown. In religious education priority is placed on the length of study. Authority is established in terms of years of devotion accorded to a few works or specific areas within Islamic theology rather than the salience of insight of the scrutiny. This structure is reflected in the dynamics of how the "brothers" (colleagues in the Islamic movement) approach their deliberations. Arguments are frequently heated and debates intense, but what decision ensues usually centers around keeping the procedures of deference intact. Criticism of seniors is usually viewed as the complaining of the immature rather than as a necessary challenge. No matter how incisive criticism may be, the mechanisms for attenuating its impact are reaffirmed by its very presence. Everyone may have a right to speak (and Sudanese take full advantage of it), but the efficacy of speech is tightly bound to social position.

In a similar fashion, heterogeneity or idiosyncrasy of personal character and belief is limited to serving as an example of the fundamental tolerance of the larger group—it is seldom allowed to have a radicalizing effect. One colleague, no longer a Jabha member but a professional associate of a Jabha-related organization, repeatedly displayed an icono-clastic viewpoint and style of interaction. Although this individual's per-formance was not subject to the public repudiation and criticism that such performances often engender in Khartoum, the idiosyncratic ele-ments simply were not paid attention to. Instead, they were utilized to obfuscate differentiating forces existing among other colleagues—i.e., to make them look more similar than they were.

What I must stress here is that these practices of talking do not radi-cally differ from those found in all cultures—some espousing radically different ideological positions and worldviews. But this is precisely the point: Whereas observers are led to believe that the fundamental pre-suppositions underlying political differences engender antagonism and competition among groups holding different beliefs, the discursive prac-tices used to elaborate and control this antagonism manifest a sup-pressed complicity—a "working together" of the differences. The pre-sumed distance of superficially divergent political agendas is visible only as a two-dimensional representation of a process where the mimetic space of political narration folds in on itself. Understanding how poli-tical differences "work together" requires assessing similarities, diver-gences, and complementarities in how political groups in specific cul-tures talk about groups external to them.

In National Islamic Front decision making, participant efforts are geared toward constructing a functional homogeneity. This is not so much an attempt to suppress individual points of view and possible po-larities as to constitute a language that appears common. Within the NIF there are many tendencies, interpretive strategies, points of view, and competing agendas. As in any political movement, there are fierce rival-ries, bitter feelings, and ideological conflicts apparent to everyone. Yet, the invisibility of these divergences is constructed more from what does not get said publicly than from what is uttered. Gossip and rumor cer-tainly play a part in this process, but in a very specific way. Gossip and rumor establish the reputation of a particular participant, create an im-age of how he is to be known. When various participants are assembled, the existence of tensions or differences of opinion are suspected when particular individuals do not assume the ideological and tactical postures that rumor has established them as representing. Again, it is not what is said that enables participants to know the internal dynamics of the group, but rather what is viewed as omitted. Although contributing to an apparently fluid working relationship among participants, such con-structed homogeneity results in matters being frequently deferred to other settings—things are settled without being settled. As a result, opinions are not foreclosed, but neither are policy decisions fully implemented. Generalities are then obstinately pursued in order to reaffirm the coherence of the movement.

During the all-night deliberations held by the NIF in 1988 over whether to join a national government with the two other ruling parties, an outside observer might have concluded that a clear ideological debate was finally emerging that might advance the internal complexity of the movement. Eventually a decision was made to join the government, but the vote was so evenly divided across the ideological spectrum and social complexion of the NIF that this seemingly fundamental division was able to connote a sense of unity.

The ambiguous status of Sudanese as both African and Arab, and the continued relevance of ethnicity as a vehicle of urban mobility, render Sudanese vulnerable to the prospect of any kind of marginalization. Their intense desire to participate in the political process—a source of strength for contemporary Sudanese political culture—inclines Sudanese to appear homogenous in the practice of sociality. On the other hand, many young Sudanese have vacated politics in recent years. Both of these factors have contributed heavily to a general sense of sedentariness. When divergence does occur in social exchanges, it frequently assumes an intense quality that provides for a reassertion of ethnic particularism and antagonism. A colleague of mine working for a daily newspaper wrote a series of articles that raised questions concerning traditional Islamic modes of interpreting literary texts. An influential Islamicist and poet announced to a study group that he ran (one attended by many journalists) that the writer was a Communist in disguise. This accusation precipitated an intense period of threats and counter-threats which involved two distinct ethnic groups and a series of lawsuits. What appeared to provoke the fierceness of the dispute was the threat of marginalization and the power existing within Khartoum politics to marginalize. Many players, including prominent NIF leaders, attempted to resolve the dispute. But the questions of theory initially raised were left unaddressed. In the end, reference was made to the attempts of both parties to engender a vibrant and relevant Islamic sensibility.

This factor raises another issue related to discursive politics among the Islamicists. In an Islamic movement, the Quran and *Sunna* (the practice of the Prophet) must play major parts in informing the procedural dynamics of everyday political practice as well as ideology. But since discussion more often "passes through" Quranic citation and reference than finds justification and elaboration for particular points of view there, invocation of Islamic texts and principles posits a normalizing function that limits the opportunity for a deliberated multiplicity of perspectives. In other words, as the Quran is an immutable space of divine guidance and injunction, it, as a text, does not "respond" to interpretations and uses made of it. It is autonomous for human usage, despite the fact that it is interpreted in a myriad of ways.

Because of the absence of reciprocal influences, the Quran is to be viewed by Sudanese as a common space and shared sensibility rather than a means to sustain, alter, or restructure particular points of view. With both reverence and appreciation, individuals can acknowledge one another joined together within this space. In fact, the space exists in order to join together and assemble individual differences into a fundamental unity of purpose. This does not mean that theological debates are absent in Sudan either within or outside of political contexts. The Sudanese love to argue as much as anyone, and politics is their great passion. But the extent to which Quranic reference assumes a differentiating function within and between distinct political articulations is limited by virtue of individuals being inscribed within highly codified structures for reading and using it.

The attempt by Mahmoud Muhammad Taha to provoke a reconsideration of this traditional hermeneutic was construed as dangerous, not so much on religious terms but because of its radical implications for the position of Quranic interpretation within Sudanese political culture. Within the Islamicist community, a secularist is not so much one who has abandoned the faith or ceases religious practice, as one who refers to the Quran and Sunnah to legitimate a differentiating point of view.

GETTING THE POINT ACROSS

Applied Islamic discourse asserts a sense of commonality and accessibility, but mystifies as well. Much of the way Islamicists talk with one another reflects Abner Cohen's point about how symbolic practices tend to mystify as well as clarify the nature of relationships among people operating within various settings.[6] It is the ambiguity of the symbolic that is the source of its power to hold attention and attenuate questioning about either the authenticity or efficacy of social relationships. Persons engaged in a ritual activity are unable to conclude precisely whether the activity caters to their internal needs and sensibilities or to some larger agenda of the social group to which they belong.

Having participated in many discussions with NIF members, I often found it difficult to decide just what was being "done" to me by virtue of this participation. I was always warmly welcomed and invited to share in most deliberations, but it was clear that they were not going to give me a clear role. Because of this ambiguity I tended to gear my actions toward maintaining some form of inclusion, to keep the possibilities of some ongoingness open. I did this, not because I wanted to know "better" what they thought or maintain sources of information, but simply in order to make sense of their approach to me. One is treated fairly but impersonally, listened to but ignored—one is the object of generosity both sincere and perfunctory that permits an easy dismissal of one's presence. At times, moves I made to delink myself were met with great consternation, as they conveyed how much my input was needed in certain areas. When I took some initiative in those areas, I was met with an equal amount of distress. Importance confidences were at times easily divulged. At other times, the most insignificant details were treated as state secrets. Allah was to be mightily praised for involving an American Muslim in the movement, but this fact was often viewed as having no practical implication and no concrete reason for being important.

Decisions can be consensually agreed upon only to be undone in consensus elsewhere. The mystification generated by inclusion in the Islamic discourse makes it difficult to operate with the social bearings that are necessary to introduce functional heuristic thinking into political discussions. One day one thing is said, the next day something different. The inconsistency is not to be seen as a contradiction but as an indication of the fact that the social positions of individuals are fluid, subject to change as others change. I was always bemused at how some of my colleagues kept shifting the status of certain persons when they talked about their social networks. Persons who were considered trusted partners one day were often seen as antagonists the next, and then trusted collaborators a few days later as if nothing had happened.

A discursive strategy that "announces" the masking of the expedient, self-aggrandizing, and manipulative aspects of politics is simultaneously used by activists to protect themselves against becoming objects of political expediency. When the "sacred" gets too unwieldy, the "base" is emphasized, and vice versa. Each covers for the other. Everyone seems to know the game is being played. The banal dynamics of party politics are masked. Yet the masking operation is apparent, even at times joked about. But thus masked, these dynamics cannot always be effectively challenged without precipitating displays of the "we are all brothers" language referred to earlier. As a result, withdrawal becomes the most familiar means of resistance.

The predominance of religiously styled talk does not mean that the movement shies away from other media or means of provocation. In its attempt to exert hegemony over the political applications of religious thinking and discourse, the Islamic movement views control over the terms of derogation, humor, and insult as significant to its task. During the post-Numayri period, *Al-Wan*, an independent daily newspaper closely aligned with the NIF, gained the largest circulation in Sudan largely because it reframed reporting on everyday national political events as an ongoing cartoon series. The strategy worked by anticipating the need of readers to laugh and reflected their attitude that politics was simply a joke. More importantly, it acted to convince readers that the current state of Sudanese politics was explicable and comprehensible only on the level of a cartoon or soap opera. Reversing the traditional format in which cartoons were relegated to back sections, *Al-Wan* foregrounded the ongoing saga of a menagerie of thinly disguised political actors as the significant news.

Taking advantage of the tendency of the prime minister to deliver lengthy speeches for every possible occasion, attributions were falsely made to him, but these were rarely challenged effectively since his voluminous nature convinced most everyone that no single person could possibly remember what he did or did not actually say. With fictional stories taking precedence over hard news, stories from other contexts documenting real events were often included, leaving out markers that would identify the event's actual location. Readers would more than likely conclude that these stories, actually about situations in other countries, were taking place in Sudan. Fabrication, irony, parody, simulation, and hyperbole, in addition to unrivaled critical analysis, enabled *Al-Wan* to radically alter the public nature of political talk in Khartoum.

PEDESTRIAN DISCOURSE

Because the Islamicists do such a good job of handling the inventiveness of public talk, they tend to act as if they are afraid of it and emphasize absolutism over provisionality. This wariness is compounded by the urbanization process taking place in Khartoum. Although people still reside in highly territorialized neighborhoods largely ethnically defined, the enormous growth in population is rapidly changing this structure. Diverse peoples are brought into greater contact with one another. These intersections of diversity open up new forms of sociality and diffuse new ways of talking that displace, supplement, or alter intact discursive styles.[7] The social body grows more intricate and so do the resultant means for negotiating and traversing it. What de Certeau calls a "pedestrian rhetoric" is accentuated—a bricolage of common sayings, over-heard conversations, allusions, and ellipses that represent the fluidity of a changing social environment.[8] Not yet installed as the voice of any particular institution, it is an occasion for singularity and idiosyncrasy.

In Khartoum, a plethora of new ways of talking are emerging. Many young members of the NIF, faced with the amplified urbanity of their living space, spend long hours simply walking around different neigh-borhoods without a clear agenda or purpose, seeing Khartoum, as one friend remarked, "for the first time." What is seen is the multiplicity in-herent in the structure of their identity. Although it doesn't necessarily alter their sense of religious commitment, this new view expands the range of what they consider necessary in order to live out a religious commitment. Sometimes it shifts their desire for inclusion/participation away from the context of Islamic politics toward some kind of nebulous participation in the potential cultural vitality of Sudan.

A new discourse, precipitated by this experience, was subject to at-tack in various Islamic newspapers as a "creeping disrespect for the lan-guage of religion."[9] Note here that it is not religion itself that is dis-respected, but its language. Religious consciousness is inextricably linked to the use of a specific discourse. But this new language, as a manifestation of cultural interpenetration, is a source of danger, a chal-lenge to the Islamicists to open up the parameters of the ways they talk about politics. Although the Islamicists talk about Khartoum as a city to be remade, the implications of this agenda are not as clear to them as is the need to couch an ideally transformative politics in a rhetoric calling for the preservation of the traditions of the "old city." Yet, in this practice of walking Khartoum, and the talk that represents it, identity is up for grabs.[10]

THE SUPPRESSION OF PROVISIONALITY

Islamicists consider rhetorical strategies that emphasize provisionality and a detachment from moralism and authenticity to be legitimate in-struments of political warfare. But in their internal thinking and modes of sociality, they do not view these same strategies as legitimate tools for creating political understanding. Although often calling for the opening of the gates of *ijtihad* (the realm of new interpretations and pro-visional formulations), the Islamicists are reluctant to engage in intellec-tual play or experiment with personal demeanor. It is difficult to ascer-tain whether this reluctance is an intrinsic limitation of the movement's relationship with Islam or stems from the particular role the movement plays for the majority of its adherents. The movement understands that to some extent it has substituted itself for kinship loyalty. As economic conditions have deteriorated progressively over the last decade, the ability of kinship ties to adequately ensure the economic well-being of relatives has been sorely strained. As political parties have themselves largely reflected the convergence of kinship, ethnic, and religious loyalties, many young people have turned to the political arena almost as an extension of family, even if very few of their family members were actually involved in the NIF.

Just as household discourse is tightly bounded by terms of propriety, invocations of paternal/maternal responsibility, and mediation, the internal discourse of the Islamic movement is also conscious of the boundaries within which it must operate. But the agenda of the movement is not to substitute itself for kinship. Although valuing the sanctity of family life, the movement would like to detach Sudanese from the sedentary and "tribal" aspects of those relationships. It sees itself as unable to accomplish this, however, if the internal discourse of the movement is viewed as too divergent from that of family life.

The fundamentalist spirit embodied by the NIF is not a rejection of social progress but emanates from an understanding that social progress is all too necessary. Women are viewed as essential players in national development and must involve themselves in politics. Still, the involvement of women in the movement must be handled with care. They are expected to spend long hours away from home, to attend meetings at night. Potential conflicts with the family are avoided by presenting the movement in terms they can understand. Who can deny a daughter leaving the house at night if she is participating in a meeting or rally that will restore Islamic law to the land?

By foregrounding religious talk, Islamicists create the impression that everyone can be involved in the political process by virtue of being a Muslim, that Islamic identity is the most important criterion for political participation. The movement can thus theoretically draw upon the masses kept out of politics—long seen as the exclusive domain of a few families. Of course, questions concerning who controls the terms of Muslim identity remain.

The suppression of provisionality in Islamicist discourse is not motivated simply by political expediency. There are aspects of Sudanese culture that tend toward absolutism when it comes to the management of cultural imperatives. This tendency is probably best seen outside of the religious sphere. One of the complaints often heard in the NIF is that many Sudanese practice their secularism religiously. That is, they have such rigid and determined ideas about keeping religion out of their lives, for the sake of individual freedom and intellectual openness, that they might as well have not abandoned religion in the first place.

Although exaggerated, the extremes of this sentiment occasionally evidence themselves. I was asked to do psychological consultation on a case involving a highly educated young couple with a three-year-old son experiencing aphasia. The couple considered themselves thoroughly modern Sudanese, educated abroad and disenchanted with traditional mores which they thought left the society in a permanent state of underdevelopment. Both had high positions working for foreign interests in Khartoum. Their attitudes of modernism extended to the raising of their one child. While both worked, the child was left with a caretaker who was instructed to keep contact to a minimum. For most of the day, the child sat in front of a video recorder watching an assortment of movies. Upon arriving home, each parent spent twenty minutes with the child, curtailing frivolous play and instead attempting to coax the child into giving a report of the movies he had watched. The child was raised to be completely independent. Time with the child was scheduled and an agenda was set. Contact with extended family was limited because the couple thought they would spoil him. Physical affection was offered only as a reward for impulse control and then meted out without passion.

The interesting thing about this situation was not its apparent pathological character but the fact that the parents were fighting back their own instincts, subsuming them to a distorted picture of how the "modern" person develops. Little flexibility or resilience was ever demonstrated. It was as if modernism had its own sacred text to which adherence was being paid. What is significant here is that the suspicion accorded the provisional in political and social discourse may be informed by religious stricture but extends beyond religion to encompass aspects of life and styles of thinking superficially antithetical to it.

Within everyday Sudanese social relations a certain complementarity of religious and secular talk has been effected. Relations and situations can be improvised or bargained with precisely because some absolute reference exists contiguous to anything that is fluidly made and remade. The historical overlay of Arabic culture and language on the Sudanese body engineers its articulators into what at times appears to be a beguiling indirectness. Anger and direct criticism are to be circumvented, perhaps because once started, disputes and bickers are hard to de-escalate. But more importantly, it is the view of many Sudanese that religious discourse embodies all the possibilities for directness and honesty.

This view, usually associated with the Sudanese scholar Dr. Jaafar Sheik Idris, notes that honesty is seldom expedient; it doesn't necessarily make things go better. Relying on the Quran as the voice of judgment and evaluation, sticking close to its terms as informing everyday social practice, obviates the need for humans to approach one another as mutual evaluators. Evaluation is performed and judgment is made, but it is not individuals themselves who do this, but individuals as representatives of God's law, in which individuals do not intervene. If human individuals were to assume the responsibility of judgment based on grounds of their own making, all justice would be arbitrary. By adhering to the word of Allah, something potentially knowable by all, each individual has the opportunity to be treated fairly in any encounter, knowing in advance the grounds on which he will be marginalized or punished. Provisionality is thus associated with the nonjudicious, since it relocates the power to disrupt social ties as the arbitrary power of individuals. Whatever ensues from difficult or problematic interactions is the will of God.

On several occasions colleagues remarked to me in meetings that they thought certain invocations of religiosity were simply shams. But rarely did they say so outright, since they found it hard to resist the notion they were socialized to uphold, that is, that the terms of such criticism do not belong to them.

Again, this does not mean that bitter disputes and challenges do not occur. I've seen small arguments blow up into major confrontations that take days of constant negotiation to resolve. But such eruptions exist more to strengthen the implicit determination of political players to adhere to proper procedures than they do to restructure the discourse through which politics is played.

There is much in the Quran that is not easy to abide. Despite the Prophet's concern that religious devotion not ask too much from Muslims and be simple in its expectations, anachronistic aspects of Quranic injunction are now frequently used to impose a measure of clarity on complex social and political affairs. The complexity of these affairs can be directly attributable to the unwillingness of Muslims to deal directly and honestly with their lives. As Dr. Idris states, hand-cutting for theft may strike people as crude and archaic, but if we are honest in our relationship with God we will acknowledge a very difficult thing, i.e., that this is what our religion calls for and the message is direct. Our attempts to invent the terms of directness with one another can only result in a relationship of indirectness with God.[11]

URBAN IMMERSION

Despite the sacrosanctity of Islamic values, NIF activists are increasingly confronted with a country that frequently veers out of the range of any rational apprehension. In a strange way, many Islamicists have not shied away from facing the issue of cultural and religious differences in the country. Hassan al-Turabi was almost killed during a visit to Wau when thousands of people surrounded the building in which he was speaking; three of his aides were killed.[12] Given the security situation in the South at the time, one might reasonably conclude that it was foolish for him to go there. The same was said about a close friend of mine, Zubair Bashir Taha, who, during a speech in Karton Karol, an anti-Arab stronghold of Khartoum, was shot at several times.

Younger activists, living off minimal professional salaries, have been forced to find housing and purchase land for building homes in illegally occupied residential areas. In many such areas the government has turned a blind eye, and in some cases, has been forced to provide basic services. In the end, however, the state retains the authority to eliminate these neighborhoods and has selectively done so in the past eight years. But the significant issue for this discussion is that Islamicists, for economic reasons, are increasingly "thrown" into culturally and religiously heterogeneous neighborhoods where for the first time some have prolonged contact with Southerners and with a second economy that frequently depends on activities at odds with Islamic principles.

In these neighborhoods, Islamicists must confront the realities and myths inherent in the ways they and the Islamic movement have understood the changing realities of Khartoum. Previously quick to attribute the surge of drinking, theft, and whoring in Khartoum to Ethiopian and Southern refugees, they discover that these people make every effort to avoid these activities as a means of economic survival. Notions of the pagan and animist as devoid of religious practice and discipline cannot help but dissipate in the efforts Southern Sudanese make to maintain orderly households in the face of awesome adversity.

A great deal of drinking, crime, and illicit sex does occur in Khartoum. But they stem from dislocation, urban psychological stress, and economic hardship and are not a fundamental aspect of any particular cultural identity. From Halfayet to Hag Yousif to Umm Baddah, Islamicists who are not part of the merchant class have had to rethink the nature of their relationships to non-Northerners and non-Muslims.

This rethinking assumes various forms. It does not necessarily adhere to a liberal Western idea of tolerance for plurality or a postmodernist celebration of difference. Whoever the other is, they are not to be left alone in their otherness. In this position of coresidence, differences are not simply left to coexist. Nor is there the conception of reciprocal confluence, in which some new synthesis of worldviews and essential practice is posited. What emerges is the need to further elaborate an Islamic sensibility that is able to be present in all situations and eventually bring all situations under a discernibly Islamic framework. Islamicists living in these neighborhoods do not avoid day-to-day interactions with those culturally strange to them. Neither do they attempt to convert them or extend kindness with a hidden agenda (this would come only later as part of an intensified effort at policing the periurban areas). They make full efforts to understand the terms of their lives within the other's own terms.

With this effort it is thought that points of convergence between Islam and non-Muslims are increasingly elaborated. Within the concept of *tawhid*—the notion increasingly applied by Ikhwan scholars to connote an essential oneness in the social order of the universe ruled by God—there is no aspect of life "hidden" from Islam or outside the basic interlocking divergences that extend God's will. Differences are not to be apprehended by the terms that are familiar, but rather, Muslims must familiarize themselves with the multiple perspectives from which sociality has been configured by God. Talking about others and otherness within this notion of *tawhid* is a process of worship.[13] Generating a knowledge of the other is the means of identifying oneself, but not in a schema of bifurcation, e.g., "I know myself by what I am not;" rather: "Where I am is not in the place I thought myself to be." Unlike Lacanian notions of a self always absent to its apprehension, the knowledge of both other and self in Islam is not only possible but is a religious imperative and a fulfillment of history.

Since nothing exists outside of Islam, everyone is potentially a Muslim. It is the responsibility of the Muslim to address the other in such a way that brings the potential for Islamicity to the fore. In order to do this, Islamic discourse cannot simply be forced upon or proselytized to the non-Muslim. The other cannot simply be considered a deficient Muslim amenable to corrective measures. After all, Muslims are accountable to God for their representations of others. Islam will emerge in non-Muslims, but not from the weakness inherent in their identity (for weakness deceives and protects its dysfunction to the end). Rather, it is the sheer strength and viability of alternative views that enables them to open up "onto" Islam as a natural culmination of their own wisdom. Unless the Muslim then understands and appreciates the nature of that wisdom, there is no way the other will be brought to Islam. And since nothing exists outside of Islam, the mode of convergence between these two realities is Islam.

Within the notion of *tawhid*, otherness is not an irreconcilable philosophical or political chasm, a problem to be solved, or a sign of an essential plurality. Otherness is instead an opportunity for a broader human fulfillment for everyone. It makes both self and other something neither were before (but were essentially the whole time).[14]

What the experience of living in multiracial and multireligious neighborhoods has meant to many young Islamicists is the discovery and elaboration of this particular interpretation of *tawhid*. The experience has not forced them to suspend their Islamic outlook; indeed, for many, it has served to intensify it. What may seem to outside Western observers as the abnegation of otherness and the denial of an irreducible cultural heterogeneity is rarely perceived in this manner by Islamicists. It is not heterogeneity that is denied, but its implications in terms of deriving a practice of interchange and mutuality. This does not mean that there are not some Islamicists whose sensibility is profoundly altered by their interactions with non-Muslims. Certainly, there have been NIF activists who, forced to live with Dinka, Nuer, Shilluk, Taposa, Azande, etc., radically changed their commitment to Islam—but this is not the general pattern.

At times the consideration of the other's worldview as an aspect of Islamic principle is effectively communicated to some non-Muslim residents of Khartoum. The practice has antagonized others who conclude hidden agendas or misinterpret intentions. At times even a certain amount of envy is involved. As one Dinka woman, Annuel Deng, told me, "The young Jabha are so certain with their ways; even we are not able to disturb them, yet we get so bothered by them . . . maybe we are not as good at knowing what we are."

Whether the position of otherness connoted by this interpretation of *tawhid* acts as a hidden form of cultural imperialism or a reasonable instrument for overcoming some of the practical dilemmas involved in cross-cultural relations cannot be argued in any general way. It is a matter of contexts, conflicting perceptions, and provisional opportunities. What is clear, however, is that within the context of cultural, political, and religious conflict in Sudan, reconciliation is not simply a matter of overcoming Arab racism, promoting understanding, or appreciating cultural differences.

What is also clear is that the new Jabha-dominated regime has not curtailed, and in some events has actually encouraged, a total contravention of these notions of *tawhid*. In the rush to establish the "rule of God," basic human rights among residents in the periurban areas, both Muslim and non-Muslim, have been largely trampled. Forced and enticed conversions are the order of the day.

What these "shortcuts" to Islamicization indicate is that those components of Islamic practice that are seemingly so important to informing a reasonable politics of building a coherent and functioning city are both conceptually and practically the most difficult to inscribe within a broader political practice. Instead of seeing Islam enriched in its adoption by the dark-skinned, animist, or Christian, the tendency too often is to view Islam as a civilizing mission. Additionally, the strategy of approaching the situation of otherness embodied in the *tawhid* is not only conceptually complex but depends on the willingness of the other to be engaged.

At this point, Southerners will largely suspect any initiative by Islamicists, no matter what it is. Southerners are demanding the right to make initiatives themselves as well, to be accepted not only as capable but inherently eligible to direct engagements both on the micro- and macropolitical levels. The Islamicist conception of otherness may indeed contain important seeds and viabilities. But something else will need to happen before the seeds are able to "take."

TALKING ABOUT THE SOUTH

If the everyday conception informing the progressive Islamicist's interaction with the non-Muslim is difficult to translate into practical terms, the problem has been confounded, as stated earlier, by the actual policies of the present regime. Its official rhetoric has reflected a gradual progression toward hysteria and moral indignation in its characterization of national events. Islam is increasingly seen as the only way to defend the integrity of the country.

The conflation of religious and national sentiments has not always won popular support in the recent past. In early 1989 street demonstrations in Omdurman expressed frustration with the single-mindedness of the Islamic agenda, especially given the dire economic circumstances.

For its part, the NIF was frustrated by the SPLA's continuous reassertion of the same preconditions for the settlement of the conflict. It felt that the South had been provided all the guarantees necessary to assuage its concerns about the protection of religious freedom and the NIF's commitment to the economic development of the region. Essentially the NIF was saying, "We are prepared to leave you alone." But the message was interpreted by the South as an autonomy by default—an autonomy secured by a fundamental nonparticipation in the definition of the country.

The Quranic verses accompanying NIF explication seemed to drive home this point: "If they come to you, give them your judgment or let them be" (Surah al-Ma'idah: 42). Citing this surah in the NIF's statement on the new Islamic laws presented to the Constituent Assembly in August 1988, Dr. Al-Mikashfi Taha al-Kabbashi (head of the Court of Appeals under Numayri) stated, "As long as non-Muslims remain in their own regions, we should leave them alone and leave their laws and judgments alone."[15] He felt it was sufficient to say that the provisions dealing with alcohol, apostasy, plunder, and adultery would not apply to the Southern regions unless a defendant requested that they apply.

But, as Amin Makki Medani of the University of Khartoum pointed out in an article in *Al-Ayyam* (in 1988), although the *hadd* punishments are suspended for these activities, they are still defined as *hadd* crimes for both Muslims and non-Muslims alike. Non-Muslims may not be stoned for premarital sex, but premarital sex is still defined as a crime.[16] By doing this, the NIF ignores the commitment in its charter to respect the customary practices and social conventions of non-Muslims.

In addition, the NIF's Sudan Charter of January 1987 states that Muslims are identified as the majority. "The Muslims therefore have a legitimate right by virtue of their religious choice, of their democratic weight and of natural justice to practice the values and rules of their religion to their full range—in personal, familial, social, or political affairs" (p. 2). Then one paragraph later, after acknowledging that minorities should not be subjected to prejudice or restrained, "Non-Muslims shall, therefore, be entitled to freely express the values of their religion to the full extent of their scope—in private, family or social matters." Note the absence of political affairs in this statement.

The South doesn't want to be left alone; its adamancy regarding the preconditions for giving up armed conflict is an insistence upon being recognized as a national, not regional or separatist, force. The Islamicists, who increasingly portrayed the war as an abberation manipulated by foreign forces intent upon destroying Islam, were seen by the South as unwilling to recognize the rationale for the conflict, let alone any sense of its legitimacy. Economic disparity and underdevelopment did sow the seeds of Southern antagonism—both sides concur with this understanding. But the Islamicists view the disparity as a remnant of colonialism; the Southerners view it as the result of purposeful Northern hegemony. What results is that the more the South presses for recognition of an existent logical basis for armed struggle, the more this is denied by the North.

The official NIF statement regarding the Democratic Union Party–negotiated accord with the SPLA in November 1988 indicates, "We regret the capitulation agreement because it is an unequivocable recognition of the rebellion. . . . We will not allow anyone with the military establishment to have loyalty to anyone but God and country."[17] Preoccupied with the possibility of losing their own identity and value by recognizing the rebellion, the Islamicists assume that there really is no identity or value inherent in the Southerner to capitulate to. The fight of the Southerner is then partly a fight against internalizing the structure of this disparity. As Maj. Yusuf Kuwahi, the SPLA's former second in command, has said, "We're fighting an inferiority and superiority complex. We feel inferior but when we bear arms, we feel equality. There are people in the grip of a superiority complex, but when they hear bullets, feel weakness and inferiority and begin to come down. We want both sides to be equal."[18]

But equality becomes increasingly difficult to acknowledge when an internal political conflict is increasingly defined as a last-ditch defense of an entire faith. The venom expressed in the NIF peace accord statement toward the SPLA was turned Quranically against the party who had sat down with the "enemy" in Addis Ababa—something that almost every political group but the DUP had already done in previous years. Referring to the secularists in the DUP, the statement cites Surah al-Tawbah (47): "Had they taken the field with you, they would only have added to your burdens." "They would have wormed their way through your ranks, seeking to sow discord amongst the faithful: and amongst you there were some who would have gladly listened to them. Allah knows the evildoers."[19]

Much of the NIF's emphasis in recent years has been to search out and expose the evildoers. Perceiving insult added to injury, Southerners feel that the NIF's intensive attention to rooting out the "fifth column" (Northern collaborators) implies that the SPLA would never be able to sustain the conflict by themselves. Although the interconnections among region, friendship, and political party do establish all conceivable levels of complicity, the Islamic press seems to exaggerate the dependency of the SPLA on various Northern intelligence sources.

Intelligence gathering is, however, an entrenched part of the political game in Khartoum. Most of the political parties had their own secret divisions that were funded to gather and fabricate information, as well as guard against infiltration from the outside. An observer would be excused for being skeptical about the ingenuous way documents dealing with espionage plots are found lying casually in desk top drawers. The degrees of interpretive elaboration can also be impressive. For example, the Baath Party issued a ten-page analysis of an intricate NIF plot supposedly contained in an otherwise seemingly innocuous three-sentence letter.[20]

In December 1987, following the temporary fall of Kurmuk, a border town officially considered part of the North, war hysteria was at a fever pitch. Members of the DUP were seen getting in and out of army helicopters at the front; other Arab countries were pressed to supply more arms. For a time, appeals to deep-seated Sudanese sentiments regarding the sacredness of land and nation served to distract attention away from the acute economic crisis and generated appeals for a national reconciliation government that could mobilize general support.

The context of this reconciliation attempt served to exacerbate the underlying conflicts between the parties and to reveal the weakness of each as a self-contained ideological and political unit. In the Umma/DUP/NIF triumvirate, each party seemed to focus its energies on precipitating and playing off conflicts between the other two. Each upheld the inviolability of particular institutions or democratic processes when the others made moves to generate radical shifts in war and economic policy. For example, Ali al-Hajj Muhammad, NIF Director of Political Affairs and former trade minister, insisted that no peace accord could contain preconditions since it was the role of the constitutional conference to propose political arrangements that had to be then approved by the Constituent Assembly. Democratic institutions had to be upheld at all costs.[21] This was the same man who, as trade minister, had no objections to his ministry conducting emergency, extralegal courts to try black marketeers.

The implosive character of the political process in Khartoum increased its vulnerability to the very external forces that the Islamicists sought to defend against. Conversely, the situation accentuated the nature of Sudan's dependency on the external inputs it received from other nations. The resumption of United States aid in early 1989 was tied to the government's taking steps to end the war in the South. Other Arab nations were demanding that internal politics be clarified before they would provide more arms. The masses were waiting hours in line for bread; the United States was complicating the renewal of previous wheat agreements. The Islamicists, their power in eclipse after having dominated the political scene for the better part of 1988, called for an end to the politics of accommodation. Too many parties—Ethiopia, Libya, Chad, the United States, Kenya, Iran, Iraq, Egypt, and Saudi Arabia—had to be pleased and catered to.

Articles appeared in the Islamic press calling for the renewal of self-sufficiency, imploring Muslims to please themselves and God rather than focusing on other parties, whether they be fraternal or not. Muhammad Taha Muhammad Ahmed, in an article in *Al-Rayah*, said: "Why hide our flaws . . . the Prophet accepted the siege in the desert of the Arabian peninsula. Why shouldn't we accept a siege? Why not set a siege around the sorghum stalks, with sorghum being as abundant as it is in al-Qadarif? Why not put our trust in God? He will provide our subsistence just as He provides for the birds that come hungry and fly out with full stomachs."[22]

The NIF considered the most realized form of self-sufficiency to be support for the dedication and suffering of the armed forces. As in many wars, an appreciation for the situation of the combatant was belated. Political capital rather than the welfare of the soldier was often the chief priority. Settlement of the war was increasingly framed as a betrayal to the sacrifices of the sons of Sudan. If the Sudanese were not able to support those who supported their freedom and religion, Sudan would not be able to do anything, let alone build a functioning economy. Although draining the economy, the million dollars spent on the war every day was, after all, not enough to do the work that would be necessary to resuscitate the economy in the long run. Commitment to canonical Islamic law was the ultimate expression of loyalty to the nation. In fact, any talk of accommodation was a form of defamation of the blood spilled.

Instead of consolidating support among young Sudanese, this strategy of effusive support for the armed forces bifurcated their political sentiments. Increasingly, commitment to the Islamic agenda ran parallel to a commitment to find all available ways to end the war. What contradictions ensued from this dualist position simply weren't paid attention to. Many soldiers themselves expressed marked ambivalence about the war. They began to feel that they were an irrelevant factor in a game being played by other parties and forces. Some agreed with the Islamicists that a solution had to be imposed once and for all; others hoped that some workable peace could occur so they could move to the South, some Northerners having fallen in love with its natural abundance and economic potential.

The Islamicists had been organizing in the army over the course of several years. Attention to the armed forces was not something that came overnight. There had been coup whisperings in Khartoum for eighteen months. Partly this reflected Sudanese aspirations that something concrete be done about the economic situation. It was not that the Sudanese preferred military rule; rather, they were exasperated with the insidiousness of the constant political maneuvering.

Following the ultimatum issued by the army to the government in early 1989, it became evident to the NIF that continued participation in the government would further erode its base of support. The military was applying pressure on the Constituent Assembly to defer the implementation of *Shari'a*. Under the auspices of their commitment to Islamic law, the NIF withdrew from the government in March. As the Sudanese conflict found itself more internationalized—a process which the NIF had implicitly encouraged by pointing to outside intervention as the raison d'être of the war's continuation—the NIF carved out its return to the opposition in broad international terms.

It was as if the NIF was saying, look, we are tired of all of this debate and concern over who we are as a people; we know who we are and the world, especially our Arab brothers, should take cognizance of this. As Turabi stated when explaining the NIF's refusal to join the new government, "One might say that the Arab brothers have abandoned Sudan, a country where the Arabs belong to Islam in Africa, to be the target of whatever [it] is subjected to in their stead. The Sudan shields them from the arrows aimed at them. However, if Sudan falls, these arrows will penetrate into what lies beyond Sudan, and the hatred for the Arab world will move to other borders of Sudan."[23]

Although much of the NIF's public rhetoric in the last few years has been an exercise in political propaganda, playing upon the general Sudanese passion for the political (where the political is the vehicle for passion), it reflects other dynamics as well. Perhaps, as evidenced by Turabi's statement, the North displaces its frustration with its historical marginalization from the Arab world onto the South. On the other hand, Islamicists doubt whether there are any benefits to be gained by mutual accommodation anyway—what is the future of a country that may always have to work exceedingly hard to be one?

The intricacy of the theological position regarding otherness in Islam makes it difficult to translate into a political agenda. The complexities of *tawhid* are certainly not understood by the majority of Muslims. Yes, there is the apprehension that a fundamental unity underlies all existence, both natural and social. But the politics of interaction derived from this notion of unity, in which radical difference must be supported in order to manifest unity, is a distant abstraction. This is especially true in a situation where the concept of being religious entails living out certain obligations in a specified way. The confrontation with differences can get in the way, despite the fact that Islamic cultures have multiple and rich legacies for negotiating the relationship of religious compliance with social contingency.

The Islamicists in Sudan have not compromised their position. Some will say this is a matter of Machiavellianism, political expediency, and the absence of any other unifying issue. Certainly these factors have been involved to varying degrees. But it is not clear that the NIF would have destroyed itself by compromising or changing its position on *Shari'a*. Still, in a political arena of shifting loyalties, vague ideologies, invaginated political and religious affiliations, and incessant turnabouts, the sheer consistency of their commitment to *Shari'a* distinguished the Islamicists from other political forces.

All politics has its murkiness. This reality must be confronted by those who play the political game. The Islamicists knew that the murkiness could not be fully avoided (and indeed they played the game better than anyone in Sudan). But because they obstinately clung to their principles, even to the point of sustaining the war, they were viewed as the only political force with integrity by a large proportion of Khartoum—even though the content of that integrity may not have been universally supported.

The government of Sadiq al-Mahdi kept power by holding real policy decisions in abeyance. More decision-making bodies were set up during his tenure than in probably the entire history of the nation. For three years he made himself indispensable as the manager of uncertainty—where rule is maintained not by virtue of what you do but what you can make others think they are doing. Within this calculated fluidity, *Shari'a* became a constant—an issue acquiring power by everyone's progressively affirming its inevitability but, at the same time, never quite becoming inevitable.

Existence in a combined multiracial and religious society is difficult in most places. Differences of race but similarities of religion provoke conflicts in themselves, and vice versa. Southerners and many Northerners have called for secularization. But many Sudanese are not convinced that secularization is the framework that will allow for the harmonious existence of people from different cultural backgrounds.

Nor is secularism in itself some intrinsic threat to the efficacy and totalizing function of Muslim institutions. Rather, the call for secularism is often interpreted by Islamicists as a call for homogenization, for some artificial equilibration of character, worldview, and passion. For the Islamicists, secularization ushers in a world where the important choices of life are left to individuals. Therefore, there is no enforced occasion of struggle in which people must deal with obligations not of their own making. Since it is only in such a contest that the character of a person is shaped or manifested, secularism is seen as an avoidance of selfhood. In the West we often construe religious people as hiding behind their religiosity. But in Muslim societies, secularism leads to a collective hiding of selfhood, becomes a mechanism for avoiding essential confirmation and thus the process of struggle that differentiates character. In this interpretation, secularism erodes and neutralizes the fundamental contours of life. Individuals are atomized, become manipulable. For some Islamicists it would have been better for Southerners to call for a society based on Dinka or Nuer religion or customary law rather than advocate for a secular state.

Issues of pride and toughness are laid over the religious focus. To protect religion is to protect manhood and womanhood. Not that religious identity, gender identity, and sexual fortitude are equivalent zones of cultural elaboration. Rather, the Islamicist response to secularism is an indication of the muscular and emphatic energy invested in maintaining the body of religion, as if there is concrete physicality to its presence. Its physicality, however, is not something to be sheltered away from the possibility of wounding; it does not pass the hours in sanguine reflections on its intactness and health. The religious body is combative and merciful, sufficiently above the fray not to pick needless fights, but prepared to slug it out in the service of what is right.

Islam emerged from a culture accustomed to prolonged bouts of combat, where war was the clearest application of cunning and knowledge.[24] Support of secularism is seen by many Islamicists as the concession of vitality, the relinquishing of the fighting spirit. Even the highly educated and urbanized offspring of the Ansar, the fighters for the Mahdiyyah who waged many battles in the last century, recount their ancestors' unequivocally courageous, if often futile, battle behavior with a sense of great pride. Of course this kind of aggression can devolve into seemingly interminable cycles of wanton violence. But I suspect that the civil war continues in part out of a perceived need of Northern Sudanese to reinscribe a very physical sense of determination into the collective psychology.

That secularism poses the danger of homogenization is a perception that emanates from a historically rural reluctance to assimilate into the administrative normalcy of the city.[25] In this rural African Islamic worldview, the natural world is the actual word of God rather than the statements of the Quran or the Prophet.[26] The Quran may be an aspect of this word, but it is not seen as the voice of God in its entirety. Literacy was an activity for the cities, but in the country, the Muslim read the stars and the moon. It is not a practice that is completely dead. A legal scholar at the University of Khartoum returned to his sheep in the rural area, giving up a brilliant career so that he could regain what for him was the eternal experience of direct reflection on the source of religion, i.e., the unmediated sense of creation itself.

The emphasis on literality and literacy—the normative interpretations of divine text and the calibration of conduct to scriptural specification that have emerged in urban Islam over the centuries—exerts a homogenizing force that must be attenuated.[27] Such attenuation is difficult since the coherency of urban administration requires the systematicity of codification—be it theological or economic.[28] But in an international context, where the plurality of the Muslim world is curtailed by culturally dystonic forces (in this case the West), this very systematicity must somehow be disrupted if the Muslim is not to be viewed as inextricably complicit with those forces impinging upon the autonomy of Islam. For example, in the Muslim world's eagerness to demonstrate parity with the West, major efforts have been made to Islamicize the different academic disciplines. There are textbooks in Islamic psychology, Islamic economics, and so on. There is nothing debilitating to Islam about these efforts. But what must be recognized is that they reaffirm and legitimate the saliency of an organization of knowledge and discipline that is primarily Western.

For some Sudanese the infusion of a personalistic, practical Islam complements the textual focus of urban movements and structures. The urban emphasis on *taqwa* (the evaluation of efficacy by the measurable standards of a person's moral responsibility) is thus complemented by the elliptical eruptions of *ruh* (spiritual visions that are conceptually fuzzy but emotionally direct). The latter opens up religious sensibility for all to participate in; it is always negotiating the terms of its application, always finding its way. This sense of spiritual abundance frequently appears under the cover of something else.

For example, the very personal sense of individual faithfulness and the emphasis on staying within God's "sight lines" that is manifested by the Burno (from Western Sudan) often masks itself in social relationships that operate outside conventional urban exchange circuits. In the central area of Khartoum adjacent to Souk Shaby—the main transport hub— is Hillat al-Nuer, an urban reassemblage of a large Nuer village with a semilegal status (in the sense that a school has been allowed to exist within it, even though no other services are provided).

The Nuer have always been suspicious of both Christians and Muslims. More precisely, they have distrusted the institutionalization of religion. Yet, Burno traders have moved in among them and have used the apparent ethnic homogeneity of the encampment as a cover for their own petty trade and a practice of Islam that animates itself in the magic of recitation. Among the Burno, recitation is an ongoing and active dialogue with the multiplicitous nature of Allah. Within the market they have constructed one of the most aesthetically powerful mosques in Khartoum, a structure built entirely of metal scrap and refuse. As Gellner has pointed out, the "homogeneity of nomenclature" in textual Islam masks an incessant heterogeneity of organization, singularity, and egalitarianism.[29] At times this heterogeneity has been actively suppressed. At others, the unambiguous and transethnic norms of propriety generated by classical urban Islam have permitted unimpeded applications of imagination and creative energy from more eschatological motivations.

Too often the characteristics of Islam in Khartoum have been discussed from the point of view of a resurgent Islam and the renewal of systematicity. Through this renewal, effective political organizations have been formed. But what is often not discussed is the notion that current limitations in the articulation of religious and political development in Sudan also follow from the demise of Sufism—not as a particular institutional structure, but as a constellation of cognitive orientations that might have tempered some of the political rigidities of the renascent Islamic movement.

By forming political parties and synchronizing themselves with state institutions, the turuq (Sufi brotherhoods) lost much of their capability of promoting an autonomous religious sensibility that could "come and go" in its dealings with other aspects of everyday life. In other words, the traditional Sufi emphasis on the practice of having access to the intervention of Allah and to a sociality informed by the mutual efforts of individuals to construct an arena of spiritual immediacy has been vitiated. A state apparatus has been constructed upon it.

When Sadiq al-Mahdi waged an intense battle with his uncle, Ahmed al-Mahdi, in an attempt to become the imam of the Ansar, a threshold had perhaps been long crossed. The Mahdiyyah had become an administrative entity, an arena of patron-client relationships, that had normalized operations within the confines of the state and thus became increasingly unable to operate as a context of liminality.[30] The more patrons dispensed favors and opportunities, the more they seemed to decline as the bearers of *barakat*—a fundamental grace endowed directly by Allah to the devout which can be dispersed and multiplied. It was this prospect of having *barakat* rubbed off on one that motivated the proximity the faithful would maintain to shaykhs and others of the brotherhood.

Sufism has coexisted uneasily with urban reform movements. In West Africa, the decline of the *turuq* in some areas has been associated with the emergence of a self-conscious Islam more aware of its political positioning in the national and regional context and adamant about rebuilding its image as a modern political and economic force. But it is possible that such shifts will attenuate the cognitive resiliencies and social skills that have gone into engineering complex interwoven networks of economic and social affiliation for Muslims. These networks inculcated a sense of physical mobility and psychological maneuverability within Muslim political consciousness.

This is not to say that an urban, textual Islam is inevitably wedded to calcified administrative structures. In Khartoum, the Islamic movement has facilitated rather than impeded clientalism—social relationships that necessitate a large measure of flexibility so as to allow connections to be made outside kinship and primary groups. Clientalism is free-enterprise leadership, in which influence groups cohere around a series of individuals who can legitimate their authority through displays of strategic effectiveness and their ability to withstand challenges from others engaged in frequent and open competition.

Clientalism in Khartoum frequently exceeds ideological divisions. In sectors of Deim and Sahafa, theoretically breeding grounds for Islamicist influence, Baathists and Communists maintain control because they can protect the adjustments the population has had to make to deal with urban conditions. Long-term personal contacts, control of trade unions, and connections with local administrative councils and police have solidified the support for these parties over the years. This has occurred despite the fact that their political power in general has greatly diminished.[31]

THE ARBITRARINESS OF THE ISLAMIC VISION

The ideology of the Islamic movement has frequently advocated policies of economic rationalization that seem to obviate the predominance of clientalism. But these policies seem to be a mask for the actual hegemony of such structures. Certainly, the clientalist-centered structure of Islamic banking and its financing of the second economy (allowing small merchants to circumvent their marginalizing dependence on traditional sources of credit) has operated in ways that lessen the need to appeal to people on the basis of shared ideology or common codes of ethics and rules. In other words, the Islamic movement has resuscitated and enlarged the spread of socioeconomic relationships that "speak their own language," that seem not to need an Islamic ideology at all. The discourse of Islamic renewal has precipitated a situation in which the Islamic movement is economically and politically powerful in part because it is not dependent on Islamic discourse at all.[32]

Given this result, it becomes difficult not to question whether an aspect of the adamant sustenance of Islamicism is an attempt to mask this structural lack of dependency on Islam. Even if we take into consideration the differentiating roles of ideology and economic rationality as manifested in many other cultures—where the relative autonomy of these functions is necessary to their ability to elaborate each other—the degree of their divergence seems particularly significant in Sudan.

Islam is a discursive shortcut. It doesn't require a great investment of energy or time to serve as a link among people. It allows cognizance of mutual benefit derived from social relationships while downplaying the prospect that mutual benefit is the primary motivation behind the relationship. Additionally, relationships can be defined as being cemented by mutual obligation when it is expedient to do so, e.g., "I had to offer assistance since he is my brother in Islam." For the NIF, clientalism has helped to create the impression that its agenda is supported by the majority of the population. It has worked hard to develop contacts with schoolteachers, financing their educations and finding positions for them, because teachers "control" large numbers of students who can be mobilized for demonstrations, propaganda, and organizing work.

The denial of clientalism often leads the NIF to act as if it is not beholden to anything but itself. Since it exists to uphold Islam, Islam is part of it. Since it knows no allegiance to anything but Islam, it in effect owes no allegiance but to itself. In other words, it acts as if it is not accountable to anything outside of itself, to any sense of otherness.

In this practice, the Islamic movement risks cultivating a false sense of self-sufficiency. Tactical alliances with others are necessary to further its aims, but relations with others are not considered essential to the furtherance of Islamic principles, understandings, or visions. Religion and politics risk being confused in such a way that the two simply cancel each other out—in contrast to the Islamic view that both religion and politics are terms that point to the same sense of unity. Godzich states in his discussion of the development of political institutions that, "The principal difference between a society that submits to what I will call, for lack of a better term, a religious order, and one that submits to a state-organized one lies in their attitude toward otherness. . . . The first type makes the other an absolute other, whereas the second turns into an inner component of the same."[33]

Paranoia is clinically defined as the universal applicability and relevance of the individual and/or social body to all domains. It is the stance of individuals who believe that their existence is central to all persons, conversations, and interactions. There is nothing outside of themselves. Since paranoids cannot control all those people and events they believe themselves relevant to, they worry incessantly about the extent to which they are controlled by those others. The external, which after all doesn't really exist, is to be defended against.

In its attempt to mask its very lack of dependence on the Islam it is the sole upholder of, the Islamic movement is vulnerable to a structural paranoia which might marginalize its capacity to remain a long-term political force in Sudan. Islamicist voices have been known to reach histrionic tones when they insist that they embody the will of the majority. Harborers of the divine who speak for the will of the majority often are led to define dissent and alternative conceptualizations as evil. They recognize no need for complementarity since they are complete within themselves.

It is this spirit of totalization which leads overzealous university administrators to force renowned academics into writing sophomoric paeans to the regime and which produces a network of "safe houses" where prominent professionals have been detained and perhaps tortured.

Zubair Bashir Taha, one of the NIF's most respected activists, frequently pointed out when encouraging Muslims to visit the "marginal" mosques of Khartoum—those of the Burno, Hausa, Midab—that a vital spirit of Islamic personhood is moved back and forth within these communities like circulating blood in a heartfelt urgency to know God. In these communities, Taha would say, people have a real sense that their skin extends into other skin as a corridor to Allah.[34] Without this sense of personal bonding and of personalizing the divine, what will the movement of Islam have fought for, what kind of society will have been formed?

But it is exactly this personalized vision of the social body that a movement, anxious that it has precipitated occurrences that cannot always be controlled in the terms through which it has been engendered, will find increasingly difficult to understand. The movement will conclude that it must protect itself against these possibilities.[35] Inner reality will become increasingly peripheralized.

The Islamic movement, rooted in textuality, specifies the abstract right of egalitarianism and justice while vitiating the social forces that ensure the possibilities of egalitarianism. The protection of difference makes equality a meaningful concept. A legalistic notion of equality attained by persons all subject to the equilibration of the disciplinary regime tends to erode that sense of difference. How to use and incorporate that which remains undecidable and dispossessed of clear meaning is perhaps the most challenging political question. How else is a movement motivated to exceed itself, maintain its agenda in different forms, or recompose itself in a shifting economy of available resources and terms of recognition?

The long-term survival of the Islamic movement seems to depend on how it will make the most of conditions it cannot anticipate and utilize ways of talking that it at times cannot understand or control. As Lincoln points out, if a religious movement is to transform itself from a mode of resistance to a revolution, "it must overcome its insularity and begin to recruit actively, incorporating new adherents from segments of society previously absent from its membership."[36] The forced inclusion of large numbers of Nuba men from the destroyed villages of Jebel Nuba in Islamic training camps outside Khartoum is a distorted step in recognizing this need. Any sense of completeness is premature, a sign of danger, not of success.

What further complicates the position of the NIF is the existence of the Muslim Brothers, an extraparliamentary group deriving from *Ikhwan* but parting ways with the NIF in 1985. Led by Nur al-Da'im, the Muslim Brothers are reluctant participants in the political process and prefer to conduct Islamicization away from the murkiness of state politics. They have been highly critical of many of the political practices of the NIF and have cast aspersions on the sincerity of the NIF's commitment to *Shariʿa*, even going so far as to pointedly state that the conditions for the functional adherence to Islamic law do not exist in Sudan. Nur al-Daʿim states in the Cairo newspaper *Al-Iʿtisam*:

> As is well known God's law is not embodied only in the penal code. People are contending and debating only in this narrow field, which, whatever its importance, represents a truncated view of Islam and the Muslim cause. One need only realize that we have not yet agreed on the sources of legislation and on the fundamental principles of the rules. In the absence of the comprehensive broad view that the Muslim Brotherhood has continuously propagated, and in the absence of a fitting model in the area of public activity, and given the disintegration, fragmentation, and conflict that lead to failure and lost effort, as well as the lying, deceit, hypocrisy, and lack of truth with God, oneself and others, there is not hope of establishing the law of God. God's law first demands of all sincerity of attitude, devotion to God, and the freedom from selfish interests and desires. It demands decisive resolve, strong will, generous sacrifice, and pure altruism. These are qualities completely absent from the scene.[37]

The sense of self-sufficiency in the NIF is sustained in part because like the West, Islamicists tend to see modernity as a complete package, an indefatigable oneness that inevitably leads in one direction. It is true that individuals within the movement have been very adept at dissociating technological proficiency from moral decline and do view the West as the source of important contributions. But this proficiency has not significantly altered the view that Western modernity is the frightening specter of imminent human dissolution. Only the insertion of Islamic values can surgically pick and choose the elements of neutrality from the midst of the cancerous organ. Islamic values themselves are acknowledged as aspects of a complete wholeness. Sudanese culture, as a result, is not relieved of wholes, or the primacy of the container.

At the same time, the Islamic movement perceives that it must disperse the wholeness of modernity, deprive it of its claim that it contains a universal rationality and applicability that defines the evolutionary process for all societies. Yet, the substitution of one artifice of wholeness for another may not be adequate to the Sudanese attempt to actively deconstruct the West.

The particular circumstances in which Sudan finds itself have to a large extent been arbitrarily configured. Recognition of this arbitrariness is necessary to the belief that efficacious Islamic political and cultural formations are indeed possible. To change something, one has to assume that there is no frozen or fixed reason why things have to be the way they are in the first place. It is true that scenarios could occur became they are willed by God. Yet, in Islam, man is necessary to God's will to assure that things proceed in one direction and not others. Allah does not fix events, as He makes use of whatever transpires and incorporates it into His will.[38]

Many Sudanese believe the myth that political life is condemned to alternate between military coups and democratic regimes. Each current situation finds precedence in the accumulated failures of all prior regimes. The new is thus linked to the fate of the old—people believe that some underlying structural weakness reflecting both colonial domination and an internal political logic repeats the scenario.

Whether this assessment is true or not, the important idea is that the cycle need not be inevitable. It is not unreasonable for people to question the sources of their current predicament. However, such a focus should open up the interpretive possibilities and not foreclose talk about the present situation. A psychological climate has existed in Khartoum which "invites" arbitrariness—i.e., the insertion of political agendas that do not make sense into conventional paradigms of social development. The current strength and weakness of Islamic politics has much to do with the implicit attitude of the movement toward its own arbitrariness. Unlike Marxism, which understands political relations in terms of structural determinism, the Islamic movement has not substantially elaborated the historical functions of its current predicament. Rather, it conceives its work as insertable at any given time or place—even though it has a long and complex history.

Much of the movement's appeal to the young rests in their belief that Islam can exert a transformative force in its own terms—terms that do not have to be linked to historical or situational contingencies. The young have grown up in an era of rapid and seemingly arbitrary change. Things have changed fast without apparent explanation. Despite Turabi's patient and methodical approach to taking power, an impression has been created that change can occur if it is simply willed. Transformations need not make sense in terms of historical precedents, economic infrastructure, or relations of production. Necessity is substituted for feasibility, inversion for progress. For example, a frequent argument for the application of *Shari'a* posed by university students is that *Shari'a* will necessarily foster the conditions that will make *Shari'a* possible. When asked how *Shari'a* can be expected to bring about a situation that itself makes *Shari'a* effective, the characteristic response is: The act of faith makes the reality of faith possible—we make faith contingent upon nothing but itself, it relies on neither what comes before or after, but is the only vehicle capable of linking before and after, and therefore must be present in both. What is being implied here is that the very arbitrariness of *Shari'a* enables it to act independently from the economic and political forces it is to transform. Because it doesn't have to have anything to do with them, it is free to rearrange them in its own terms.

At the same time, this sense of change unchained to either determinant historical necessity or situational logic reinvents the ideal of an essential autonomy. This opens the way for systems of repression or punitive guilt-inducing disparagement when failure occurs. If change is possible simply because one wills it to occur, what happens when change does not come about? Is failure as arbitrary as success? Or does the person or movement involved in the failed transformation condemn themselves or others? How is the loss of face compensated for; how is it explained? If the forcefulness of the call for change was motivated by its absolute necessity (in theological terms), what happens when the situation stalls? How does one explain failure to God? How does a movement maintain a realistic assessment of its capabilities? How does one understand one's position as a result?

The Islamic movement has not brought about its larger transformative agenda. In its concentration on *Shari'a* law, the movement has hedged its bets on the more radical agenda of transforming Sudanese culture. Taking note of the saying, "New dreams emerge from inside the safety of the father's house," the Islamic movement did try to reduce the arbitrariness of the agenda by struggling to root the Sudanese firmly within the Islamic orbit. Now that this may have been put on hold by the new regime, it remains to be seen how the movement will handle the arbitrary nature of its ups and downs, whether while in power it can sustain the momentum for change in Islamic terms. How closely will it pay attention to and seek to address the massive changes that have taken place in Khartoum since the civil war—changes no bulldozer can completely eradicate? How will it address a collapsing infrastructure and economic debt? Will it insist on an Islamic agenda that need not take these realities into any fundamental consideration, or work miracles in the account books in order to buy time? Whatever it does, it will find a difficult hand to play, a difficult discourse to talk.

BIG TEXTS PRODUCE SMALL PARTICULARISMS

For all the maneuvering that has taken place within the past decade, there have been reversals in the apparent political stasis and intractability. As the guarantor of Muslim plurality, the NIF exerts a homogenizing trend over forms of Islamic expression and insists on a nonnegotiable litmus test of authentic political progress. Much of the political leadership does not really intend this, but finds its hands largely tied by all the diverse social, theological, and client strands it is forced to hold together.

The insistence on *Shari'a* has also spawned the multiplication of small particulars that the movement must try to coordinate into a rationalized process of urban political and cultural development. The more the movement acts against these small excesses, however, the more excessive the particulars seem to be. The more the movement curtails the scope of individual autonomy in the interest of securing a space of larger cultural freedom, the more autonomous individuals actually become as both political and cultural actors, despite the regime's repression. The more the movement implicitly acts to preserve the ethnic and cultural homogeneity of Khartoum, through pursuing policies implicitly maintaining the civil war, the more ambiguous the religious and ethnic composition of Khartoum becomes.

No one really knows who is actually in Khartoum. The Muslim majority in the capital is not an overwhelming one. This intersection of divergent peoples proceeds in largely unpredictable directions. On the one hand, polarization has increased. Sharing the same city does not necessarily make people the best of friends or contribute to antagonists' appreciating one another more. Subtle racism is not so subtle. Complex intricacies characterizing long-term affiliations at a distance redefine themselves in often resoundingly crude simplicities when made proximate. A bus ride from Khartoum to an outlying district in the afternoon will confirm this. On the other hand, a city cannot sustain anyone if people are fighting all the time. And in unexpected ways, people of diverse backgrounds are cooperating, seeing in one another unforeseen possibilities.

The drinking house, the anathema of the Islamicist and the thing to be finally eliminated under *Shari'a*, is an institution of greater importance than ever before. It is the locus of an institutionalized and obvious clandestinity that allows people to talk to one another when no other place is either legitimate or safe. It occasions an actual intimacy in a world of formalized interchanges. For example, a young man, son of an important Islamic leader, tells a group of young Azande men that he really doesn't believe any of that "shit" about *Shari'a*. Yet in public life, he is a compliant and seemingly dedicated party activist. He gives his drinking partners information about smuggled goods coming into a particular market, which he heard about from his uncle. He can't operate on the information himself because of family pressures, but if his "partners" want to take advantage of it, they should go ahead and perhaps think about giving him just a small percentage of the take. Each day there are hundreds of scenarios like this, where people "step out" of their inscribed positions—their adherence to ethnic, religious, family, professional, and occupational "scripts"—to engineer relationships that are askew, that circumvent normative strictures.

Although it is not as important as the mosque, it is still hard to imagine how urban life would be negotiated without the drinking house. This is not to say that the intensified consumption of alcohol is itself a useful thing. The Islamicists have a valid concern with the social and economic costs of such consumption. But the more they move to exert definitive control over the differentiating patterns of interchange and the localized organization of everyday life, the more the drinking house becomes reified as a "source of opposition" to the mosque and the values it embodies. Its position is an artificial one largely created by the Islamic movement as a means of legitimating a radical transformative vision.

Islamicists make as much out of the issue as they can. But the talk gets wilder, the affiliations more arbitrary, the second economy more dominant, and the fears that motivate much of the campaign of moral rectification stronger. The Islamic movement is pushed toward being a force of confrontation and a guarantor of purity and away from its original agenda of reconfiguring political culture in a way that works for all.

In an interview with *Al-Tadmun* (London, 25 April 1987), Turabi indicated that the Islamic movement was still in the stage of "thwarting falsehood rather than achieving truth."[39] This focus is seen at work in the way the Islamic movement quickly and clandestinely sought to shore up its position with the military regime. The regime quickly demonstrated a dubious capacity for generating effective social and economic policies, instead proving fairly adept only at exercising a policing function that halts any transformation in the terms through which the significant political and cultural conflicts facing Sudan are to be understood. In this collaboration, the movement concedes to its own self-perceived weaknesses. Turabi: "Islam as a historical reality is a phenomenon which unfortunately does not exist today. In their confusion and certainty that what exists today is not Islamic, Muslims sometimes take refuge in a history and take from it something that represented religious righteousness at that time [the time of the Prophet] but that perhaps does not represent the requirements of religiousness today."[40]

Turabi and the Islamic movement face a potentially debilitating contradiction. The quest for Shari'a sought to end the dualistic nature of political and cultural life—a life with Shari'a courts and civil courts; secular education and religious education. Such dualism marginalizes Islam. Islam as marginalized cannot be productive and resourceful in the development of modern agendas. Turabi has always insisted that he is not a fundamentalist, that he is interesting in seeing Islam as a progressive force in social and economic development, but that this could not happen if Islam were compartmentalized as an aspect, rather than being the foundation of society. Pursuit of this agenda is why Turabi has in the past always downplayed the international aspects of Ikhwan.

Once Islam assumed an unequivocally dominant position, Islam would then be able to generate fresh and vital frameworks for contemporary life. When the marginalization of Islam becomes the primary issue, however, the kinds of inputs, interpretive practices, confidence, and imagination that will have to intersect with an unmarginalized Islam in order to engender the creative process will be increasingly marginalized themselves. An inverted dualism takes place in which people are driven outside the confines of Islam in a concerted effort to make sure everyone operates within it. As Jiris As'ad of the University of Khartoum stated in an interview with al-Ayyam (Khartoum, 16 October 1988), "Practicing politics in the name of religion or dealing with religion as a matter of politics turns religion into endless wars, ceaseless factionalism, undying struggles, and an unquenchable furnace."[41] As a result, Islam may be strong, but will there continue to exist an arena—a progressive process of social development—in which it can practice its strength?

According to John Lonsdale, "If politics is not always to be in an uproar, nor production fail, it follows that rulers cannot govern exclusively in the chief class supporters' interest. . . . For the moment it is enough to establish that to share out power is in a very real sense to create it. . . . The contested accountability of power appears to be essential to its productivity even in class-divided societies."[42] This remark is relevant to a process of realpolitik that takes place in theological terms.

The Islamicists will have to learn how to sustain their political vision while negotiating creatively with non-Muslims, even if the object of such negotiations is to create two separate Sudans. They will have to take into consideration the terms through which non-Muslims understand the important issues and agendas. In large part this consideration was the most incisive aspect of the Prophet's political skill.

Although Islamicists have been active in the development of human resource institutions in the South, this effort has been deployed through institutions, such as Da'was Islamiyyah, that work with local populations in very limited ways. Although the former director of this organization, Mubarak Gasmallah, a Southerner from Malakal, is a very sensitive and proficient organizer, its sources and implementors of funding are not as adept at taking into consideration the divergent worldviews of non-Muslims.

Whatever relationship between the terms of religion and politics emerges, it will have to do so over a period of time when all Sudanese have the freedom to define each term. A relationship cannot be defined when there are so many different ideas about what religion and politics are. In Sudan, ambiguity seems more workable than clarity. Africa has a long legacy of making sure that the uncoded openness of what constitutes both religion and politics is not foreclosed by either internal or external imposition.[43]

No team of national experts will be able to decide a suitable relationship between religion and politics—as was proposed by General Bashir. It is the almost permanent contestation of this relationship that has provided pockets of maneuverability for Africans. What limited power urban Africans have is to continuously allude to a shift in what phenomena might be political at any given time, so that any activity may or may not signify political ferment.[44] In these conditions people do not stick to clearly demarcated territories or regions, political or historical blocs. To thrive increasingly depends on striving to operate outside of the "ghetto" to which you have been assigned, even as others try to "ghetto-ize" increasingly expanded spaces. The Islamicists, themselves refusers of Western notions of what politics is and where it belongs, end up trying to tell others where they belong. But the war shows that this "deviation" from their own rebelliousness isn't doing the Islamicists any good. The more they say to Southerners, go back to the South, the more determined the Southerners are to live in the North.

THE SOUTHERN RESPONSE

What Garang has always demanded until lately is the ability of the Southerner to aspire to and contribute to a national agenda, to define the terms of a national political culture and not simply exercise authority over the nature of Southern interests. Although forced by internal power struggles to assume a more separatist position in 1992, Garang had become more insistent upon the broader focus the more he concluded that the issues of *Shari'a*, Pan-Arabism, and majority rule simply masked the intention of the North to make sure this national role for the South never happened. Indeed, when Bashir announced a referendum on Islamic law, Garang pointed out that, "It is blasphemous for Al-Bashir to say that God's law should be taken for human judgment."[45]

In an address to the nation on 27 May 1985, Garang made it clear that he was inserting himself as a national player. "Negotiations in the context of the so-called Southern problem is against the national interest and a recipe for disaster. Suppose we solve the problem of the South. We will soon have to sole the problem of the Nubah because the Nubahs can also take up arms. After that the problem of the Bijahs and so forth. It is a national problem, not a Southern problem that we might address."[46] He claims that the SPLA has been the only consistent driving force in Sudanese politics as a whole during the past six years—that governments come and go largely on the basis of what it does. Although the SPLA is criticized by many as simply a bunch of mutineers, the self-imposed military regime presently in power sweeps away the salience of that criticism.

In an interview with *Al-Tadmun* (London, 6 May 1989), Johannes Akol, spokesman for the Bloc of Afro-Sudanese Parties, rejects completely the sectarian terms of the conflict. "This is a conflict between one group which is being exploited and another which is doing the exploiting. . . . This is a healthy struggle that unites Christians and Muslims as well as Arabs and blacks of the same class and brings them together in one front. This means struggle against those who monopolize power whether they be Christian, Muslim, Arab, or black."[47]

There is general agreement among many Southerners and Northerners that the NIF has monopolized the terms through which the political situation is addressed. This view comes from people even within the NIF itself. Not even the language through which the conflict is talked about can be negotiated, let alone the terms of a solution, because the Islamicist owes "No Allegiance to Anyone But God" (the most popular slogan of the NIF). The Southerner is reduced to a challenge, an obstacle to be overcome. As NIF Politburo member Ahmad 'Abdal-Rahman told *Al-Nur* (Cairo, 17 June 1987), "Most of its [the South's] inhabitants are heathens who worship stones, trees, crocodiles, the sun, etc. . . . All this presents a civilized challenge to all of us as Arabs, because there were heathens and Jews at the time of the Prophet, and we know how the Muslims treated Christians and Jews."[48] Southerners are not credited with sense of historical development or progressive engagement with the world.

When Southerners are criticized for their lack of unity, Garang responds by begging the question—why should the South be any more unified than the North, and the North is certainly not a unified whole. In fact, whatever unity exists, Garang claims, is a negative one—the North is unified against the South. Garang asks why the South should repeat this bad habit. The only basis for unity is within a framework of political pluralism, he insists. But such pluralism "must be a reflection of social differentiation and ease of administrative development, rather than religious, regional, or ethnic cleavages. For while the former would ensure better interest articulation by the party on behalf of its constituents, the latter would only serve to highlight cleavages that militate against national unity."[49]

War is a bad thing. Both the NIF and SPLA have been roundly criticized for maintaining hard-line positions that have resulted in the deaths of perhaps four hundred thousand people in the last three years. Why don't they reconcile in the interest of a more vital economy, a more stable living environment, or human decency? What is so important about the positions assumed, that the country is being progressively torn apart?

What is not helpful at such times is to look at the conflict through liberal sentiments that simply recount the suffering and detail the oppression. As indicated earlier, the civil war has largely been a fight for Khartoum-for access to the center. The war has resulted in the center being irreversibly changed. The myth of majorities is a thing of the past. People have indeed paid a huge price to kill this myth. Southerners have borne the brunt of the toll. Their lives in Khartoum are difficult, mostly unwanted. But yet they are there. If given the opportunity, probably most would return to the South. But the development of a viable rural infrastructure in the South is now decades away. The divisions that existed with regional separation have been replicated in conditions where diverse peoples live close to one another. In Khartoum, Northerner and Southerner, Muslim, Christian, Africanist for the most part go their separate ways. But there has been increasing interaction—not usually sought out but still an implication of people having to share aspects of the same space. This recomposition has and will continue to have an impact on the perceptions of the generation who will rule next.

This intersection does not necessarily mean that things will get better in forthcoming years. There is probably a lot more blood to be spilled. But in an important way, the polarization of positions on both the part of the Islamicists and the SPLA will accrue a strange efficacy in the long run. Their significance is not simply that they will have been "responsible" for reconfiguring a different urban society—a precursor to any new political culture. Rather, their significance rests in the sense that both their discourses simultaneously embody the death of old political ideas and signal the provisional future of new political cognitions and imaginations. Perhaps this is what all politics does, but the conflict in Sudan represents most pointedly the precarious intricacies the Third World will have to go through in order to put together viable political identities.

Unlike Eastern Europe, the Third World is a geopolitical arena where neither the definitive death nor birth of political ideologies is possible. For the Sudanese at this point, a compromise of political vision might be a waste of time. It is not now possible to talk about the invention of new forms of cultural coherence and freedom (as embodied by the Islamicization process), as it is not yet fully possible to talk about the invention of a coherence of multiplicities in which differences can continue to exist with a sense of autonomy (as embodied by the SPLA position).

In fighting each other, however, both positions are able to survive as forceful political visions—neither has killed the other off yet; it seems neither will. This political survival is one of the brutally fascinating aspects of the civil war—brutal because wars of ideas always involve bodies. Perhaps in Africa's unconscious, it is known that if Sudan works its situation out, it will be immediately catapulted into the position of one of the most important countries on the continent. If the children of Khartoum find a way to survive that doesn't cost too much, much will be learned from their political sensibility in the future. Their political talk will have a lot to say.

Chapter Seven

The Politics of Cultural Revival

Attempts at cultural revitalization are fraught with worries about whether people are doing the right thing. For an African society whose process of organic cultural development has been interrupted and perhaps dominated out of existence, there can be considerable alarm over the varying directions pursued by its members. The anxiety concerning cultural authenticity, however, seems to be the preoccupation of the economically privileged. The desperate conditions of everyday material life have long forced the majority of Sudanese to find a myriad of small ways to reproduce or reinvent the cultural frameworks that imbue their meager lives with some kind of meaningful impetus.

Islamicists believe that *Shari'a* is a form of definitive cultural liberation, a breaking free of the psychological bondage that has forced the Islamic world to pay attention to Western mores and cultural imperatives. Equipped with such an affirmative renunciation of these imperatives, the Sudanese people will finally be able to mobilize their collective energies and build a postcolonial society free of external domination. Although the Islamic heritage is rich in the juridical, economic, and social thinking essential to such a process, the insistence upon *Shari'a* in Sudan also reflects the difficulty inherent in conceptualizing such a process of extrication in the postindustrial era. The problem faced by the Islamic movement is not that it is simply trying to bring back old tunes without a sense of historicity, but that it believes a tune of cultural liberation can be sung outside the framework of an emerging international cultural order.

Of course the Islamic movement seeks to posit its own sense of universality and internationalism. But in order to aspire to this agenda, it must employ a method of cultural creation and governance that has yet to be constructed. Ikhwan in Sudan has believed that such a method is only possible when the movement can control the fundamental social dynamics of a society. *Shari'a*, then, has consolidated a movement that seeks to realize itself in ensuring access to fundamental social power so that whatever method is engendered is provided a necessary framework of action, and can resist disputes over its scope.

For Turabi, the method is essentially that of *tawhid*, a balancing of reason and revelation, elitism and populism, originality and tradition, code and interpretive freedom. In its organizational principles, platforms, and tactics, the Islamic movement has attempted to demonstrate such a balance. Yet if the balance is to be more than a seesaw of swings, contradictions, and indecisiveness, a framework of power is necessary in order to assure that these divergences nurture and remain a simultaneous presence to one another.[1]

The only authority capable of effecting such balance is that of God; so the responsibility of the movement, elevating itself into government, is to ensure that individuals and collectives have complete freedom to pursue their understanding of God's will—that there be no interference with the worship and knowledge of God.[2]

The history of the Sudanese demand for *Shari'a* demonstrates how this instrumental value of Islamic governance is risked in the symbolic trappings of the religious state. In a geocultural arena that necessitates the capacity to maneuver with elasticity through interpenetrated sectors of power and cognition, a focus on the symbolic integrity of a society concedes to others the ability to shape and direct technological, psychological, and broadly cultural dynamics affecting the larger international arena. Instead of generating tactics to interact with Western media, social practices, behaviors, and production networks, a singular determination to establish an Islamic state coheres a sense of self-identity at the cost of devitalizing religion as an exemplar of dynamism and adaptability.[3] Perhaps it is unreasonable to ask religion to act as such an exemplar. But implicit within the Islamic vision is precisely such a capability. The singular focus ignores the multiplicity of social and political problems endemic to past Islamic regimes unable to reconcile aspiration with the practical problems of running a state.

Traditionally, Muslim communities have preferred a minimum of governance in their lives. Its absence has accorded them the autonomy to be fully engaged with their religion in a timeless fashion and reproduce everyday practices of devotion unencumbered by the incursions of other cultural realities. Though this separation of state and religious practice is often pursued by Muslims today, it is a decreasingly viable option in a world where no one leaves anyone else alone. Withdrawal into the integrity of some pristine geopolitical and psychological territory is now a virtual impossibility.[4]

Intellectuals in the Islamic movement insist that the formation of the Islamic state in no way cuts them off from substantive interactions with the larger world. In fact, they have nothing against Western technology. The movement simply wants to cut off and filter out destructive moral practices. The focus of the masses should be on their own indigenous way of life; they need to be exposed to the West only to gain from it the skills necessary to make an Islamic society feasible. The question remains, who assumes the control and authority to determine what in the outside world is appropriately useful or valuable and what gets in the way of worshipping and knowing God?

The call for *Shari'a* is justified as the expression of the will of a people who, upon subjecting themselves juridically to the immutable will of Allah, abnegate to a large degree any further expression of "their" will. The masses have spoken loudly, but there is no provision for them to speak again. The problem inherent in Turabi's emphasis on *tajdid* (renewal or revival) is that it may articulate an important disengagement from the West, but it threatens to liberate people from the very act of culture-making itself—a process that by nature is messy, conflictual, and frequently irrational.[5] The balances of a new order do not come from an authority simply engineering a specific relationship between intact, well-defined opposing categories—for the interaction of ideas and objects changes their definitional boundaries. Balance, rather than an ideal, is perhaps more a process of learning and compensating for unanticipated results and directions, of making sure all that is considered potentially important has an opportunity to be known and effective.

On the other hand, because expediency and symbolism are predominant values in the political world today, it is not difficult to understand the emphasis placed on the reimposition of *Shari'a* laws as the quickest and most instrumental form of social transformation. As Zeidan Hassan Zeidan, a professor of philosophy at the University of Khartoum, so elegantly stated to one of his classes, the Third World is always being judged by a different, and higher, standard of political efficacy and cultural enlightenment. He says that the Third World is always forced to be more rational, more careful, and more substantial than the West in its plans and aspirations, yet at the same time is rarely viewed as capable of such care and rationality. If the Reagan presidency was largely symbolic manipulation, then why shouldn't the Islamic movement in Sudan demonstrate that it has learned how to do something that the political analysts say works?

For those anxious to "resolve" those intricate questions, the implementation of *Shari'a* seems to be a reasonable expedient to getting the process of identity and legislation over with so that other aspects of national development, implicitly being held in abeyance in light of those questions, can proceed. To many Sudanese, however, the issue of national identity and social cohesion is not a dilemma to be simply "gotten over." The legal framework of the state cannot resolve questions of identity, it can only ensure a fair distribution of opportunities for citizens to participate in the "authorship" of identity over time. Practically, the judicial process in both Western and Islamic traditions can only establish a framework that allows for the perpetuation of religious identities and the conduct of everyday life according to valued religious principles.[6]

One of the reasons for the fierceness of the *Shari'a* debate, as expressed by Mohammed Omar Bashir, former head of the Sudan Human Rights Association, is the fear that once *Shari'a* is imposed, debate over the direction of the country will no longer be possible since distinctions between political resistance and religious apostasy will be matters of arbitrary judicial interpretation rather than constitutional definition.[7] The law emanates from Allah's concern that man not overstep the bounds of his freedom and that the community be guided by firm structure. Yet, the Sudanese see the primary violation of Quranic principles in the perceived lack of freedom they have to express and develop their lives. The immorality that terrorizes the imams and moulanas is not so much indicative of the "victory" of the West as it is a manifestation of the frustration felt by people unable to exert meaningful control over their own lives. Those who are "seduced" by Westernization are those who can afford to leave the country every time they want to have a drink or fool around.

On the other hand, *Shari'a* may be an instrument that the Sudanese cannot do without. Hassan al-Turabi has said many times that the nature of *fiqh* (Islamic jurisprudence) will have to be altered, that it is possible to generate forms of Islamic law that are compatible with the development of Sudanese society, but that these changes must take place only in the context of a society that has consciously legislated its envelopment within Islamic law.[8] In other words, the mutability of Islamic law can only come from the paradoxical acceptance of its immutability.

Turabi believes that to make changes in *fiqh* outside of this framework would be to challenge and abnegate the inviolability of Islamic principles. The challenge is: if *Shari'a* must precede context-specific applications, who then is empowered with the authority and access to establish the terms through which these changes take place? Whose *ijtihad*—the interpretation of salience through personal exertion which the Prophet deemed a necessary form of Quranic exegesis—will take precedence? Whose *ijma*—collaborative consensus to determine the general interest—will constitute the ultimate mediation? As in other Islamic societies, whoever musters sufficient political power and sways the theocratic establishment will more than likely dominate. Questions concerning the distribution of power and the mechanisms through which civil society can hold the state accountable for its actions still remain undeliberated.

Turabi does understand that Sudan must live in a world where the need to interpret, the need to act, outpaces the need to align every action to some unyielding framework. But the test of just what adjustments need to be made comes only from seeing just exactly what a movement or a leadership can reasonably get away it. In other words, if the Sudanese community must temper its aspirations because it lives in a multireligous, multitextured political and economic world, the precise nature of how it adapts to the world cannot be determined in advance of full and principled efforts to carry out the Islamicizing agenda.[9]

If *tawhid* is to be the method that generates a functional political practice, Islamicization must then, according to Turabi, be capable of finding various niches and opportunities for manifestation. One is always playing with fire—but as long as *Shari'a* remains a part of the picture, then the passion of renewal is not likely to burn down the entire edifice. One can have a preference, as Turabi states in his basic commitment to democracy, for certain processes in which to "renew" the *umma*, but a commitment to *tawhid* necessitates that significant advances be made no matter what the prevailing political and economic conditions.[10] The world exists for the service of Allah, and Muslims must be ever opportunistic, seeking to discover any and all openings in whatever does exist to pursue the advancement of humanity in the worship of God. Again, striking this balance between the need to pay attention to the consequences of the Islamic movement's actions in the world and the need to bring about renewal in every present moment produces actions and discourses that themselves rush in seemingly opposite directions so as to steady the "dirigible" of the Islamic agenda.[11]

Though Turabi has seemed patiently, almost mercurially, calculating throughout the past two decades, plotting step-by-step his and the movement's ascent to power, Ikhwan's political history is better characterized by an incessant search for openings and opportunities to act as if power were already in their hands. The process of coming to power was in itself an education for the Muslim people, an aspect of society's Islamicization—which makes *Shari'a* more of an essential marker of progress than the end-all or be-all of the movement.

Likewise, Islamicization does not culminate in control of the state but must subordinate itself to the dictates of *Shariʿa*. As soon as the state tries to assume total responsibility for its own compliance, it becomes totalitarian. The state can nourish the personality of the Muslim, but it cannot enforce every Islamic rule.[12]

Here, Turabi seeks to emphasize that whatever the present Sudanese state looks like now, it should not be taken as a definitive form—for after all, in the end it serves a limited function. A predominant role for the state was never intended by the Prophet or his early companions. A sense of absolutism set in only when Umar was forced to fire several officials.

A space must be assured outside of the state where the functions of the state can be continuously monitored and coherence imposed upon the making of legislation and the accumulation/distribution of wealth. For Turabi, this space is defined and claimed by a judiciary—which on the surface ensures the compliance of the state apparatus with Islamic principle. But it appears that in many ways such a justification is subsumed by another aim: to posit an institutional structure which informs the practicalities of governance—because it is the purveyor of "divine injunction"—but which can incorporate great latitude in elaborating its own frameworks of interpretation.[13] At times, *Shariʿa* seems to be for Turabi a way to buy time and power simultaneously in order to work the ideological framework that would usually be necessary to legitimate the assumption or maintenance of power.

Partly out of conviction, partly out of his mastery of public relations, Turabi has said many times that less than 5 percent of existing exegesis is relevant to informing a viable framework of political *fiqh*—practical law.[14] *Ijtihad* is not a question of one verse matched to one situation, but a bringing together of a thousand verses into a complex weave. The role of the state may be limited, but its presence is everywhere and transparent. What the state is at any given point in time is not apprehendable, for in the carrying out of its practical administrations it aspires to a general sense of applicability, yet it is neither universal or context-specific. As a function "in between," it must be continually subject to the application of a political *fiqh* that is itself being continually worked out.

It is never precisely clear when one talks to Jabha intellectuals and jurists just exactly who and what mechanisms are going to interweave those thousands of verses. Turabi may state that the Islamic movement has achieved the theoretical maturity to engineer this process—after all, the movement, according to most Jabha leadership, has planned the current state of affairs so far. But even within the internal operations of the judiciary there is incessant wrangling over procedures, references, and authority of interpretation. Given the social tensions and structural instabilities in Sudan today, this dissention is actually quite heartening, and acts as a check on the excesses of the more "activist" judges.

Turabi himself concedes that the process contains more rough edges than anything. Sudan has inherited a colonial state, experienced a totalitarian socialist state. Religiosity can never be completed at a single moment, but entails a constant struggle with particular ideas crystallized at given points in time.[15] Sometimes it seems that the entire process comes down to old-fashioned politicking within highly elaborate, perhaps convoluted, arguments.

For example, the location of real power often appears to be intentionally ambiguous—something to which Islamic discourse provides a nearly perfect foil. The use of a military regime as the official mode of governance has gone beyond mere ruse. At times, the military uses its association with the Islamic movement to reconsolidate the opportunities for economic accumulation that were prevalent during the Numayri regime; the Islamic movement, in turn, uses the affiliation almost as a way to undermine the very authority of the army while purportedly ensuring respect for it.

The collaboration between these two forces appears as a convenient way to get rid of an old elite and establish a new one—hardly a revolutionary agenda. For too long, Turabi states, the state has protected a division between the educated classes and the populace—a division overdetermined in the distinctions made between civilian and military rule. The pact the Islamic movement made with the military should actually be seen as a pact that both made with the masses,[16] since the military is the guarantor of the masses' ability to demand that the elite account for their actions. The Islamic movement opened up the space for the army to assume its Islamically appropriate role as an arm of deliverance. The army was not immune to the trends and forces that the rest of the society experienced (i.e., nationalism in the fifties, leftism in the sixties), so the present government of collaboration is part of the social evolution of society as a whole.

This concert of sectors, each pursuing their convergence as a result of "natural" developments, has not for a moment stopped local speculation about who in the end, Islamic movement or army, really controls whom. Statements were made frequently during early 1993 that the army would step down soon, only to be vociferously retracted. Despite purges and failed coup attempts, many junior officers are bound by deep-seated loyalties to the Ansar—whose control over vast sections of Omdurman remains intact, along with substantial caches of weapons.

The popular civilian defense forces initiated by Jabha are viewed as one vehicle through which the Islamic movement is appropriating military authority, even though the army supervises their actual operations. Jabha has claimed that many of the recent successes on Southern battlefields were due to these "volunteer" forces. It is not clear whether the increased militarization of urban society is a means of entrenching the army's authority or a way for the Islamicists to hold it in check. The army has long been the most heterogeneous institution in the country and, despite the protracted civil war, views itself as the embodiment of Sudanese identity. Though the top brass is frequently more concerned with business than with "preparedness," the rank and file exude generally populist attitudes. Many are not amused by a new Islamic elite of fat cats whose ostentation can exceed that of the Umma or Democratic Party leaders and who, in turn, are starting to play soldier.

Turabi now insists that every Muslim is a soldier—a stance that has provoked rumblings in the barracks over its implicit deprofessionalizing of the soldier's job. Turabi says that all Muslims desire to become *mujahid*, and when the state comes closer to the Islamic spirit, the door will be open for every level of daily life to approximate the life of a military person—there will be no difference between an "official" and an "unofficial" soldier.[17]

Whether Jabha bases this conclusion on Islamic exegesis or a cynical reading of postcolonial Sudanese political history, the effort to dissipate the division between civilian and soldier is viewed as the most important strategy in uniting the Sudanese people. For it was this division that continually exacerbated power struggles at the state level and weakened society as a whole.[18]

At the same time, the Islamic movement cannot be burdened with the day-to-day administration of governance—especially since the apparatus of governance is focused on the confines of specific national boundaries and territories. Though Islam must be related to every reality in its specificity, the Sudanese Islamic movement is universal in its trajectory. Given Sudan's specific position at the crossroads of cultures, it is forced to be a locus of renewal (*tajdid*) and universality, which is why, despite the immediate political problems, it cannot underplay the primacy of religion. For, as the Quran states, "The final consequence will be for those who are God fearing."

Although the movement has no boundaries, its current focus on exporting Islamicism to surrounding countries and aiding new governments could be viewed as a way of ensuring the present boundaries of Sudan. By supporting long-dormant Muslim communities in Ethiopia, Somalia, Uganda, northern Kenya, and even the Central African Republic, the regime may hope to squeeze Southern non-Muslims into eventual submission, if not conversion, to Islamic doctrine. The movement feels justified in playing this international role because (1) very few movements have had their experience in attempting to simultaneously govern and decenter the state from the primacy of governance, and (2) very few movements have waited patiently for other ideologies and strategies to exhaust themselves. That the Islamic movement gave other dispensations time to work (and fail) means that they, above others, can legitimately claim to have a global perspective.

When asked about the resistance of much of black Africa to wholesale Islamicization and the obvious racism of many Jabha ideologues, Turabi combines a distorted poststructuralism with the trappings of Arab paternalism. Most of Africa, says Turabi, is too indebted to the imperialists to think independently at this point. The West is forcing Africans to accept multipartyism as democracy, which will only exacerbate fragmentation and *fitna*.

Freedom is a symbol of monotheistic faith, insofar as every individual is free to worship God and stand up for justice.[19] But the Christians in Africa have engaged in a deceptive practice: In order to install their own version of a unitary deity, they have harped away at the multiplicity of gods in the pantheon of indigenous peoples, distracting them from the concepts of a single creative force and Being that already existed within their cosmologies. This practice has caused both fragmentation and dependence on external powers.

According to Abdallah Mekki, the coordinator of Muslim Youth, the Islamic movement is the only structure coming indigenously from within Africa that presently has the ability to ensure the ability of individuals to exercise their belief in God. As this belief is the glue that unifies societies, the Islamic movement has an obligation to be involved beyond the borders of Sudan.

As far as prejudicial attitudes are concerned, the more closely the Muslim community connects with its *iman*, the less prejudice will be a factor. What might look prejudicial in the short run will actually undo parochialism in the long run; that is, the adoption of Islamicism will eventually engineer a new configuration of individual attitude and self-efficacy.

Increasingly Turabi has come to identify the psychological as the locus of a new political model. Whether this is an attempt to obscure the vicissitudes of having to run the country for the past four years or an evasion of having to commit himself to visible structures and programs is still unclear. Popular movements will unfold into a dispensation neither that of military rule, adversarial multiparty politics, nor a one-party state—but a system uniting the people on a higher level. At this point, Turabi is prone to break into excessive rhetorical flourishes of inspiration.

Turabi explains everything from his miraculous recovery from serious head injuries inflicted during the attack in Ottawa to recent bountiful harvests as the will of God—long the common sense of Sudanese cultural practice. The basics have been set in motion: a rudimentary *Shari'a*, a system of public discipline, renewed capacity on the battlefield, a new system of Islamic education and material accumulation. But there is no immediate prospect for resolutions: resolving the civil war and a viable structure of national governance; roles for democracy, the military, and civilian legislatures; a unified structure of judicial reference and interpretation; a long-term strategy for economic development. In this way, the Islamicists parallel other Sudanese governments—great plans of social engineering are initiated, the basic skeleton implemented, and then trust is placed in God for the rest.

The Islamic movement perhaps can do little else at this point. Because it has drawn such a tightly defined universe within which its integrity, legitimacy, and ultimate effectiveness is to be judged, it must resort to a broad, vague, and frequently mystifying discourse in which to chart future developments.

THE ROAD TO FREEDOM

Inherent in this process of Islamicization is a legacy of inconsistency, contradiction, and political struggle. There is nothing wrong with this; it is best acknowledged. The conservatism and reticence of the great law schools of the eighth and ninth centuries, especially the Maliki and Hanifa systems, acted to attenuate many of the mechanisms of flexibility adopted by the Prophet and his companions to resolve intricate legal issues during and immediately after his lifetime.[20]

Muslims have willingly been mobilized to throw their bodies into resistance and loyal admonition. But the history of Islamic politics has not found adequate means for engaging the masses in the process of interpretation and institution building. Faced with the challenge of enacting religion in a world radically transformed primarily by others and in which resistance has been the predominant form of Muslims' contribution to this transformation, the Muslim finds it difficult to use his religious faith as a methodology for creating social existence in ways that are more than a parody of either the Islamic or the Western legacies.

Quranic exegesis has remained circumscribed by religious circles and only recently is being deemed the purview of social and physical scientists. As Abdallah Botchway, former head of the Federation of Ghanaian Muslims, stated, "Muslims must begin to see that the inconsistencies in the Quran, its gaps, its conflation of logical levels is not inherently troubling or necessitating of strict dependencies on the endeavors of those most proximate to the advent of Islam."[21] For these people often repressed ambiguities and elasticities in both *Surah* and *Sunna* in order to force feasible theological and political systems, given the specific political and social circumstances faced by the Muslim *umma* at the time.

Botchway goes on to indicate that it is possible to sustain the belief in divine revelation—that everything Allah said was indeed from Him—without having to interpret its every injunction as universally applicable. For revelation must always reconcile instructions given to a people being taught for the first time with injunctions projected beyond the life of the immediate recipients in anticipation of audiences yet to be born and who, by their nature, will be different in outlook and capacity from those who preceded them. The inviolability of Islam is to be found in the fact that in almost every conceivable circumstance and historical period since the time of the Prophet, people have given themselves to the religion. If this has not always meant strict adherence to every tenet, at least people have aspired to create the social conditions of their existence within the spirit of Islam.

The conditions in which individuals exercise their freedom to submit to the will of Allah are varied, often ambiguous, and endlessly mutable. The power of Islam is that since people must come to it through their own volition, submission itself becomes the signifier of man's essential freedom. Thus, preservation of this freedom to submit must be preserved if Islam is to be preserved. Man must always use this freedom to strive to discover the law to the extent that it applies to actual situations in his life.[22]

In these terms, the will of the majority to live Islamically makes little sense since Islamic values are not expressions of a statistical majority. Majorities implement policies that can be evaluated only in terms of prevailing international standards. In other words, to advocate the imposition of *Shari'a* as a religious exercise because a supposed majority demands it takes the process of law-making outside a religious purview.

For submission before Allah, a submission exercised out of human freedom, is acceptance of the fundamental equality of all people. To submit is an act of homeostasis because individuals subject their lives to He who created all life. It is from this recognition of equality that the Muslim is commanded to create the conditions in life that will allow others to come close to Allah. By this recognition the others will see themselves equipped with the freedom necessary to make the choice of submission. Freedom, by definition, will not compel or produce the inevitability of submission. Rather, it is the only condition under which actual submission can take place. Therefore, the consolidation of the *umma* is of little value if that community does not act in ways that make it possible for others to volitionally accept Islam. It is certainly clear that the conduct of Islamic politics in Sudan has not done what it could to create the conditions through which Dinka, Nuer, Taposa, and Nuba peoples could move closer to Islam.

Much of the fight over *Shari'a* has little to do with its actual content. The lack of political integration in Sudan has resulted in different regions adhering to their own customary practices. This situation will take a long time to change even if a new legal framework is adopted.

First, the Islamic parties are asking for an ideological commitment to a theological content of Islam that does not run deep in the bulk of the Sudanese population. The original advantage of the Islamicization process to the Sudanese centuries ago was that it meant incorporation into a broad and thriving social system that had clear material and cultural benefits. Islam facilitated the circulation of bodies and goods. Often conversion was based on political expediency, as is often suggested in the case of the Funj Sultanate of Sennar.[23]

Although an increasing percentage of Sudanese now live in the cities, the psychological orientation of most Muslims is still to the desert or bush. The dislocations and ruptures that have been experienced are still addressed by most Sudanese through an internal emphasis on the curative and charismatic elements of religion and not through abstractions of jurisprudence or theology. The precariousness of existence necessitates a religious-cultural instrument that posits a form of access to the direct intervention of a God who is personally present rather than abstractly immanent. As the contradictions involved in the incorporation of more of the population into the world economic system intensify, so does the need to seek intercession from one's God. Although the strength of the established Sufi brotherhoods is waning, this does not mean that the role of spiritual intermediaries is declining in importance.

The Islamicists may be embarrassed by the archaic devotion still displayed by the Sudanese masses to an array of *shaykh*s and *faqir*s, yet they recognize that they have not been able to generate a passionate sense of commitment cutting across class, ethnic, and educational lines as have these traditional holy men. In one sense, the laissez-faire operations of the *shaykh*s manage to preserve a sense of autonomy and independent choice for the singular needs of a particular devotee—they are a manifestation of his or her need for a personal relationship with God in a religion that places doctrinal emphasis on the community of believers. The power and efficacy of the *shaykh*'s knowledge seem to embody the possibilities of such singularity.

The *shaykh*'s apparent tools are quite limited: *bukhrat*—inhaling the burnt ash of the Quran; *hijab*—wrapping a piece of the Quran in leather or skin; *minhaia*—drinking the ink of the Quran when soaked in water; *azeima*—the blowing of breath during Quran recitation. An almost limitless number of situations are addressed with these implements, not in some mechanical fashion but through the ability of the *shaykh* to make God accessible. *Shaykh*s don't speak about how they do what they do precisely because their ability stems from the uncodifiable nature of their relationship with the divine.

Quranic revelation engendered practices that emphasized the homogeneity of the community. Whereas rupture is often culturally induced, the illnesses that proceed from such rupture are usually construed by Sudanese as stemming from their own moral culpability; and indeed, the afflicted are marginalized or differentiated from community life. Healing necessitates that the differentiating forces be brought under some kind of control. The *shaykh*, who has separated himself from community life so as to engage in a life of study and devotion, is the signifier through which the unspeakable separateness of the afflicted is read and then brought back to sense again.

Although there is nothing formally anti-Islamic about the *shaykh*'s practice, it does posit a space within the orthodox Islamic state that is not readily compatible with the state's aims of reasserting the homogeneity of the *Sunna*, i.e., conformity to the practices of the Prophet and His community. What has been viewed as especially terrifying by the Islamicists are efforts to reframe this indigenous Sufi tradition within a contemporary and socially conscious intellectual framework.

The work of Mahmoud Muhammad Taha, a former head of the Department of Law at the University of Khartoum, was seen as particularly alarming and was subjected to brutal repression. Shortly before his ouster, Numayri had Taha hanged for apostasy and his corpse displayed by helicopter over the city. The complicity in this execution of the presiding judges, Hassan Ibrahim al-Mahalawy, al-Mikashfi Taha al-Kabbashi, and el-Hag Nour, considered some of the keenest minds of the Islamic movement, has proved a difficult matter for the movement to live down as years pass.

Taha commanded great love and respect among the young; many have indicated that they learned who Allah was through him. Over the years, his primary contention was whether the "humanistic" principles and moral exigencies developed by the Prophet in Mecca, then altered and pragmatically reworked when he was faced with the contingencies of administering the state in Medina, were actually abrogated (naskh). Taha's interpretation was that they were merely to be held in abeyance until that time when the Muslim community was fully able to consolidate its social order. He always stated that he understood the political realities which necessitated a series of qualifications of the liberating spirit of early Islam and the construction of an edifice of codes and rules that came to dominate it. The essence of Islam, insisted Taha, was not to be found in such a legal framework.

Taha considered Shari'a perfect, but only because it involves the process of an interaction between God and the people He guides. The perfection of Shari'a consists "precisely in its ability to evolve, assimilate the capabilities of individual and society, and guide such a life up the ladder of continuous development, however active, vital and renewed such social and individual life may be."[24] For Taha, the history of the umma counted for something, since that history marked a continuous evolution of getting closer to God. The codes governing the relationship between person and God would have to change as the relationship itself changed. From Taha's point of view, Shari'a exists as a mechanism of moral encouragement, an experiential legacy of homeostasis. The law is to actively interact with persons as they grow into their independence and freedom—a freedom based on their greater knowledge of God. Shari'a is to move with individuals through their progress (tatwir al-tashri'). Penalties should never be motivated by vengeance or a debilitating wounding, since the purpose of the law is to restore and train the body to manifest the attitudes necessary for it to operate freely.

For the Sudanese ulema, such a philosophical position suggested their eventual obsolescence, and they in turn acted as if Taha's position constituted a direct threat to their authority. This, coupled with his fearlessness, forceful advocacy of women's rights, and refusal to be silent, made him a marked man. Yet, to this day, he continues to embody the religious (if not political) aspirations of many young educated Sudanese.

THE INSERTION OF THE FRINGE
INTO THE CENTER

In addition to these Islamic trends, even explicitly non-Islamic practices such as the *zar* cult have flourished in Khartoum. *Zar* is practiced primarily by women for women who have been possessed by one or several of the twenty-four archetypal *zar* personalities carried by *rih ahmer* (the red wind). Conducted by a *kudiya* assisted by other women initiates, *zar* has its own ritual language *(ratma)* which is enveloped in the incessant beating of drums used to identify the possessing personality. Within Khartoum's neighborhoods, it constitutes a vehicle for the assertion of women's own specific communal positions. For women facing both greater opportunities and greater restrictions, *zar* is the voice of transformation and hope.

In Darfur, although people profess and adhere to Islamic formalities, religious practices are deeply engrained in a cosmology that affirms the omnipresence of various spirits, sorcery *(sahin)*, and the practice of magic. The latter is especially contained in a tradition of female *tkedjir* that are widely sought out in Khartoum by Muslims and Christians alike for their interpretation of dreams. Despite the fact that the formal Sufi brotherhoods have been in a progressive state of decline, either being transformed into formal political parties and urban fraternal organizations or ignored for their anachronistic models of social affiliation, the sentiment they embody—the possibility of transcending the rational order—remains.

Shaykhs are increasingly free from the demands of sustaining a cohesive group of followers. Although *zawiyat* (lodges) and Quranic centers are still maintained, often providing refuge and sustenance for large numbers of people, *shaykhs* are more inclined to operate as independent agents involved in the urban economy, generating diffuse networks of affiliations within it.

Interest in Sufism is being expressed by the educated as well. Here, the emphasis is to mine these traditions, not for religious models, but for an indigenous intellectual and cultural tradition that can be incorporated into the process of modern institution building. Increasingly, the dilemmas posed by secular exigencies, cultural stagnation, and continued religious commitment are being framed as psychological considerations.

The University of Khartoum has one of the largest psychology departments in Africa and has been involved in an international effort to elaborate Islamic conceptions of social and psychological processes.

One of the primary interests of students is methodologies of cultural regeneration, renewal, and transformation. This interest has ushered in a process of self-reflection and self-consciousness heretofore absent in the culture. Embedded in a religious-cultural framework that emphasizes the indivisibility of everyday life and rigidly specifies the parameters of individual conduct, these students attempt to understand what has occurred in a society increasingly experiencing pervasive depression and anxiety and a seeming inability to utilize its substantial intellectual and spiritual resources to halt its spiraling decline into a kind of national abjection.

More than perhaps any other discipline, the undertaking of psychology posits the greatest source of discordance with Islamic thought. At the same time, it provides students with a new conceptual toolbox as it, conversely, acts as a seal on their suspicions that cultural transformation in Sudan is virtually impossible. Islam is a paradigm of thought affirming the ultimate ability of people to conceptualize their existence and motivations with rationality; it does not readily provide guidance for people confronted with the irrationality of the objects of their contemplation.

In part, secularization connotes a sense of impersonality and perfunctoriness in public relations. For example, psychiatrists on average spend less than five minutes in a session with a client. One can walk into a psychiatric clinic at 8:00 A.M. and see seventy-five patients waiting to be seen. By 10:00 A.M. (breakfast time) the place is empty. In contrast, the *faqir* (*shaykhs* specializing in medical healing) are seen as giving careful and personalized attention to their clients, even if the modality of intervention seems as mundane and redundant as the psychiatrist's prescription of drugs and electroshock. This is just one example of what young Sudanese intellectuals see as the "limited reading" provided by the secular, or, more precisely, the complaint that the secular in Sudanese hands tends to ignore the particularities and complexities of Khartoum.

While the Islamicists worry about the threats to Islam posed by accelerating secularization, a sector of young Sudanese express the concern that the secular, as experienced both at home and abroad, is itself insufficient for liberating them from the overstultifying regimen of Sudanese social practices. So even as they express contempt or indifference for the formal Sufi orders, the notion of *haqiqa* (the reality attained through inward vision of divine power or *mushahadat*) remains a powerful aspect of the young's thinking. *Shari'a* may be the basis for acting in the world, but it does not guide the youth in terms of how to think about the world. In large part, their allegiance to the religious movement is not motivated by their own religious reality.

There is much that is valued in Sudanese culture that is not ideologically compatible with the Islamic movement. During the initial period of Islamicization in Sudan centuries ago, a pantheon of spirits, intermediary processes, and elliptical cognitions could be sustained and flourish as long as the *tawhid* was not compromised.[25] The early experience of Islam in Africa was characterized by a process of "evocation"—a focus on the reality-making aspects of discourse where there was nothing pre-existent to represent, only something to redo and redo; a process of reciprocal legitimation in which the indigenous was explained in Islamic terms and the Islamic reality was explained in terms of the indigenous. Islam spread across the continent by accommodating the cultural diversities it confronted, subsuming in turn what it had accommodated. According to Joseph Schacht, "As long as it [*Shari'a*] received the formal recognition from the Muslim as the religious ideal, it did not insist upon being carried out in practice."[26] Only after its initial spread did Islam operate as a war machine dissipating prior social groupings and subsequently offer itself as the vehicle of social reconstitution.

What has become clear in recent years is that the intensified experience of Westernization has motivated young Sudanese to initiate a new level of comprehension of their religion, to probe more deeply into questions about the identity of God, and to analyze the worldview of Islam and its conceptions of creation and social responsibility. In part this process is a product of Western education itself. Young Muslims have increasingly familiarized themselves with the analytical techniques and discursive practices necessary to carry out an elaborated intellectual commitment to their religion. This does not mean that the capacity for abstraction and conceptualization was in any way absent from traditional Islamic cultures. Rather, for most Muslims, the pedagogical tools for apprehending the religion have been limited, oftentimes consisting of only recitation, memorization, and exposure to the exegeses of others. Little emphasis has been placed on using Islam as the site for the application of their own analytical abilities.[27]

Many Sudanese say that the work of Mahmoud Muhammad Taha had to be stopped because much of the *ulema* recognized that for the first time a broad wave of Sudanese youth were beginning to take the content of religion seriously. Taha represented the catalyst of youth's exploration of the issues related to institution building, the formulation of legal foundations for society, the legitimation of authority, and even matters of cosmology and authenticity. Because Taha was popular with the young, despite the fact that many disagreed with him politically, the question became one of who was going to control the terms and structure of this new level of engagement with religion.

The controversy over Shari'a, which eventually sealed Taha's fate, is a continuation of a long-term political strategy of consolidating political power by maintaining a highly contentious and fragmented body politic. Instead of working in the Islamic spirit, in which law could be seen as the culmination of cohesiveness, the debate over Shari'a provides access to the national political arena for those sectors of society facing crises of legitimacy. If the content of the bulk of Islamic legislation proposed was not framed as Islamic, it is doubtful whether the passions generated would be so intense. Yet, it often seems that labels are the things that are important.

ISLAM AS THE SEARCH FOR COMMON BONDS

During the time of the Prophet, the specifics of Shari'a were an attempt to displace the demands and structures of ethnic particularism. An Islamic tradition became important because respect for tradition was the means the Prophet used to wean people away from blind adherence to their former traditions. Some jurists argue that the relative harshness of Shari'a punishments was intended to challenge the very notions of property and community, to get those who sit in judgement to find a compelling reason behind every wayward action. Some have even argued that anything that exists in nature, such as food, cannot be stolen since it is the property of the earth which all people share. The essential idea was to compel people to pay attention to those aspects and elements that linked them together, that brought them together in an essential complementarity and mutual responsibility.[28] In a strange way, Sudan may indeed desperately need Shari'a, but the fight for Shari'a frequently seems totally counterproductive to these harmonizing aims.

Although such a sense of coalescence is the intent of many Sudanese Islamicists, the controversy over Shari'a has become the badge of a seemingly intractable divisiveness. Southern Sudanese vehemently oppose the law, feeling that it institutionalizes them as permanent strangers in their own country. Although the NIF repeatedly states that it welcomes the Southern presence in Khartoum as a means of demonstrating the vitality and flexibility of Islam and of definitively showing Islam to be the embodiment of justice and dignity, it also clearly indicates that their presence is welcomed only as long as it does not obstruct the basic aims of Islamic revitalization.

For the educated Southern elite, the project of Islamic law portends a double estrangement. In Dinka society, religion has exerted a power no less forceful than that of Islam; the secular and the religious are interwoven in a way that permits no easy conceptual or experiential distinction. When Dinka sought out Western, Christian education, traditionalists considered it a disruption of enlightenment and wisdom, a "piercing" of the universe.[29] Khartoum became the context for a new enlightenment, being as it was the axis of secular, Christian, and English institutions. The process of arabization not only estranges these Southerners from their assumed identity but intensifies the experience of estrangement from their own traditions which now, in the devastation of their "home" territories, will be almost impossible to resume. As a result, Southerners acclaim vague but deeply felt virtues of being African and try to "fill" public space with their own ideas and images of Africanity.

For Arabs, conversely, the public space outside of trading relationships and the mosque always portends the potential for chaos (*fitna*) and unprincipled pragmatism—a kind of carnival of the secular. Since it is within this public space that many Southerners have been compelled to insert themselves, Northerners often feel threatened by their presence. This is why Southerners consider NIF claims that *Shari'a* laws are directed toward the Muslim majority and not toward them disingenuous. Islamicists say that Christians (not "pagans") have a protected place within an Islamic social order. The issue, Southerners respond, is what place? Is it to be assigned, or will any place be theoretically occupiable? Although the Bashir regime has made sure that Southerners occupy ministerial posts, only recently has a Southerner been given a major portfolio.

Turabi attempts to posit the Islamic movement as the epitome of reasonableness, capable of directing itself to people's immediate concerns and offering a dynamic message perfectly suited to a developing country.[30] He insists that there is no problem working within the framework of any political order as long as its operations are based on *Shari'a*. Capital accumulation should be in accordance with a fair distribution of wealth. Free universal education should be established, and guarantees accorded to freedom of expression and assembly. Avenues for widespread political participation should be developed as a necessary corollary to economic restructuring. In all, Turabi presents a picture of a progressive political and economic agenda familiar to the West. The difference is that the Islamicist believes that such an agenda is not attainable without a structure governing appropriate individual and social behavior. The fundamental question becomes how an ideology of universal and reciprocal accountability will be operationally translated into the specifics of a given society. Now that a form of *Shari'a* is in place, the NIF claims that the absence of democratic structures is attributable to the state of emergency imposed by the war. As soon as the war is over, the democratization of society can begin—even though the war is largely about what is perceived to be the structural impossibility of democratization in Islamicist hands.

NIF legal scholars express their right to be independent of Western civil law and criminal procedure. Yet, it is their very familiarity with these Western traditions that makes them the most dangerous applicants of *Shari'a* in Southern eyes. Southern politicians view the very grounding of Islamicist jurists in Western notions of discipline, punishment, and retribution and the literality of legal codification as making them the least likely to view *Shari'a* in the way conceptualized by its original formulators—i.e., as a general guideline that facilitates the endurance of community life. Southerners are fond of pointing out that if the laws are considered immutable and closed to basic revision by virtue of their being the best possible codification of Allah's will, and authored by those in the most advantageous position to apprehend His will, then they will stand as the laws for Muslims regardless of the stance taken by the state.

If a Muslim is a Muslim, then submission to the law should be a prerequisite for sustaining this identification. As the Prophet has indicated, the cohesion of the *umma* must be based on faith and the propagation of a framework for enhancing interpersonal relationships.[31] Through *Shari'a*, the Islamicists may be able to gain the political power necessary to enhance the process of development in Sudan, but the struggle for political power has not exemplified the values of benevolence, trust, generosity, and kindness that Sudanese diligently seek in their social life and which constitute the desires inherent in their aspiration for the rule of law.

Any political movement must carry its adherents with it into any new regime to become the embodiment of its resources and capacities. Democracy in Sudan became a vicious vortex drawing both the eager and the reluctant into a seemingly endless bicker. A constantly uneasy stasis was maintained. Relations among colleagues, workers, offices, and institutions were intensely politicized, resulting in endless transfers and staff reassignments. A receptionist who had remained stationary in his post at the cultural ministry for a long duration remarked to one of the many hundreds of new employees he has greeted during his tenure, "Good luck, nothing has happened here for seventeen years."

Perhaps the proliferation of factions, newspapers, and tendencies that had reemerged after the May 1985 uprising served the function of providing opportunities for political and cultural expression stifled during the Numayri years. Eventually, this plurality would cohere into viable ideological options able to coalesce a workable consensus among the various sectors of civil society. Yet, when cabinet members do not speak with each other and depend on their squabbles to secure public attention, the particularism of the political process, enjoying no real autonomy of operation, will have to identify a common agenda.

Turabi asserts that there can be no acting out of expediency with Allah's law, no compromising of His will. The history of the direction of Islamicist thought since World War I reflects, however, the importance of political expediency in the conceptualization of the Islamic state. The first major political theorist following the demise of the Ottoman caliphate, an Egyptian named Sayyid Muhammed Rashid Rida, posited a new paradigm for Islamic governance. Although primarily heuristic in scope, his conception of *Shari'a*, in which he restored the distinction between laws governing devotional and religious acts *(ibadat)* and those pertaining to the realm of social relations *(mu'amalat)* is of particular interest. Social relations were to be the purview of novel, man-made legislation undertaken by an *ulema* educated in the sciences as well as in theology and jurisprudence, as long as they adhered to general religious principles and did not tamper with matters concerning "nearness to God."[32]

Rida called for the participation of women in all social roles, with the exception of the imamship (chief leader), head of household, and prayer leader, and asserted the predominance of *ijtihad* as a methodology governing the application of the prophetic tradition to contemporary concerns. He called for diversity of social practices and autonomy for Christians and Jews to conduct their personal lives as long as it did not hurt Islam.[33]

Sayyid Muhammed's work established the theoretical framework for the appearance of Ikhwan in 1939—initially as an Egyptian youth and cultural organization. The political conflicts and ideological struggles prevalent in Egypt during the ensuing decade propelled Ikhwan into an increasingly militant political role. Egypt's internal volatility, coupled with the advent of the state of Israel, motivated the Islamic movement to consolidate its ideology in increasingly conservative terms. The movement called for strict adherence to the precise terminology of Islamic law and for the recreation of the Islamic order as manifested by the first caliphates.[34]

Muhammed Ghazzali exemplifies this return to a monolithic conception of a social order in a text written in 1949 (*Minjuna na'lam*) calling for a uniform interpretation of all laws as divine and subjecting everyone equally. The Arab defeat by Israel in 1967 and the Westernization of urban areas further solidified this reversal of Sayyid Muhammed Rashid Rida's formulation. Because of the threat of Western cultural imperialism and the relative weakness of the Arab states, the freedoms of individuals, particularly those of women, had to be balanced with the increasingly important need to sustain the integrity of family life and religious commitment.[35]

The Muslim body politic sought to assert its difference from the West—a psychological need that gave further credence to calls for governance unequivocally enunciating the uniqueness of Islam. Even though there is much in Islamic thought and tradition that argues against any definitive bifurcation with the West, these elements are frequently repressed in any large-scale effort to resist the imposition of an "alien" cultural framework.

The Islamic movement in Sudan embodies many of the intricate paradoxes of this project. At one and the same time, Ikhwan has had to assert both its role as the protector of purity and its capacity to apply a set of often ingenuous, anachronistic, and unelaborated injunctions, traditions, examples, and formulations to the development of a modern state. It has had to assert its ability to codify legislation drawn from divine revelation and prophetic example which cannot embody (either in textual or conceptual form) the consistency, generality, or specificity necessary for the structuring of polity. As such, Islamicists have claimed their willingness to move away from literality. But this movement has opened the way for a wide range of nonliteral religious thinking to vitiate the fundamentalist's role as protectors of the faith.[36]

Attempting to maneuver out of this paradox, Turabi states that the *umma* must be articulated to the literalness and uniformity of *Shari'a* because this is the only grounds on which God will then guide it to suitable reinterpretations to meet contemporary situations. Over and over again, Turabi implores his audiences to believe that Islamic society is not static, but that the only way to go anywhere is to go there (to the implementation of the most familiar version of *Shari'a*) first.[37]

The Islamicists argue that what matters to people is a concise and unimpeachable assertion of their identity. What better source of governance is there than that which gave our people their difference? The dilemma for Sudan is that there do exist various Islamically rooted options for different kinds of specifications of Islamic principle than the one presently in focus. The turbulent recent history of Arab politics and the place Sudan occupies within it, however, seem to conspire against an interweaving of different Islamic discourses that might generate popular appeal. The kind of interweaving of social dialectics and Islamic devotion posited by 'Ali Shari'ati in Iran appears implausible given the Islamicists' ingrained practice of consolidating support by undermining other tendencies, particularly leftist ones. Even so, the strong threads of both millenarian leftist and religious discourse running through Sudanese culture are key to the emergence of a distinct and culturally syntonic political vision.

As indicated earlier, Sudan's internal divisions are maintained in part by the behavior of other Arab countries, who view Sudan as their beach-head in Africa. Four states with distinct political orientations, Libya, Saudi Arabia, Iran, and Egypt, all vie for the attentions of Sudan in terms of its potential as a leverage in other parts of Africa. However, Sudan's Afro-Arab positioning is more apparent than real—the understanding Northern Sudanese have of their Africanity is highly limited.[38]

If the Sudanese had anything approaching a comprehensive understanding of Dinka and Nuer societies, for example, it is clear that the nature of their perceived threat would be mitigated and the basis for a working sense of commonality would be maximized. Additionally, such an understanding would have meant that Northern Sudanese would have been aware of the massive starvation taking place in the South from 1987 onwards. Most Northerners when initially confronted with news of this situation found it impossible to believe.

The continuation of the civil war and the tendency of the government to quickly blame other East African countries for undue interference in internal affairs has severely constricted Sudan's maneuverability in its relationships with sub-Saharan Africa. Having been politically and economically depleted through its involvement in competing Arab interests, Sudan finds itself increasingly dependent on this Arab political game in order to fund its own internal politics and feed its people. Alliances, bilateral agreements, declarations of territorial unification, and affirmations of support between Sudan and the Arab players are continuously offered, denied, abrogated, or qualified. Diplomats are repeatedly flying to Teheran to undo what another did in Tripoli.[39]

During the past decade, (in the meantime), the educated youth have passed through Sufi orders, communist parties, nationalist parties, and Islamic fronts. They search for some vehicle that might instrumentally represent the sociocultural complexity of their own social positions and personal character. There is general frustration. At the same time, there is the invocation of hope for some political form that embodies their aspiration to live as Muslims and to create a viable economic and cultural order capable of creative thought, diversity of opinion, a fair distribution of wealth, and a sense of social vitality and enthusiasm. Movements of cultural revitalization may simply leave more movements for cultural revitalization in their wake.

Chapter Eight

The Religion of Race, the Race for Religion

The prevalent conception of Sudan's difficulties as the polarization of the African Nilotic ethnic groups and the Arabized groups of the North makes the reference to race inevitable. In actuality, this over-simplified demarcation fails to take into account the intricate process of intermingling that tends to homogenize the diversity of cultural inter-relationships that have gone into making both Northern and Southern identity. The basic North-South distinction is an overdetermined one, bearing the intersection of not only racial, but religious, cultural, linguistic, and political conflicts as well.

On the one hand, what race consciousness means is clear at those times when Sudan resembles a South African apartheid situation. On the other hand, this consciousness is fraught with many subtle ambiguities, especially since religious, racial, and cultural terms are not organized in unequivocal forms. Sudanese culture has acted in various historical eras to constrain the operation of these ambiguities. It is this constraint that impedes attempts to undermine a racialist social order. These ambiguities of identity both confirm the severity of Sudan's racial problems and render any definitive stratification of individual bodies a nearly impossible task.

Consider, for example, several specific individuals. The first is Abu Gassim Goor Hamid, a thirty-three-year-old journalist and critic who was the cultural affairs officer for the province of Kordofan. Ethnically he is a Baqqara—his father was a Baqqara *shaykh* and his mother part Azande, Dinka, and Baqqara. Gassim is dark-skinned, African-featured. A shepherd as a child, he worked his way up through the provincial schools to earn a degree in theater at the University of Khartoum. His family were strong supporters of Sadiq al-Mahdi, and he was not without political connections that he could manipulate if he chose to do so.

Having spent a year in prison as a Communist during his late teens, he, like many others, left the Party because of its persistent advocacy of policies deemed culturally insensitive and overly doctrinaire. He later joined the National Islamic Front and was considered by both his party and his district to be a leading candidate for the next parliamentary elections in 1990 (which never took place). In 1981, he co-founded *Al-Wan*, which was to become Khartoum's leading newspaper. Although deeply religious, Gassim often addressed Islamically sensitive cultural issues and repeatedly challenged the authority of the *ulema* to control the interpretive apparatus of Muslim ideology.

The salient issue regarding Gassim's position is that his advocacy of autonomy was frequently viewed by others (even by some of his colleagues) as a manifestation of his blackness. Although a co-founder of the newspaper, he was not the man with the money. The publisher paid Gassim's meager salary over the years and gave him space for his idiosyncratic and provocative texts, but maintained him in a perpetual state of marginality in the organizational structure.

Following his graduation, Gassim searched for a place to live. He was willing to put out almost all his $40-a-month salary to find some shelter away from the university hostel. Despite the advantages gained by the NIF in having Gassim as a member of the party, they were unable to locate accommodations for him. Often he received tips about available rooms only to find them unavailable upon his arrival. At work, there was a preponderance of partly joking, partly antagonistic interchanges with colleagues in which he was referred to as "the son of my slave." Although considered Khartoum's premier theater-cultural critic, he was always prevented from occupying any real position of power in the cultural establishment, despite the fact that his opinions and perspectives were constantly solicited.

Being one of the few NIF members in a traditionally solid Umma Party region, Babanousa, Gassim was constantly courted by the Islamicists and distanced by them at the same time. Top Islamic organizations extended him invitations to conduct seminars, and then would fail to pay him. His writing would be awarded top prizes, but he would be omitted from lists of participants attending international conferences, contestants placing second and third going instead.

When Gassim expressed his intention to spend some years in the United States, a steady stream of NIF intellectuals pleaded with him to stay in Sudan. When he requested $400 from the party so he could get married, it was unable to come up with the funds, and in fact, intervened to get a son of a party official a lucrative scholarship to Great Britain by erasing Gassim's name on the application and inserting the party official's son's in its place.

Gassim's favourite topic of conversation was a structure of theater he called *bhaksa*, derived from a Dinka concept passed on by his mother, which basically referred to an architecture of staging. The actors would basically be pursuing different scenarios on stage—different events, stories, conversations—but in each scenario would be a linking action or character that was open to the distinct events being played out in contiguous separation. Thus a multiplicity of small "plays" all separately going on at the same time would be simultaneously linked. All events have their unfolding in space—an architecture of bodies—and it was the form of social architecture that designates separateness through linkage, and vice versa, to which this notion of *bhaksa* referred. It was Gassim's vision of the Sudan.

Nadia is a thirty-two-year-old woman whose family had lived in Khartoum for several generations, originally having come from the lowland Nuba—an ethnicity that had been Islamicized for nearly a century, unlike their counterparts, the "mountain" Nuba, who fiercely clung to animist traditions. Sectors of the Muslim Nuba community in Khartoum had been cultivated as an elite, ensconced as trusted members of the civil service.

Nadia has a degree in chemical engineering and is also one of Sudan's top actresses. Unlike many professional women who embed their sexuality in a traditional quietism necessary for them to pursue their careers, she used her relative security as a consultant to the UN before the 1989 coup to launch a frontal assault on the rules governing public demeanor. (Now, of course, current *Shari'a* legislation would make such an "assault" a punishable form of assault.) At public gatherings she would be the first to say prayers at the appointed minute, even though she dressed in fashions more appropriate to Kinshasa nightclubs. She repeatedly entered the domains of religion and bureaucracy where she was not welcome but, surprisingly, was not always refused. Even though she "fronted" a forbidden image, her behavior was otherwise a model of propriety and integrity. She has worked hard to embed her lifestyle within an Islamic framework. For this she was simultaneously admired and hated.

More clandestinely, she made a concerted effort to know and mingle with Nuba people living in some of the most miserable shantytowns in Khartoum. She grew up never really knowing this to be her ethnic heritage. Nadia had assimilated the common habit of disparaging the "paganism" of Nuba culture. It was only when she struck up a friendship with a visiting anthropologist while attending the university that she found out from documentary histories the anthropologist was working with that she was a Nuba. Later, her grandmother confirmed this for her.

There was really no need for Nadia to attempt to reestablish these ethnic connections. At that point in her life, she was on her way to a promising career. Her father had the connections that could circumvent her African features, and a postgraduate scholarship in Britain was a likely possibility. But the discovery of her Nuba roots directed her attention to a sense of ceremony and ritual that she had discredited. Nadia then began to act in the plays of friends attending the drama institute and received wide critical acclaim.

Building connections to Nuba communities in Khartoum was more difficult than Nadia had envisioned. The people were distrustful and reluctant, bewildered as to why someone successfully assimilated into Northern culture over the generations would want to venture out of such a position. She talks of being allowed to visit several Nuba households, but having to wear the traditional robes of Northern Sudanese women to mark her distinctiveness. This undertaking made her reluctant to leave Sudan, even though she had several opportunities to do so.

Though she was forced to leave Sudan shortly after the coup and married an African "from somewhere else," Nadia rarely expressed any intense anger about the oppression of women and blacks in the Sudan, indicating that "no one in the country listened to anger anyway." "I am a professional, an artist, an African, a Sudanese, a woman, and I will always act as if there will be no problem being all of them."

Given the polarizations and conflicts endemic to Sudanese culture in relation to the above designations, the degree to which Nadia was not shunned, not excluded, not made the object of constant derision, is surprising. Just as some people can be fooled into letting down their guard, others can be temporarily numbed and prevented from advancing their attack. Shortly after the June 1989 takeover, however, the regime came after her; she barely got out. She had not wanted to leave, but being considered a threat to the Islamic order, she would have been treated as a whore, as are thousands of other Nuba women with no place to go.

Outside of the racial killings that take place weekly in Khartoum, racial dynamics often take on a burlesque sensibility. Territorialization of activities along ethnic lines is depended upon as a means of subverting the very stratification connoted by it. Young African Muslims from Darfur are often seen with sunglasses and hats attending Sunday services at St. George's Cathedral so that they can mingle with the informal "parade" that occurs afterward from the church to the Mahata Wusta bus station. This parade is a congenial saunter of well-dressed, joking Southerners stopping off for cold drinks and playful banter and street jive before heading home. It is one of the few accessible moments of a public Africanity.

Despite being astute handlers of the diplomatic complexities inherent in their assignments, most foreign missions and nongovernmental organizations tend to staff their operations with Southerners and socialize with them as well. This sets up a situation in which Khartoum Arab elites often find themselves seeking favors from Southerners having lower social status in order to expedite their access to certain sectors of the foreign community. A common game played by the sons of dark-skinned Muslim elites is to feign employment with the top private security agency (SSI), which guards most of the foreign companies, offices, clubs, and missions. The agency employs mostly Southerners. These Southern-expatriate attachments are based primarily on the greater fluency of Southerners in the English language. But they are also based on the implicit belief of expatriates that Southerners will be more tolerant of their behaviors and lifestyles and more dependable, not only as workers but as co-observers of their life in Khartoum.

Deprived of substantial economic opportunities, Southerners are dependent on these affiliations, not only for work, but as a source of moral support and as a means of vitiating excesses on the part of the Sudanese government. As would be expected, Khartoum Arabs are antagonized by these relationships. They are quick to perceive outside interferences in internal affairs. These hostile attitudes came to the fore especially during times like August 1988, when the image of the Virgin Mary appeared in the portrait of a local Coptic Christian family and was displayed to thousands of visitors, Muslims and Christians alike, in a church in Khartoum North. To assuage any widespread curiosity about Christianity, the government has gone out of its way to paint a distorted picture of it. During recent assemblies the government has organized to "prove" its respect for human rights, the most marginal and extreme of international Christian groups are brought together with Muslim delegates to simultaneously elicit fringe support and embarrass local Christian organizations.

THE COMPLICITY OF AVOIDANCE

At a seminar on the nature of Sudanese identity, one finds two of Sudan's most prominent intellectuals, one Dinka and one Hamiliyya, in dialogue with each other. Both rely on a translator to go from English to Arabic, Arabic to English, even though both are fluent in each language, as is the audience on this occasion. Afterwards at a private reception, the Dinka and his colleagues break into the Southern-based Juba Arabic dialect for conversation among themselves, and the Hamiliyya and his colleagues take up a Khartoum slang English for the same purpose. The two scholars have been close friends for many years. Perhaps the friendship has been possible because visible concessions to accommodation are unyieldingly resisted.

There is nothing particularly unique about such a situation. In Khartoum, this posturing is merely intensified to the point where the mutual assimilation of language and culture is viewed as the total collapse of each group. At the same time, Southerners and Northerners have each become inextricably dependent on the other as a necessary reference in affirming their own identities. The years of conflict and the endless manipulations by external colonial forces, both Western and Arab, that have unsettled efforts to cohere national identity have also made it difficult for either Northerners or Southerners to consolidate a vision of themselves in their own terms.

Many young Sudanese have been delinked from their cultural traditions and psychological frameworks through factors independent of this internal conflict. What racial conflict has done is to arbitrarily and artificially maintain youth in a superficial proximity to their traditional identifications and cultural "homes." It adheres them to loyalties otherwise fatigued or problematic. What ensues is a lack of the breathing room and maneuverability necessary for them to rethink and reorganize the sources and methods of cultural affinity and to enliven and adjust what it means to be a Dinka or a Shaygiyya to postcolonial life. As the conflict continues year after year, it generates a situation in which the mutual avoidance and hostility of the antagonists becomes a compensation for the lacks in self-sufficiency and cultural confidence that are perpetuated by the conflict itself.

More young people indicate that they are tired of being caught up in the protracted war because they see it ending up depleting themselves. Although youths from the North and South mostly express their frustration about not knowing what to say to each other or how to conduct relations with each other, they are especially tired of feeling that they are under some obligation to know what to do with each other. They want to proceed with their own lives and are more threatened by internal pulls than by the presence of the other. In some ways this "selfishness" portends the continuation of the conflict even if, at the same time, it expresses the desire to be done with it.

I frequently chatted with groups of Northern youth while they smoked hashish after finishing the night prayers. A common theme of their discussions was the mixture of both respect and contempt for the Southerner. "We have nothing else to prove to the world . . . you take

Islam away from us and you take away our only weapon." "Look what happens to the Dinka . . . you take away his cows and he is nothing." "We were brought up with the purpose of fighting for Islam before we fight for ourselves." Islam coheres them into a group; it is their shared value, their civil society. It grows in proportion to their perception that without Islam they are defenseless against the Southerner, whom they see as more proficient at fighting and hustling themselves. Additionally, Southerners are viewed as more inclined to stick together—a coalescence that doesn't bother with ideology but is instead enforced by the Southerner's position as a minority.

The Northern majority, according to these kids, has to find a way to act as the majority. The significance of prayer cannot be underestimated as a glue that cements relationships in a collective submission to an authority that is both external to and the heart of these social relationships. If one were to hypothetically assess Northern social relationships having no access to the conventionalizing practices of Islam—examining the psychological dependencies, the intense way communities scrutinize their members, and the great tendency of individuals to distrust the intentions of others—one would find a great potential for debilitating rivalries and jealousies. These jealousies certainly exist in Sudanese everyday life, but without Islam, they probably would overwhelm social relationships, friendships, and kin ties.

Both Southern and Northern youth now prefer to just live their separate lives. But with approximately 40 percent of Khartoum identifying itself as African, according to a 1989 survey of a small sample of various types of neighborhoods conducted by the Department of Geography at the University of Khartoum, it is difficult to see how the state could coordinate a definitive separation of cultural lives while providing for power sharing. There are few attempts at integration. The Sisters of St. Francis have fostered an integrated educational environment, but this is mostly due to the fact that they operate the best affordable private school in Khartoum. The young children are acutely aware of the cultural schism and tend to avoid all but necessary social contact with the other group.

Religious strife as a metaphor for racial antagonism has been the customary way of looking at the conflict between North and South. But just as importantly, the racial conflict in Sudan has become the enunciation of a displacement of genuine religious conflict. In Sudan, as has been the case in much of Africa, ruptures in the social fabric of cultures have been addressed religiously. In other words, religious discourse and cognition have been appropriated as a methodology for political operations because they are posited as the most effective means of forging new instruments of social organization, disseminating information, and coordinating competing groups.[1] As Fields points out, daily life takes shape by "now resisting, now accommodating the unseen forces that define human existence. . . . Once embodied in the ordinary, the unseen forces become seen facts . . . ritual was one of the "languages" in which all activity, including [political] rule, was experienced, described and legitimated."[2]

Religion is the vehicle through which people orient themselves to their society, as well as a means of reconstructing their psychological relationship to a given social order or political predicament. It is especially salient in the African context where the agenda of national development often remains thoroughly oblique to most of the population living in the clarity of destitution and the seemingly permanent ambiguity of cultural drift.[3] In fact, to many Sudanese, the prospect of such development is an alarming one since it augurs the prospect of increased accountability and responsibility to a state presently favored more as a nonobtrusive symbol of national integrity rather than as an engineer of social construction.

As Khalid Younis Hassan, a Khartoum journalist for *Al-Midan*, points out, there is a stability in economic instability for the Sudanese masses. Such instability fosters a situation in which people are left to their own devices. Although antithetical to a coherent pattern of capital accumulation, such an attitude does reflect the wariness of many at being "captured" as "citizens" with well-defined and prescribed social and economic roles. Even for the Southerner, the intrusion of Christianity in large part precipitated the internal cultural crises that propelled the South into becoming the active antagonist in the North-South conflict. Going to war became a means of regaining a sense of identity put into question when the traditional religious order had been disrupted.

An ironic aspect of this North-South, Muslim-Christian and animist conflict is that the Southerner, most particularly the Dinka, argues for the separation of the social and religious (for politically understandable reasons)—a position that is antithetical to the traditional Dinka conception of everyday life.[4] In the Dinka heritage, religion motivates all aspects of daily life, authorizes the structure of social relationships, and informs the basis for the interpretation of political and social events. The terms of the present struggle, however, compel the Southern antagonists (for the most part educated Christians, educated through Christianity) to defend their right to affiliate with and live by a religion that has largely been unsympathetic to or ignorant of the disruption it has engendered in the cohesiveness of its Sudanese flock.

Instead of devoting energy to molding a Christian discourse and ritual suited to their worldview and the various dilemmas of African existence (as has occurred in most of the rest of Africa), Southerners have had to maintain a little-desired proximity to the edifice of Western Christianity in order to protect any opportunity they might have to one day move away from it.

Southerners are caught in an additional dilemma: As long as they adhere strongly to their relationship with the established church, they will be viewed with suspicion by the Northerner as people easily prone to outside manipulation, as a symbol of the Christian conspiracy against Islam. (This, despite the fact that Khartoum may have more foreign agents and spies per square inch than anywhere else in the Arab world). The established church, however, with its interconnections with Western developmental aid programs, provides the only concrete context through which the Southerners can at this moment enunciate their perceived and valued cultural distinctiveness. Engendering religious activities and movements independent of the established church would threaten the limited external protection and religious autonomy that does exist. The North disdains the established church, but it is more prepared psychologically to adapt to its presence than it would be to face a host of rapidly proliferating indigenous Christian movements.

Southerners are adamant about preventing any formal consolidation of Islam as the law of the majority, not because it threatens them with the diminution of a Christianity they are deeply invested in, but because it threatens to constrict the space from which they might reintegrate religious sentiments with aspects of their cultural heritage. It is through this reintegration that they might reinvent themselves as vehicles for a religious power that once breathed life into family units (now largely fragmented and moribund) and established a fierce sense of collective pride.

Northerners, on the other hand, blame the Southerner for impeding their attainment of a new moral order that they believe will restore a sense of equanimity and trust to social relations. Equally important is their not-so-hidden anticipation that the assumption of this order will upend the corrupt strata of an *ulema* whose authority cannot be challenged directly but who themselves cannot legitimately challenge the discourse, i.e., the implementation of *Shari'a*, through which their anticipated demise is framed. This aspiration is present even though Sudan has long warded off the consolidation of a specifically religious class. Merchants and politicians have masked themselves with religious roles.

An aspect of Northern resentment is that Southern resistance deprives them of a methodology for political vindication and renewal. There is no guarantee that the implementation of *Shari'a* would actually sweep away the deadwood at the top, as is anticipated by the masses. But the point is that Sudanese believe there is no other way but *Shari'a* to make such a change happen.

The successive bursts of democracy alternating with prolonged periods of military rule, informed by ever-shifting ideological commitments, have not sustained a believed-in vision of a better life. Instead, democracy appears to most of the masses to merely amplify the demise of their well-being. A popular Sudanese saying indicates that ideals have a way of quickly becoming unfriendly dogs. *Shari'a* is viewed as a means to ensure a greater measure of accountability in political life. Additionally, it is hoped that it will serve as an immutable standard to which most Sudanese politicians will fail to measure up and thus condemn themselves to the wayside. As one nineteen-year-old in Saganna summed up, "I love to drink and I love to screw, but I'll gladly give them up if it means Allah will help us get rid of all these motherfuckers and liars who have forgotten who we are."

Part Three

A Reference from
Another Africa

Chapter Nine

Advantageous Marginalities
A South African Critique of the Islamic Movement in Sudan

M y role in Sudan was problematic from the outset. I was in Khartoum to buttress a marginal aspect of the Islamic movement that
my hosts believed had to be maintained as marginal. The movement was
sufficiently perspicacious to realize that it needed a cutting edge, a small
wing of committed Muslims who were capable of challenging orthodoxy and inserting Islamic discourse into domains with which it had
been reluctant to engage, such as cultural studies, criticism, psychology.
But this cutting edge was never to challenge the precepts of the movement itself.

To operate at the margins is problematic for those who work there.
Some feel comfortable because the margins provide a relative respite
from excessive scrutiny and evaluation. For those with diminished confidence in their capabilities or who are adamant about pursuing directions in thinking and lifestyle that they consciously acknowledge as
nonnormative, the margins are an institutionalized shelter. For others,
the margins are a place of involuntary exile, a launching pad for repeated
attempts at acceptance and legitimacy. Not only is one relegated to the
shadows, but one is forced to evaluate one's own complicity with this
position, to ask what one did wrong.

At the same time, the larger society must keep tabs on what transpires
at the margins. A society knows implicitly that its margins exist partially
as a space to which it can relegate thinking and discourses it considers
dangerous and destabilizing. Yet, every social order is in some way obligated to the margins for its existence.[1] The marginal is the negative
mirror of the normative; it enables the normative to see and advertise
itself as normal. It provides the normative its "magisterial" quality, i.e.,
its status as the official discourse for "real" human behavior, which allows
it to enforce its view of the marginal as the place of incapacity and irrationality. But in this announcement of supremacy, the normative requires
a "beyond," something that exceeds itself, in order to exist, because this

is how the normative has presented itself in the first place—as something that has legitimacy because it exceeds what has gone on before.

The modern is beyond primitivism; Islamic values are beyond the decadence of the West. The margins, as the concrete manifestation of this beyond (not yet cohered as normal), are thus the place of the fragmentary, the dissolute, hostile, and nonconsensual. The new order comes from the margins but must act as if this is not the case.

Islam has had trouble dealing with its margins.[2] The more it has tried to remove them, the more they are created. In the Sudanese movement, the margins are expected to be productive and to do so within conversational bounds—they are to generate a sense of radical momentum but stay under strict control. Margins don't operate this way. The Islamicists wanted to find a way to keep several promising activists in the fold. They gambled on the chance that an American Muslim might provide a way for these activists to exercise a sense of daring and yet maintain their affiliation with the movement. It was, as I indicated earlier, a strange reality based on a reasonable yet misplaced interaction of assumptions. I assumed the movement was more flexible than it was; the movement assumed I was more conventional than I appeared.

From the beginning I wondered how to appear. The group of activists and I were thrown together. Indirectly, I was to assuage their discontent. Indirectly, they were to show how progressive the movement really was. Indirectly, we were to temper each other. Additionally, we were encumbered with the task of trying to show the movement that certain collaborations were possible. The movement was not really interested in this possibility, or was interested only to the extent that it became an academic exercise. Since these collaborations involved non-Muslims in urban areas where too many un-Islamic activities occurred, Islam had to dominate or have no presence at all. Collaborations cannot be effected on that level.

How can we be Muslim, political, culturally progressive Sudanese and practical players all at the same time? This seemed to be the question these activists were trying to address. The National Islamic Front seemed to dominate the terms of active Islamic focus in the political sphere. Secularists and leftists appear to claim the territory of cultural progressives and thus viewed Islamicism generally as an anathema. University intellectuals could carve out a wide variety of singular spaces and syntheses, but would have little effective role in the political process unless as part of a political party or syndicate. The Islamic movement was where these activists generally wanted to be. But most felt that it

Chapter Nine

was impossible to maintain their affiliation for long. There were too many contradictions, rigidities, manipulations, ethnocentricisms.

For some, the only way to maintain the vibrancy of religious faith was to dissociate it from social and political involvements, even though the tenets of faith mandated those involvements. Others faced the prospect of having to subjugate a nascent learning of the interpretive breadth of Islam to the exigencies of a mass movement and were resentful, but practical. One person wanted to join the SPLA, but felt that, in addition to becoming an outlaw, he would end up being used and made to look foolish. Still others in the group thought about little else but getting away, seeing the entire Sudanese situation as hoeplessly intractable.

LOOKING OUTSIDE

Having worked as a psychologist with communities going through difficult crisis periods, I have learned that it is often useful for the community to step outside of itself and consider things going on elsewhere. It is especially useful if the situation looked at has a radically different composition or set of problems. Particularly in Sudan, it seemed important for people to take a look at situations external to themselves, since the internal dynamics of everyday life had become so complex and frustrating, so prone to distortion. I remember arguing with a group of Southern students who insisted that there were no black Muslims in America.

Such a focus does more than simply provide fresh ideas or a temporary vacation from one's problems. It not only emphasizes unforeseen possibilities of thinking and action but can reframe what exists internally as an indication of a set of other possibilities. Things may make sense that didn't before.

How is the outside to be looked at? Specific movements are wedded to their social contexts. Their theoretical, ideological, and behavioral suppositions and styles are the products of the interaction of persons with specific social histories, economic conditions, worldviews, and political cultures. Movements are inscribed in these contexts yet actively invent them at the same time. It is a reciprocal process of mutual shaping. Local realities must be addressed in sensible ways. Yet what those realities are and how they are interpreted and what they will become in the future is not solely determined by the histories, economies, or politics they engender.

It is true that some things work in one context and not in others—that certain ideas, ideologies, and social and religious practices have efficacy and applicability in some cultural domains while remaining strange in others. Yet, possibilities circulate, take shape in different forms and translations. Their site of emergence is not necessarily their destination. Today, especially, it is not clear where anything definitively belongs. Culture has become increasingly internationalized. Ideas and practices might work best in places where, on the surface, they wouldn't seem to work at all. The realization of a vision may require a set of problems unavailable to it in its place of inception. Experiences and concepts have always been used in ways never originally intended. Whatever use the possibilities of such an exchange offer, groups and movements must look outside of themselves in a manner that sees more than themselves.

It is ironic that one part of an extremely small Islamic movement in South Africa might provide a useful external referent to Sudan, given the way that Sudanese Northern hegemony over Southerners has been compared to South African apartheid. Sudan and South Africa are obviously two different places. They have very little in common—in fact, Sudan was the last country in Africa to refuse entry to South African passport holders. Yet on the African continent, these are the two places where Islam has substantially exceeded its conventional role. One country has used an Islamic agenda as a tool of cultural reconfiguration; the other uses Islam as a vehicle to obligate political resistance to an unjust non-Muslim regime and, more importantly, to justify a process of Muslims working conjointly with people and groups of different religious and ideological backgrounds to accomplish this task.

Despite the cultural and political differences, there is a strong thread of common Islamic practice that runs through all parts of the Muslim world. Islam is a religion that specifies clear and, for the most part, unequivocal behavioral coordinates, and these show up everywhere. Under this umbrella of sameness, a multitude of subtle differences exists. Islam must be articulated to a vast variety of environments, and the nature of these articulations affects the attitudes and actions of Muslims. Even though Islam is being used as a political instrument in both Sudan and South Africa, one is hard-pressed to think of situations where Islam looks more different than it does in these two countries, or, more precisely, in the two distinct movements operating there.

While living in Sudan, I became interested in facets of the South African Islamic movement that would resolve conceptually (or at least attenuate) some of the problems endemic to the Sudanese situation.

What Sudanese claimed they could not do as Muslims, South Africans saw as fulfilling their obligations as Muslims. What many Sudanese considered heresy, South Africans framed as legitimate possibilities. As stated repeatedly in this book, vigorous debates have been going on in Islamic theology for a very long time, occasioned both by the Islamic institutions that preserve and reconstitute the integrity of the faith and by the political conditions faced by Muslims. Islam has been used to justify revolutions, reactionary regimes, democracies, monarchies, colonial rule, wars of liberation.

Though intensive periods of reform have left their mark on the corpus of Islamic thought, the nature of Islamic understanding and practice has in many ways remained unaffected by them. In South Africa, a threshold appears to have been crossed in how Islamic thinking and political practice can reshape each other. This raises many problems in terms of the apparent immutability of Islam. By understanding both these radical innovations in practice and the problems that they raise, both theological and practical, much of the thinking informing the actions of Sudanese Islamicists becomes clearer.

CONSIDERING ISLAMS

In part, this reshaping takes place because Islamic practice in South Africa exists in a highly idiosyncratic situation. Unlike the seemingly intractable Sudanese dilemma, the issue in South Africa is appallingly clear—an entire society of differential rights, access, and privilege based on racial classification. The popular belief is: elect a real democratic government and the problem is over. Although the situation is more complex than that (just listen to any discussion of what post-apartheid society in South Africa is supposed to look like), the impression is created that apartheid is the totality of the problem.

South Africa seems like an anachronistic holdover from a previous order—the last place where a liberation struggle has occurred; the last place where the dynamics of power, oppression, and disenfranchisement appear unequivocally and concretely apprehendable. An observer might be excused for concluding that whatever innovations in Islamic theology exist in South Africa are due to the extreme peculiarity of its situation. In part this conclusion is probably accurate, but it does not stop Islamic productions in South Africa from entering a larger sphere of consideration or being applied to other situations.

Although politically anachronistic, South Africa has the most advanced economy on the continent, and South African Muslims are one of the most thoroughly working-class communities in the Islamic world. A democratic South Africa will in the future come to assume a substantially larger economic and political role in Africa. At the same time as exposure to the modern world has been advanced, the legacy of colonial domination and apartheid has provided a strong measure of insularity to the Muslim community, enabling it to maintain itself as a highly cohesive unit with a strong sense of tradition and continuity. Thus, theological innovation cannot be simply construed as a by-product of the dissolution of essential Islamic values and practices.

Muslims are a small minority in South Africa, making up between 2 and 3 percent of the total population.[3] As a small minority they will never assume substantial formal political power, and thus do not have to face many of the issues of governance so troubling to the Sudanese. Yet, in the mass democratic movement (MDM) and now the African National Congress (ANC), Muslims have assumed a political role whose significance far outweighs what would be expected from their numbers. In turn, they constitute the largest "ethnic" bloc of potential votes in Greater Cape Town—the country's second largest city and legislative capital. They may not be encumbered with the task of orchestrating a mass movement of Muslims, but many Muslims have taken on the responsibility of helping to direct a mass movement in which many different religions and races are involved. The issues are different, but the skills needed and the importance of the tasks involved are not radically unequal.

The simultaneous consideration of Sudan and South Africa illustrates several issues. Both show that efforts to deliberate confounded social and national identities force the practice of Islam out of conventional routines and stabilities. As the Sudanese attempt to reconcile competing pulls on how they recognize themselves, Islamic practice and notions of majority reciprocally elaborate each other. In other words, the thinking is that the only basis of a majority in Sudan is its Islamic religious background. Although many have pointed out the sociological fallacy of this claim, it is a conventionally accepted social fact.[4]

If Islam is then the predominant and overarching characteristic of social organization, it must be intensified and clarified. Islamic identity must take precedence over any other identity so that a national identity, which is seen to rely on this predominance, can be put in place. Such considerations outweigh the obvious attenuation of national identity in the conflicts precipitated by making Islam the ultimate priority. Instead of Muslims concluding that they can rest comfortably with a non-Muslim minority, since they are the supposed majority, and not feel threatened with dissolution, the opposite occurs. Confidence in the salience and efficacy of this renewed commitment to Islam must be constructed.

Yet, there often appears to be a deep-seated lack of assuredness that Islam can fulfill the task of serving as a vehicle for national development. This is not to say that the Sudanese are not deeply religious or wedded to their faith. Rather, this faith now bears an additional responsibility as a positive framework for social transformation, and thus risks simultaneously being used as a collective defense mechanism against it. In the social domain, then, Islamicization in Sudan proceeds from a fundamental ambiguity of national and cultural identity and is not simply the projection of a religiously clear sensibility on the social field.

In South Africa, the Islamic movement to which I will refer, made up of two organizations in particular, the Call of Islam (COI) and the Muslim Youth Movement (MYM), is a small movement in a minority community. As in Sudan, ambiguity of identity is engendered by the particularities of South Africa's location on the geopolitical map. In general, however, the details of the ambiguity are very different. But this difference is what makes the two situations comparable. Both "explain" the directions the other takes. In other words, substantial analysis of the South African situation seems to facilitate comprehension of why the Islamic movement in Sudan takes the course it does, and vice versa.

As indicated earlier, the integrity of the Muslim community in Cape Town has been maintained in part by colonial and apartheid policies that have substantially restricted the nature of work, political rights, and social and physical movement. An apparatus of oppression has served as an apparatus of social cohesion. This situation has been particularly acute for the so-called Cape coloreds. Officially categorized as Malays under the government of Magnus Malan in 1950, the community had its origins in enslaved political dissidents from Java who were brought to the Cape in the late seventeenth century. Only 1 percent actually came from the Malay Peninsula. Over the years, this original community mixed with freed African slaves, people from India, Shan Khoi ethnicities, Afrikaaners, and other whites to constitute the "colored" community of today.[5]

Initially the designation "colored" referred to all non-Europeans, and it was not until 1904 that the term was used to refer to mixed-race peoples. The combination of economic depression and intensified racialist ideology at the beginning of the twentieth century led to a progressive exclusion of coloreds from the construction trades and artisan craft unions. Non-Bantu-speaking coloreds began to differentiate themselves from Bantu speakers—a move further substantiated by Islamic practice and the use of the proto-Afrikaans language. The invocation of colored identity became a defense in a period when franchise rights were being eroded and social Darwinism informed social structures.[6]

The state assumed a more active stance in constructing functional divisions between African and colored communities. In 1901, the plague epidemic in Cape Town provided an excuse for the advent of racial segregation. Henceforth, a policy of influx control was pursued which limited the number of Africans permitted to live in the cities. The African People's Organization, set up by A. Abdrahman to protect the political and economic interests of colored people, excluded black Africans. A prolonged period of mutual exclusion in colored and black organizations during the 1920s and 1930s further solidified the split, as did colored exemption from influx controls. An ambivalent state policy was directed at the colored community. On the one hand, their economic interests were protected by curtailed competition with Bantu-speaking Africans. On the other, their economic advancement was undermined; for example, by the Apprenticeship Act of 1922, which set a minimum educational requirement for skilled jobs.[7]

When Christian Nationalists seized power in 1948 through a slim plurality, the situation for coloreds changed rapidly. Afrikaaner hegemony was to be maintained through a policy of enforced group identity and territorialization. This policy was predicated on terminating the practice of coloreds passing for whites (indeed, in the 1930s, perhaps as many as 40 percent of the colored community passed as whites.)[8] In the Population Registration Act of 1950, coloreds were given an imprecise and ambiguous definition—in some instances resulting in an overly arbitrary designation. A colored nation was to cohere and be assigned a territory, although there was little basis for coherence. To achieve this, Afrikaaners passed legislation to register the population and limit miscegenation.

In 1953 coloreds were given formal preference in employment in the Western Cape in an attempt by the state to develop a colored middle class capable of providing the intellectual and economic leadership for a separate nation. A policy of removing Africans from Cape Town was also pursued, and by 1962, thirty thousand Africans had been expelled. Viewing colored representation as a threat to their slim majority in parliament, the Afrikaaners rescinded direct coloured participation in 1956. The Non-European Unity Mobement and the South African Coloured Peoples Congress attempted to prevent the reassertion of colored identity during this time, but with limited impact.

In Cape Town, the colored community is now equally divided between Christians and Muslims. Not sharing the basic tenets of religion with either the majority of the population, the Xhosa and Zulu (both Christians and traditionalists), or the ruling Afrikaaner and English cultures, and being racially distinguished from them as well, the Muslims have felt doubly marginalized within South Africa. This marginalization has been contributed to by the fact that they have found themselves in the middle between the extremes of oppressor and oppressed. Muslims have been deeply resented by black Africans for the way the former have managed them in work and commercial activities. The virulence of Muslim racism has frequently been on a par with that of the Afrikaaner. Yet, the most the Muslim could aspire to was the status of "honorary white."

This position bred an internally motivated insularity to go along with external impositions. This insularity had precedents in the beginning of the nineteenth century, when the first mosque in Cape Town was built. The community became virtually a state within a state, where *Shari'a* law was fully applied. It became a center of cultural autonomy from British colonial structures. This autonomy, coupled with an ideology that emphasized human equality, attracted sizable numbers of "free" blacks. A host of ancillary institutions were formed which framed relations between Muslims and blacks and legitimated the structure of their economic collaborations.[9]

After emancipation in 1838, the Muslim community experienced a tenfold increase until 1850, when alarm over the growth of Islam prompted intense Christian missionary work. As the community grew, there was a rapid proliferation of mosques. Such expansions prompted a variety of disputes over land ownership, zoning, and so forth, which were used by the British to institute a system of civil adjudication. As an autonomous community within a larger structure of confinement, the Muslim community appropriated Azharite codes of the Shafi school of Islamic law, which emphasized the predominance of the will of Allah—that one's position in society is largely preordained. This appropriation, born out of a need to explain one's social position, served to further legitimate social relations based on maintaining internal autonomy by minimizing concerted challenges to the overall structure of state power. Within this relatively closed system, a religious class was formed which was basically restricted to a few families that intermarried among themselves for several generations. These families are the ancestors of much of the local *ulema* today.

The Call of Islam and the Muslim Youth Movement have attempted to break Muslim dependence on insularity as the guarantor of Muslim identity. Seeing that this dependence has produced a general tenor of political conservatism and reticence, these organizations encourage Muslims to utilize and accept the fundamental ambiguity of their identity within South Africa as a positive instrument. Part of this thrust is necessitated by changing circumstances as South Africa "normalizes" itself within the international community.

In the Muslim community, the question on everyone's mind is what will happen under the ANC government. The changing situation affects conceptions of Islamic practice—many of the current theological disputes in the community seem to emanate directly from concerns expressed about this new order. What is clear is that the institutionalization of the historically localized autonomy of the Muslim community (the autonomy to govern the practice of Islam, its culture, and its institutions) will change. The question of what direction this change will take is engendering divisions in the apparent unity of the community.

Both COI and MYM believe that the ongoing viability of Islamic identity depends upon full participation in the struggle for a new South Africa. These two organizations basically differ only in COI's unequivocal commitment to the congress (ANC) movement, whereas the MYM believes it should refrain from explicit commitment to any political organization, even though today the majority of its black participants are members of the ANC. Otherwise, engagement with diverse communities, religious backgrounds, and discourses, rather than separateness, is seen by both organiztions to be the best means for ensuring the relevance of Islam within the national context. It can be argued that as a minority community, Muslims have little other choice. But what is intriguing about COI is that its participation in the United Democratic Front (a broad coalition of anti-apartheid organizations formerly allied with the ANC) did not simply entail a strategy of expediency—i.e., Muslims going with the flow to protect their conception of religious and community interests. Rather, an Islam is being articulated that not only justifies this involvement but provides the framework for a singular role in and contribution to the larger struggle. In other words, submergence to common struggle in order to protect religious difference is not the way COI participation in the UDF was viewed. Rather, the difference of Muslim identity was to emerge through the character of Muslim participation in the common struggle.

This emphasis reflects the fact that Muslims have shared the struggle to maintain everyday existence with colored Christians as well as the vast majority of black Africans. Until the Group Areas Acts of 1950, 1957, and 1966, which removed black and colored populations from the bulk of central Cape Town and relocated them to the flatland areas southeast of the city, Cape Town showed glimmers of a progressive, multiracial city. Even a small African middle class existed in parts of what is today Rondebosch—a residential area of cottages on tree-lined streets with parks all around.

District Six, a dense neighborhood rising from the harbor to the east of downtown, was the center of Muslim and colored life. Everybody knew everyone else. Tightly organized gang structures (e.g., the Globes, Killers) integrated coloreds of different religious and ethnic backgrounds into a generalized social-urban identity in the same way religious institutions integrated their respective communities. Intensely fought competition, characteristic of the patterns established by immigrants in American cities, was coupled with well-established networks of social support and basic community trust. District Six embodied the sense of autonomy and self-sufficiency that had been the vital compensation for the lack of access to political rights and real economic power.

When District Six was destroyed in 1966 during the reengineering of social space, coloreds were forcibly relocated to specially constructed government townships. Some of the original ones, such as Hanover Park, Mannenburg, and Retreat, were nothing more than glorified army barracks built on sand flats, cold and damp even in the summer months. Soon to follow were Bontheuwel, Athlone, Landsdowne, Primrose Park, Elsie's River, Grassy Park, Belhar, Bishop Lavis, and Mitchell's Plain. Rail lines, highways, and industrial zoning were all used to separate and ghettoize each individual township.

Colored and African townships were interspersed to preclude the development of large homogenous racial territorial blocs. The township scheme was used to stratify the colored population according to class as well, with the better-off and stably employed populations securing better housing in Rylands, Surrey Estate, Bellville, Strand, and Walmer Estate. Each township had two access points with a police station at each one in order to maintain surveillance.

In most townships, homes consist of simple cement block constructions with three rooms. As many as fifteen people are sheltered in each house; many live in small shacks that have been constructed in the back yards. Today there is an extreme shortage of housing stock for both black and colored populations throughout the country. Small quarters are overcrowded. Marriages are often delayed or face the strains of living in households where as many as four generations reside. Meanwhile, there are an estimated thirty-five thousand vacant residential quarters in Cape Town's white areas.[10]

The class division of the colored community reinforced conservative and protectionist trends in the Muslim community and facilitated the growth of the Tabliq Jaamat, a conservative Muslim international organization originating in India and Pakistan that emphasizes religious discipline and business acumen. The territorialization of Cape Town was rigidly enforced. Although people are by law now free to live anywhere, de facto segregation is the rule. Much time is spent commuting to factories, stores, and construction sites. Wages are substantially depressed, with an average factory worker in Cape Town bringing home a little over $200 a month. Elaborate networks of informal credit have been established, and Muslim women have formed mutual aid societies that link poor and wealthier Muslim communities. But for the most part, colored populations have internalized the physical segregation applied as the basis for their own attitudes in dealing with socioeconomic differences within the community.

For most of the past two decades, the young have assumed the primary burden of keeping some kind of political pressure alive. During the years prior to the state of emergency decrees, 1984 and 1985, Cape Town was the site of a sustained insurrection unlike anything that had existed since those of the early 1960s. Muslim youth engaged the police in armed combat, closed schools, organized widely, and cemented relationships with African youth. As elsewhere in South Africa, funerals of slain comrades became focal points of political dissent, often the only occasion when large groups of people were permitted to assemble.

Youth maintained attacks on township surveillance operations conducted by police in armored trucks. Commercial vehicles were attacked, buses stoned, train lines stalled. Roadblocks of burning tires were set up nightly in attempts to cut off police reinforcements. Student and youth congresses fought for the right to convert schools into contexts for political organizing. The state came down hard on these activities. The death of one young organizer, Ashley Kriel from Bontheuwel, shot by police in his aunt's house, particularly galvanized the colored community.[11]

In 1985, faced with increasing violence and unrest, the Muslim Judicial Council (MJC), the primary Muslim legislative body in Cape Town, called a prayer service on 16 October to protest against the harshness of police repression. The "Trojan Horse incident" had been especially embittering—three young children were shot and killed in Athlone by security forces that jumped out of a Coca-Cola truck to disperse a demonstration. The security forces then refused to release the bodies to the parents and placed severe restrictions on the conduct of the funeral. This turned out to be an especially sensitive issue to the Muslim community since it is the practice of Islam to bury the dead as soon as possible.

The subsequent prayer meeting was held at St. Athans Road Mosque in Athlone and was attended by over five thousand people, both Christians and Muslims. Moulana Farid Esack, one of the founders of COI, told the meeting, "My proudest moment as a Muslim was when I rushed up to three students who were being dragged into a police van to ask their names. The cops tried to stop me and when I persisted, the officer shouted, 'You Muslims, must watch out! We've had enough of you Moslems,' I felt *alhamdulillah*, the oppressors are recognizing the *ummah* of Muhammed (S.A.W.) as an element in their destruction."[12]

While the meeting was in progress, a police van provoked a crowd moving toward the mosque and a small skirmish ensued. A half hour later armored troop carriers approached the mosque from all directions, but the congregants had used their own cars and other barricades to cushion the mosque. Inside the mosque, people were taking the decision to march to the morgue where the children's bodies were being kept the following day. Aware that a large police contingent has amassed outside, participants were urged to go straight home without confrontation.

As the initial part of the crowd exited there was both tear gas and rifle fire. One unidentified man in the forecourtyard of the mosque pulled out a pistol and shot a policeman in the stomach. Police then fired openly at people in the mosque and lobbed tear gas inside.[13] One man, Abdul Friddie, was fatally wounded and three others seriously wounded. The siege continued past midnight, and was ended only after international pressure was placed on the state to withdraw.[14]

Thirty thousand people attended Friddie's funeral. Not since the murder of Imam Abdullah Haroon, a politically active Muslim killed by security police while in detention in 1969, had the Muslim community been so up in arms. Farid Esack addressed the *jenaza:* "Freedom does not lie in the hands of white liberals . . . freedom lies in my hands, and your hands—the hands of the people. Let them know that this system is responsible for all the indiscipline and destruction of human values. . . . Let them know that this *ummah* of Muhammed is only starting now. . . . We will only be able to lead a full Islamic life on the ash-heap of racial capitalism."[15]

The imposition of the state of emergency during this time further emphasized, for increasing numbers of Muslims, the sense that their ability to practice Islam was only possible if the struggle for a nonracial democracy was successful. Under the state of emergency, people could basically be detained for any reason. Many children were arrested, many as young as twelve and thirteen. Internal police review of the detention was not mandated prior to thirty days.[16] Any activity conceivably political was banned, and most political organizations were also banned. Ebraiham Rasool, a founding member of COI and treasurer of the UDF, was detained.

Political activity took a psychological toll on individuals and family life. Many young activists were forced into long periods of hiding. The accumulated stress of political activity and the requirements of political discipline often resulted in an attenuation of religious discipline—activists took refuge in the comfort of sexual intimacy, alcohol, and marijuana. Families, accustomed to being tight-knit, had to get used to children being out of contact for long periods of time. Some even left the country for guerrilla training with the ANC. Detention of children exerted the biggest psychological cost as families had to go through the arduous process of tracking down where the children were being kept, trying to get some access to them. In some instances children would simply disappear. The police would categorically state in such instances that those in question had left the country for "training;" it is presumed that some were simply killed by the security forces.[17]

In some Muslim households, wide schisms were opened between parents and children. Parents could not longer effect any control over their children's political activities. Employers often threatened parents with dismissal if the more publicly known of their children didn't cease their activities. Activists arrested on serious charges at fifteen, sixteen, or seventeen would often face delays in adjudication until their eighteenth birthday, when harsher sentences could be applied. Parents were often forced to witness their children being ushered into police helicopters for a "ride over the ocean."

Making hajj, the annual pilgrimage to Mecca, is an important part of a Muslim's life. It has taken on great importance for South African Muslims, who take the opportunity to spend several months in the holy city. Families save for years and accrue great status in the community by making the pilgrimage. For Muslims, the experience seems to be a concrete confirmation of an identity that exceeds that of a South African colored, pulling together disparate histories and the stark reality of social "confinement" into a more realized and fulfilled self-image. The surprising

Chapter Nine

aspect of the making of hajj is that it seems to introduce a conservative force into the Muslim community. Parents who might have been somewhat sympathetic to the anti-apartheid struggle return from hajj more critical of such political activity. Many feel that they worked hard to aspire to and obtain this new status and are content to stabilize themselves within it. They feel they have accomplished an internationalized identity that is able to symbolically exceed the particulars of their local situation. For many of the young, although religious values and identity are important, this identity is not enough.

In the poorer townships there has been a legacy of mutual assistance among Christians and Muslims. Survival has dictated that people cooperate and take care of one another. This sense of solidarity is a holdover of the District Six ethos. The demise of District Six has had a lasting effect on Muslim and colored consciousness. It is endlessly referred to by everyone who lived there. An entire corpus of stories detailing the physical and psychological demise of individuals wrenched from this vibrant community has been built up. The bulk of District Six remains a startlingly empty space aside the downtown section—the state was afraid to develop the area following the controversy over the forced removals. Taking a drive through the area with any older former resident will bring to life rich details and stories about notorious figures, liminal festivals, gang victories, nights filled with the singing of Christian hymns, saxophones from nightclubs, muezzins reciting the Quran during Ramadan, and the whir of all-night tailors at their sewing machines. A rich and multifaceted urban life has been decimated.

What remains in the austere ghettoes of the new townships is the sense of mutual help and solidarity among people of all backgrounds. The COI, in its emphasis on working with people of all religions, was simply foregrounding what had been a long-standing cultural practice. Never did this multireligiosity vitiate the integrity of Muslim identity. In every Muslim house, one immediately finds a picture of the Kaaba and a Quran—no matter how poor the family, no matter to what extent they adhere to Islamic strictures.

This sense of solidarity has become one of the few means of resistance to a state that has both explicitly and implicitly sought to stamp it out. The advent of a tricameral legislative system in 1986, when coloreds and Indians were given separate houses of parliament to govern their own affairs (i.e, housing, education, and employment), was an attempt to introduce levels of fission into the community, as well as to legitimate the facade of a progressive democracy. The colored community rejected this ploy as well as other policies that reaffirmed the viability of group identities. Despite the money the state poured into these communities in attempts to buy votes and cajole cooperation, only 15 percent of the population have voted in the two national elections held since the policy was implemented.[18]

THE SOCIAL IMPACT OF ISLAM IN SOUTH AFRICA

Years of oppression and state violence have made South Africa a violent society. Especially since the advent of the state of emergency, the level of local and random violence has been extraordinary—a problem which the official end of apartheid has done little to solve. Unemployment is rampant. Groups of "skollies," young men without anything to do, stand on corners in every township amassing frustration and bitterness. After sunset in many townships there is a wanton ritual of bloodletting— gangs patrolling territory, challenging for territory, resolving internal disputes, abducting young girls, coercing people to join gangs, and preying on those in the community who hold jobs or are known to have certain possessions.

Young people, ashamed of the way the society has "broken" their parents, having almost no access to recreational activities, and generally enraged at facing lives of utter meaninglessness, look to the gangs to provide opportunities for status, as well as a way to spend time outside the drab confines of overcrowded homes often torn apart by severe family conflicts engendered by poverty and the overburdening of women as breadwinners, caregivers, and household managers. One of the pastimes of gangs is the smoking of *dagga* (marijuana) with mandrax, a practice of drug-taking unique to South Africa.

In contrast to their crackdown on political activism, the police have barely intervened to curtail the level of gang activity and violence. In many ways gangs serve their interests: people are confined to their homes, and gang activity serves to justify increased levels of police presence in the townships. At times it is difficult to persuade people to attend meetings or social events in the evenings if they don't have cars because of concerns for safety. Gangs have frequently cooperated with police in going after members of political organizations and are used as informants in prison.

Parents have been known to implicitly encourage gang participation as a way of mitigating their own feelings of being overextended and unable to control what is going on at home. These homes suffer a high incidence of alcoholism, wife abuse, and incest. Embedded in a variety of social ills, households grow progressively more reclusive—especially Muslim households—in attempts to hide the problems from public view. As sociality grows more privatized, gang structures predominate as compensation for the lack of other available social and public domains.

Muslim organizations in Cape Town have made the renewal of a sense of sociality an integral goal of their work. Learning, propagation, reflection, and political activity must be balanced with opportunities for people to have fun, enjoy one another's company, and develop productive friendships and intimacies. The struggle is not only for political rights, but for the right to live a decent life, to be able to maintain a functional household and attain a measure of psychological well-being.

The nature of these issues reflects South Africa's peculiar position with one foot solidly in the First World and the other even more entrenched in the Third. Economic survival in the colored community is a struggle, but on terms that approach those of abject poverty in the West rather than in the more urbanized peasant economies of the rest of Africa. A basic Westernized infrastructure is in place. A visit to one of the hypermarkets—huge grocery stores the size of football fields stocked with every conceivable consumer item—is a strange experience. In line at the cash register can be found well-dressed English yuppies and barefoot mothers with swollen-bellied, barely dressed children in tow. For the colored community, access to education (however bad) and media have inculcated a strong sense of Western values and desires.

When poverty is coupled with extreme political and social oppression, a deadly mix ensues. Muslim organizations have attempted to intervene with a strong sense of purpose and a psychologically sophisticated effort to convey a new language that seeks to resolve the accumulated tensions inherent in the position of coloreds, that is, the ambiguity involved in their own consideration of themselves. The struggle thus is both political and psychological. As the COI states in a brochure, "It is in the sharing of our deepest selves that we come to know who we really are . . . because we need those who allow us to be as we are on our own." [19]

The particular theological contributions of the COI have emerged, then, within the very particular dynamics of colored life in Cape Town. This theology has been developed not only as the intellectual exercise of an enlightened Islamic attempt to produce a Muslim equivalent to Christian liberation theology, but as a means of addressing the substantial dilemmas faced by the Muslim community. A measure of its radicalism is the comparison to the kind of Islam that has existed for decades in South Africa, whose level of consciousness has not exceeded frequently precious doctrinal disputes between Deobandi and Barelvi sects—disputes that have their origin in India and basically relate to the degree of flexibility allowed in religious practice.

This is not to say that issues of substance have not existed. Whether to engage in relationships with Christians and other religious groups has become a major issue. Both COI and MYM have emphasized a willingness to work with other religious groups largely because there is no other choice if Muslim political participation in the liberation struggle is to have any impact. Equally importantly, however, this collaboration is an attempt to draw Muslims away from internalization of state-promoted obsessions with the preservation of cultural and ethnic identities. At times, the preoccupation of Muslims with their own collective "purity" borders on the fanaticism that white Afrikaaners exhibit in relationship to their own identity. By willingly working with other religious groups, Muslims resist the imposition of the state that has sought to preclude such collaborations. In fact, it was the willingness of Muslims to participate in broad-based political activities and reach out to the black African community that prompted white alarm over the potentially insidious role of Islam within the country.[20]

Yet, COI, MYM, and others insist on initiating collaborative work because it undermines the structure of their being minorities. Since Christians have tended to determine when there will be interreligious interaction and what the content of that interaction will be—the attitude of the dominator—Muslims symbolically undo this by taking the initiative. Additionally, Muslim-Christian collaborations have been facilitated by the nature of the apartheid system itself. As official church structures have historically supported various forms of white domination while propagating their "civilizing mission," a framework was created for the articulation of African nationalism with the African Christian church.

The enforcement of separate institutional structures fostered a climate for diverging theological developments. This divergence attenuated Muslim perceptions of Christianity as a univocal and monolithic force to be rigidly defended against. The nature of these relationships often took convoluted forms. The early development of Black Theology in the 1970s, with its initial emphasis on black separatism, was comforting to more militant Muslims who were able to see this move as homologous to their own interest in amplifying the difference of Islam from other religions. They were thus able to cooperate in a sort of marriage of convenience with black political elements rooted in this separatist stance. The work of Achmied Cassiem and Yusuf Patel with the Pan-

African Congress is particularly exemplary of this phenomenon. Cassiem is an imam in Cape Town who has spent much of the past fifteen years in prison for his uncompromising advocacy of Islamic revolution.

The increased political participation of Muslims in the anti-apartheid movement and the heightened visibility of Muslim missionary work in the black African community prompted increased white concern about Islam. The quadrennial General Synod of the Nededuitse Gereformeede Kerk (NGK, or Dutch Reformed Church), representing 40 percent of South African whites, passed a resolution in October 1986 denouncing Islam as a "false religion which poses a threat to Christianity in South Africa, Africa, and the contemporary world."[21] Muslim outrage over the resolution gained strong and unequivocal support from important Christian and Jewish anti-apartheid leaders. This amplified split in Christian thinking made it possible for select Christian-Muslim alliances to proceed, as the anger of Muslims did not result in general rejection of Christians.

At the center of the policy debate about Islam in the NGK was a report commissioned four years earlier and tabled at the synod—compiled by Professor Dione Crafford, Head of the Theology Faculty at the University of Pretoria. The report was primarily a fairly balanced reiteration of common sociological knowledge concerning the basic principles of Islam and its history in Africa. It closed with a conciliatory advocacy for better understanding and peaceful coexistence among groups, and, at the same time, a qualification that such harmony can "never mean that Christians sacrifice their mission to convert Muslims for Jesus Christ."[22]

Special attention was given to strengthening the independent black church—long viewed by the NGK as inauthentically Christian—as a bulwark against the spread of Islam: "The growth of the churches causes thousands of supporters of traditional religions to be drawn in and thus snatched away from possible influence of Islam."[23] But in all events, the report indicated, dialogue should be promoted. Such recommendations were not heeded by the synod, which instead followed the sentiments expressed by the chaplain-general of the South African police, Rev. Stoffel Colyn, that the church not cooperate with something that is a threat to it.

Shortly after the storm of controversy that ensued, the NGK called for reconciliation talks to deal with what it called a mere religious squabble. This provided an opportunity for progressive Muslim groups to use the issue to their political advantage: (1) it highlighted the extent to which questions of doctrine and theology serve implicit political agendas; (2) in rejecting proposed talks with the NGK, Muslim groups were able to experience a sense of unity, as progressives were provided with a context to reject dialogue in the interest of Muslim integrity and thus vitiate some of the negative reaction generated by their past involvement with Christians; and (3) it reaffirmed solidarity between Christians and Muslims in the liberation struggle, as Christians were compelled to be more specific in enumerating the uniquely Muslim contributions to the struggle and thus convey the message that Muslims were not conceived as participants to be subsumed under a Christian-dominated agenda.[24]

Although the majority of Muslims held fast to their intention not to deal with the NGK until the resolution was rescinded, a breakaway group of local imams in Cape Town, the Islamic Council of South Africa (ICSA), held talks with the NGK in February 1987. ICSA had everything to gain by a resolution that provided a theological basis for rooting out Muslim activists opposed to apartheid, even though ICSA took a strong stand against the resolution in these talks. The talks, which were widely construed as a means of curtailing Muslim activism, provoked more Muslims to join activist ranks. The connection between Islam and political activism was further solidified. The NGK resolution generated division within the NGK itself.

What is demonstrated here is the potential strength a minority has when it does not act like a minority, that is, when it acts as if it has the potential to be an agent of general social transformation and not simply the mediator of things done to it by a majority. If a minority is not simply to be obstructionist and is to provide itself opportunities for such general change, it must at times affirm its uniqueness through interweaving itself with other forces and groups.

Applying this notion to Sudan, the role of the minority SPLA in contributing to the stalemate in the civil war becomes clearer. They have played one aspect of a counter-minoritarian discourse very well—i.e., they act as if they can orchestrate a government for all of Sudan. But they have not yet evolved a means of interweaving themselves with other forces in the country, and thus they limit their power to deterring resolutions to the conflict.

A NEW ISLAMIC HERMENEUTIC

The formation of a new Islamic hermeneutic by COI has involved the pulling together of several disparate points and strands of reformist thinking that have existed for centuries. Below I delineate what I consider to be the key aspects of this hermeneutic.

1. A counter-discourse of Muslim activism has emerged from the process of individual activists taking on, one by one, the rationalizations used by Muslims to avoid political struggle. In speeches, writings, and discussions, COI activists have prioritized spelling out just what these rationalizations are, identifying the kernel of truth at the core of them, and then presenting a picture of how that truth could be manifested in different ways. Conversely, they have reframed minor considerations within larger, overarching rubrics of responsibility and obligation. For example, the duty to protect the interests of Muslims is affirmed as long as those interests have been acquired in an Islamic manner, and never if defending the good means using the evil.[25] This manner of engagement with Muslims allows COI to maintain its identity as part of the larger Muslim community; it has not sought a special, breakaway, or autonomous position that simply defines its own agenda. The organization does define an agenda, but does so by anticipating and actively dealing with those in the larger Muslim community who disagree with it. The intent of the organization is not simply to be oppositional, but to incorporate the doctrinal opposition as an aspect of its own agenda. To a large extent, what COI and MYM can undertake both theologically and politically depends on how they can use the typical objections concerning political activism.

For example, many Muslims point out that they enjoy religious freedom; they can practice religion according to its tenets. COI raised the questions: yes, that may be true, but can we worship, and isn't worship (*Ibat'allah*) a necessary aspect of religion? "And what is worship? It is more than praying prayers; it is making connections with the poor, and those connections inevitably lead to trouble with the government."[26] COI and MYM always make a wide range of voices a part of their own voices. In this way the organizations insist on maintaining themselves as "members of the family." This enables the organizations at times to act like mass movements even though they are far from being so.

2. In the South African movement, as in Islamic movements elsewhere, the affirmation of Islamic identity takes precedence over ethnic or national identity. Yet, the nature of Muslim identity is viewed in a way that means that Muslims cannot rest comfortably if someone else is suffering or being exploited, regardless of their background. As political activists, community organizers, or protesters, Muslims are operating as Muslims. They are not subsuming their Islam to any higher authority or objective. Regardless of whether activists hold high positions in the

ANC, COI affiliates view their participation there as a display of their Islamicity.

Surah ul Ma-un from the Quran is frequently cited to elaborate this position: "Have you the person who denies religion? He is the one who is rough to the orphan. And does not encourage the feeding of the poor. Curse upon those who make *salah* (prayer) and yet ignore the consequences of their *salah*. Who want to be seen. And yet prohibit acts of kindness." The implication of this Quranic surah is that the preservation of Muslim identity means little if the person inscribed in that identity does not act to implement its significance—to make it substantially real rather than simply affirming a sociological position or artifice.

At the same time, the fundamental arbitrariness of identity is also connoted. The predominance of Muslim identification is not abandoned, and thus COI members are forced to "stand" with others taking widely divergent positions while, at the same time, insisting upon calling themselves Muslim. When all is said and done, people can identify with that they will—only God can definitively judge whether authenticity has been achieved. This point is important because COI members have never said that others who don't share their point of view are not real Muslims. They may be pointedly critical of their behavior, but the criticism does not attack the validity of the other's self-identification. Rather, COI insists upon its own right to account for what it does as emanating from the central role Islam plays in its life. Despite theological codification, this is a maneuver that depends on the notion that all identity is in some way arbitrary.

3. The Prophet Muhammed is to be considered a political activist and theorist as well as the Messenger of God (in fact, the role of being the Messenger of God necessarily implies such activism). His leadership of the Muslim community is not to be viewed only as an inspirational example for personal demeanor but also as a source of tactical knowledge for contemporary political movements.

Here, the example of the Treaty of Hudaibiyyah is frequently invoked by COI:[27] The Prophet had decided to make the lesser pilgrimage (*umrah*) to Mecca from Medina, where Muslims had been accepted as a ruling exile community. In the war with the Meccans that had gone on for nearly six years, the month of *Dhul Qa'dah* (sacred to the Arabs) was expected to be free of hostilities. Still, the Meccans refused to let pilgrims enter. Negotiations were opened between the two sides, and a treaty was eventually concluded: All war would stop for ten years; there would be no pilgrimage this year, but one during the following year; all Meccans coming over to the Prophet's side would be allowed to return to their homes; there was no obligation for the Meccans, however, to reciprocate. There was much complaining in Muhammed's camp about the unequal nature of the treaty. Many worried that the Meccans had won an unnecessary victory. But the treaty, from a politically strategic point of view, ensured interaction among previously noninteracting peoples. In this interaction, new converts rallied around the Prophet, eventually providing him the superior political advantage.

The example of this treaty is used by COI to justify its willingness to negotiate with the current South African government. More importantly, it affirms the political strength to be gained by maintaining and nurturing interactions among diverse, even competitive, groups. Dangers of negative cultural diffusions, homogenization, and detrimental influences notwithstanding, the fluidity of interactions will only serve to sustain Islam.

For South African Muslims (mirroring Muslim communities in many other places), survival has often meant a kind of self-encapsulation and defensiveness that in the long run impedes their capacity to engage the larger world. The more withdrawn and self-protective a community becomes, the more it turns in on itself and sees the outside world as hostile and threatening to its existence. Subsequently, the community turns even further inward.[28]

Acknowledging the existence of profound international changes affecting the Muslim community, COI seeks to ensure that the community can make productive use of them. At times the community may have to accept changes and conditions that seem to put it at a disadvantage, but it is thought that the community will ultimately be enhanced by them if these conditions maximize the presence of Muslims and Islam in various sectors and walks of life.

4. In common practice, Muslims usually make *iman* (faith) the ultimate priority, and see it as the key to social and economic progress. COI, instead, thinks that such an emphasis is often simply an Islamicized reiteration of Western notions separating the spiritual from the material and is, therefore, not Islamic. Most movements of Islamic renewal have emphasized the strengthening of faith—if faith can be substantiated and dedication to the religion affirmed, then a wide range of social and political problems will be straightened out by Allah by virtue of this commitment.

COI emphatically believes that anti-system politics is the only vehicle for proving one's faith in today's world. There can be no neutrality in political matters; political engagement is a *fard kafiyah* (an obligatory act). Citing a *hadith* of the Prophet, COI states, "When anyone of you sees an evil being committed, he should use his hands to prevent it and if that is not possible then the tongue should be used, and if this is even impossible, then the heart. And this (the heart) represents the lowest level of faith" (Hadith Muslim).[29] *Iman* can only be strengthened in an ongoing conflict with what is not *iman*. To work only on one's faith outside a context of this conflict is to suggest that Allah is presently only a spectator in history.[30] As Farid Esack, former COI national coordinator, puts it:

> Our understanding of struggle differs from that of some other groups in the House of Islam. Some of them are committed to a comprehensive Islam but feel that a lot of thinking must go into all of this intellectually before they can get involved. They also feel the need to Islamicize their own lives and produce good Muslims who will not be swept away by un-Islamic behavior or ideas. Others again feel that they must stick to working on their faith and Allah will sort out the rest. The idea that patterns of Islamicization can be worked out before action is strange to the *sirah* [the Prophetic precedence]. They are worked out whilst one is involved.[31]

Crucial to this agenda of activism is the use of Islam as a vehicle for political training. If a framework of social relations is to be built out of concrete action, then that action must generate an Islamic vision. Islamicists in Sudan have also committed themselves to a concept of an Islamic society brought about by applied action. Many Sudanese are sophisticated activists, but there is little training in the movement about how to be an Islamic political activist. The ambiguities and uncertainties of this position have led to an overreliance on the need to impose Islamic law as a kind of shortcut recognition that people are moving in the right direction. COI believes that immediate action is necessary even though it is not clear exactly what is going on or being done. It accepts that mistakes will be made.

In the small cells of COI, i.e., the *halqat*, much effort goes into understanding clearly the individual motivations that people have for getting involved in the movement. Within the COI ethos, only self-aware activists have the capability of linking their activism to the realization of social transformations compatible with an Islamic ethos. Equipped with such self-awareness, there is less of a chance that the movement will be "hijacked" by expediency and self-interest, or degenerate into interminable power struggles consuming time and energy. There will be occasions when "awareness" is even more important than activity. "Sometimes we underestimate the importance in the changes in our attitudes, mentalities and values. This is expressed—not so much in the sense of doing things—as in a different way of being; a different way of looking at reality, especially the awareness of the self. It is self-awareness that enables us to discover who we are and allows us to discover the real reasons behind our involvement."[32]

This self-awareness is considered important because it keeps people focused on the causes of the oppression they are trying to change and on the relationship between the social conditions that have precipitated political involvement and the motivations of their behavior as activists. Unlike Islamicists in other countries who might try to form a new Islamic man and woman by forcing adherence to canonical law or legislation, the COI asserts a psychological unfolding of reflection in action coupled with a strong sense of fellowship. The objective may be the same, but the implications are radically different.

Most Muslims ascertain the necessity of collective responsibility. The COI sees the evolution of a substantialized experience of personal responsibility as necessary to the revitalization of Islam. Esack:

> We assume personal responsibility for our own lives. Most of us start off in the group with some idea that it will contribute to our growth. Personal responsibility actually means that we are going to be the main characters in that growth; but people should actually see their destiny in their own hands; that they come to a meeting with certain ideas of what they are going to put in instead of what they are going to get out of it. Another aspect of formation which is slightly more difficult is to work towards becoming a self-propelling individual, i.e. someone that does not have to be pushed into activity and critical awareness but who actually functions on his or her own.[33]

These arguments would seem, on the surface, to go against the importance of social harmony and the submergence of individual strengths in the collective good—values that have been traditionally viewed as important in Islam, especially in the Shafi tradition largely appropriated by South African Muslims. But the purpose of individual growth is to facilitate the evolution of a more productive society:

> In order to reform the earth [islah fil ard] members of a community have to be properly formed as individuals. Without properly formed individuals the human community will not be able to execute the message of universal brotherhood [ukhuwwa], active mutual good will [tawasi] and cooperation [ta'awun]. According to the

Quran, the individual is to be formed on the basis of *taqwa*. Literally, *taqwa* means to be on one's guard or alert.[34]

According to the COI, individual spiritual development cannot take place outside of involvement to ensure the development of all people.

5. To enjoin the good and to forbid the evil, the primary Quranic injunction, means searching out alliances with the good from other religions. COI and MYM have worked with Christians, Hindus, Jews, and traditionalists in the democratic struggle. Of all its activities, this aspect of COI's work seems to be the most troubling to many. To justify this position religiously, COI often points out the example of the *Hilful Fadul*—the noble alliance with polytheists that the Prophet Muhammed joined to help the weak and oppressed. Even though his participation occurred before his prophethood, he indicated years later that he would do it again.

If alliances based on mutual good were not made, this would indicate implicit tolerance of the bad people who share the Islamic faith (at least by designation). In other words, the forbidding of badness would be tempered by the consideration of common identity. The formal aspects of identity would take precedence over the content of identity. It is true that the Quran warns against cooperation with Christians, but it indicates that avoidance is necessary only when faith and adherence is in danger of being submerged by the pragmatic necessities of such a relationship. As COI states repeatedly, participation with Christians in the anti-apartheid movement was undertaken because Muslims are Muslims. A Muslim is "used" or manipulated only when a movement does not provide an enhanced space of autonomy to be a Muslim.

Each year COI evaluates its work in the ANC and its affiliations with Christians. Its decision to renew these alliances is based explicitly on their not compromising Islamic values for the sake of efficient political relationships, and COI is committed to withdrawing from these alliances if such compromises are made. Additionally, cooperation with Christians is needed so that distinctions made between Christians and Muslims will simply be distinctions of religious fact and nothing else. Such distinctions are not to be used as purveyors of hypocrisy. For example, Muslims will often not let blacks use their toilets because they are non-Muslim, but will let their white employers use them even though they are also non-Muslim.

Participation with Christians is also justified by COI as a means of ensuring that Muslim activists in so-called "progressive" structures have Muslims around to guide them and advocate for their Islamicity. "We have a task to reclaim Muslims who have fallen by the wayside and who have abandoned the comprehensive morality of Islam. We know that many are in struggle organizations and we pray to Allah that the COI's arrival on the scene is none too late to reclaim them. . . . As for un-involved Muslims who want to get involved, we want them to do so through an organization like ours where we can also care for each other and nurture our commitment to Islam even as we struggle alongside others."[35]

As Muslims, members of COI feel compelled to be witness bearers to the world around them and consider the realities of people from all walks of life. Invoking the Quranic injunction, "Whosoever does not judge by that which Allah has revealed, they are indeed the oppressor," they believe that they have a responsibility to go where people are, whether they are being detained, beaten, jailed, killed, stoned, ne-glected, or silenced.

Having worked with COI for several months in 1989, I found them to be a unique Muslim organization. Their active participation in a highly publicized and long-lasting political struggle makes them more than an interesting idiosyncrasy. Although they are by no means repre-sentative of any large-scale Muslim trend, their unique positioning at the crossroads of the First and Third Worlds renders their experience significant and potentially fruitful for Muslims everywhere despite the peculiarity of their status (which, in turn, has much to do with the pecu-liarity of South Africa within the larger world).

What was immediately and continually striking about COI was the degree of political sophistication among people who were mostly quite young. Even considering the fact that for many South Africans political education begins at a young age, the degree of discipline, conceptual clarity, efficiency, and reliability exuded by these young Muslims was impressive to me, as well as to their compatriots in other organizations. The focus on mutual nurturance, fellowship, and personal development enabled these Muslims to be much less psychologically battered and scarred by the vicissitudes of political activism—the constant meetings, mutual suspicions and paranoia, and the repression of former years.

As with most aspects of South Africa, there is a conflation of extremes in the movement; a profound sense of personal openness and intimacy coupled with despair and cynicism; vibrant determination and gnawing fatigue; enormous resources of resiliency and flexibility coupled with glaring defensiveness and inhibition.

In the context of Islam, the COI's incorporation of a variety of psychologism—the language of self-development and awareness, of personal growth—appears radical. In contrast to the Western postmodern focus on arbitrary identities, the inextricable complicity between social reality and simulation, and the irreconcilable divergence of sense from social necessity, this language seems somewhat odd and out of date. Perhaps this is the arrogant reflection of a jaded psychologist. The use of this psychological language may provide a sense of immediacy in a way that Sufism perhaps did in the past. It relocates Islamic sensibility from the doctrinaire to the personal, giving Islamic commitment a measure of direct vitality and urgency. In a country that has squelched opportunities for self-empowerment and development, such language may be a necessary compensation for years of enforced solemnity. Like similar trends in Christianity, the infusion of psychological discourse may be especially persuasive to the young who seek some sense of healing and integration in a rapidly changing and often alienating world.

In the attempt to mediate theological reflection and political activism with reliance upon the language of growth psychology, both theological and political understandings risk becoming confused. When individuals are trying to manage religious obligations and, at the same time, subsume individual needs to the exigencies of organizational politics, discourses that emphasize developing human relationships of substance can make individuals vulnerable to being manipulated by those who are skilled in using such language.

Of course this is true of any language. But the psychological terrain is especially dangerous since it concerns the means through which people regard themselves and their capacities. Interpersonal analysis can become a hidden means of self-aggrandizement, and decision making can become increasingly murky and drawn out.[36] How the growth of social relationships can be translated from a small group setting to viable Islamic institutions remains a highly problematic issue. In the history of reformist Islamic movements, the psychological saliency of new patterns of religious practice has tended to falter when attempts were made to organize mass movements around them.[37]

The interesting connection here is to the Sudanese psychology students who tended to form the liberal wing of the Islamic movement in Sudan. The psychology department at Khartoum University was the center for the conceptualization of new Islamic institutions and practices. But this work was framed by steady referencing to a strong sense of Sudanese Islamic tradition and a highly codified set of religious practices. Even within this rubric, the psychologization of Islamic practice was highly provisional and tentative.

In South Africa, people are operating in another kind of uncertainty. The determination to institute a democratic system of governance is the only thing that is clear—in a way homologous to the use of *Shariʿa* in Sudan as the sole instrument of clarity in the Islamicization process. In Sudan, *Shariʿa* was to form the basis for the development of an Islamic society—a work in progress. In South Africa, a new Islamic hermeneutic, supplemented in large measure by growth psychology, was to carry a historically tight-knit community into a new age without any really clear idea about where it was going, but knowing it had to take an active stance about going somewhere.

In Sudan, psychology was still primarily used as a way of understanding the impact of rigidities of culture and was not appropriated as a modus operandi of Islamic practice. At most, it was a way of opening up Islam onto a renewed sense of relevance for everyday matters still largely determined by tradition. Given a world where the locus of power includes the visible and invisible, the macro and the micro, the personal and the political, the very means of attempting to negotiate spaces of individual autonomy can easily become instruments for vitiating it.

The attempt of COI to make Islam an everyday psychological reality, with its concomitant focus on self-awareness and interpersonal growth, posits substantial possibilities for fostering Muslim engagement with the larger world, especially if it is done without Muslims feeling that they must compartmentalize the Islamic aspects of their identity. On the other hand, this process is potentially murky and confounding. It tends to detract from the highly visible significations of moral authority, social coherence, and continuity inherent in movements that establish reference to *Shariʿa* as an overarching value—where things are crystal clear, this or that, for everyone to see, know, and have access to; a kind of common sense. Additionally, it is difficult to see how these two positions can be brought together in any kind of functional balance. Perhaps they better serve the Muslim world as active polarities, introducing a potentially valuable measure of internal theological conflict and upheaval.

PROGRESSIVE THEOLOGY AND HARDBALL POLITICS

What tempers COI's tendency toward an excessive reliance on psychological discourse is its ability to play direct, hardball politics—something for which, as we have seen, the Islamicists in Sudan are criticized. Ironically, when I speak to liberal Muslims familiar with both Sudan and South Africa, progressive theological and political positions appear buttressed by the capacity to engage in political expediency in one context, while the political use of traditional modes of thinking tends to be met with accusations of hypocrisy in the other. There perhaps will never be any clearer determinant notion of what role and function this kind of politics should have within Islam. As can be expected, Muslims of different ideological persuasions evaluate this function differently.

COI has allied itself with the Muslim Judicial Council (MJC) on numerous occasions, securing important positions on several committees. The MJC is the legislative body that represents the majority of the ninety mosques in the Cape Town area. The body is made up of the imams who are chosen by each community. The MJC handles matrimonial matters, oversees the authorization of *hallal* foods (religiously permitted), supervises Islamic education, arbitrates mosque disputes, and, in general, is the voice of the Muslim community on religious and social matters. Despite the fact that progressive Muslims widely disparage the body, COI has made sure not to distance itself from it. In part, this is a move to accrue increased legitimacy to itself in the eyes of the Muslim community and to carry out its aim of bringing the community with it step by step in the formation of its own form of *tajdid* in South Africa.

"Unity" has been a significant trope for Muslims in South Africa ever since their arrival three centuries ago. Unity enabled Islam to survive the first century when religious practice had to be maintained in secret. Unity enabled Muslims to carve out a distinct position in the racialist restructuring of South African society. It is a trope that stirs great emotions. As South Africa and Muslims confront massive change, just what unity is to mean becomes subject to dispute and protracted conflict.

During 1989, a major controversy erupted in Cape Town's Muslim community over the timing of the celebration of *Eid al-Adha*, the feast of sacrifice that marks the end of the pilgrimage to Mecca. The controversy centered around whether the community should continue to follow Cape tradition, which relies on the local sighting of the *hilal* (the new crescent), or synchronize the celebration with Mecca, which would mean adherence to an astronomically determined date. The controversy precipitated a strange amalgamation of progressives and conservatives taking both sides of the question.

The initial crisis began in 1987 when Jamiat al-Ulama, a judicial group in Transvaal, declared *Eid al-Adha* a day later than Muslims in the Cape and Natal regions. The dispute subsequently affected Transvaal's calendar for the start of Ramadan (the month of fasting), making it a day later than in the rest of the country. The split between Transvaal and the rest of the country generated splits within Transvaal itself. The MJC, in conjunction with its counterparts in Transvaal and Natal, formed a national committee in an attempt to restore a unified date. In July 1988, sixty-nine imams at an MJC meeting unanimously resolved to "firmly strive for the celebration of both the day of *Wuquf* (the day when pilgrims meet on the plains of Arafat outside Mecca) and the day of *Eid al-Adha* in conformity with Mecca next year, *Insha'Allah* (God willing)."[38]

What the MJC was after was unity on the issue. However, the issue itself was used to accentuate divergent positions, undercurrents, and power struggles taking place in the community. The Islamic Council of South Africa and Majlis as-Shura, another breakaway organization representing fifteen mosques, supported coordination with Mecca (a reversal of the position they had taken a year earlier). ICSA head Shaykh Najar was intent upon embarrassing the current head of the MJC, Shaykh Nazeem, who had deposed him from the MJC chairmanship several years earlier. It was widely thought that ICSA was intent upon taking an obstructionist position as a continuation of its collaborationist role—it had been accused of sanctions-busting activities and collusion with the tricameral parliamentary system.

Conversely, many theological progressives in the Cape supported immediate coordination with Mecca, seeing it as a means for Muslims to come to terms with the complexities of modern sociopolitical developments and affirm the South African *umma* as an integral part of a larger Muslim community that places little importance on geographical or national distinctions. It was argued that since Muslims live in an increasingly internationalized arena, it was important for Muslim empowerment and coherency that Muslims throughout the world at least mark important religious days at the same time.[39]

As part of the MJC effort to get local mosques to change policy, a *fatwa* (a judicial decision) was elicited from the rector of al-Azhar University in Cairo, Shaykh Jad al-Haq Ali Jad al-Haq. The decision rendered encouraged Muslims to follow Mecca: "It is incumbent on all Muslims of South Africa and others to celebrate the blessed *Eid al-Adha* with all the *jujjaj* (pilgrims) in Makkah in spite of the different time factors as previously explained. . . . Just as it is permissible for them and others to accept the news on the day of Arafat through the broadcasting or other means of communication on condition that it emanate from a Muslim country."[40]

A translation of the *fatwa* appeared in the main Cape Town newspaper. However, a subsequent controversy was stirred over the translation itself. Usually the word "incumbent" in Arabic is *wajib*, but this word does not appear in the text. Rather the word *ala* is used (meaningless in itself) coupled with *qarinah*, which renders the clause as meaning "permissible." A second *fatwa* from Al-Azhar arrived in May 1989 indicating, "As to the fixing of the day of *Eidul Adha* and the fasting of *Wuquf* for Muslims who are not on *Haj*, whatever is applicable to the month of *Ramadan* is applicable here, i.e., those who do not accept the sighting of the moon from another country, their *Eid* will be determined as it is for *Eidul Fitr*" (i.e., through the local sighting of the moon).[41] Basically, Muslims could do as they wanted.

In June 1989 the MJC split on the issue and voted to continue the tradition of local sighting, stating that it had not succeeded in persuading all in its ranks to change. Therefore, it would have to strive for "absolute unity" and "greater theological clarity;" till then it would follow local convention.[42] Two weeks later, ICSA and Majlis as-Shura, as well as the MYM, reaffirmed their earlier decision to celebrate with Mecca. COI, although theologically inclined to dispense with the convention of the local sighting, rallied to support the MJC position (in fact, authoring the MJC justification for its decision).

The tension surrounding the issue increased as 13/14 July approached. Some mosques in the heavily working-class areas of Hanover Park, Mannenburg, and Mitchell's Plain formed vigilante groups to intimidate and harass key members of the MJC and their congregations. The dispute was widely publicized in the press, and the South African state took the opportunity to portray the Muslim community as widely divided and coming apart in ugly scenes of internecine violence.

Some theologians attempted to portray the crisis as actually a sign of increased sophistication on the part of Muslims. "There is nothing more crucial in understanding that every crisis is also a moment of reconstruction. Nothing is dismantled without putting something new in its place. This is entirely a new concept of crisis and power . . . it forces existing organizations to take new initiatives and examine their modus operandi and it also creates space for new ones . . . but it takes place at the cost of disrupting the status quo in Cape Town's Muslim community."[43]

Indeed, *Eid al-Adha*, typically a day of great joy and festivity, was marked with an overwhelming sense of depression and fatigue. Families were divided at a celebration that emphasizes family togetherness. Every Muslim in Cape Town had been forced to take a political decision over something that had for generations been devoid of politics. The issue was political, as Ebraiham Moosa, a theologian at the University of Cape Town, puts it, because "what we presently witness in the Western Cape is a contest for authority and power to interpret and manipulate the religious symbols of Islam in contemporary South Africa."[44] Competing concerns for unity and different levels and concepts of unity have produced a situation of disunity.

ISLAMIC FUTURES

It remains to be seen whether COI will be able to maintain and coordinate the expansive scope of its agenda. It does its best to anticipate and plan for an uncertain future. Young men are sent to Pakistan to be trained as imams so that a progressive *ulema* might be built. Family members and parents are included in many organizational activities to assuage potential conflicts or divisions. The organization is working with unions, who in many respects hold the key to the shape of a future South Africa. COI has never hesitated to go door to door, mosque to mosque, church to church, street to street.

Because the heart of the progressive organizations lies in the Cape region, the swelling numbers of black Muslim converts in the largely conservative, Indian-dominated Transvaal region largely remain unaddressed and hidden. The MYM has now largely refocused itself as a primarily black organization, trying to cut through the massive disparities in access to materials, opportunities, and knowledge that have tended to create an increasingly bitter division between black Muslims and the rest of the Muslim community. As long as black Muslims were content to play marginal roles and amplify their dependence on those "born to the faith," relations remained functional. But as the Indian community, in particular, tires of being viewed as a source of endless charity, and the black Muslims grow more bitter about paternalism and Muslim "apartheid," relations among ethnicities will prove to be the test of whether new Islamic movements in the country will continue to be relevant.

As black Africans assume state power and face the country's enormous needs for capable workers and the redistribution of resources, what role Muslims will play as Muslims remains up for grabs. Certainly the internal cohesiveness facilitated by both apartheid and the struggle against it will be subject to great strains and will have to find other forms. This is an inevitable process in a situation where Muslims, like Africans, will have political rights, yet still exist very much as a minority community.

Will black Africans in power feel more comfortable sharing it with coloreds who are Christian? Will the important positions assumed by both Muslim and Christian coloreds by virtue of their better access to education and economic opportunity carry over into a post-apartheid society? These and a host of other questions will be important in terms of where COI goes with its progressive Islam. The uncertainty and risks entailed perhaps "explain" why Islamic movements elsewhere, such as in Sudan, attempt to mitigate the vagueness of the future by attempting to apply the so-called clarity of the past. The question becomes whether dependence on this clarity precludes the ability of a social movement to transform and innovate.

As we have seen, both radical innovation and restoration are vulnerable to abduction by base political interests. The situation in Sudan might be vastly different if the kind of Islam purveyed by COI had taken root. The elimination of Mahmoud Muhammad Taha prevented that from happening. Too many young people in Sudan convinced themselves that the COI version of Islam could not exist and was not possible even as a conceptual instrument, let alone a political strategy.

What the South African situation demonstrates is that there are few political shortcuts; political transformations must be adamant and persistent. Sudanese students went along with many things that may not have otherwise been acceptable to them because they tended to believe in the power of such shortcuts. Nonetheless, given a society for which Islam has very clear and limited definitions, it is difficult to conceive of other ways Sudanese could have constituted a viable Islamic political practice. The problem in Sudan was not so much the advocacy of the Islamicization of society as it was the curtailing of the divergencies permitted within the definition of the process. One has to remember that in the 1985 election following the overthrow of Numayri, there were thirty different political parties all espousing rather vague and unrealistic platforms. *Shari'a* was the only clearly differentiating issue, carved out the only terrain on which a real choice could be made. The problem was that Islamicists too often forgot the dictate of Imam Shafi, one of the four major legal scholars of Islam's formal codification: "I am correct with the possibility of my opponent also being correct."

What COI seems tentatively able to do is to effect what Mazrui calls a convergence between "Islam from above and Islam from below"—a provisional reconciliation of Islamic religious authority and learning with the particular political and social realities faced by Muslims.[45] COI has been able to accomplish this partly because there may be nothing else to gain outside of the goal of national liberation. In Sudan, the stakes are state power and control of the machinery of policy making and resource distribution necessary to transform society. The political platform had to be simple and clear.

COI may be accepted because of the degree of oppression existing in the country; its theological hermeneutics are understandable (if not comprehensible) in circumstances of oppression. Islamic agendas were appropriated by political activists in Sudan in part to attenuate resistance to the socioeconomic and cultural restructuring they proposed once state power was attained. Their problem was that there was limited consensus in the movement about what that restructuring would look like, and that their pursuit of state power was not coupled sufficiently with grassroots education and mobilization. Therefore, Islamicists had to worry about the implications of a failed vision: If the Islamicists in Sudan had unilaterally controlled the state apparatus, how would an innovative Islamic agenda be judged; what would happen if the new practices, applications, and institutions failed to take root in a country nearly bankrupt and holding onto strong religious conventions? Would such a failure lead to a general questioning of the efficacy of Islam, or would Islam be turned to as a vehicle for increased cultural conservatism?

The attempt to go after state power has enormous risks for Islamic thought—any intentions of fostering widespread social transformations end up necessitating the use of political strategies that tend to undermine those very intentions. At the same time, not to go after something concrete (such as control of the state apparatus) also has risks for Islamic thought—ideals tend to dissipate into vagueness and a loss of authority. Other forces cohere to operate against them. The question must be asked: Is the new hermeneutic (as embodied by COI) simply an academic exercise, or does it really help to put more bread on the table or provide more people concrete freedom in living their lives? For too many people, help is sought from God in any way they can get it.

Many choices exist in constructing relationships between religious and political practice. Evaluating the efficacy, authenticity, and implications of each choice within a single context poses enormous complexities. What does seem clear is that the scope, significance, and viability of each choice is increased by the existence of a climate in which individuals are convinced that such choices do exist and feel that they have the opportunity to freely make them. In both countries, Islamicists have sought to gain hegemony over defining the nature of Islamic practice. Although politically pragmatic in the short run, this is a strategy that quickly declines in value as each movement is deprived of contrary positions that could remotivate the scope of its own parameters and thought.[46]

In the future, both movements will require a substantial dose of each other's present status quo; both movements can perhaps only be enhanced by heavily borrowing from each other's ideological, tactical, and theological positions. Each movement generates a wide range of reactions and produces realities that it cannot completely anticipate. The COI and MYM are bringing a lot of Muslims with them, but by virtue of this, they are prompting more conservative elements to find their own voice by doing everything possible to undermine the organizations. COI will need to make concerted efforts to convince most facets of the Muslim community that what it is doing it is doing for the advancement of Islam—an emphasis that has been effective in Sudan.

In Sudan, there are many in the Islamic movement who are waiting to see whether Islam is capable of doing anything other than applying canonical punishment or rooting out so-called enemies of the faith (i.e., of doing something other than doing something for the formal institutions of Islam). Will Islamic frameworks generate the motivation, capability, and strategic acuity needed to provide for people's basic needs? Given the complexity of Sudan and the degree of economic and urban degeneration there, new hermeneutics will have to be considered as at least a possibility, a matter of choice.

In a country in which there is no chance of significantly Islamicizing national politics, the COI and MYM can instead emphasize the use of Islam as a way of protecting and nurturing spiritual, psychological, political, and economic realities of substance in the unyielding desperation of African existence. Their long-term vision is to symbolically energize the political capacities of Muslims in various parts of Africa, and they fully expect these efforts to take diverse forms. Given the close ties that exist between COI and the ANC, there is a possibility that COI will eventually have some continent-wide impact: young Muslims in several African nations are growing increasingly frustrated with the political and economic marginalization fostered by traditional religious authorities. These youth tend to be suspicious of Arab-based efforts to organize their frustration into so-called revivalist movements yet are intent upon bringing their commitment to Islam into political life.

What is important here is that the possibility of Islamic thought and practice making significant social, cultural, political, and economic contributions be foregrounded over and differentiated from an emphasis on Islam's own self-aggrandizement. Where Muslims are a majority, the process of Islamicization frequently becomes inseparable from the process of advancing the political and economic interests of the religious class and its related institutions.

The Muslims I was "assigned" to work with in Khartoum frequently complained about how they were continually marginalized and used to convey an openness in the movement that didn't really exist. My purpose in getting actively involved in the South African movement was to see whether it might be possible for my Sudanese colleagues to maximize their impact by accepting their minority status, their marginalization.

In a shrinking and internationalized world in which political space in the West becomes more and more homogeneous and, at the same time, more differentiated from an African world growing poorer and poorer—a world dominated by structural readjustment policies in the formal sector and disengaged social and economic structures of enigmatic resiliency in the informal—minoritarian status is provocative simply because it is something to be seemingly avoided at all costs. But if one is inscribed within that status there is no need to necessarily internalize its apparent structural and psychological implications.

In the Third World, state power in most countries means less than it did at independence. People are making it and surviving because they have managed to free themselves from total incorporation into larger governmental and economic structures and instead employ a wide range of microtactical maneuvers and informal spaces to feed themselves and run their lives. They do this even though the scope of their autonomy may be substantially narrow.[47]

The crucial difference between COI and the Islamic movement in Sudan rests not so much in doctrinal divergences or hermeneutics, or in the fact that one is a mass-based political party and the other a small grassroots movement. Rather, the key difference is in psychological posture. COI is a minority movement for a minority population, yet it tends not to act like one. Instead, it integrates the political struggle into its agenda as a Muslim organization and does not subject its Islam to the dictates of any political organization. In most respects, the entirety of the democratic movement in South Africa is considered a Muslim movement because it is doing Muslim things and, for the most part, implementing a Muslim practice (albeit without officially bearing such a designation). Since the democratic movement is thus a "Muslim" movement, COI as "actual" Muslims are by default, if not by explicit definition, the actual "leaders" of the movement. COI members do not go around proclaiming this kind of arrogance, but it is a psychological construct that is present to keep the organization from feeling overwhelmed by any doubts about what it is doing—the doubts of a minority. At times, COI leaders have been accused of arrogance and the usurping of leadership roles, but this has been countered by their discipline, reliability, and tactical skill.

On the other hand, the Islamicists in Khartoum are a majority that tend at times to act like a minority. They attempt to integrate everything into an overarching rubric because they fear that if they don't, they might disappear. The movement is unable to rest comfortably with antithetical positions or countervailing discourses; it incessantly finds itself protecting its positions rather than using its position to do something that exceeds the status quo. It sees threats everywhere that must be defended against. At times those most confident about Islam being the way of the future act as if they have no confidence in Islam at all—as if they feel that it is about to be attacked or debilitated at any moment.

Trends toward cultural homogenization in Sudan may in the end be complicit with the thrust of Westernization. That is, by defending themselves so vigorously against Western influence, the Islamicists may be reproducing the cultural and cognitive structures of the West, albeit in different guise. It is, after all, the West that most powerfully advocates notions of standardization—in definitions of intelligence, processes of learning, and economic structure. It is in the West that everything must be known, coded, taken apart, reproduced, exhibited, relayed, magnified, distributed, analyzed, blown up, assessed, simulated. Despite the West's plurality of backgrounds and its celebration of diversity as a cultural pastime, it homogenizes cultural difference in terms of the need for optimal behavior and the pragmatics entailed in being successful in career and family. It is the West that parades out social workers, counselors, psychologists, and self-help groups in an attempt to regulate and normalize social behavior.

As Ali Mazrui indicated in an address to Muslims in New York several years ago, Islamic movements may be the only viable counter-discourse to Western homogenizing trends. Therefore, Muslims must be careful not to replicate Western behavior in this regard.[48] If Islam has always ascertained the integral linkage of the personal, religious, and political; if it adheres to a vision of an essential entity with all aspects of life; and if it begins with a strong sense of public responsibility (as it did in Sudan), then the movements that purvey Islam have no choice but to take theological and political risks. In other words, they must feel confident that diverging hermeneutics and applications of principle will not destroy the essence of Islamic faith or sensibility. The movement must not simply be the West in Islamic garb.

There are moments in South Africa when one does not know who is an Islamicist and who is not—there is nothing about their speech, dress, demeanor, or even public thinking that would give them away. In Sudan, the identification of Islamicism depends on just these very aspects. Neither ambiguity or clarity, overcoding or undercoding of identity, is clearly better or worse in the abstract. But the ability to switch back and forth while maintaining a strong sense of who one is and what one is working for is the real accomplishment.

In an important ethnography conducted by Gerd Bauman in a Southern Nuba Miri village, the significance of micropolitical postures is evident in terms of the future viability of Sudan.[49] What from an urban standpoint appears to be the economic integration of the village into a developing national economy and labor market is experienced by the villagers as their own active integration of rural development and urban economic opportunities into communities that remain essentially self-sufficient (either by subsistence farming or work in the agricultural development schemes). Their process of being integrated into Muslim Northern Sudan is reexperienced as the local integration of a more satisfying and respectable doctrine *with* the maintenance of a natural order. Divergent positions don't fight to the death, but rather find some larger rubric that allows them to exist side by side without diminishing the integrity or viability of either position. This process is what Bauman calls "redintegration" (the restoration of a sense of wholeness and unity to superficially fragmented and marginalized social spaces).

This concept does not connote an opposite to processes of national integration, nor a negation of it, since the "locally integrative experiences are already an amalgamation of autochthonous traditions with originally urban ideas."[50] Rather, it is a process in which national integration proceeds in a way that can be found or acted upon by localities as a means to reconstitute their own traditions and sense of efficacy. In the village studied, Islam exists side by side with certain Nuba traditions of dancing and music without either being applied as an explicit or implicit criticism or attack upon the other. Each has been lived in such a way that neither traditional practice nor Islamic practice obviates the other. This is not synthesis, but a functional parallelism.

In the West, distinct groups, tendencies, and worldviews increasingly assume that each has something to do with the other; that each has to take the other into consideration; that somehow what the other is doing is a necessarily relevant factor to be reckoned with. It is in this incessant act of comparison that homogenization takes place. If Islam is to be about everything that exists, then this comprehensiveness may find its viable contemporary form in the ability of Islam to be taken seriously, referred to, and aspired to in all situations—even those apparently inimical to it. In other words, Islam's comprehensiveness may find its very valorization in a situation of coexistence with the non-Islamic—in the fact that it can operate and thrive in a contiguous position with all that it is not, and yet still be itself.

Internationally, Islam will have to live side by side with non-Muslims, and will have to interpret their behaviors in ways that don't construe everything they do as having direct relevance to itself. Whether Muslims control state governments will mean little—this is something acknowledged even by Islamicists themselves in their concept of a larger *umma* that transcends national boundaries. No matter how valuable it is for Muslims to govern themselves by God's law, if a particular implementation of this law destroys an opportunity to develop new ways for Muslims and non-Muslims to coexist in mutually productive ways, or an opportunity to bring more people to Islam, then the loss is for Muslims everywhere. In such a situation, Muslims are thinking only about themselves rather than assuming their religious responsibility to oversee all of God's creation.

Sudan has been encumbered by its unique position at the crossroads of the African and Arab worlds. Although full of intellectually interesting possibilities in terms of cross-cultural studies and liberal notions of pluralism, its nearly four decades of independence have been exceedingly difficult. In response to these difficulties, Sudan has sought to normalize its inclusion within the Arab world by taking the initiative to realize long-sought Islamic values in action. More importantly, it foresaw an opportunity to reaffirm its basic Islamic commitment by setting an example for all Muslims of how Islam could prosper. It would show the relevance of Islam in a world where increasingly no one belongs anywhere, where differences in national boundaries lose significance— a world rapidly being reconfigured to simultaneously include and exclude everyone.

It is perhaps asking too much of Sudan to do what no other country has effectively done—create a truly multiracial and multireligious society. It faces tasks that few nations face. But perhaps it can at least begin to operate with more autonomy if it accepts some of the impossibility of the task and the intractability of the situation. Perhaps it will find a way to use marginality and impossibility to its advantage. Nothing could renew or extend Islam more.

Notes

Chapter One

1. D. Zahan, *The Religion, Spirituality and Thought of Traditional Africa* (Chicago: University of Chicago Press, 1979), 154.

2. Ibid., 48.

3. H. H. Bhabha, "Signs Taken for Wonders: Questions of Ambivalence and Authority under a Tree outside Dehli, May 1817," *Critical Inquiry* 12, 1 (1985): 144–165.

4. See H. Bucher, *Spirits and Power: An Analysis of Shona Cosmology* (Cape Town: Oxford University Press, 1980); W. MacGaffey, "African Ideology and Belief," *African Studies Review* 24, 2/3 (1981); J. Comaroff, *Body of Power, Spirit of Resistance: The Culture and History of a South African People* (Chicago: University of Chicago Press, 1985); K. Fields, *Revival and Rebellion in Colonial Central Africa* (Princeton, N.J.: Princeton University Press, 1985); T. O. Ranger, "The Mwari Cult and Peasant Experience in Southern Rhodesia," in W. V. Binsbergen and M. Schoffeleers, eds., *Theoretical Explorations in African Religion and Society in Central Africa* (Chicago: University of Chicago Press, 1986).

5. T. O. Ranger, "Religious Movements and Politics in Sub-Saharan Africa," *African Studies Review* 29, 2 (1986): 1–69.

6. J. Fernandez, "African Religious Movements," *Annual Review of Anthropology* (1978): 228–29.

7. E. Zuesse, *Ritual Cosmos: The Sanctification of Life in African Religions* (Athens: Ohio University Press, 1976).

8. R. Pelton, *The Trickster in West Africa: A Study of Mythic Irony and Sacred Delight* (Berkeley: University of California Press, 1980).

9. A. Cohen, *Two Dimensional Man: An Essay on the Anthropology of Power and Symbolism in Complex Societies* (Berkeley: University of California Press, 1974).

10. See C. Geertz, "Religion as a Cultural System," in M. Banton, ed., *Anthropological Approaches to the Study of Religion* (London: Tavistock, 1966), 1–39; C. Geertz, *The Interpretation of Cultures* (New York: Basic Books, 1973); B. Wilson, *The Contemporary Transformation of Religion* (London: Oxford University Press, 1976); B. Wilson, *Religion in a Sociological Perspective* (London: Oxford University Press, 1982).

11. See particularly D. Lam, *Guns and Rain: Guerillas and Spirit Mediums in Zimbabwe* (Berkeley and Los Angeles: University of California Press, 1985); W. Beinhardt and C. Bundy, *Hidden Struggles: Rural Politics and Popular Consciousness in South Africa* (London:

University of California Press, 1986); D. D. Laitin, *Hegemony and Culture: Politics and Religious Change among the Yoruba* (Chicago: University of Chicago Press, 1988).

12. See Laitin, *Hegemony and Culture,* for discussion of the elaboration of Yoruba ethnicity and ancestral authority as a means for submerging potential Christian-Muslim political segmentation in the context of the multireligious and multiethnic Nigerian state.

13. Comaroff, *Body of Power, Spirit of Resistance.*

14. M. G. Schatzberg, *The Dialectics of Oppression in Zaire* (Bloomington and Indianapolis: Indiana University Press, 1988).

15. A. Hussein, "Islamic Reawakening in the Twentieth Century: An Analysis and Selective Review of the Literature," *Third World Quarterly* 10, 2 (1988): 1005–23.

16. See J. Waardenburg, "Official and Popular Religion in Islam," *Social Compass* 25, 3/4 (1978): 314–41; I. M. Lewis, "The Past and the Present in Islam: The Case of African "Survivals," *Temenos* 19 (1983): 55–67; C. C. Stewart, "Introduction: Popular Islam in Twentieth Century Africa," *Africa* 55, 4 (1985): 363–69. Stewart posits popular Islam as movements falling under one of the following rubrics: (1) anti-establishment, political movements in Muslim societies that are articulated in a Muslim mode; (2) cultural expressions of Islamic identity; (3) the rather more elusive, dynamic process wherein notions of "popular" and "establishment" may change place over time, and/or a symbiotic relationship in which "popular" and "establishment" practice serve to reinforce each other (363).

17. S. Zubaida, "The Ideological Conditions for Khomeni's Doctrine of Government," *Economy and Society* 1, 2 (1982): 138–73.

18. M. C. Hudson, "Islam and Political Development," in J. L. Esposito, ed., *Islam and Development: Religion and Sociopolitical Change* (Syracuse, N.Y.: Syracuse University Press, 1980).

19. H. Roberts, "Radical Islam and the Dilemma of Algerian Nationalism: The Embattled Arians of Algiers," *Third World Quarterly* 10, 2 (1988): 559.

20. P. M. Lubeck, *Islam and Urban Labor in Northern Nigeria: The Making of a Muslim Working Class* (Cambridge, New York: Cambridge University Press, 1986); E. Burke III and P. M. Lubeck, "Explaining Social Movements in Two Oil Exporting States: Two Divergent Outcomes in Nigeria and Iran," *Contemporary Studies in Society and History* 29, 4 (1987): 643–65.

21. P. J. Vatikiotis, "Islamic Resurgence: A Critical View," in A. J. Cudsi and A. H. Dessouki, eds., *Islam and Power* (London: Croom Helm, 1981).

22. See references to the Iranian revolution in S. A. Arjomand, "The Rule of God in Iran," *Social Compass* 36, 4 (1989): 539–48.

23. M. de Certeau, *The Practice of Everyday Life* (Berkeley and Los Angeles: University of California Press, 1984).

24. See A. G. Frank, *On Capitalist Underdevelopment* (New York: Oxford University Press, 1975); B. S. Turner, "Orientalism, Islam and Capitalism," *Social Compass* 25, 3/4 (1978): 371–84; E. R. Wolf, *Europe and a People Without History* (Berkeley and Los Angeles: University of California Press, 1982).

25. See particularly V. Y. Mudimbe, *The Invention of Africa: Gnosis, Philosophy, and the Order of Knowledge* (Bloomington and Indianapolis: Indiana University Press, 1988).

26. Weber proferred dissonant attitudes regarding Western and Third World religions. He would often see the constitution of religious edifices in the West as motivated by the acknowledgement of the position of God and the need to adjust to this position, whereas Third World religions continued as a means of coping with material suffering. See *The Sociology of Religion* (Boston: Beacon Press, 1963), and R. Robertson, "Weber, Religion, and Modern Sociology," in *Meaning and Change: Explorations in the Concept of Sociology in Modern Societies* (New York: New York University Press, 1978), 50–102. As far as Islam is concerned, Weber accorded too much significance to the transformation of asceticism into a warlike, expansionist culture—seeing this as the key impediment to capitalist development in the Muslim world. However, his argument that the persistence of the prebendal state, which limited access to state-owned land to those providing services to the state (a practice that impeded economic and political autonomy), inhibited speculative capital continues to be a useful description of the historic structural precursors of many African states. See B. S. Turner, *Weber and Islam* (London and Boston: Routledge and Kegan Paul, 1974).

27. D. Hervier-Leger, "Tradition, Innovation, and Modernity," *Social Compass* 36, 1 (1989): 71–81.

28. J. F. Bayart, "The Historicity of African Societies," *Journal of International Relations* 46, 1 (1992): 73.

29. P. Ekeh, "Development Theory and the African Predicament," *African Development* 11, 4 (1986): 1–40.

30. A. Mbembe, "Provisional Notes on the Postcolony," *Africa* 62, 1 (1992): 3–37.

31. S. Berry, "Social Institutions and Access to Resources," *Africa* 59, 1 (1988): 40–55.

32. J. Paden, ed., *Values, Identities, and National Integration: Empirical Research in Africa* (Evanston, Ill.: Northwestern University Press, 1980).

33. N. Kofele-Kale, "The Impact of Environment on Ethnic Group Values in Cameroon and National Political Culture," in Paden, *Values, Identities, and National Integration;* E. Nwabuzor, "Ethnic Propensities for Collaboration in Cameroon, ibid.

34. N. Chazan, "State and Society in Africa: Images and Challenges," in D. Rothchild and N. Chazan, eds., *The Precarious Balance: State and Society in Africa* (Boulder: Westview Press, 1988), 325–41.

35. J. F. Bayart, "Populist Political Action, Historical Understanding, and Political Analysis in Africa," in B. Jewsiewicki and D. Newbury, eds., *African Historiographies* (Beverley Hills, Calif.: Sage, 1986), 261–68; J. W. Fernandez, "Edification by Puzzlement," in I. Karp and C. S. Bird, eds., *African Systems of Thought* (Bloomington: Indiana University Press, 1980); P. Padervand, *Listening to Africa: Developing Africa from the Grassroots* (New York: Praeger, 1989).

36. C. F. Fisiy and P. Geschiere, "Sorcery, Witchcraft and Accumulation: Regional Variations in South and West Cameroon," *Critique of Anthropology* 11, 3 (1991):

251–78; P. Geschiere, "Sorcery and the State: Popular Modes of Action Among the Maka of Southeastern Cameroon," *Critique of Anthropology* 8, 1 (1987): 35–65.

37. J. Friedman, "Narcissism, Roots and Postmodernity: The Constitutions of Selfhood and the Global Crisis," in S. Lash and J. Friedman, eds., *Modernity and Identity* (Oxford and Cambridge, Mass.: Basil Blackwell, 1992); Mudimbe, *The Invention of Africa.*

38. F. Eboussi Boulaga, *Christianity without Fetishes* (New York: Orbis, 1984); J. B. Chipenda, "Theological Options in Africa Today," in K. Appiah-Kulli and S. Tori, eds., *African Theology en Route* (New York: Orbis, 1977); A. Mbembe, *Afriques indociles, Christianisme, pouvoir et état en société postcoloniale* (Paris: Editions Karthala, 1988).

39. V. Azarya and N. Chazan, "Disengagement from the State in Africa: Reflections on the Experience of Ghana and Guinea," *Contemporary Studies in Society and History* 29, 1 (1987): 106–31; Crawford Young, "Patterns of Social Conflict: State, Class, and Ethnicity," *Daedalus* 111, 2 (1982): 71–98; A. Gupta and J. Ferguson, "Beyond Culture: Space, Identity, and the Politics of Difference," *Cultural Anthropology* 7, 1 (1992): 6–24; O. J. Ingue, "L'officiel, le parallèle et le clandestin," *Politique Africaine* 9 (1983): 32–45; T. Bierschenk, "Development Projects as Arenas of Negotiation for Strategic Groups: A Case Study from Benin," *Sociologia Ruralis* 28, 2/3 (1988): 146–60.

40. T. M. Callaghy, "The State as Lame Leviathan: The Patrimonial Authoritarian State in Africa," in Z. Ergas, ed., *The African State in Transition* (Houndmills, Basingstoke, Hampshire: Macmillan, 1987); R. Lemarchand, "The Dynamics of Factionalism in Contemporary Africa," ibid.; R. Lemarchand, "African Transitions to Democracy: An Interim (and mostly pessimistic) Asssessment," *African Insight* 22, 3 (1992): 178–85; M. Mamdani, "Contradictory Class Perspectives on the Question of Democracy," in P. Nyong'o, ed., *Popular Struggles for Democracy in Africa* (London: Zed, 1987).

41. T. M. Shaw, "Reformism, Revisionism, and Radicalism in African Political Economy During the 1990s," *Journal of Modern African Studies* 29, 2 (1991): 191–212.

42. C. Meillassoux, "Development and Population Growth," *Southern Africa* 5, 1 (1991): 30–37; J. Guyer, ed., *Feeding African Cities* (Indianapolis: Indiana University Press, 1987); S. Strichter and J. L. Papart, eds., *Patriarchy and Class: African Women in the Home and the Workforce* (Boulder: Westview Press, 1988).

43. Gupta and Ferguson, "Beyond Culture"; see also F. Cooper, "Urban Space, Industrial Time and Wage Labour in Africa," in F. Cooper, ed., *Struggles for the City: Migrant Labour, Capital and the State in Urban Africa* (Beverley Hills, Calif.: Sage, 1983).

44. J. L. Roitman, "The Politics of Informal Markets in Sub-Saharan Africa," *Journal of Modern African Studies* 28, 4 (1990): 675.

45. A. Melucci, *Nomads of the Present: Social Movements on Individual Needs in Contemporary Society* (London: Hutchinson Radius, 1989).

Chapter Two

1. A. El-Affendi, "Studying My Movement: Social Science Without Cynicism," *International Journal of Middle East Studies* 23, 1 (1991): 87.

2. M. Ottaway, "Post-Numeiri Sudan: One Year On," *Third World Quarterly* 9, 3 (1987): 891–905.

3. I. A. Rahman, "Urgent and Social Duty," *Sudanow* 10, 6 (1985): 17.

4. J. Derrick, "Topping Up an Empty Basket," *African Events* 2, 1 (1986): 34–36.

5. *World Bank Annual Report* (1983).

6. A. A. Gadir Ali, "The Sorcerer's Apprentice," *African Events* 2, 1 (1986): 27–30.

7. S. Umbadda and E. F. Din, "IMF Stabilization Policies: The Experience of Sudan 1978–1982," in Ali Abdel Gadir Ali, ed., *The Sudan Economy in Disarray* (London: Ithaca, 1985).

8. Derrick, "Topping Up an Empty Basket."

9. Gadir Ali, "The Sorcerer's Apprentice."

10. Derrick, "Topping Up an Empty Basket."

11. V. Bernal, "Coercion and Incentives in African Agriculture: Insights from the Sudanese Experience," *African Studies Review* 31, 2 (1988): 89–108.

12. A. R. Al Rayah Mahmoud, "The Machinery of Economic Management," in M. Abd-al-Rahim, et al., eds., *Sudan since Independence: Studies in Political Development since 1956* (Aldershot: Gower, 1987).

13. K. El Wathig, *Corruption as a "Fifth" Factor of Production in Sudan* (Uppsala: Institute of African Studies, 1985).

14. M. al Assam, "Bureaucracy and Development in the Sudan," *Journal of Asian and African Studies* 24, 1/2 (1989): 28–48.

15. Interview with Murtada Hasan," *Al-Dustr*, 13 July 1987, 36–37.

16. C. Gurdon, *Sudan at the Crossroads* (Cambridgeshire: Middle East and North African Studies Press, 1984).

17. "Interview with D. Bedawi Babkr 'Uthman, Director of Rural Development, Faisal Islamic Bank," *Joint Publications Research Service-Near East*/North Africa 806 (1988): 2. Cited hereafter as JPRS-NEA.

18. E. H. Bilal Omer, *The Donagla Traders of Northern Sudan: Rural Capitalism and Agricultural Development* (London: Ithaca, 1985).

19. "Interview with D. Bedawi Babkr, 'Uthman," 22.

20. Omer, *The Donagla Traders.*

21. Ibid.

22. *Indian Ocean Newsletter*, 25 May 1991, 8.

23. *Al-Midan*, 26 May 1989, 6.

Chapter Three

1. Figure obtained by the Sudan Red Crescent Society in Khartoum and confirmed by staff at USAID.

2. *John Garang Speaks* (London: Kegan Paul International, 1987).

3. "Interview with John Garang," *Sudan Times*, 3 August 1988, 2; "The National Address of John Garang of 14 August 1989," *Foreign Broadcast Information Service: Daily Report*, Near East and South Asia (18 August 1989), 17–21. Cited hereafter as *fbis*.

4. *Africa Research Bulletin/Political Series* 30, 1 (1993).

5. Based on the investigations of Abu Gassim Goor Hamid, correspondent for *Al-Wan.*

6. *Africa Confidential* 29, 24 (1988): 6.

7. *JPRS-NEA* 051 (1988): 5–7.

8. M. O. Bashir, *The Southern Sudan: From Conflict to Peace* (London: C. Hurst, 1975).

9. D. Wai, *The Southern Sudan: The Problem of National Integration* (London: Frank Cass, 1973).

10. J. Markakis, *National and Class Conflict in the Horn of Africa* (Cambridge and New York: Cambridge University Press, 1987).

11. Ibid.

12. M. O. Bashir, *The Southern Sudan: Background to the Conflict* (London: C. Hurst, 1968); L. P. Sanderson and N. Sanderson, *Education, Religion and Politics in Southern Sudan 1899–1964* (London: Ithaca, 1981).

13. Wai, *The Southern Sudan;* Markakis, *National and Class Conflict.*

14. *The Vigilant* (Khartoum), 4 October 1965.

15. R. O. Collins, "Bastion Against Islam: The Upper Nile in the Twentieth Century," in G. R. Warburg and U. M. Kupferschmidt, eds., *Islam, Nationalism and Radicalism in Egypt and the Sudan* (New York: Praeger, 1983).

16. R. O. Collins, *Shadows in the Grass: Britain in Southern Sudan 1918–1956* (New Haven: Yale University Press, 1983).

17. M. K. Nhial Arou, "Devolution and the Southern Problem in Sudan," in *Post-Independence Sudan* (Center for African Studies, University of Edinburgh, 1980), 114–42.

18. P. S. Magga, *The Addis Ababa Agreement* (London: Khartoum University Press, 1977); A. B. El Obeid, *The Political Consequences of the Addis Ababa Agreement* (Stockholm: Liber, 1980); P. Bechtold, *Politics in the Sudan: Parliamentary Rule in an Emerging African Nation* (New York: Praeger, 1976).

19. M. B. Hamid, "Confrontation and Reconciliation within an African Context," *Third World Quarterly* 5, 2 (1983): 320–29.

20. R. H. Ahmed, "Regionalism, Ethnic and Sociocultural Pluralism: The Case of Southern Sudan," in M. O. Beshir, ed., *The Southern Sudan: Regionalism and Religion* (Khartoum: Khartoum University Press, 1984).

21. A. M. Lesch, "Confrontation in the Southern Sudan," *Middle East Journal* 40, 3 (1986): 410–28.

22. "Interview with Sadiq al-Mahdi," *JPRS–NEA* 039 (1988): 24.

23. Gurdon, *Sudan at the Crossroads.*

24. For much of this section of the NIF I am indebted to A. El-Affendi, *Turabi's Revolution: Islam and Power in the Sudan* (London: Grey Seal, 1991)

25. *John Garang Speaks.*

26. Gurdon, *Sudan at the Crossroads.*

27. Ibid.

28. Ibid.

29. *African Confidential* 26, 9 (1985): 3.

30. M. K. Ndur and E. Hooper, "The Battle for Juba," *New African* 228 (1986): 18.

31. *Africa Confidential* 27, 10 (1986): 5

32. Ibid., 4.

33. "Interview with Taysir Muhammad Ahmad 'Ali," *JPRS-NEA* 040 (1987): 21–30.

34. *JPRS-NEA* 053 (1989): 38.

35. J. S. Migdal, *Strong Societies and Weak States: State-Society Relations and State Capabilities in the Third World* (Princeton, N.J.: Princeton University Press, 1988).

36. *JPRS-NEA* 040, (1987): 52–54.

37. *Africa Confidential* 29, 18 (1988): 3–4.

38. *Le Monde Diplomatique* 24 December 1988, 4.

39. *Africa Confidential* 29, 24 (1988): 7

40. *Africa Research Bulletin* 26, 2 (1989): 9193.

41. A. El-Affendi, "In the Heat of the Storm," *African Events* 5, 4 (1989): 24–26.

42. *Africa Confidential* 30, 6 (1989): 4.

43. *Africa Confidential* 30, 14 (1989): 5.

44. *FBIS* 105 (1989): 8.

45. *FBIS* 116 (1989): 12.

46. *JPRS-NEA* 039 (1989): 43.

47. *FBIS* 122, (1989): 20.

48. Ibid.

49. *FBIS* 123 (1989): 8; *FBIS* 124 (1989): 13; *FBIS* 126 (1989): 7

50. *Africa Research Bulletin* 26, 7 (1989): 9352–55.

51. *Africa Confidential* 30, 15 (1989): 1–3.

52. El-Affendi, *Turabi's Revolution*.

53. U. A. Mahmoud and S. A. Baldo, *Ed Da'ein Massacre: Slavery in the Sudan*, 1988. Unpublished version circulated to the Faculty of Arts, Khartoum University.

54. *FBIS* 159 (1989): 7–14.

55. *FBIS* 154 (1989): 10.

56. *FBIS* 182 (1989): 13.

57. *Sudanese Islamic Legislations* (National Islamic Front, 1988), 221.

58. Ibid., 205.

59. *African Confidential* 32, 2 (1992).

60. *Indian Ocean Newsletter* 477, 4 May 1991.

61. Nhial Arou, "Devolution and the Southern Problem in Sudan."

62. *Sudan Times*, 12 June 1988, 5.

63. Nhial Arou, "Devolution and the Southern Problem in Sudan."

64. K. Gwado-Ayoker, "Interpreting the South," in M. Abd-al-Rahim et al., eds., *Sudan since Independence* (Aldershot: Gower, 1987), 65–74.

65. E. Goffman, *Frame Analysis: An Essay on the Organizaton of Experience* (New York: Harper and Row, 1974).

66. M. Foucault, *Power/Knowledge: Selected Interviews and Other Writings* (New York: Pantheon, 1980).

67. M. J. Shapiro, *Language and Political Understanding: The Politics of Discursive Practices* (New Haven: Yale University Press, 1981).

68. M. Castells, *The City and the Grassroots: A Cross-Cultural Theory of Urban Social Movements* (London: Edwin Arnold, 1983).

69. D. L. Hamilton and G. D. Bishop, "Attitudinal and Behavioral Effects on Initial Integration of White Suburban Neighborhoods," *Journal of Social Issues* 32 (1976): 47–67; R. Sherwood, *The Psychodynamics of Race* (Brighton, Sussex: Harvester Press, 1980).

70. See particularly T. M. Shaw, "Toward a Political Theory of the African Crisis: Diplomacy, Debates and Dialectics," in M. Glantz, ed., *Drought and Hunger in Africa: Denying Famine a Future* (Cambridge: Cambridge University Press, 1986), 127–47; J. F. Bayart, "Civil Society in Africa," in P. Chabal, ed., *Political Domination in Africa: Reflections on the Limits of Power* (Cambridge and New York: Cambridge University Press, 1986), 109–25.

71. C. Geertz, *Local Knowlege* (New York: Basic Books, 1983); L. Rosen, *Bargaining for Reality: The Constitution of Social Relations in a Muslim Community* (Chicago: University of Chicago Press, 1984).

72. J. O'Brien, "Sowing the Seeds of Famine: The Political Economy of Food Deficits in the Sudan," in P. Lawrence, ed., *World Recession and the Food Crisis in Africa* (London: James Currey, 1986), 193–200; "Toward a Reconstitution of Ethnicity: Capitalist Expansion and Cultural Dynamics in the Sudan," *American Anthropologist* 88, 4 (1986): 898–907.

Chapter Four

1. Mohammed Mahjoub Harron, interview with author, 21 February 1988.

2. See particularly the works of Syed Abul Ala Maudoodi, the reference of Islamicists seeking the implementation of an Islamic state: *First Principles of the Islamic State* (Lahore: The Islamic Publications, 1974); *The Islamic Movement: Dynamics of Value, Power and Change* (Leicester: The Islamic Foundation, 1984); *Witness Unto Mankind: The Purpose and Duty of the Muslim "Ummah"* (Leicester: The Islamic Foundation, 1986). Also see: S. Qutb, *Milestones* (Kuwait: International Islamic Federation of Student Organizations, 1978); I. Ahmed, *The Concept of an Islamic State: An Analysis of the Ideological Controversy in Pakistan* (New York: Coronet, 1985).

3. F. Rahman, *Islam and Modernity: Transformations of an Intellectual Tradition* (Chicago: University of Chicago Press, 1984).

4. B. S. Turner, "Orientalism, Islam and Capitalism," *Social Compass* 25, 3/4 (1978): 371–84.

5. S. Zubaida, "The Ideological Conditions for Khomeini's Doctrine of Government," *Economy and Society* 11, 2 (1982): 138–73.

6. R. M. Unger, *False Necessity: Anti-Necessitarian Social Theory in the Service of Radical Democracy*, pt. 1, *Politics, A Work in Constructive Social Theory* (New York and Cambridge: Cambridge University Press, 1987).

7. Abu Gassim Goor Hamid, "A Presentation to the Sudan Writers Union," Khartoum, 23 July 1988.

8. Personal communication.

9. See particularly J. R. Willis, "Introduction," in Willis, ed., *Studies in West African*

Islamic History, vol. 1 (London and Totowa, N.J.: Frank Cass, 1979); M. Hiskett, *The Development of Islam in West Africa* (New York: Longman, 1984); N. Levtzion and H. J. Fisher, eds., *Rural and Urban Islam in West Africa* (Boulder: L. Rienner, 1986).

10. S. Y. Najm al-Din, "The Historical Antecedents of Sudanese Identity" (Paper presented to the International Institute for Islamic Thought Conference on the Behavioral Sciences in Islam, Khartoum, July 1986).

11. Personal communication.

12. A. J. Cudsi, "Islam and Politics in the Sudan," in J. P. Piscatori, ed., *Islam in the Political Process* (Cambridge: Cambridge University Press, 1983), 36–55.

13. T. Niblock, *Class and Power in the Sudan: The Dynamics of Sudanese Politics 1898– 1985* (Albany: State University of New York Press, 1987).

14. A. Shariati, *On the Sociology of Islam* (Berkeley: Mizan, 1979).

15. L. Binder, *Islamic Liberalism: A Critique of Development Ideologies* (Chicago: University of Chicago Press, 1988).

16. Shariati, *On the Sociology of Islam,* 46.

17. A. Shariati, *What Is to Be Done: The Enlightened Thinkers and an Islamic Renaissance* (Houston: Institute for Research in Islamic Studies, 1986).

18. See L. Gardet, "Muslim Views of Time and History," in UNESCO, ed., *Culture and Time* (Paris: UNESCO, 1976); A. H. el-Zein, "Beyond Ideology and Theology: The Search for an Anthropology of Islam," *Annual Review of Anthropology* 6 (1977): 229–54; E. Gellner, *Muslim Society* (Cambridge and New York: Cambridge University Press, 1981).

19. See F. Rahman, *Islam* (Chicago: University of Chicago Press, 1979); A. Shariati, *Red Shiism* (Houston: Free Islamic Literatures, 1980); I. al Faruqi, "The Quran," in I. R. al Faruqi and L. L. al Faruqi, eds., *The Cultural Atlas of Islam* (New York: Macmillan, 1986); M. Arkoun, "The Topicality of the Problem of the Person in Islamic Thought," *International Social Science Journal* 117, (1988): 407–22.

20. el-Zein, "Beyond Ideology and Theology."

21. See A. Chiragh, "Islam and Change," in J. J. Donahue and J. L. Esposito, eds., *Islam in Transition: Muslim Perspectives* (New York: Oxford University Press, 1982), 44–47; S. P. Manzoor, "Thinking About a Future Civilization of Islam," *Inquiry* 2, 12 (1985): 32–36; W. E. Roff, "Islamic Movements: One or Many," in Roff, ed., *Islam and the Political Economy of Meaning* (London: Croom Helm, 1987); Binder, *Islamic Liberalism.*

22. A. Nandy, *The Intimate Enemy: Loss and Recovery of the Self Under Colonialism* (Dehli: Oxford University Press, 1983).

23. J. Berque, *Arab Rebirth: Pain and Ecstasy* (London: Al-Saqi Books, 1979).

24. H. Hanafi, "The Relevance of the Islamic Alternative in Egypt," *Arab Studies Quarterly* 4, 1/2 (1982): 54–74.

25. Bayart, "Civil Society in Africa," 120.

Chapter Five

1. M. O. El Sammani, et al., "Management Problems of Greater Khartoum," in R. E. Stren and R. R. White, eds., *African Cities in Crisis: Managing Rapid Urban Growth* (Boulder, San Francisco, London: Westview Press, 1989), 247–75.

2. Ibid.

3. Ibid.

4. A term popularized by Dr. Zubair Bashir Taha of the University of Khartoum and National Islamic Front.

5. F. B. Mahmoud, "Businessmen and Politicians," in Abd-al Rahim et al., *Sudan since Independence*, 7–19.

6. P. J. Vatikiotis, "Islamic Resurgence;" H. Enayat, *Modern Islamic Political Thought* (London: Macmillan, 1982).

7. J. O. Voll, "The Evolution of Islamic Fundamentalism in Twentieth Century Sudan," in Warburg and Kupferschmidt, *Islam, Nationalism and Radicalism in Egypt and the Sudan*, 113–42.

8. El-Affendi, *Turabi's Revolution*.

9. H. A. Ibrahim, "African Initiatives and Resistance in N.E. Africa," in A. Boahen, ed., *Africa Under Colonial Domination 1880–1935* (Berkeley: University of California Press, 1985); L. Kapteijns, *Mahdist Faith and Sudanic Tradition: The History of the Masalit Sultanate 1870–1930* (London: Kegan Paul International, 1985); J. O. Voll, "Abu Jummayza: The Mahdi's Musaylim," in E. Burke III and I. M. Lapidus, eds., *Islam, Politics and Social Movements* (Berkeley and Los Angeles: University of California Press, 1988), 97–114.

10. Ibrahim, "African Initiatives."

11. G. R. Warburg, *Islam, Nationalism and Communism in a Traditional Society: The Case of the Sudan* (London: Frank Cass, 1978).

12. Ibid.

13. Voll, "Evolution of Islamic Fundamentalism."

14. F. B. Mahmoud, *The Sudanese Bourgeoisie: Vanguard of Development?* (London: Zed, 1984).

15. *JPRS–NEA* 29, 24 (2 December 1988): 7.

16. For a description of the *zariba* system see particularly G. A. Schweinfurth, *The Heart of Africa: Three Years Travels and Adventures in the Unexplored Regions of Central Africa 1868–1871 by Dr. Georg Schweinfurth* (London: S. Lowe Marton Lowe Searle, 1873). See also R. L. Hill, *On the Frontiers of Islam* (Oxford: Clarendon, 1970); E. Tonido and R. L. Hill, eds., *The Opening of the Nile Basin: Writings by Members of the Catholic Missions to Central Africa on the Geography and Ethnography of the Sudan 1842–1881* (London: C. Hurst and Co., 1974); L. Mire, "Al-Zubayr Pasha and the Zariba Based Slave Trade in the Bahr al-Ghazal 1855–1870," in J. R. Willis, ed., *Slaves and Slavery in Muslim Africa*, vol. 1 (London: Frank Cass, 1985), 101–22.

17. Mire, "Al-Zubayr Pasha and the Zariba Based Slave Trade."

18. S. K. Mohsen, "The Legal Dimension," in D. Peretz, R. U. Moench, and S. K. Mohsen, eds., *Islam: Legacy of the Past, Challenge of the Future* (New York: New Horizon Press, 1984), 99–128.

19. See R. Horton, "On the Rationality of Conversion," *Africa* 45, 3/4 (1975): 219–35, 379–99; Willis, *Studies in West African Islamic History*, vol. 1; V. Azarya, "Jihads and Dyula States in West Africa," in S. N. Eisenstadt, M. Abitbol, and N. Chazan,

eds., *The Early State in African Perspective: Culture, Power, and Division of Labor* (Leiden, New York: E. J. Brill, 1988) 109–33.

Chapter Six

1. M. Foucault, *The Archaeology of Knowledge* (New York: Pantheon, 1972).

2. J. Rajchman, *Michel Foucault: The Freedom of Philosophy* (New York: Columbia University Press, 1985).

3. J. F. Lyotard and J. L. Thebaud, *Just Gaming* (Minneapolis: University of Minnesota Press, 1985).

4. M. Foucault, "Questions of Method: An Interview," *Ideology and Consciousness* 8 (1981): 3–14.

5. P. L. Brown, "Epistemology and Method: Althusser, Foucault and Derrida," *Cultural Hermeneutics* 3 (1975): 147–63; J. Arac, "The Function of Foucault at the Present Time," *Humanities in Society* 3 (1980): 73–86; Rajchman, *Michel Foucault*.

6. Cohen, *Two Dimensional Man*.

7. See J. Gumperz, *Language in Social Groups* (Palo Alto: Stanford University Press, 1971); W. Labov, *Sociolinguistic Patterns* (Philadelphia: University of Pennsylvania Press, 1973); S. Tyler, *The Said and the Unsaid: Mind, Meaning and Culture* (London: Academic Press, 1978); S. Bochner, "Cultural Diversity: Implications for Modernization and International Education," in K. Kumar, ed., *Bonds without Bondage: Explorations in Transcultural Interactions* (Honolulu: University of Hawaii Press, 1979); E. Goffman, *Forms of Talk* (Philadelphia: University of Pennsylvania Press, 1981); P. Heelas and A. Lock, eds., *Indigenous Psychologies: The Anthropology of the Self* (London: Academic Press, 1981); T. Kochman, *Black and White Styles in Conflict* (Chicago: University of Chicago Press, 1981).

8. de Certeau, *The Practice of Everyday Life*.

9. *Al-Wan* (Khartoum), 4 February 1988, 3.

10. de Certeau, *Practice of Everyday Life*, 103.

11. Conference of the Institute for Muslim Minority Affairs, City College of the City University of New York, 28–29 October 1989.

12. *Africa Confidential* 27, 3 (1986): 4.

13. This is also the concept of Abu Bakr Shingiety of the University of Massachusetts. See also A. M. Mutahhari, *Fundamentals of Islamic Thought: God, Man, and the Universe* (Berkeley: Mizan, 1985).

14. A. Shariati, *On the Sociology of Islam*.

15. *Al-Rayah* (Khartoum), 8 July 1985, 5.

16. *Al-Ayyam* (Khartoum), 12 October 1988, 2.

17. *Al-Rayah* (Khartoum), 20 November 1988, 7.

18. *JPRS–NEA* (1988): 30.

19. *Al-Rayah* (Khartoum), 20 November 1988, 7.

20. *Sudan Times* (Khartoum), 1 February 1988, 3.

21. *JPRS-NEA* 014 (1989): 56.

22. *Al-Rayah* (Khartoum), 2 January 1989, 5.

23. *Al-Siyasab* (Khartoum), 20 March 1989, 3.

24. See M. Meeker, *Literature and Violence in North Arabia* (Cambridge: Cambridge University Press, 1979); al Faruqi and al Faruqi, *The Cultural Atlas of Islam.*

25. Gellner, *Muslim Society.*

26. al-Zein, "Beyond Ideology and Theology."

27. C. Geertz, *Islam Observed* (New Haven: Yale University Press, 1968); L. Rosen, *Bargaining for Reality: The Constitution of Social Relations in a Muslim Community* (Chicago: University of Chicago Press, 1984).

28. D. Harvey, *Consciousness and the Urban Experience* (Oxford: Oxford University Press, 1985).

29. Gellner, *Muslim Society.*

30. This is a pattern that has befallen many Islamic Sufi orders in Africa. See D. B. C. O'Brien, *The Mourides of Senegal* (Oxford: Clarendon, 1971); J. Paden, *Religion and Political Culture in Kano* (Berkeley: University of California Press, 1973); A. H. Nimtz, *Islam and Politics in East Africa: The Sufi Order in Tanzania* (Minneapolis: The University of Minnesota Press, 1980); D. B. C. O'Brien and C. Coulon, eds., *Charisma and Brotherhood in African Islam* (Oxford: Clarendon, 1988).

31. S. T. Barnes, *Patrons and Power: Creating a Metropolitan Community in Metropolitan Lagos* (Manchester: Manchester University Press, 1986).

32. See, for example, "Revealing the Truth Behind the Faisal Islamic Bank," *Arabia: the Islamic World Review* 4, 42 (1985): 66–67; "Interview with Sayed El Tayib Abdel Majied, Head of the Bank Oversight Committee," *Sudan Times* (Khartoum), 27 April 1987, 2.

33. W. Godzich, "Religion, the State and Post(al) Modernism," in S. Weber, *Institution and Interpretation* (Minneapolis: University of Minnesota Press, 1987).

34. ProSeminar on Islamic Psychology, University of Khartoum, 23 January 1988.

35. G. R. Warburg, "Islam in Sudanese Politics," in M. Curtis, ed., *Religion and Politics in the Middle East* (Boulder: Westview Press, 1981), 307–21.

36. B. Lincoln, *Religion, Rebellion, Revolution* (London: Macmillan, 1985), 276.

37. *JPRS-NEA* 055 (1989): 62–64.

38. F. Rahman, *Major Themes of the Quran* (Chicago: Bibliotheca Islamica, 1980); J. M. Pessagno, "On Al Maturidi's Notion of Human Acts;" in I. al Faruqi, ed., *Islamic Thought and Culture* (Washington, D.C.: International Institute for Islamic Thought, 1982).

39. *JPRS-NEA* 072, (1987): 48.

40. Ibid.

41. *JPRS-NEA* 085 (1988): 47.

42. J. Lonsedale, "Political Accountability in African History," in Chabal, *Political Domination in Africa*, 137.

43. T. O. Ranger, "Religious Movements and Politics in Sub-Saharan Africa," *African Studies Review* 29, 2 (1986): 1–69.

44. Schatzberg, *The Dialectics of Oppression in Zaire.*

45. *FBIS-NES* 89–159, 13.

46. Ibid., 9.

47. *JPRS-NEA* 053 (1989): 41.

48. *Al-Nur* (Cairo), 17 June 1987, 4.

49. *FBIS* 159 (1989): 12.

Chapter Seven

1. Hassan al-Turabi, "Manhajiyyat al-Fiqh wa'l-Tashri' al-Islami" (International Institute for Islamic Thought, Conference on Islam and the Behavioral Sciences, January 1987).

2. Hassan al-Turabi, *Al-Iman: Atharuhu fi Hayat al-Insan* (Manshurat al-'Asr al-Hadith, 1984).

3. Although most Islamic social theorists do not condemn attempts to establish Islamic states, many see the need to focus on more significant issues that tend to get lost in the singular focus on an Islamic political agenda. See M. Nuwayhi, "A Revolution in Religious Thought," in Donahue and Esposito, *Islam in Transition*, 160–68; M. Taliqani, *Society and Economics in Islam* (Berkeley: Mizan, 1982); Rahman, *Islam and Modernity*; S. P. Manzoor, "Thinking About a Future Civilization," *Inquiry* 2, 12 (1985): 32–36; Z. Sardar, *Islamic Futures: The Shape of Ideas to Come* (London and New York: Mansell, 1985).

4. See J. Galtung, *The True Worlds: A Transnational Perspective* (New York: Free Press, 1980); A. M. M. Hoogvelt, *The Third World in Global Development* (London: Macmillan, 1982); J. N. Rosenau, "A Pre-Theory Revisited: World Politics in an Era of Cascading Interdependence," *International Studies Quarterly* 28, 3 (1984): 245–305; J. Halloran, "International Democratization of Communication: The Challenge for Research," in J. Becker, G. Hedebro, and L. Paldan, eds., *Communication and Domination: Essays in Honor of Herbert Schiller* (Norwood, N.J.: Ablex, 1987), 241–48.

5. C. Levi-Strauss, *Structural Anthropology*, vol. 2 (New York: Basic Books, 1976).

6. See C. Fluerh-Lobban, *Islamic Law and Society in the Sudan* (London: Frank Cass, 1987); M. M. Taha, *The Second Message of Islam* (Syracuse, N.Y.: Syracuse University Press, 1987); A. al-Azmeh, ed., *Islamic Law: Social and Historical Contexts* (London and New York: Routledge, 1988).

7. *Sudan Times* (Khartoum), 18 June 1988, 5.

8. Hassan Turabi, interview with author, 3 April 1988.

9. Hassan al-Turabi, *Al-Harakah al Islamiyya fi al-Sudan* (translation by the Africa Muslim Agency, Kuwait, 1992).

10. Hassan al-Turabi, "Manhajiyyat al-Fiqh wa'l-Tashri' al-Islami."

11. See particularly the lofty and effusive language of Hassan al-Turabi in *Al-Imam: Antharuhu fi Hayat al-Insan* (Manshurat al-'Asr al-Hadith, 1984).

12. Hassan al-Turabi, *Al-Harakah Islamiyyah fi al-Sudan*.

13. Ibid.

14. Hassan al-Turabi, *Tajdid al-Fikr al-Islami* (Khartoum: Jam'iyat al-Hady al-Qurani, 1982).

15. El-Tijani Abdul Kader Hamid and Hassan al-Turabi, "As-Sudan wa Tajiribah al-Intiqal lil Hukm al-Islami" ("Interview with Dr. Turabi: Sudan and the Experience

of the Transition toward Islamic Rule"), *Political Readings* 2, 3 (Tampa, Fla.: World Islamic Studies Enterprises, 1992).

16. Ibid.

17. Ibid.

18. Hassan al-Turabi, *Al-Harakah al-Islamiyyah fi al-Sudan*.

19. El Tijani Abdul Kader Hamid and Hassan al-Turabi, "Interview with Dr. Turabi."

20. See particularly Enayat, *Modern Islamic Political Thought;* J. O. Voll, *Islam: Continuity and Change in the Muslim World* (Boulder: Westview Press, 1982).

21. Seminar on Islamic Education, Department of Religion, University of Ghana, March 21, 1989.

22. See F. Hassan, *State and Law in Islam* (Washington, D.C.: University Press of America, 1981); I. al Faruqi, *Tawhid: Its Implications for Thought and Life* (Wyncote, Pa.: International Institute for Islamic Thought, 1982); S. H. Nasr, *Traditional Islam in the Modern World* (London: Kegan Paul International, 1987).

23. J. S. Trimmingham, *Islam in the Sudan* (London: Frank Cass, 1965); R. S. O'Fahey and J. Spaulding, *Kingdoms of the Sudan* (London: Methuen, 1974).

24. Taha, *The Second Message of Islam*, 39.

25. R. S. Humphreys, "The Contemporary Resurgence in the Context of Islam," in A. E. H. Dessouki, ed., *Islamic Resurgence in the Arab World* (New York: Praeger, 1982), 67–83.

26. J. Schacht, "The Law," in G. von Grunebaum, ed., *Unity and Variety in Muslim Civilization* (Chicago: University of Chicago Press, 1955), 78.

27. M. Arkoun, "The Topicality of the Problem of the Person in Islamic Thought," *International Social Science Journal* 117 (August 1988): 407–22.

28. See S. Mahmasani, "Adoption of Islamic Jurisprudence to Modern Social Needs," in Donahue and Esposito, *Islam in Transition,* 181–87; S. K. Mohsen, "The Legal Dimension," in Peretz, Moench, and Mohsen, *Islam,* 99–128; N. Kielstra, "Law and Reality in Modern Islam," in E. Gellner, ed., *Islamic Dilemmas: Reformers, Nationalists and Industrialization* (Cologne: Mouton, 1985), 10–21.

29. F. M. Deng, *Dinka Cosmology* (London: Ithaca Press, 1980).

30. See interviews with Hassan al-Turabi: *The Middle East,* (London), 5 September 1979, 7–8; *New Statesman* (London), 15 October 1985, 14–17. See also J. M. Abun-Nasr, "Militant Islam: A Historical Perspective," in Gellner, *Islamic Dilemmas,* 73–93.

31. A. Shariati, *An Approach to Understanding Islam* (Houston: Free Islamic Literatures, 1980).

32. Binder, *Islamic Liberalism.*

33. H. A. Faris, "Heritage and Ideologies in Contemporary Arab Thought: Contrasting Views of Change and Development," *Journal of Asian and African Studies* 21, 1/2, (1986): 89–103.

34. See M. I. Husayni, *The Muslim Brethen: The Greatest of Modern Islamic Movements* (Beirut: Khayat College, 1956); H. Al-Banna, *What is Our Message?* (Lahore: Islamic

Publications, 1974); A. K. Audah, *Islam Between the Ignorant Followers and Incapable Scholars* (Kuwait: International Islamic Federation of Student Organizations, 1977).

35. Enayat, *Modern Islamic Political Thought.*

36. Ibid.

37. Hassan al-Turabi, Address at the University of Khartoum, 13 July 1988. See also S. Safwat, "Islamic Laws in the Sudan," in Al-Azmeh, *Islamic Law.*

38. D. M. Wai, "Afro-Arab Relations: Interdependence or Misplaced Optimism," *Journal of Modern African Studies* 21, 2 (1983): 187–213.

39. A. El-Affendi, "In the Heat of the Storm," *Africa Events* 5, 4 (1989): 24–26.

Chapter Eight

1. Fields, *Revival and Rebellion.*

2. Ibid., 260.

3. See B. Jules-Rosette, "The Veil of Objectivity: Prophecy, Divination and Social Inquiry," *American Anthropologist* 80, 3 (1978): 549–70; Fernandez, "Edification by Puzzlement;" J. Fabian, "Missions and the Colonization of African Languages: Developments in the Former Belgian Congo," *Canadian Journal of African Studies* 17, 2 (1983): 165–87; Boulaga, *Christianity without Fetishes;* T. O. Ranger, "Taking Hold of the Land: Holy Places and Pilgrimages in Twentieth Century Zimbabwe," *Past and Present* 117, (1987): 158–94.

4. F. M. Deng, *Tradition and Modernization* (New Haven: Yale University Press, 1986).

Chapter Nine

1. J. Derrida, "Living On: Borderlines," in H. Bloom et al., eds., *Deconstruction and Criticism* (New York: Seabury Press, 1979).

2. Berque, *Arab Rebirth;* M. Tamandonfar, *The Islamic Polity and Political Leadership: Fundamentalism, Sectarianism and Pragmatism* (Boulder: Westview Press, 1989).

3. F. Esack, "Three Islamic Strands in the South African Struggle for Justice," *Third World Quarterly* 10, 2 (1988): 473–98.

4. J. Voll and S. P. Voll, *The Sudan: Unity and Diversity in a Multicultural State* (London: Croom Helm, 1985).

5. Achmat Davids, interview with author, Cape Town, South Africa, 14 July 1989. Davids is considered to be the key historian of Cape Muslims and has published many studies of the community, among them *The Mosques of the South Kaap* (Athlone, S.A.: Institute of Arabic and Islamic Studies Research, 1980); *The History of Tana Baru* (Cape Town: Committee for the Preservation of Tana Baru, 1985); "Politics and Muslims in Cape Town: A Historical Survey," in *Studies in the History of Cape Town* (University of Cape Town Press, 1983), 174–220.

6. I. Goldin, "The Reconstitution of Coloured Identity in the Western Cape," in S. Marks and S. Trapido, eds., *The Politics of Race, Class and Nationalism in Twentieth Century South Africa* (London and New York: Longman, 1987), 156–81.

7. Ibid.

8. I. Goldin, *Making Race: The Politics and Economics of Coloureds in South Africa* (London and New York: Longman, 1988).

9. Achmat Davids, interview with author.

10. *Grassroots* (Cape Town), July 1989, 3.

11. See S. M. Davis, *Apartheid's Rebels: Inside South Africa's Hidden War* (New Haven and London: Yale University Press, 1987); M. Murray, *South Africa: Time of Agony, Time of Destiny, The Upsurge of Popular Protest* (London: Verso, 1987); W. Cobbett and R. Cohen, eds., *Popular Struggles in South Africa* (London: James Currey, 1988).

12. *The Call of Islam* (Cape Town, December 1985): 1.

13. *Africa Events* 1, 11 (1985): 1.

14. *The Call of Islam* Cape Town, November 1985, 1.

15. *Africa Events* 1, 11 (1985): 11.

16. Repression Monitoring Group, Essa Moosa and Associates, Athlone, South Africa.

17. Ibid.

18. "Apartheid Barometer," *Weekly Mail,* 12 August 1989.

19. *The Call of Islam* (May 1987), 5.

20. G. Lubbe, "Christians, Muslims and Liberation in South Africa," *Journal of Theology for Southern Africa* (University of Cape Town) 53 (1985).

21. "Chapter and Verse," *Africa Events* 2, 12 (1986): 30–38.

22. Ibid., 38.

23. Ibid.

24. R. Omar, "Muslim-Christian Relations in South Africa: The Case of the 1986 NGK General Synod Resolution on Islam." (Department of Religious Studies, University of Cape Town, January 1989).

25. F. Esack, *Our Task: Questions and Answers About Muslims and Their Involvement in the Struggle for Liberation* (Cape Town: Call of Islam, 1988).

26. Ibid., 8.

27. Ibid., 14–18.

28. G. Simmel, *Conflict and the Web of Group Affiliations* (New York: Free Press, 1955).

29. *The Struggle* (Cape Town: The Call of Islam, 1988), 54.

30. Ibid.

31. Ibid., 37–38.

32. Ibid., 61.

33. Ibid., 74.

34. M. E. Moosa, "Muslim Response," Paper presented at symposium, Believers in the Struggle for Justice and Peace, hosted by the Institute for Contextual Theology, World Council for Religion and Peace, South Africa, 27–29 May 1988, 31.

35. F. Esack, *Side by Side with Non-Muslims* (Cape Town: The Call of Islam, 1989), 30.

36. Foucault, *Power/Knowledge.*

37. Binder, *Islamic Liberalism.*

38. M. E. Moosa, "Power Struggle Behind the Eid Issue," *South* (Cape Town, 13 July 1989, 24.

39. Ibid.

40. "The Muslim Judicial Council Speaks" (Cape Town, 4 July 1989) 10–11.

41. Ibid., 12.

42. "Our Decision," Claremont Main Road Masjid (Cape Town, 2 July 1989), 2.

43. Moosa, "Power Struggle Behind the Eid Issue," 24.

44. Ibid.

45. A. Mazrui, "National Trust and Cohesion," *Sudanow* 10, 5 (1985): 12–15.

46. See C. Boggs, *Social Movements and Political Power* (Philadelphia: Temple University Press, 1986); R. Kothari, "On Human Governance," *Alternatives* 11, 3 (1987).

47. See C. Newbury, "Dead and Buried or Just Underground: The Privatisation of the State in Zaire," *Canadian Journal of African Studies* 18, 1 (1984); J. MacGaffey, *Entrepreneurs and Parasites: The Struggle for Indigenous Capitalism in Zaire* (New York and Cambridge: Cambridge University Press, 1988).

48. Address to the Conference on Muslim Minority Affairs, Roosevelt Hotel, New York, N.Y., 23 October 1989.

49. G. Bauman, *National Integration and Local Integration: The Miri of the Nuba Mountains* (Oxford: Clarendon, 1987).

50. Ibid., 194.

Index

'Abbud, Major General, 91
Abd-al-Majid, Osman, 89
'Abdal-Rahman, Ahmad, 165
'Abd-al Rahman al-Mahdi, 111
Abdrahman, A., 212
Abdullah, Khalifa, 111
Abu Harira, Mohammed Yousif, 113
Addis Ababa Agreement, 49, 50
Adultery, 69
Africa: associational groups in, 19; black Africans' resistance to Islamicization, 176; Burkina Faso, 18–19; Cameroon, 74; Chad, 61; Christianity and African religious concerns, 4; church and mosque as power centers in, 17–18; colonialism, 3–4, 6; cultural construction of community in, 19; cultural development interrupted by colonialism, 3–4; democracy in, 21; discontinuity between identity change and value change in, 16–17; Egypt, 61–62, 72, 188, 190; Ethiopia, 66; indigenous solutions sought for, 83; Kenya, 74; Liberia, 21; Libya, 54, 190; postcolonial era, 5, 14, 15; recolonization feared in, 8–9; religion and cultural development in, 3–5; religious attachments in postcolonial, 5; shantytowns, 106–9, 122; state and civil society in, 13–22, 98; states' anarchic and repressive actions, 4–5; sub-Saharan Africa, 25; Togo, 21; Uganda, 74; underdevelopment in, 127; urban life in, 104–5, 119; West Africa, 89, 154; youth in, 125. See also South Africa; Sudan
African National Congress (ANC): and Call of Islam, 214, 230, 240; Muslim role in, 210; and Muslim Youth Movement, 214
African Peoples Organization, 212
Agriculture, 35–36; bank financing of, 37;

capitalist development of, 79; cotton, 35, 39; farm labor, 35, 79; sagiy system, 38; subsistence agriculture destroyed in the South, 79; wheat, 39
Ahmed, Abdallah Muhammed, 59
Ahmed, Muhammad Taha Muhammad, 148
Akol, Johannes, 165
Akol, Lam, 43
Alcohol use, 69, 107, 108, 114, 161–62
'Ali, Fathi Ahmad, 63, 70
'Ali, Taysir Muhammad Ahmad, 56, 65
Alier, Abel, 49, 50
Amm ath Thwara, 64
ANC. See African National Congress
Ansar al-Mahdi, 32, 100, 111, 154, 175
Anya-Nya, 47, 48, 49
Anya-Nya II, 49, 53, 56
Apprenticeship Act of 1922, 212
Arabs, 79–80
Arens, Moshe, 60
Arok, Machur, 64
As'as, Jiris, 163
Associational groups, 19
Atta, Hasin al-, 91
Atem, Aquot, 53, 54
Aujong, Deng, 55
Awad, Aminah, 66
Azande, 117, 118
Azanian National Front, 47

Baath Party, 147, 154
Banks: Faisal Islamic Bank, 36, 65; Islamic banks, 37, 155; regulatory discrepancies, 36
Banna, Hassan al-, 65
Baqqara, 29, 32, 41, 113
Barakat, 154
Bar al-Ghazal, 41, 43, 47, 50, 58, 72, 116–17

Barelvi sect, 221

Bashir, Mohammed Omar, 171

Bashir, Omar Hassan Ahmed al-: accusation of Saudi support for SPLA, 80; clampdown on Khartoum, 66–67; coup, 62–64; democracy ended by regime of, 62–72; economic policy problems, 38; Garang on regime of, 65; *hudud* held back by, 99; proposal on relationship between politics and religion, 164; proposed referendum on Islamic law, 165; *Shari'a* implemented by, 63, 68–69; Southerners in government of, 186

Basilica of Yammousoukro, 18

Basri, Shaykh Abdel, 65

Bauman, Gerd, 243

Bayart, Jean-François, 14, 98

Bhaksa, 194–95

Bieli, Hassab Ismail el, 65

Black Theology, 222

Bloc of Afro-Sudanese Parties, 165

Boigny, Houphouët, 18

Boma incident, 53

Botchway, Abdallah, 178

Brock, R. C. G., 47

Bruhani sect, 80

Burkina Faso, 18–19

Burno, 153, 156

Call of Islam (COI): and African National Congress, 214, 230, 240; agenda of, 237–41; attempt to break Muslim dependence on insularity, 213–14; hardball politics of, 233; in Islamic movement in South Africa, 211; Islamic movement in Sudan compared to, 241; Muslim Judicial Council alliance, 234, 236; new Islamic hermeneutic of, 224–33; on objectives of activism, 224–25; theological contributions of, 221; undermined by conservative elements, 240; and United Democratic Front, 214; working with people of all religions, 219, 222, 230

Cameroon, 74

Cape coloreds. *See* Coloreds

Cape Town: Africans removed from, 212, 215–16; coloreds removed from, 214–15; District Six, 215, 219; *Eid al Adha* controversy, 234–36; insurrection of 1980s, 216; Majlis as-Shura, 235, 236; Muslim Judicial Council, 216, 234–36; Muslim population of, 210; *Shari'a* in, 213; Trojan Horse incident, 216–17

Capitalism: and Islam, 11; penetration in Sudan, 38; in Sudanese agriculture, 79; and underdevelopment, 12

Cassiem, Achmied, 222

Chad, 61

Chol, Gordon Koang, 43

Christianity: and African religious concerns, 4; Black Theology, 222; Christian fundamentalism, 7; government treatment of, 196; and Muslims in South Africa, 221–24, 230; Sisters of St. Francis, 198; and Southerners, 199–200

Cirillo, Peter, 64

Civil service, 36, 39, 102, 194

Civil society: Islam as the civil society of Northerners, 198; and the state in Africa, 13–22, 98

Civil war, 41–80; between Arabized North and Africanized South, 13, 20, 29, 41; context for resolution of, 72–75; Dinka in, 41; ethnic tensions exacerbated by, 41; as fight for access to the political center, 166; historical roots of, 46–48; martyrdom ideology in, 45; and the *Shari'a*, 31–32; Sudan People's Liberation Army in, 31; Westerners in, 42

Clientalism, 154, 155

Cohen, Abner, 134

COI. *See* Call of Islam

Colonialism, 3–4, 6

Coloreds (Cape colored): current status, 213–19; history, 211–13; Muslims among the, 212–13; removal from central Cape Town, 214–15; and tricameral legislature, 219; Western values and desires among, 221

Colyn, Stoffel, 223

Communist Party (Sudan). *See* Sudanese Communist Party

Compaore, Blaise, 19

Constituent Assembly, 57

Corruption, 36

Cotton, 35, 39

Council of State, 60

Crafford, Dione, 223

Currency controls, 37

Currency reform, 39

Daf'allah, Jazuli, 56, 61

Dahab, Suwar ad-, 52, 55, 61

Da'im, Nur al-, 157, 158

Dar es Salaam, 68, 120

Darfur, 36, 68, 182

Da'was Islamiyyah, 164
Dawiyy, Salah al-, 62
Debry, Idris, 61
Debt service obligations, 34
Democracy: in Africa, 21; end of in Sudan, 62–72; failure of in Sudan, 57–60; National Islamic Front on absence of in Sudan, 187; restoration of in Sudan, 55–57; the Sudanese masses on, 201
Democratic Front, 115
Democratic Unionist Party (DUP), 32, 37, 59, 63, 113, 146
Deng, Aldo Ajo, 58, 59
Deng, Annuel, 143
Deng, Francis Mading, 26, 73
Deng, William, 46, 48, 58
Deobandi sect, 221
Din, Ibrahim Shams al, 72
Din, Shams al-Din Yunis Najm al-, 89
Dina, Shaykh Amadou, 94
Dinar, 39
Dinka: and Anya-Nya split, 53; in the civil war, 41; economic and social conditions of, 73; Equatorian conflict, 55; ethnic identity, 29; fear of Nuer collaboration with the government, 43; in Khartoum multiethnic theft rings, 20; Messeriyya conflict, 56; Northern misunderstanding of, 190; Nuer fear of, 49; playing off the Arabs against the Azande, 117; religion, 186; on separation of religious and social, 199; in SPLA factional split, 44
District Six (Cape Town), 215, 219
Djamous, Hassan, 61
Donagla, 38
Drinking. See Alcohol use
DUP. See Democratic Unionist Party
Dutch Reformed Church (Nederduitse Gereformeede Kerk; NGK), 223–24

Egalitarianism, 157
Egypt, 61–62, 72, 188, 190
Eid al Adha, 234–36
Equatoria, 41, 50, 55
Esack, Moulana Farid, 217, 228, 229
Ethiopia, 66
Ethnicity: discontinuities in ethnic identity, 16; divisions among Southern ethnic groups, 32, 68; ethnic neighborhoods of Khartoum, 136; ethnic tensions exacerbated by civil war, 41; hostility among ethnic groups, 29; as mechanism for asserting sense of commonality, 14; in

neighborhood organization and social affiliation, 67; and political discourse, 133; regional conflict based on, 20; in the shantytowns, 107–8; among South African Muslims, 237. See also Race
Export commodities, 34

Fadala, Burma, 30
Faisal Islamic Bank, 36, 65
Faith (iman), 227–28
Faqir, 180, 183
Farm labor, 35, 79
Federalism, 72
Fernandez, James, 4
Fiqh, 171, 173
Foreign earnings, 38
Foucault, Michel, 130
Freedom, 178–79, 181
Friddie, Abdul, 217
Fur (people), 61
Futa Jallon, 12, 123

Gangs, 220
Garang, John Maribor de: attending to rifts in the ranks, 44; on Bashir regime, 65; demand for national political role for the South, 164–65; as leader of SPLA, 41, 53; meeting with Arens, 60; negotiation with Mahdi, 56–57; refusal to negotiate with transitional government, 44; reported deposition of, 43; on Southern unity, 166; strategy of, 42
Garang, Joseph, 48
Gasmallah, Mubarak, 164
Gatati South Mayo, 120
Gezira, 38
Ghazzali, Muhammad, 189
Godzich, W., 156
Government. See State, the
Greater Cape Town. See Cape Town
Group Areas Acts, 214–15
Gulf War, 38

Habre, Hissein, 61
Hadd. See Hudud
Hajj, 218
Hamdi, Abdel Rahim, 38
Hamed, Ahmed Sayed al-, 113
Hamid, Abu Gassim Goor, 88, 192–94
Hamidallah, Farouk, 91
Hanafi, Hassan, 97
Hanifa legal system, 177
Haqiqa, 183

Harakah al-Qawmiyyah, Al- (National Movement for the Rectification of the Situation), 62

Haroon, Mohammed Mahjoub, 83

Haroon, Abdullah, 217

Haroon, Omar, 89

Hassan, Khalid Younis, 199

Hilful Fadul, 230

Hillat al-Nuer, 153

Hudaibiyyah, Treaty of, 226–27

Hudud (hadd), 69: Bashir regime's holding back on, 99; in Islamic movement's policies, 84, 85; National Islamic Front on, 85; for non-Muslims, 145; relaxation of after Libyan bombing of Omdurman, 54; in the September laws, 26, 33; Turabi on, 85

Ibadat, 188

Ibrahim, Osman Hamid, 106, 109

ICSA (Islamic Council of South Africa), 224, 235, 236

Idris, Jaafar Sheik, 140

Ijma, 172

Ijtihad, 137, 171, 173, 188

Ikhwan (Muslim Brotherhood): acting as if power were already in their hands, 172; on conditions of cultural creation, 168; dual role in Sudan, 189; Islamic movement influenced by, 12; and Islamic universalism, 95; National Islamic Front criticized by, 157–58; National Islamic Front's roots in, 51–53; and Numayri, 52; and Rida, 188

Iman, 227–28

Interim Council for the South, 58–59

International Monetary Fund (IMF), 8, 33, 34, 39

Iran, 71, 190

Islam: Africanization as threat to, 76; Barelvi sect, 221; Bashir regime's use of, 68; and capitalism, 11; Deobandi sect, 221; *Eid al Adha*, 234–36; faith, 227–28; *faqir*, 180; *fiqh*, 171, 173; hajj, 218; Hanifa legal system, 177; homogeneity and heterogeneity of, 153; *ijma*, 172; *ijtihad*, 137, 171, 173, 188; as instrument of political and social change, 6; as internal focus for politics, 109; Islam from above and Islam from below, 238; Islamic banks in Sudan, 37, 155; Islamic ideology and the Islamic movement, 155–60; Islamic politics, 94–97, 179, 206; Islamic state, 97–99; in

Khartoum, 153; literacy emphasized by, 152; Maliki legal system, 177; marginalized by political-cultural dualism, 163; and its margins, 206; need for a versatile religion, 91–94; new Islamic hermeneutic of Call of Islam, 224–33; and Northerners, 198; as organizing force, 122–25; on otherness, 150; and political activism, 228; politicization of, 97–98; popular, 246n.15; progressive theology and hardball politics, 233; *qisas*, 33, 69; the Quran, 95, 133–34, 140, 152, 178, 180; on race and culture, 32; reconciliation with modernism, 7; the religious and the secular in the Sudan, 89–91; Shafi legal system, 213, 229, 238; *shaykh*, 180, 182; social impact of in South Africa, 220–24; in South Africa, 208–44; Southerners on, 200; and the state, 123; strength relative to other forms of political consciousness, 87; and Sudanese identity, 77–79; Sudanese Islamicism and West African Islam, 89; Sudanese Muslim population, 25; Sudan's nineteenth-century Islamic regime, 12; Sufism, 32, 80, 111, 153–54, 179, 182; the Sunnah, 133–34, 178, 180; Tabliq Jaamat, 216; universalism of, 95–96; Western view of, 5–6; in the *zariba*, 117. *See also* Ikhwan; Islamicization; Islamic movement; *Shari'a*; *Ulema*

Islamic Charter Front, 51

Islamic Council of South Africa (ICSA), 224, 235, 236

Islamic Front for the Constitution (IFC), 51

Islamicism. *See* Islamic movement

Islamicization: black Africans' resistance to, 176; compromising of and compromising Islam, 123; historical conditions of, 177; Muslim Brothers' approach to, 157; and the political elite, 109–10; shortcuts to, 144; subordinate to the *Shari'a*, 173; in the Sudan, 83–99, 179; Turabi on, 172; where Muslims are a majority, 240

Islamic Liberation Movement, 51

Islamic movement (Islamicism; Islamic fundamentalism; Islamic resurgence): on alcohol use, 161–62; arbitrariness of, 159–60; as bridge between the state and civil society, 22; challenge of generating forms of religious expression compatible with personal understanding of God, 91; and cultural revival in Sudan, 168–77; discursive practices of, 129–67; *hudud* as

lies to support the army, 62; refusal to join the government, 61, 149; and the Revolutionary Command Council, 64–66; *Shari'a* implementation supported by, 92, 150, 161; on Southerners in Khartoum, 185–87; splits in, 66; strength in Khartoum, 53, 63; Sudan Charter, 145; Turabi's leadership, 28, 51–52; on underdevelopment in the South, 73; and urban diversity, 141–44; ward committee election defeat, 71; on women, 66, 138. *See also* Turabi, Hassan al-

Nationalists (South Africa), 212

National Movement for the Rectification of the Situation (Al-Harakah al-Qawmiyyah), 62

National Salvation Revolutionary Command Council (RCC): clampdown on Southerners, 66–67; establishment, 62; federalism supported by, 72; meetings with SPLA, 65; and the National Islamic Front, 64–66

NDA (National Democratic Alliance), 70

Nederduitse Gereformeede Kerk (NGK; Dutch Reformed Church), 223–24

NGSH (National Gathering for the Salvation of the Homeland), 53, 55

NIF. *See* National Islamic Front

Nile Provisional Committee, 48

Non-European Unity Movement, 212

Northerners: cultural homogeneity of the North, 77; desire to move to the South, 149; and Islam, 198; North-South antagonism in Khartoum, 74; overdetermination of North-South distinction, 192; particularism among, 32; power sharing resisted by, 67; on *Shari'a* implementation, 200–201; and Southerners, 20, 75–77, 118, 186, 190, 197–201; in Sudanese civil war, 13, 20, 29, 41; on *ulema*, 200; war weariness, 45

Northern Province, 38

Nour, Babiker al-, 91

Nour, el-Hag, 181

Nuba, 20, 73, 157, 194, 243

Nuer, 43, 49, 153, 190

Numayri, Jaafar, 48–50; and a constitution for Sudan, 91; exorbitance of, 34; expulsion of Westerners from Khartoum, 101; and Ikhwan, 52; and the Islamic movement, 52; *kasha* policy, 68; and Libyan bombing, 54; overthrow of, 13, 55; political strategy of, 87–88; September laws,

26, 33, 52, 54; state apparatus of, 102; Taha executed by, 180; trip to Chad, 62

Nur, Zeidan, 88

Nus, El Tayeb al, 65

Oduho, Joseph, 44, 46, 47, 54

Omdurman, 54, 100, 101, 114, 144, 175

125th Street, 119, 122

Orientalists, 11

Otherness, 142, 143, 150, 156

Paranoia, 156

Patel, Yusuf, 222

Political parties: Baath Party, 147, 154; Bloc of Afro-Sudanese Parties, 165; Democratic Front, 115; during democratic period, 57–58; Democratic Unionist Party, 32, 37, 59, 63, 113, 146; formation after overthrow of Numayri, 55; impotence of, 115; and kinship ties, 138; Sudanese Communist Party, 48, 49, 51, 112; Sudanese Socialist Union, 52; Sudan United Party, 47; and the Sufi brotherhoods, 153; Umma Party, 28, 32, 101, 112–13, 114

Politics: of cultural revival in Sudan, 168–201; Islam and political activism, 228; Islamic politics, 94–97, 179, 206; murkiness of, 150; political discourse of the Islamic movement, 131–36; progressive theology and hardball politics, 233; and religion, 156, 163–64, 239; and religion in Sudan, 22–23, 32; in Sudan, 109–14, 165; Sudanese attitude toward, 87, 114–16; Sudanese political coherency, 24, 27; women's role in, 138

Population Registration Act of 1950, 212

Postcolonial era, 5, 14, 15

Privatization, 21, 39

Provisionality, 137–41

Public sector, 37

Qisas, 33, 69

Quran, 95, 133–34, 140, 152, 178, 180

Qutb, Sayyid, 92

Race, 192, 195, 197–99. *See also* Ethnicity

Racial segregation, 212

Racism, 75, 213

Rafsanjani, 'Ali Akbar Hashemi, 71

Rasool, Ebraiham, 218

Rassa, Gismella, 50
RCC. *See* National Salvation Revolutionary
    Command Council
Regional Covenant Act, 50
Religion: church and mosque as power cen-
    ters in Africa, 17–18; under colonial rule,
    6; and cultural development in Africa,
    3–5; in Dinka society, 186; and lan-
    guage, 137; need for a versatile religion,
    91–94; and politics, 156, 163–64, 239;
    and politics in Sudan, 22–23, 32; and ra-
    cial antagonism, 198–99; religious attach-
    ments in postcolonial Africa, 5; and the
    secular in the Sudan, 89–91; Weber on,
    9, 10, 11. *See also* Christianity; Islam
Rida, Sayyid Muhammad Rashid, 188
Rizaygat, 41, 56
Roberts, Hugh, 7
Ruh, 152

Sagiy system, 38
Sahloul, 'Ali Ahmed, 67
Sankara, Thomas, 18, 122
SANU (Sudan African National Union), 47
Saudi Arabia, 79, 80, 110, 190
Sayyid 'Abd-al Rahman al-Mahdi, 111
Schacht, Joseph, 184
Schuster, Sir George, 47
Secular, the, 89–91, 183
Secularism, 139, 151–52
Secularization, 151, 183
September laws, 26, 33, 52, 54, 56
Shaban uprising, 52
Shafi legal system, 213, 229, 238
Shail system, 37
Shamasa, 126–27
Shantytowns, 106–9, 122
Shari'a: Bashir's implementation of, 63,
    68–69; in Cape Town, 213; economic
    consequences of, 33; as form of cultural
    revival, 168, 170–74; function of in Su-
    dan, 232–33; implementation to create
    conditions of the possibility of, 159–60;
    as internal focus for Sudanese politics,
    109; Islamicization subordinate to, 173;
    Islamic movement on, 31, 83–84, 89, 98,
    123–24; in Khartoum, 124; military sup-
    port for circumvention of, 61, 149; Mus-
    lim Brotherhood on, 158; National Dem-
    ocratic Alliance disagreement on, 70;
    National Islamic Front support for, 92,
    150, 161; Northerners on implementa-
    tion of, 200–201; and religious reality,

183; Rida on, 188; the September laws,
    26, 33, 52, 54, 56; and Southerners,
    185–87; and Sudanese civil war, 31–32;
    and Sudanese identity, 30, 78; supporters
    and opponents of, 31; as supposed major-
    ity demand, 178–79; and Taha, 181, 185;
    Turabi on 173, 177, 189. See also *Hudud*
Shari'ati, 'Ali, 91, 92, 190
Shaykh, 180, 182
Sisters of St. Francis, 198
Skollies, 220
Sokoto, 12
Sorcery, 17, 182
Souk Libya, 102
South Africa: African National Congress,
    210, 214, 230, 240; African Peoples Or-
    ganization, 212; Apprenticeship Act of
    1922, 212; gangs in, 220; Group Areas
    Acts, 214–15; Islam in, 208–44; Islamic
    Council of South Africa, 224, 235, 236;
    Islamic movement in, 211; mass demo-
    cratic movement, 210; Muslim popula-
    tion of, 210; Nationalists, 212; Non-
    European Unity Movement, 212; Popula-
    tion Registration Act of 1950, 212;
    skollies, 220; social impact of Islam in,
    220–24; South African Coloured Peoples
    Congress, 212; Sudan compared to, 208,
    210–11, 224, 232–33, 238–40; town-
    ships, 215; tricameral legislature, 219;
    ulema, 213, 237; United Democratic
    Front, 214; women in, 220. *See also* Call
    of Islam; Cape Town; Coloreds; Muslim
    Youth Movement
South African Coloured Peoples Congress,
    212
Southern Command, 46
Southerners: Addis Ababa Agreement, 49,
    50; in Bashir government, 186; as cheap
    labor, 72; and Christianity, 199–200; de-
    population of the South, 45; economic
    and social conditions of, 72–74; ethnic
    and religious divisions among, 32, 68; ex-
    pulsion from Ethiopian refugee camps,
    42; following independence, 46–48; in-
    formal work, 40; Garang's demand for na-
    tional political role for, 164–65; Interim
    Council for the South, 58–59; on Islam,
    200; and the Islamic movement, 118,
    141, 144–49, 164–67; Jonglei Canal op-
    posed by, 72; in Khartoum, 67, 101,
    185–87, 195–96; Muslims in Southern
    Sudan, 110; National Islamic Front's poli-

cies on the South, 144–49; Nile Provisional Committee, 48; and Northerners, 20, 75–77, 118, 186, 190, 197–201; Northerners' desire to move to the South, 149; North-South antagonism in Khartoum, 74; under Numayri regime, 48–50; oil deposits, 45; overdetermination of North-South distinction, 192; purported attack on Malakal by, 43; response to the Islamic movement, 164–67; Revolutionary Command Council clampdown on, 66–67; on separation of religious and social, 199; share of national development budget, 73; and the *Shari'a*, 185–87; South administered from Khartoum, 45; Southern soldiers transferred to Khartoum, 50; Southern Sudan Liberation Front, 53; Southern Sudan Liberation Movement, 48; Southern Sudan Provisional Government, 48; subsistence agriculture destroyed in the South, 79; in Sudanese civil war, 13, 20, 29, 41; underdevelopment in the South, 73. *See also* Sudan People's Liberation Army

Southern policy, 47–48
Southern Sudan Liberation Front, 53
Southern Sudan Liberation Movement, 48
Southern Sudan Provisional Government (SSPG), 48
SPLA. *See* Sudan People's Liberation Army
SPLM. *See* Sudan People's Liberation Movement
SSPG. *See* Southern Sudan Provisional Government
State, the: anarchic and repressive action of African state, 4–5; apparent incompetence of, 18; as broker for development money, 18; church and mosque as more important power centers than, 17–18; civil service, 36, 39, 102, 194; and civil society in Africa, 13–22, 98; conditions for a strong state, 57; decline of in Third World, 241; and Islam, 123; Islamic movement as bridge between civil society and, 22; Islamic movement's quest for state power, 84–85, 98; Islamic state, 97–99; in Liberia, 21; merchant domination in Sudan, 112; Numayri's state apparatus, 102; postcolonial, 14; and the shantytowns, 107; Sudanese, 102, 112, 173; in Togo, 21; Turabi on the Sudanese, 173
Sub-Saharan Africa, 25

Sudan: Addis Ababa Agreement, 49, 50; Afro-Arabism of, 76; agriculture, 35–36, 37, 38, 39, 79; Arab identity in, 79–80; army ultimatum to Mahdi government, 60–62; Azanian National Front, 47; Bashir coup, 62–64; as beachhead in Africa for other countries, 190; Boma incident, 53; capitalist penetration of, 38, 79; civil service, 36, 39, 102, 194; Constituent Assembly, 57; constitution for, 91; corruption, 36; Council of State, 60; cultural homogenization of, 241; currency controls, 37; currency reform, 39; debt service obligations, 34; democracy ended by Bashir regime, 62–72; democracy restored in, 55–57; democracy's failure in, 57–60; dependence on foreign countries, 147–48; divide and rule policy, 41; economy, 33–40; emigration, 104; export commodities, 34; foreign earnings, 38; Islamic and African trends in, 30–33; Islamic Charter Front, 51; Islamic Front for the Constitution, 51; Islamicization in, 83–99, 179; Islamic Liberation Movement, 51; Islamic politics in, 96–97, 179, 206; Jebel Ladu scheme, 35; Koka Dam accord, 55; Little Almira incident, 58; Muslim population, 25; national debt, 33; National Democratic Alliance, 70; National Gathering for the Salvation of the Homeland, 53, 55; National Islamic Front on absence of democracy in, 187; National Salvation Revolutionary Command Council, 62, 64–67, 72; nineteenth-century Islamic regime, 12, 111; oil deposits in the South, 45; oil pipeline controversy, 53–54; political coherency in, 24, 27; politics, 109–14, 165; politics and religion in, 22–23, 32; politics of cultural revival in, 168–201; privatization, 21, 39; public sector, 37; purchasing power, 34; race in, 192, 195, 197–99; racism in, 75; recolonization feared in, 8–9, 93; Regional Covenant Act, 50; the religious and the secular in, 89–91; the September laws, 26, 33, 52, 54, 56; Shaban uprising, 52; South Africa compared to, 208, 210–11, 224, 232–33, 238–40; the state, 102, 112, 173; and sub-Saharan Africa, 25; Sudan African Closed District Union, 46–47; Sudan African National Union, 47; Sudanese attitude toward politics,

United Democratic Front (UDF), 214
United States, 147, 148
Upper Nile, 41, 43, 50

Wad al-Abbas, 35
Wan, Al- (newspaper), 136, 193
Ward committees, 70–71
Wau, 45, 48, 73, 118, 141
Weber, Max, 9, 10, 11, 247n.26
West Africa, 89, 154
Westerners: informal work, 40; in Khartoum, 67, 101; in Sudanese civil war, 42
Wheat, 39

White Nile Tannery, 39
Women: Islamic movement on, 125; National Islamic front on, 66, 138; Rida on, 188; in South Africa, 220; in the work force, 102; and *zar* cult, 182

Yassin, Mohammed el Hassan Abdullah, 113

Zaire, 5
Zar cult, 182
Zariba, 116–17
Zeidan, Zeidan Hassan, 170
Zein, Abdul Hamid al-, 95

THE PENGUIN POETS

TWENTY LOVE POEMS AND A SONG OF DESPAIR

Neftalí Ricardo Reyes, whose pseudonym was to be Pablo Neruda, was born in Parral, Chile, in 1904. He grew up in the pioneer town of Temuco, briefly encountering Gabriela Mistral, who taught there for a time. In 1920 he went to Santiago to study, and the following year published his first collection of poetry, *La Canción de la Fiesta*. A second collection, *Crepusculario*, brought him critical recognition; and in 1924 the hugely successful *Veinte Poemas de Amor y una Canción Desesperada* appeared. From 1927 to 1943, Neruda lived abroad, serving as a diplomat in Rangoon, Colombo, Batavia, Singapore, Buenos Aires, Barcelona, Madrid, Paris, and Mexico City. This is the period that saw the publication of the first two volumes of his celebrated *Residencia en la Tierra*. He joined the Communist Party of Chile after World War II, was prosecuted as a subversive, and began an exile that took him to Russia, Eastern Europe, and China. Already the most renowned Latin American poet of his time, he returned to Chile in 1952. He died there in 1973, having just seen the fourth edition of his *Obras Completas* through the press. In receiving the Nobel Prize in 1971, he had said that the poet must achieve a balance "between solitude and solidarity, between feeling and action, between the intimacy of one's self, the intimacy of mankind, and the relevation of nature."

W.S. Merwin has published several volumes of verse, among them *A Mask for Janus*, *The Dancing Bears*, *Green with Beasts*, and *Moving Target*. His *Selected Translations, 1964–1968* appeared in 1968.

Twenty Love Poems

AND A SONG OF DESPAIR

Pablo Neruda

Translated by W. S. Merwin

PENGUIN BOOKS

Penguin Books Ltd, Harmondsworth,
Middlesex, England
Penguin Books, 40 West 23rd Street,
New York, New York 10010, U.S.A.
Penguin Books Australia Ltd, Ringwood,
Victoria, Australia
Penguin Books Canada Limited, 2801 John Street
Markham, Ontario, Canada L3R 1B4
Penguin Books [N.Z.] Ltd, 182–190 Wairau Road,
Auckland 10, New Zealand

20 *Poemas de amor y una Canción desesperada* first published in
Chile 1924
This edition translated from the Spanish and first published in
Great Britain by Jonathan Cape Ltd 1969
First published in the United States of America by
Grossman Publishers 1969
Published in Penguin Books 1976

Reprinted 1977, 1978, 1980, 1981, 1983, 1984

LIBRARY OF CONGRESS CATALOGING IN PUBLICATION DATA
Neruda, Pablo, 1904–1973.
Twenty love poems and a song of despair.
(The Penguin poets)
Translation of Veinte poemas de amor y una
canción desesperada.
Parallel Spanish texts and English translation.
Bibliography: p. 66.
I. Title.
[PQ8097.N4V413 1969]   861   76-29006
ISBN 0 14 042.205 6

Printed in the United States of America by
Halliday Lithograph Corporation, West Hanover, Massachusetts

Contents

Twenty
Love Poems

AND A SONG OF DESPAIR

I

Cuerpo de Mujer

Cuerpo de mujer, blancas colinas, muslos blancos,
te pareces al mundo en tu actitud de entrega.
Mi cuerpo de labriego salvaje te socava
y hace saltar el hijo del fondo de la tierra.

Fui solo como un túnel. De mí huían los pájaros,
y en mí la noche entraba su invasión poderosa.
Para sobrevivirme te forjé como un arma,
como una flecha en mi arco, como una piedra en
   mi honda.

Pero cae la hora de la venganza, y te amo.
Cuerpo de piel, de musgo, de leche ávida y firme.
Ah los vasos del pecho! Ah los ojos de ausencia!
Ah las rosas del pubis! Ah tu voz lenta y triste!

Cuerpo de mujer mía, persistiré en tu gracia.
Mi sed, mi ansia sin límite, mi camino indeciso!
Oscuros cauces donde la sed eterna sigue,
y la fatiga sigue, y el dolor infinito.

I

Body of a Woman

Body of a woman, white hills, white thighs,
you look like a world, lying in surrender.
My rough peasant's body digs in you
and makes the son leap from the depth of the earth.

I was alone like a tunnel. The birds fled from me,
and night swamped me with its crushing invasion.
To survive myself I forged you like a weapon,
like an arrow in my bow, a stone in my sling.

But the hour of vengeance falls, and I love you.
Body of skin, of moss, of eager and firm milk.
Oh the goblets of the breast! Oh the eyes of absence!
Oh the roses of the pubis! Oh your voice, slow and
    sad!

Body of my woman, I will persist in your grace.
My thirst, my boundless desire, my shifting road!
Dark river-beds where the eternal thirst flows
and weariness follows, and the infinite ache.

II

En Su Llama Mortal

En su llama mortal la luz te envuelve.
Absorta, pálida doliente, así situada
contra las viejas hélices del crepúsculo
que en torno a ti da vueltas.

Muda, mi amiga,
sola en lo solitario de esta hora de muertes
y llena de las vidas del fuego,
pura heredera del día destruido.

Del sol cae un racimo en tu vestido oscuro.
De la noche las grandes raíces
crecen de súbito desde tu alma,
y a lo exterior regresan las cosas en ti ocultas,
de modo que un pueblo pálido y azul
de ti recién nacido se alimenta.

Oh grandiosa y fecunda y magnética esclava
del círculo que en negro y dorado sucede:
erguida, trata y logra una creación tan viva
que sucumben sus flores, y llena es de tristeza.

II

The Light Wraps You

The light wraps you in its mortal flame.
Abstracted pale mourner, standing that way
against the old propellers of the twilight
that revolves around you.

Speechless, my friend,
alone in the loneliness of this hour of the dead
and filled with the lives of fire,
pure heir of the ruined day.

A bough of fruit falls from the sun on your dark
    garment.
The great roots of night
grow suddenly from your soul,
and the things that hide in you come out again
so that a blue and pallid people,
your newly born, takes nourishment.

Oh magnificent and fecund and magnetic slave
of the circle that moves in turn through black and
    gold:
rise, lead and possess a creation
so rich in life that its flowers perish
and it is full of sadness.

III

Ah Vastedad de Pinos

Ah vastedad de pinos, rumor de olas quebrándose,
lento juego de luces, campana solitaria,
crepúsculo cayendo en tus ojos, muñeca,
caracola terrestre, en ti la tierra canta!

En ti los ríos cantan y mi alma en ellos huye
como tú lo desees y hacia donde tú quieras.
Márcame mi camino en tu arco de esperanza
y soltaré en delirio mi bandada de flechas.

En torno a mí estoy viendo tu cintura de niebla
y tu silencio acosa mis horas perseguidas,
y eres tú con tus brazos de piedra transparente
donde mis besos anclan y mi húmeda ansia anida.

Ah tu voz misteriosa que el amor tiñe y dobla
en el atardecer resonante y muriendo!
Así en horas profundas sobre los campos he visto
doblarse las espigas en la boca del viento.

III

Ah Vastness of Pines

Ah vastness of pines, murmur of waves breaking,
slow play of lights, solitary bell,
twilight falling in your eyes, toy doll,
earth-shell, in whom the earth sings!

In you the rivers sing and my soul flees in them
as you desire, and you send it where you will.
Aim my road on your bow of hope
and in a frenzy I will free my flock of arrows.

On all sides I see your waist of fog,
and your silence hunts down my afflicted hours;
my kisses anchor, and my moist desire nests
in you with your arms of transparent stone.

Ah your mysterious voice that love tolls and darkens
in the resonant and dying evening!
Thus in deep hours I have seen, over the fields,
the ears of wheat tolling in the mouth of the wind.

IV

Es La Mañana Llena

Es la mañana llena de tempestad
en el corazón del verano.

Como pañuelos blancos de adiós viajan las nubes,
el viento las sacude con sus viajeras manos.

Innumerable corazón del viento
latiendo sobre nuestro silencio enamorado.

Zumbando entre los árboles, orquestal y divino,
como una lengua llena de guerras y de cantos.

Viento que lleva en rápido robo la hojarasca
y desvía las flechas latientes de los pájaros.

Viento que la derriba en ola sin espuma
y sustancia sin peso, y fuegos inclinados.

Se rompe y se sumerge su volumen de besos
combatido en la puerta del viento del verano.

IV

The Morning Is Full

The morning is full of storm
in the heart of summer.

The clouds travel like white handkerchiefs of
    goodbye,
the wind, travelling, waving them in its hands.

The numberless heart of the wind
beating above our loving silence.

Orchestral and divine, resounding among the trees
like a language full of wars and songs.

Wind that bears off the dead leaves with a quick raid
and deflects the pulsing arrows of the birds.

Wind that topples her in a wave without spray
and substance without weight, and leaning fires.

Her mass of kisses breaks and sinks,
assailed in the door of the summer's wind.

V

Para Que Tú Me Oigas

Para que tú me oigas
mis palabras
se adelgazan a veces
como las huellas de las gaviotas en las playas.

Collar, cascabel ebrio
para tus manos suaves como las uvas.

Y las miro lejanas mis palabras.
Más que mías son tuyas.
Van trepando en mi viejo dolor como las yedras.

Ellas trepan así por las paredes húmedas.
Eres tú la culpable de este juego songriento.
Ellas están huyendo de mi guarida oscura.
Todo lo llenas tú, todo lo llenas.

Antes que tú poblaron la soledad que ocupas,
y están acostumbradas más que tú a mi tristeza.

Ahora quiero que digan lo que quiero decirte
para que tú me oigas como quiero que me oigas.

El viento de la angustia aún las suele arrastrar.
Huracanes de sueños aún a veces las tumban.
Escuchas otras voces en mi voz dolorida.

Llanto de viejas bocas, sangre de viejas súplicas.
Ámame, compañera. No me abandones. Sígueme.
Sígueme, compañera, en esa ola de angustia.

V

So That You Will Hear Me

So that you will hear me
my words
sometimes grow thin
as the tracks of the gulls on the beaches.

Necklace, drunken bell
for your hands smooth as grapes.

And I watch my words from a long way off.
They are more yours than mine.
They climb on my old suffering like ivy.

It climbs the same way on damp walls.
You are to blame for this cruel sport.
They are fleeing from my dark lair.
You fill everything, you fill everything.

Before you they peopled the solitude that you
    occupy,
and they are more used to my sadness than you are.

Now I want them to say what I want to say to you
to make you hear as I want you to hear me.

The wind of anguish still hauls on them as usual.
Sometimes hurricanes of dreams still knock them
    over.
You listen to other voices in my painful voice.

Lament of old mouths, blood of old supplications.
Love me, companion. Don't forsake me. Follow me.
Follow me, companion, on this wave of anguish.

Pero se van tiñendo con tu amor mis palabras.
Todo lo ocupas tú, todo lo ocupas.

Voy haciendo de todas un collar infinito
para tus blancas manos, suaves como las uvas.

But my words become stained with your love.
You occupy everything, you occupy everything.

I am making them into an endless necklace
for your white hands, smooth as grapes.

VI

Te Recuerdo Como Eras

Te recuerdo como eras en el último otoño.
Eras la boina gris y el corazón en calma.
En tus ojos peleaban las llamas del crepúsculo.
Y las hojas caían en el agua de tu alma.

Apegada a mis brazos como una enredadera,
las hojas recogían tu voz lenta y en calma.
Hoguera de estupor en que mi ser ardía.
Dulce jacinto azul torcido sobre mi alma.

Siento viajar tus ojos y es distante el otoño:
boina gris, voz de pájaro y corazón de casa
hacia donde emigraban mis profundos anhelos
y caían mis besos alegres como brasas.

Cielo desde un navío. Campo desde los cerros:
Tu recuerdo es de luz, de humo, de estanque en
    calma!
Más allá de tus ojos ardían los crepúsculos.
Hojas secas de otoño giraban en tu alma.

VI

I Remember You As You Were

I remember you as you were in the last autumn.
You were the grey beret and the still heart.
In your eyes the flames of the twilight fought on.
And the leaves fell in the water of your soul.

Clasping my arms like a climbing plant
the leaves garnered your voice, that was slow and at
    peace.
Bonfire of awe in which my thirst was burning.
Sweet blue hyacinth twisted over my soul.

I feel your eyes travelling, and the autumn is far off:
grey beret, voice of a bird, heart like a house
towards which my deep longings migrated
and my kisses fell, happy as embers.

Sky from a ship. Field from the hills:
Your memory is made of light, of smoke, of a still
    pond!
Beyond your eyes, farther on, the evenings were
    blazing.
Dry autumn leaves revolved in your soul.

VII

Inclinado En Las Tardes

Inclinado en las tardes tiro mis tristes redes
a tus ojos oceánicos.

Allí se estira y arde en la más alta hoguera
mi soledad que da vueltas los brazos como un
    náufrago.

Hago rojas señales sobre tus ojos ausentes
que olean como el mar a la orilla de un faro.

Sólo guardas tinieblas, hembra distante y mía,
de tu mirada emerge a veces la costa del espanto.

Inclinado en las tardes echo mis tristes redes
a ese mar que sacude tus ojos oceánicos.

Los pájaros nocturnos picotean las primeras
    estrellas
que centellean como mi alma cuando te amo.

Galopa la noche en su yegua sombría
desparramando espigas azules sobre el campo.

VII

Leaning Into The Afternoons

Leaning into the afternoons I cast my sad nets
towards your oceanic eyes.

There in the highest blaze my solitude lengthens and
    flames,
its arms turning like a drowning man's.

I send out red signals across your absent eyes
that move like the sea near a lighthouse.

You keep only darkness, my distant female,
from your regard sometimes the coast of dread
    emerges.

Leaning into the afternoons I fling my sad nets
to that sea that beats on your marine eyes.

The birds of night peck at the first stars
that flash like my soul when I love you.

The night gallops on its shadowy mare
shedding blue tassels over the land.

VIII

Abeja Blanca

Abeja blanca zumbas, ebria de miel, en mi alma
y te tuerces en lentas espirales de humo.

Soy el desesperado, la palabra sin ecos,
el que lo perdió todo, y el que todo lo tuvo.

Última amarra, cruje en ti mi ansiedad última.
En mi tierra desierta eres la última rosa.

Ah silenciosa!

Cierra tus ojos profundos. Allí aletea la noche.
Ah desnuda tu cuerpo de estatua temerosa.

Tienes ojos profundos donde la noche alea.
Frescos brazos de flor y regazo de rosa.

Se parecen tus senos a los caracoles blancos.
Ha venido a dormirse en tu vientre una mariposa
    de sombra.

Ah silenciosa!

He aquí la soledad de donde estás ausente.
Llueve. El viento del mar caza errantes gaviotas.

El agua anda descalza por las calles mojadas.
De aquel árbol se quejan, como enfermos, las hojas.

VIII

White Bee

White bee, you buzz in my soul, drunk with honey,
and your flight winds in slow spirals of smoke.

I am the one without hope, the word without echoes,
he who lost everything and he who had everything.

Last hawser, in you creaks my last longing.
In my barren land you are the final rose.

Ah you who are silent!

Let your deep eyes close. There the night flutters.
Ah your body, a frightened statue, naked.

You have deep eyes in which the night flails.
Cool arms of flowers and a lap of rose.

Your breasts seem like white snails.
A butterfly of shadow has come to sleep on your belly.

Ah you who are silent!

Here is the solitude from which you are absent.
It is raining. The sea wind is hunting stray gulls.

The water walks barefoot in the wet streets.
From that tree the leaves complain as though they
    were sick.

Abeja blanca, ausente, aún zumbas en mi alma.
Revives en el tiempo, delgada y silenciosa.

Ah silenciosa!

White bee, even when you are gone you buzz in my
   soul
You live again in time, slender and silent.

Ah you who are silent!

Ebrio De Trementina

Ebrio de trementina y largos besos,
estival, el velero de las rosas dirijo,
torcido hacia la muerte del delgado día,
cimentado en el sólido frenesí marino.

Pálido y amarrado a mi agua devorante
cruzo en el agrio olor del clima descubierto,
aún vestido de gris y sonidos amargos,
y una cimera triste de abandonada espuma.

Voy, duro de pasiones, montado en mi ola única,
lunar, solar, ardiente y frío, repentino,
dormido en la garganta de las afortunadas
islas blancas y dulces como caderas frescas.

Tiembla en la noche húmeda mi vestido de besos
locamente cargado de eléctricas gestiones,
de modo heroico dividido en sueños
y embriagadoras rosas practicándose en mí.

Aguas arriba, en medio de las olas externas,
tu paralelo cuerpo se sujeta en mis brazos
como un pez infinitamente pegado a mi alma
rápido y lento en la energía subceleste.

IX

Drunk With Pines

Drunk with pines and long kisses,
like summer I steer the fast sail of the roses,
bent towards the death of the thin day,
stuck into my solid marine madness.

Pale and lashed to my ravenous water,
I cruise in the sour smell of the naked climate,
still dressed in grey and bitter sounds
and a sad crest of abandoned spray.

Hardened by passions, I go mounted on my one
    wave,
lunar, solar, burning and cold, all at once,
becalmed in the throat of the fortunate isles
that are white and sweet as cool hips.

In the moist night my garment of kisses trembles
charged to insanity with electric currents,
heroically divided into dreams
and intoxicating roses practising on me.

Upstream, in the midst of the outer waves,
your parallel body yields to my arms
like a fish infinitely fastened to my soul,
quick and slow, in the energy under the sky.

X

Hemos Perdido Aun

Hemos perdido aun este crepúsculo.
Nadie nos vio esta tarde con las manos unidas
mientras la noche azul caía sobre el mundo.

He visto desde mi ventana
la fiesta del poniente en los cerros lejanos.

A veces como una moneda
se encendía un pedazo de sol entre mis manos.

Yo te recordaba con el alma apretada
de esa tristeza que tú me conoces.

Entonces dónde estabas?
Entre qué gentes?
Diciendo qué palabras?
Por qué se me vendrá todo el amor de golpe
cuando me siento triste, y te siento lejana?

Cayó el libro que siempre se toma en el crepúsculo.
y como un perro herido rodó a mis pies mi capa.

Siempre, siempre te alejas en las tardes
hacia donde el crepúsculo corre borrando estatuas.

X

We Have Lost Even

We have lost even this twilight.
No one saw us this evening hand in hand
while the blue night dropped on the world.

I have seen from my window
the fiesta of sunset in the distant mountain tops.

Sometimes a piece of sun
burned like a coin between my hands.

I remembered you with my soul clenched
in that sadness of mine that you know.

Where were you then?
Who else was there?
Saying what?
Why will the whole of love come on me suddenly
when I am sad and feel you are far away?

The book fell that is always turned to at twilight
and my cape rolled like a hurt dog at my feet.

Always, always you recede through the evenings
towards where the twilight goes erasing statues.

Casi Fuera Del Cielo

Casi fuera del cielo ancla entre dos montañas
la mitad de la luna.
Girante, errante noche, la cavadora de ojos.
A ver cuántas estrellas trizadas en la charca.

Hace una cruz de luto entre mis cejas, huye.
Fragua de metales azules, noches de las calladas
    luchas,
mi corazón da vueltas como un volante loco.
Niña venida de tan lejos, traída de tan lejos,
a veces fulgurece su mirada debajo del cielo.
Quejumbre, tempestad, remolino de furia,
cruza encima de mi corazón, sin detenerte.
Viento de los sepulcros acarrea, destroza, dispersa
    tu raíz soñolienta.

Desarraiga los grandes árboles al otro lado de ella.
Pero tú, clara niña, pregunta de humo, espiga.
Era la que iba formando el viento con hojas
    iluminadas.
Detrás de las montañas nocturnas, blanco lirio de
    incendio,
ah nada puedo decir! Era hecha de todas las cosas.

Ansiedad que partiste mi pecho a cuchillazos,
es hora de seguir otro camino, donde ella no sonría.
Tempestad que enterró las campanas, turbio revuelo
    de tormentas
para qué tocarla ahora, para qué entristecerla.

Almost Out Of The Sky

Almost out of the sky, half of the moon
anchors between two mountains.
Turning, wandering night, the digger of eyes.
Let's see how many stars are smashed in the pool.

It makes a cross of mourning between my eyes, and
    runs away.
Forge of blue metals, nights of stilled combats,
my heart revolves like a crazy wheel.
Girl who have come from so far, been brought from
    so far,
sometimes your glance flashes out under the sky.
Rumbling, storm, cyclone of fury,
you cross above my heart without stopping.
Wind from the tombs carries off, wrecks, scatters
    your sleepy root.

The big trees on the other side of her, uprooted.
But you, cloudless girl, question of smoke, corn
    tassel.
You were what the wind was making with illumi-
    nated leaves.
Behind the nocturnal mountains, white lily of
    conflagration,
ah, I can say nothing! You were made of everything.

Longing that sliced my breast into pieces,
it is time to take another road, on which she does not
    smile.
Storm that buried the bells, muddy swirl of torments,
why touch her now, why make her sad.

Ay seguir el camino que se aleja de todo,
donde no esté atajando la angustia, la muerte, el
    invierno,
con sus ojos abiertos entre el rocío.

Oh to follow the road that leads away from every-
    thing,
without anguish, death, winter waiting along it
with their eyes open through the dew.

XII

Para Mi Corazón

Para mi corazón basta tu pecho,
para tu libertad bastan mis alas.
Desde mi boca llegará hasta el cielo
lo que estaba dormido sobre tu alma.

Es en ti la ilusión de cada día.
Llegas como el rocío a las corolas.
Socavas el horizonte con tu ausencia.
Eternamente en fuga como la ola.

He dicho que cantabas en el viento
como los pinos y como los mástiles.
Como ellos eres alta y taciturna.
Y entristeces de pronto, como un viaje.

Acogedora como un viejo camino.
Te pueblan ecos y voces nostálgicas.
Yo desperté y a veces emigran y huyen
pájaros que dormían en tu alma.

XII

Your Breast Is Enough

Your breast is enough for my heart,
and my wings for your freedom.
What was sleeping above your soul will rise
out of my mouth to heaven.

In you is the illusion of each day.
You arrive like the dew to the cupped flowers.
You undermine the horizon with your absence.
Eternally in flight like the wave.

I have said that you sang in the wind
like the pines and like the masts.
Like them you are tall and taciturn,
and you are sad, all at once, like a voyage.

You gather things to you like an old road.
You are peopled with echoes and nostalgic voices.
I awoke and at times birds fled and migrated
that had been sleeping in your soul.

XIII

He Ido Marcando

He ido marcando con cruces de fuego
el atlas blanco de tu cuerpo.
Mi boca era una araña que cruzaba escondiéndose.
En ti, detrás de ti, temerosa, sedienta.

Historias que contarte a la orilla del crepúsculo,
muñeca triste y dulce, para que no estuvieras triste.
Un cisne, un árbol, algo lejano y alegre.
El tiempo de las uvas, el tiempo maduro y frutal.

Yo que viví en un puerto desde donde te amaba.
La soledad cruzada de sueño y de silencio.
Acorralado entre el mar y la tristeza.
Callado, delirante, entre dos gondoleros inmóviles.

Entre los labios y la voz, algo se va muriendo.
Algo con alas de pájaro, algo de angustia y de olvido.
Así como las redes no retienen el agua.
Muñeca mía, apenas quedan gotas temblando.
Sin embargo algo canta entre estas palabras fugaces.
Algo canta, algo sube hasta mi ávida boca.
Oh poder celebrarte con todas las palabras de alegría.

Cantar, arder, huir, como un campanario en las
      manos de un loco.
Triste ternura mía, ¿qué te haces de repente?
Cuando he llegado al vértice más atrevido y frío
mi corazón se cierra como una flor nocturna.

XIII

I Have Gone Marking

I have gone marking the atlas of your body
with crosses of fire.
My mouth went across: a spider, trying to hide.
In you, behind you, timid, driven by thirst.

Stories to tell you on the shore of evening,
sad and gentle doll, so that you should not be sad.
A swan, a tree, something far away and happy.
The season of grapes, the ripe and fruitful season.

I who lived in a harbour from which I loved you.
The solitude crossed with dream and with silence.
Penned up between the sea and sadness.
Soundless, delirious, between two motionless
    gondoliers.

Between the lips and the voice something goes dying.
Something with the wings of a bird, something of
    anguish and oblivion.
The way nets cannot hold water.
My toy doll, only a few drops are left trembling.
Even so, something sings in these fugitive words.
Something sings, something climbs to my ravenous
    mouth.
Oh to be able to celebrate you with all the words of
    joy.

Sing, burn, flee, like a belfry at the hands of a
    madman.
My sad tenderness, what comes over you all at once?
When I have reached the most awesome and the
    coldest summit
my heart closes like a nocturnal flower.

XIV

Juegas Todos Los Días

Juegas todos los días con la luz del universo.
Sutil visitadora, llegas en la flor y en el agua.
Eres más que esta blanca cabecita que aprieto
como un racimo entre mis manos cada día.

A nadie te pareces desde que yo te amo.
Déjame tenderte entre guirnaldas amarillas.
Quién escribe tu nombre con letras de humo entre
    las estrellas del sur?
Ah déjame recordarte cómo eras entonces, cuando
    aún no existías.

De pronto el viento aúlla y golpea mi ventana
    cerrada.
El cielo es una red cuajada de peces sombríos.
Aquí vienen a dar todos los vientos, todos.
Se desviste la lluvia.

Pasan huyendo los pájaros.
El viento. El viento.
Yo sólo puedo luchar contra la fuerza de los hombres.
El temporal arremolina hojas oscuras
y suelta toda las barcas que anoche amarraron al
    cielo.

Tú estás aquí. Ah tú no huyes.
Tú me responderás hasta el último grito.
Ovíllate a mi lado como si tuvieras miedo.
Sin embargo alguna vez corrió una sombra extraña
    por tus ojos.

Ahora, ahora también, pequeña, me traes madre-
    selvas,

40

XIV

Every Day You Play

Every day you play with the light of the universe.
Subtle visitor, you arrive in the flower and the water.
You are more than this white head that I hold tightly
as a cluster of fruit, every day, between my hands.

You are like nobody since I love you.
Let me spread you out among yellow garlands.
Who writes your name in letters of smoke among
    the stars of the south?
Oh let me remember you as you were before you
    existed.

Suddenly the wind howls and bangs at my shut
    window.
The sky is a net crammed with shadowy fish.
Here all the winds let go sooner or later, all of them.
The rain takes off her clothes.

The birds go by, fleeing.
The wind. The wind.
I can contend only against the power of men.
The storm whirls dark leaves
and turns loose all the boats that were moored last
    night to the sky.

You are here. Oh, you do not run away.
You will answer me to the last cry.
Cling to me as though you were frightened.
Even so, at one time a strange shadow ran through
    your eyes.

Now, now too, little one, you bring me honeysuckle,
and even your breasts smell of it.

41

y tienes hasta los senos perfumados.
mientras el viento triste galopa matando mariposas
yo te amo, y mi alegría muerde tu boca de ciruela.

Cuánto te habrá dolido acostumbrarte a mí,
a mi alma sola y salvaje, a mi nombre que todos
     ahuyentan.
Hemos visto arder tantas veces el lucero besándonos
     los ojos
y sobre nuestras cabezas destorcerse los crepúsculos
     en abanicos girantes.

Mis palabras llovieron sobre ti acariciándote.
Amé desde hace tiempo tu cuerpo de nácar soleado.
Hasta te creo dueña del universo.
Te traeré de las montañas flores alegres, copihues,
avellanas oscuras, y cestas silvestres de besos.
Quiero hacer contigo
lo que la primavera hace con los cerezos.

While the sad wind goes slaughtering butterflies
I love you, and my happiness bites the plum of your
    mouth.

How you must have suffered getting accustomed to
    me.
my savage, solitary soul, my name that sends them
    all running.
So many times we have seen the morning star burn,
    kissing our eyes,
and over our heads the grey light unwind in turning
    fans.

My words rained over you, stroking you.
A long time I have loved the sunned mother-of-pearl
    of your body.
I go so far as to think that you own the universe.
I will bring you happy flowers from the mountains,
    bluebells,
dark hazels, and rustic baskets of kisses.
I want
to do with you what spring does with the cherry
    trees.

XV

Me Gustas Cuando Callas

Me gustas cuando callas porque estás como ausente,
y me oyes desde lejos, y mi voz no te toca.
Parece que, los ojos se te hubieran volado
y parece que un beso te cerrara la boca.

Como todas las cosas están llenas de mi alma
emerges de las cosas, llena del alma mía.
Mariposa de sueño, te pareces a mi alma,
y te pareces a la palabra melancolía.

Me gustas cuando callas y estás como distante.
Y estás como quejándote, mariposa en arrullo.
Y me oyes desde lejos, y mi voz no te alcanza:
Déjame que me calle con el silencio tuyo.

Déjame que te hable también con tu silencio
claro como una lámpara, simple como un anillo.
Eres como la noche, callada y constelada.
Tu silencio es de estrella, tan lejano y sencillo.

Me gustas cuando callas porque estás como ausente
Distante y dolorosa como si hubieras muerto.
Una palabra entonces, una sonrisa bastan.
Y estoy alegre, alegre de que no sea cierto.

XV

I Like For You To Be Still

I like for you to be still: it is as though you were
    absent,
and you hear me from far away and my voice does
    not touch you.
It seems as though your eyes had flown away
and it seems that a kiss had sealed your mouth.

As all things are filled with my soul
you emerge from the things, filled with my soul.
You are like my soul, a butterfly of dream,
and you are like the word Melancholy.

I like for you to be still, and you seem far away.
It sounds as though you were lamenting, a butterfly
    cooing like a dove.
And you hear me from far away, and my voice does
    not reach you:
Let me come to be still in your silence.

And let me talk to you with your silence
that is bright as a lamp, simple as a ring.
You are like the night, with its stillness and constel-
    lations.
Your silence is that of a star, as remote and candid.

I like for you to be still: it is as though you were
    absent,
distant and full of sorrow as though you had died.
One word then, one smile, is enough.
And I am happy, happy that it's not true.

XVI

En Mi Cielo Al Crepúsculo

Este poema es una parúfrasis del
poema 30 de El jardinero *de*
Rabindranath Tagore.

En mi cielo al crepúsculo cres como una nube
y tu color y forma son como yo los quiero.
Eras mía, cres mía, mujer de labios dulces
y viven en tu vida mis infinitos sueños.

La lámpara de mí alma te sonorosa los pies,
el agrio vino mío es más dulce en tus labios,
oh segadora de mi canción de atardecer,
cómo te sienten mía mis sueños solitarios!

Eres mía, eres mía, voy gritando en la brisa
de la tarde, y el viento arrastra mi voz viuda.
Cazadora del fondo de mis ojos, tu robo
estanca como el agua tu mirada nocturna.

En la red de mi música estás presa, amor mío,
y mis redes de música son anchas como el cielo.
Mi alma nace a la orilla de tus ojos de luto.
En tus ojos de luto comienza el país del sueño.

XVI

In My Sky At Twilight

This poem is a paraphrase of the 30th poem in Rabindranath Tagore's The Gardener.

In my sky at twilight you are like a cloud
and your form and colour are the way I love them.
You are mine, mine, woman with sweet lips
and in your life my infinite dreams live.

The lamp of my soul dyes your feet,
My sour wine is sweeter on your lips,
oh reaper of my evening song,
how solitary dreams believe you to be mine!

You are mine, mine, I go shouting it to the afternoon's
wind, and the wind hauls on my widowed voice.
Huntress of the depths of my eyes, your plunder
stills your nocturnal regard as though it were water.

You are taken in the net of my music, my love,
and my nets of music are wide as the sky.
My soul is born on the shore of your eyes of
mourning.
In your eyes of mourning the land of dreams begins.

XVII

Pensando, Enredando Sombras

Pensando, enredando sombras en la profunda soledad.
Tú también estás lejos, ah más lejos que nadie.
Pensando, soltando pájaros, desvaneciendo imágenes,
enterrando lámparas.

Campanario de brumas, qué lejos, allá arriba!
Ahogando lamentos, moliendo esperanzas sombrías,
molinero taciturno,
se te viene de bruces la noche, lejos de la ciudad.

Tu presencia es ajena, extraña a mí como una cosa.
Pienso, camino largamente, mi vida antes de ti.
Mi vida antes de nadie, mi áspera vida.
El grito frente al mar, entre las piedras,
corriendo libre, loco, en el vaho del mar.
La furia triste, el grito, la soledad del mar.
Desbocado, violento, estirado hacia el cielo.

Tú, mujer, qué eras allí, qué raya, qué varilla
de ese abanico inmenso? Estabas lejos como ahora.
Incendio en el bosque! Arde en cruces azules.
Arde, arde, llamea, chispea en árboles de luz.

Se derrumba, crepita. Incendio. Incendio.
Y mi alma baila herida de virutas de fuego.
Quién llama? Qué silencio poblado de ecos?
Hora de la nostalgia, hora de la alegría, hora de
    la soledad,
hora mía entre todas!
Bocina en que el viento pasa cantando.
Tanta pasión de llanto anudada a mi cuerpo.

XVII

Thinking, Tangling Shadows

Thinking, tangling shadows in the deep solitude.
You are far away too, oh farther than anyone.
Thinking, freeing birds, dissolving images,
burying lamps.

Belfry of fogs, how far away, up there!
Stifling laments, milling shadowy hopes,
taciturn miller,
night falls on you face downward, far from the city.

Your presence is foreign, as strange to me as a thing.
I think, I explore great tracts of my life before you.
My life before anyone, my harsh life.
The shout facing the sea, among the rocks,
running free, mad, in the sea-spray.
The sad rage, the shout, the solitude of the sea.
Headlong, violent, stretched towards the sky.

You, woman, what were you there, what ray, what
    vane
of that immense fan? You were as far as you are now.
Fire in the forest! Burn in blue crosses.
Burn, burn, flame up, sparkle in trees of light.

It collapses, crackling. Fire. Fire.
And my soul dances, seared with curls of fire.
Who calls? What silence peopled with echoes?
Hour of nostalgia, hour of happiness, hour of solitude,
hour that is mine from among them all!
Hunting horn through which the wind passes singing.
Such a passion of weeping tied to my body.

Sacudida de todas las raíces,
asalto de todas las olas!
Rodaba, alegre, triste interminable, mi alma.

Pensando, enterrando lámparas en la profunda
soledad.

Quién eres tú, quién eres?

Shaking of all the roots,
attack of all the waves!
My soul wandered, happy, sad, unending.

Thinking, burying lamps in the deep solitude.

Who are you, who are you?

Aquí Te Amo

Aquí te amo.
En los oscuros pinos se desenreda el viento.
Fosforece la luna sobre las aguas errantes.
Andan días iguales persiguiéndose.

Se desciñe la niebla en danzantes figuras.
Una gaviota de plata se descuelga del ocaso.
A veces una vela. Altas, altas, estrellas.

O la cruz negra de un barco.
Solo.
A veces amanezco, y hasta mi alma está húmeda.
Suena, resuena el mar lejano.
Éste es un puerto.
Aquí te amo.

Aquí te amo y en vano te oculta el horizonte.
Te estoy amando aún entre estas frías cosas.
A veces van mis besos en esos barcos graves,
que corren por el mar hacia donde no llegan.
Ya me veo olvidado como estas viejas anclas.
Son más triste los muelles cuando atraca la tarde.
Se fatiga mi vida inútilmente hambrienta.
Amo lo que no tengo. Estás tú tan distante.
Mi hastío forcejea con los lentos crepúsculos.
Pero la noche llega y comienza a cantarme.

La luna hace girar su rodaje de sueño.
Me miran con tus ojos las estrellas más grandes.
Y como yo te amo, los pinos en el viento,
quieren cantar tu nombre con sus hojas de alambre.

XVIII

Here I Love You

Here I love you.
In the dark pines the wind disentangles itself.
The moon glows like phosphorus on the vagrant
    waters.
Days, all one kind, go chasing each other.

The snow unfurls in dancing figures.
A silver gull slips down from the west.
Sometimes a sail. High, high stars.

Oh the black cross of a ship.
Alone.
Sometimes I get up early and even my soul is wet.
Far away the sea sounds and resounds.
This is a port.
Here I love you.

Here I love you and the horizon hides you in vain.
I love you still among these cold things.
Sometimes my kisses go on those heavy vessels
that cross the sea towards no arrival.
I see myself forgotten like those old anchors.
The piers sadden when the afternoon moors there.
My life grows tired, hungry to no purpose.
I love what I do not have. You are so far.
My loathing wrestles with the slow twilights.
But night comes and starts to sing to me.

The moon turns its clockwork dream.
The biggest stars look at me with your eyes.
And as I love you, the pines in the wind
want to sing your name with their leaves of wire.

Niña Morena y Ágil

Niña morena y ágil, el sol que hace las frutas,
el que cuaja los trigos, el que tuerce las algas,
hizo tu cuerpo alegre, tus luminosos ojos
y tu boca que tiene la sonrisa del agua.

Un sol negro y ansioso se te arrolla en las hebras
de le negra melena, cuando estiras los brazos.
Tú juegas con el sol como con un estero
y él te deja en los ojos dos oscuros remansos.

Niña morena y ágil, nada hacia ti me acerca.
Todo de ti me aleja, como del medio día.
Eres la delirante juventud de la abeja,
la embriaguez de la ola, la fuerza de la espiga.

Mi corazón sombrío te busca, sin embargo,
y amo tu cuerpo alegre, tu voz suelta y delgada.
Mariposa morena dulce y definitiva
como el trigal y el sol, la amapola y el agua.

XIX

Girl Lithe and Tawny

Girl lithe and tawny, the sun that forms
the fruits, that plumps the grains, that curls sea-
    weeds
filled your body with joy, and your luminous eyes
and your mouth that has the smile of the water.

A black yearning sun is braided into the strands
of your black mane, when you stretch your arms.
You play with the sun as with a little brook
and it leaves two dark pools in your eyes.

Girl lithe and tawny, nothing draws me towards you.
Everything bears me farther away, as though you
    were noon.
You are the frenzied youth of the bee,
the drunkenness of the wave, the power of the
    wheat-ear.

My sombre heart searches for you, nevertheless,
and I love your joyful body, your slender and flowing
    voice.
Dark butterfly, sweet and definitive
like the wheat-field and the sun, the poppy and the
    water.

XX

Puedo Escribir

Puedo escribir los versos más tristes esta noche.

Escribir, por ejemplo: 'La noche está estrellada,
y tiritan, azules, los astros, a lo lejos.'

El viento de la noche gira en el cielo y canta.

Puedo escribir los versos más tristes esta noche.
Yo la quise, y a veces ella también me quiso.

En las noches como ésta la tuve entre mis brazos.
La besé tantas veces bajo el cielo infinito.

Ella me quiso, a veces yo también la quería.
Cómo no haber amado sus grandes ojos fijos.

Puedo escribir los versos más tristes esta noche.
Pensar que no la tengo. Sentir que la he perdido.

Oir la noche inmensa, más inmensa sin ella.
Y el verso cae al alma como al pasto el rocío.

Qué importa que mi amor no pudiera guardarla.
La noche está estrellada y ella no está conmigo.

Eso es todo. A lo lejos alguien canta. A lo lejos.
Mi alma no se contenta con haberla perdido.

Como para acercarla mi mirada la busca.
Mi corazón la busca, y ella no está conmigo.

XX

Tonight I Can Write

Tonight I can write the saddest lines.

Write, for example, 'The night is starry
and the stars are blue and shiver in the distance.'

The night wind revolves in the sky and sings.

Tonight I can write the saddest lines.
I loved her, and sometimes she loved me too.

Through nights like this one I held her in my arms.
I kissed her again and again under the endless sky.

She loved me, sometimes I loved her too.
How could one not have loved her great still eyes.

Tonight I can write the saddest lines.
To think that I do not have her. To feel that I have
    lost her.

To hear the immense night, still more immense
    without her.
And the verse falls to the soul like dew to the pasture.

What does it matter that my love could not keep her.
The night is starry and she is not with me.

This is all. In the distance someone is singing. In the
    distance.
My soul is not satisfied that it has lost her.

My sight tries to find her as though to bring her closer
My heart looks for her, and she is not with me.

La misma noche que hace blanquear los mismos
    árboles.
Nosotros, los de entonces, ya no somos los mismos.

Ya no la quiero, es cierto, pero cuánto la quise.
Mi voz buscaba el viento para tocar su oído.

De otro. Será de otro. Como antes de mis besos.
Su voz, su cuerpo claro. Sus ojos infinitos.

Ya no la quiero, es cierto, pero tal vez la quiero.
Es tan corto el amor, y es tan largo el olvido.

Porque en noches como ésta ta tuve entre nus
    brazos,
mi alma no se contenta con haberla perdido.

Aunque éste sea el último dolor que ella me causa,
y éstos sean los últimos verso que yo le escribo.

The same night whitening the same trees.
We, of that time, are no longer the same.

I no longer love her, that's certain, but how I loved
    her.
My voice tried to find the wind to touch her hearing.

Another's. She will be another's. As she was before my
    kisses.
Her voice, her bright body. Her infinite eyes.

I no longer love her, that's certain, but maybe I love
    her.
Love is so short, forgetting is so long.

Because through nights like this one I held her in my
    arms
my soul is not satisfied that it has lost her.

Though this be the last pain that she makes me suffer
and these the last verses that I write for her.

La Canción Desesperada

Emerge tu recuerdo de la noche en que estoy.
El rio anuda al mar su lamento obstinado.

Abandonado como los muelles en el alba.
Es la hora de partir, oh abandonado!

Sobre mi corazón llueven frías corolas.
Oh sentina de escombros, feroz cueva de náufragos.

En ti se acumularon las guerras y los vuelos.
De ti alzaron las alas los pájoras del canto.

Todo te lo tragaste, como la lejanía.
Como el mar, como el tiempo. Todo en ti fue
    naufragio!

Era la alegre hora del asalto y el beso.
La hora del estupor que ardía como un faro.

Ansiedad de piloto, furia de buzo ciego,
turbia embriaguez de amor, todo en ti fue naufragio!

En la infancia de niebla mi alma alada y herida.
Descubridor perdido, todo en ti fue naufragio!

Te ceñiste al dolor, te agarraste al deseo,
te tumbo la tristeza, todo en ti fue naufragio!

Hice retroceder la muralla de sombra,
anduve más allá del deseo y del acto.

The Song of Despair

The memory of you emerges from the night around
me.
The river mingles its stubborn lament with the sea.

Deserted like the wharves at dawn.
It is the hour of departure, oh deserted one!

Cold flower heads are raining over my heart.
Oh pit of debris, fierce cave of the shipwrecked.

In you the wars and the flights accumulated.
From you the wings of the song birds rose.

You swallowed everything, like distance.
Like the sea, like time. In you everything sank!

It was the happy hour of assault and the kiss.
The hour of the spell that blazed like a lighthouse.

Pilot's dread, fury of a blind diver,
turbulent drunkenness of love, in you everything
sank!

In the childhood of mist my soul, winged and
wounded.
Lost discoverer, in you everything sank!

You girdled sorrow, you clung to desire,
sadness stunned you, in you everything sank!

I made the wall of shadow draw back,
beyond desire and act, I walked on.

Oh carne, carne mía, mujer que amé y perdí,
a ti en esta hora húmeda, evoco y hago canto.

Como un vaso albergaste la infinita ternura,
y el infinito olvido te trizó como a un vaso.

Era la negra, negra soledad de las islas,
y allí, mujer de amor, me acogieron tus brazos.

Era la sed y el hambre, y tú fuiste la fruta.
Era el duelo y las ruinas, y tú fuiste el milagro.

Ah mujer, no sé cómo pudiste contenerme
en la tierra de tu alma, y en la cruz de tus brazos!

Mi deseo de ti fue el más terrible y corto,
el más revuelto y ebrio, el más tirante y ávido.

Cementerio de besos, aún hay fuego en tus tumbas,
aún los racimos arden picoteados de pájaros.

Oh la boca mordida, oh los besados miembros,
oh los hambrientos, dientes, oh los cuerpos trenzados.

Oh la cópula loca de esperanza y esfuerzo
en que nos anudamos y nos desesperamos.

Y la ternura, leve como el agua y la harina.
Y la palabra apenas comenzada en los labios.

Ese fue mi destino y en él viajó mi anhelo,
y en él cayó mi anhelo, todo en ti fue naufragio!

Oh flesh, my own flesh, woman whom I loved and lost,
I summon you in the moist hour, I raise my song to
   you.

Like a jar you housed the infinite tenderness,
and the infinite oblivion shattered you like a jar.

There was the black solitude of the islands,
and there, woman of love, your arms took me in.

There were thirst and hunger, and you were the fruit.
There were grief and the ruins, and you were the
   miracle.

Ah woman, I do not know how you could contain me
in the earth of your soul, in the cross of your arms!

How terrible and brief was my desire of you!
How difficult and drunken, how tensed and avid.

Cemetery of kisses, there is still fire in your tombs,
still the fruited boughs burn, pecked at by birds.

Oh the bitten mouth, oh the kissed limbs,
oh the hungering teeth, oh the entwined bodies.

Oh the mad coupling of hope and force
in which we merged and despaired.

And the tenderness, light as water and as flour.
And the word scarcely begun on the lips.

This was my destiny and in it was the voyage of my
   longing,
and in it my longing fell, in you everything sank!

Oh, sentina de escombros, en ti todo caía,
qué dolor no exprimiste, qué dolor no te ahoga!

De tumbo en tumbo aún llameaste y cantaste.
De pie como un marino en la proa de un barco.

Aún florecistes en cantos, aún rompiste en corrientes.
Oh sentina de escombros, pozo abierto y amargo.

Pálido buzo ciego, desventurado hondero,
descubridor perdido, todo en ti fue naufragio!

Es la hora de partir, la dura y fría hora
que la noche sujeta a todo horario.

El cinturón ruidoso del mar ciñe la costa.
Surgen frías estrellas, emigran negros pájaros.

Abandonado como los muelles en el alba.
Sólo la sombra trémula se retuerce en mis manos.

Ah más allá de todo. Ah más allá de todo.

Es la hora de partir. Oh abandonado!

Oh pit of debris, everything fell into you,
what sorrow did you not express, in what sorrow are
   you not drowned!

From billow to billow you still called and sang.
Standing like a sailor in the prow of a vessel.

You still flowered in songs, you still broke in currents.
Oh pit of debris, open and bitter well.

Pale blind diver, luckless slinger,
lost discoverer, in you everything sank!

It is the hour of departure, the hard cold hour
which the night fastens to all the timetables.

The rustling belt of the sea girdles the shore.
Cold stars heave up, black birds migrate.

Deserted like the wharves at dawn.
Only the tremulous shadow twists in my hands.

Oh farther than everything. Oh farther than everything.

It is the hour of departure. Oh abandoned one!

SELECTED BIBLIOGRAPHY

A list of the principal works of Pablo Neruda
with the dates of their first appearance

LA CANCIÓN DE LA FIESTA (Ediciones Juventud, Santiago, 1921)

CREPUSCULARIO (Editorial Claridad, Santiago, 1923)

VEINTE POEMAS DE AMOR Y UNA CANCIÓN DESESPERADA (Nascimento, Santiago, 1924)

TENTATIVA DEL HOMBRE INFINITO (Nascimento, Santiago, 1925-6)

EL HABITANTE Y SU ESPERANZA (Nascimento, Santiago, 1925-6)

ANILLOS (Nascimento, Santiago, 1926)

EL HONDERO ENTUSIASTA (Empresa Letras, Santiago, 1933)

RESIDENCIA EN LA TIERRA 1925-1931 (Nascimento, Santiago, 1933)

RESIDENCIA EN LA TIERRA 1925-1935 (Cruz y Raya, Madrid, 1935)

TERCERA RESIDENCIA 1935-1945 (Losada, Buenos Aires, 1947)

CANTO GENERAL (Private Edition and Editorial Océano, Mexico, 1950)

LOS VERSOS DEL CAPITÁN (Private Edition, Naples, 1952)

LAS UVAS Y EL VIENTO (Nascimento, Santiago, 1954)

ODAS ELEMENTALES (Losada, Buenos Aires, 1954)

NUEVAS ODAS ELEMENTALES (Losada, Buenos Aires, 1956)

TERCER LIBRO DE ODAS (Losada, Buenos Aires, 1957)

OBRAS COMPLETAS (Losada, Buenos Aires, 1957; rev. and augm., 1962)

ESTRAVAGARIO (Losada, Buenos Aires, 1958)

NAVEGACIONES Y REGRESOS (Losada, Buenos Aires, 1959)

CIEN SONETOS DE AMOR (Private Edition, Santiago and Losada, Buenos Aires, 1959)

CANTOS CEREMONIALES (Losada, Buenos Aires, 1961)

PLENOS PODERES (Losada, Buenos Aires, 1962)

MEMORIAL DE ISLA NEGRA (Losada, Buenos Aires, 1964)

Editor's note: There is uncertainty, even among experts, as to some details of Neruda's bibliography.

SOME TRANSLATIONS OF PABLO NERUDA

RESIDENCE ON EARTH AND OTHER POEMS, translated by Angel Flores (New Directions, New York, 1946)

TWENTY LOVE POEMS BASED ON THE SPANISH OF PABLO NERUDA, translated by Christopher Logue in *Songs* (Hutchinson, London, 1959)

SELECTED POEMS OF PABLO NERUDA, translated by Ben Belitt (Grove Press, New York, 1961)

THE ELEMENTARY ODES OF PABLO NERUDA, a Selection translated by Carlos Lozano (Las Americas Publishing Company, New York, 1961)

THE HEIGHTS OF MACCHU PICCHU, translated by Nathaniel Tarn (Jonathan Cape, London, 1966; Farrar Straus, New York, 1967)

WE ARE MANY, a Selection translated by Alastair Reid (Cape-Goliard, London, 1967; R. Grossman, New York, 1968)

TWENTY POEMS OF PABLO NERUDA, translated by Robert Bly and James Wright (The Sixties Press, Madison, 1967; Rapp & Whiting, London, 1968)

PABLO NERUDA: A NEW DECADE, edited by Ben Belitt and translated by Ben Belitt and Alastair Reid (Grove Press, New York, 1969)

SELECTED POEMS, edited by Nathaniel Tarn and translated by Anthony Kerrigan, W. S. Merwin, Alastair Reid, Nathaniel Tarn (Jonathan Cape, London, forthcoming)

THE PENGUIN BOOK OF LOVE POETRY

Edited and introduced by Jon Stallworthy

This intriguing anthology defines a love poem as "any poem about any aspect of one human being's desire for another." Chosen from various epochs, the selections are international and are grouped according to these categories: Intimations, Declarations, Persuasions, Celebrations, Aberrations, Separations, Desolations, and Reverberations. The poets themselves range from Chaucer to Octavio Paz, from Ronsard to Lawrence Ferlinghetti, from Sappho to W. H. Auden. Read together, their poems prove that, as Jon Stallworthy puts it, "love is a country where anything can happen."

SELECTED POEMS

Baudelaire
Translated and introduced by Joanna Richardson

All of Baudelaire's major poems are given here both in French and in new English translations. The source of symbolism, of surrealism, and, indeed, of almost all modern poetry, these poems depict the corruption and splendor of urban man—his depraved visions, his thirst for the purity of death. As Joanna Richardson writes in her Introduction: "The Baudelairean world is oppressive, alluring and unmistakeable. It is hemmed in by seas which are cruel and angry, sultry and full of pearls. It is a world of strange and varied perfumes—how strong the sense of smell in Baudelaire!—of heavy fragrances which envelop women and allure men to exotic dreams." Joanna Richardson is the author of a much acclaimed biography of Verlaine.

The Penguin Poets

John Ashbery

SELF-PORTRAIT IN A CONVEX MIRROR

John Ashbery has won a Pulitzer Prize, a National Book Award, and a National Critics Circle award for *Self-Portrait in a Convex Mirror*. Not only in the title poem, which critic John Russell has called "one of the finest long poems of our period," but throughout the entire volume John Ashbery reaffirms the poetic powers that have made him such an outstanding figure in contemporary literature. "John Ashbery's new book continues his astonishing explorations of places where no one has ever been; it is, again, an event in American poetry"— Donald Barthelme.

HOUSEBOAT DAYS

Houseboat Days is John Ashbery's first collection of poems since *Self-Portrait in a Convex Mirror*, and it is in every way as dazzlingly original, as moving, and as forceful as its predecessor. Thirty-nine poems, many of them never before published, attest again to his extraordinary powers and the unparalleled range of his style.

THREE POEMS

Three Poems is one of the most profoundly innovative poetical works yet written by an American. Meant by Ashbery as a kind of trilogy to be read in sequence, the three poems open with a spiritual awakening to earthly things. Then Ashbery moves into wry, quasi-dialectical language to tell a love story with cosmological overtones and concludes with a poem that consolidates and fleshes out the themes of the previous two, balancing them with the sometimes harsh facts of his own autobiography.

SOME PENGUIN POETS